THE CHURCH IN CRISIS:
A History of the General Councils
325–1870

THE CHURCH IN CRISIS: *A History of the General Councils, 325–1870*.

PHILIP HUGHES

HANOVER HOUSE

A Division of Doubleday & Company, Inc.

Garden City, New York

Nihil Obstat: James A. Reynolds, Ph.D.
Censor Deputatus
Imprimatur: ✠ Francis Cardinal Spellman
Archbishop of New York
September 28, 1960

BX
825
.H8
(4)

Library of Congress Catalog Card Number 61–6511
Copyright © 1961 by Philip Hughes
Printed in the United States of America
All Rights Reserved
First Edition

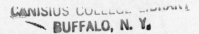

Salve, Umbria verde, e tu del puro fonte
nume Clitumno! Sento in cuor l'antica
patria e aleggiarmi su l'accesa fronte
gl'itali iddii.

        *   *   *

Tutto ora tace. Nel sereno gorgo
la tenue miro saliente vena:
trema, e d'un lieve pullular lo specchio
segna de l'acque.

Ride sepolta a l'imo una foresta
breve, e ramaggia immobile: il diaspro
par che si mischi in flessuosi amori
con l'amestista.

E di zaffiro i fior paiono, ed hanno
de l'adamante rigido i riflessi,
e splendon freddi e chiamano a i silenzi
del verde fondo.

                         Carducci.

Notre Dame du Lac
April 26, 1960

Contents

Contents

THE CHURCH IN CRISIS:
A History of the General Councils
325–1870

Introduction: On Councils
and General Councils

The history of the General Councils of the Church is a fascinating
subject, and to those unfamiliar with the history of the Church a
subject which bristles with difficulties of all kinds. This, I think,
ought to be understood from the beginning. Some of the problems
raised by this or that particular council will be considered in the
chapter devoted to it. About difficulties general to the subject I
would like to say something in this Introduction.

It is hardly possible to write the history of these twenty General
Councils as though they were sections hewn from the one same
log. They are not a unity in the sense in which successive sessions
of Congress are a unity. Each of the twenty councils is an individual reality, each has its own special personality. This is partly
due to the fact that each had its origin in a particular crisis of
Church affairs, partly to the fact that they are strung out over fifteen
hundred years of history, and that, for example, the human beings
who constitute the council can be as remote from each other as
the victims of the persecution of Diocletian in the fourth century
from the victims of Bismarck in the nineteenth. It is not through
any mechanical, material similarity of action, then, that the history
of such an institution, and its significance, can be understood.
Where the total action is spread over such vast spaces of time, and
is discontinuous, whoever attempts to relate the whole of the action is faced with problems of a very special kind. And this speciality is, of course, bound up with the fact that the body which threw
up this device called the General Council—the Church of Christ—
is itself unique in this, viz., its possession of a recorded, continuous
activity of nearly two thousand years.

Some, perhaps superficial, consideration of this vast timetable,
325–1870, may be helpful at the outset, even to the reader who is

not, by nature, chronologically minded. Reading the list of the General Councils we can see immediately two obvious groupings: the first eight were all held in eastern Europe or in Asia Minor; all the rest in western Europe, in Italy, France, and Germany. The eastern councils were Greek-speaking, the others Latin. General Councils are frequent in some ages, and in others the centuries go by without a single one. Thus, for the seventy years 381–451 there are three General Councils, then one every hundred years down to 869. For 254 years there is now not a single General Council; then, in 190 years there are seven (1123–1311). Another century goes by without a council, and in the next hundred years (1414–1512) three are summoned. The Council of Trent is called less than thirty years after the last of these three, and then 306 years go by before the twentieth council meets in 1869—ninety-two years ago nearly.

Each of these councils has a history and a character all its own. The history of the next council—how matters will go once the bishops meet—can never be foretold from the history of the last. The powers and the authority of the new council are, it is recognised, the same as its predecessors possessed. The procedure may, and will, vary. One thing is never constant: the human reaction of the council's component parts.

The first General Council met in 325. The Church had then been an established fact for nearly three hundred years. How did councils begin—i.e., meetings of bishops to discuss matters of common interest? When and where did the first church councils take place? And what about the beginnings of the "prestige" of these councils? That is, of the idea that what bishops collectively agree is law has a binding force that is greater than any of their individual instructions to their own see.

To begin with the last point, it is a safe statement that from the moment when history first shows us the Church of Christ as an institution, the exclusive right of the Church to state with finality what should be believed as Christ's teaching is manifestly taken for granted. To bring out a theory of belief, or to propose a change in morals which conflicts with what the Church universally holds is, from the very beginning, to put oneself fatally in the wrong. The immediate, spontaneous reaction of the Church to condemn thinkers with new and original views of this kind is perhaps the most general, as it is the most striking, of all the phenomena of the Church's early history, so far back as the record goes.[1]

When it was that bishops first formed the habit of coming together in council, we do not know. It is such an obvious act, on the part of officials with like problems and responsibilities and authority, that to do this was second nature surely. What we do know is that as early as the second century (100–200 A.D.) it was the custom for the bishops who came together for a bishop's funeral to take charge of the election of his successor. Here is one likely source, it is suggested, from which came the council of bishops as a recurring feature of ordinary Christian life.

About the year 190 a furious controversy as to the date at which the feast of Easter should be kept, shook the whole Church, and the pope, St. Victor I, sent orders to the places most troubled that the bishops should meet and report to him their findings. And a series of councils were then held, in Palestine, in Asia Minor, and in Gaul. Sixty years later when, with the great career of St. Cyprian, the mists clear away from Roman Africa, we perceive that the bishops' council is already a long-established practice there. The bishops of Africa meet in council, indeed, twice every year. What they decreed on these occasions was law for the whole of Christian Africa. These councils were well attended; in 220 there were seventy-one bishops present, and at another council, ninety. At St. Cyprian's council of Carthage in 256, there were eighty-seven. There was a similar, systematic conciliar action in Egypt and in Syria and Palestine.

In the early years of the next century we have records of councils in Spain (Elvira, 300) and in France (Arles, 314) with the names of bishops present and a list of the laws they enacted. The Catholic Church may, indeed, be a Church made up of churches (i.e., dioceses) but never, so this history seems to show, of dioceses where each bishop acts without any reference to the rest.

When the emperor Constantine publicly became a follower of Christ (312) he was immediately faced with the grave African problem known to history as the Donatist Schism. Necessarily, and in a

---

[1] For a succinct, popular account of which cf. my own *History of the Church*, vol. I, chaps. III, IV, passim. For an authoritative, documented account cf. Pierre Batiffol, *L'Église Naissante* (the whole book). This has been translated into English as *Primitive Christianity*.

very brief space of time, he was familiarised with the function of the council of the bishops, as an instrument of church government. It was natural, inevitable indeed, that when a few years later the Arian crisis arose, all concerned, the emperor and the bishops, should think of a great council as the first move in the restoration of order. The novel feature in 325 was that not only the bishops of the locality affected were convoked, but the bishops of the whole Catholic world.[2] This was to be not a regional or provincial council, but a council for the church in general—a General Council.

The universal belief that the Church of Christ, in its day-to-day business of teaching the doctrine of Christ, is divinely preserved from teaching erroneously, entailed the consequence that (to use a modern terminology) the General Council is considered infallible in its decisions about belief. If the official teachers *as a body* are infallible as they teach, scattered about the world in their hundreds of sees, they do not lose the promised, divine, preserving guidance once they have come together in a General Council. And once General Councils have taken place we begin to meet explicit statements of this truth. The councils themselves are explicitly conscious of it when, making their statement of the truth denied by the innovator, they bluntly say of those who will not accept their decision, Let him be anathema. St. Athanasius, who as a young cleric was present at Nicaea, can refer to its decree about Arianism as something final, the last all-decisive word: "The word of the Lord, put forth by the Oecumenical Council at Nicaea is an eternal word, enduring for ever."[3] Eighty years or so later than this the pope, St. Leo I, warning the bishops assembled at the General Council of Chalcedon to leave untouched the decisions of Nicaea about the rank of the great sees of the East, speaks of Nicaea as "having fixed these arrangements by decrees that are inviolable," and says, "These arrangements were made by the bishops at Nicaea under divine inspiration."[4] This was in the year 451. His successor, St. Gregory the Great, writing about 594 to the patriarch of Constantinople, has a

[2] The Greek word for "the whole world" is *oikouméne*, whence our modern adjective "oecumenical," which is used with reference to councils of the Church as an equivalent for "general."

[3] *Letter to the Africans*, in Rouet de Journel, S.J., *Enchiridion Patristicum*, no. 792. The full titles of all books quoted will be found in Appendix II.

[4] Ibid., no. 2185.

reference to the special prestige of the first, doctrine-defining General Councils which equates their work with that of Holy Scripture: "I profess that as I receive and venerate the four books of the Gospels, so I do the four councils," which he proceeds to list: Nicaea in 325, Constantinople in 381, Ephesus 431, Chalcedon 451. These, he says, "are the four squared stone on which the structure of the holy faith arises."[5]

Nowhere in these early centuries, in fact, do we find any member of the Church questioning the truth as the General Councils have defined it. What they teach as the truth is taken to be as true as though it were a statement of Scripture itself. The question was never raised, seemingly, that the greater or smaller number of bishops who in response to the summons attended, in any way affected the peculiar authority of the General Council; nor the fact that all but all of these bishops were from the Greek-speaking East.

How these fundamental, primitive notions developed, how all that they seminally contained matured and expanded through the centuries, this is the very subject-matter of the chapters that follow. And here will be found, in its due place, some account of the controversies that later arose as to the relation (the constitutional relation, so to speak) of the General Council to its president the pope. What the rôle of the pope has been in the General Council is, necessarily, a main topic of all these chapters. But it may be useful to say a word about this here, and something also about the nature of the bishops' rôle.

The General Council is then a purely human arrangement whereby a divinely founded institution functions in a particular way for a particular purpose. That divinely founded thing is the teaching Church, i.e., the pope and the diocesan bishops of the Church of Christ. The teaching is an activity of the Church that is continuous, never ceasing. The General Council of the teaching Church, in all the sessions of the occasions on which it has met, in the nineteen hundred years and more of the Church's history, has sat for perhaps thirty years in all, at most. It is an exceptional phenomenon in the life of the Church, and usually it appears in connection with some great crisis of that life.

Ever since the popes were first articulate about the General

[5] Ibid., no. 2291.

Council, they have claimed the right to control its action and, to take their place in it (whether personally or by legates sent in their name) or by their subsequent acceptance of the council, to give or withhold an approbation of its decisions, which stamps them as the authentic teaching of the Church of Christ. Only through their summoning it, or through their consenting to take their place at it, does the assembly of bishops become a General Council. No member of the Church has ever proposed that a General Council shall be summoned and the pope be left out, nor that the pope should take any other position at the General Council but as its president. The history of the twenty General Councils shows that the bishops —a section of them—not infrequently fought at the council the policies of the popes who had summoned the council, and fought even bitterly. But in no council has it been moved that the bishop of X be promoted to the place of the Bishop of Rome, or that the Bishop of Rome's views be disregarded, and held of no more account than those of the bishop of any other major see. There are, indeed, gaps in our knowledge of the detail of all these events; the mist of antiquity, at times, no doubt obscures our view, but through the mist at its worst the general shape is ever discernible of a Roman Primacy universally recognised, and submitted to, albeit (at times) unwillingly—recognised and submitted to because, so the bishops believed, it was set up by God Himself.

To the General Councils of the Church there have been summoned, in the last 850 years, as well as the bishops, other ecclesiastics of importance, the General Superiors of religious orders, for example, and abbots of particular monasteries. But these are present by concession. The essential elements of the General Council are, in addition to the pope, the bishops ruling their sees. And the bishops are present as the accredited witnesses of what is believed throughout the Church. This is the traditional, standard conception of their rôle on these occasions. And for typical modern statements, contained in well-known textbooks used throughout the Church today in hundreds of theological classrooms, this from Christian Pesch, S.J.,[6] may be quoted: "The bishops do not come

[6] *Praelectiones Dogmaticae* (5th ed., 1915) vol. 1, p. 313. The footnotes in this book do not give the authorities for the statements in the text, but only the source of the quotations.

together in order to think up something new out of their own minds, but in order to be witnesses of the teaching received from Christ and handed out by the Church"; and this too from Fr. Dominic Prümmer, O.P.: "The bishops gathered in a General Council are not mere counsellors of the pope, but real legislators; which is why each bishop signs the *acta* of the council as follows: 'I, James, bishop of X, defining have subscribed my name.' "[7]

As to the rôle of the General Council vis-à-vis any controversy about the Christian Faith, in connection with which it may have been summoned, this has never been more luminously stated, in a single sentence, than by John Henry Newman, with reference, indeed, to the first council of the great series, but, as history alone would show, a statement true of them all. ". . . it must be borne in mind that the great Council at Nicaea was summoned, not to decide for the first time what was to be held concerning our Lord's divine nature, but, as far as inquiry came into its work, to determine the fact whether Arius did or did not contradict the Church's teaching, and, if he did, by what sufficient *tessera*[8] he and his party could be excluded from the communion of the faithful."[9] And Newman's own great hero, St. Athanasius, writing only thirty-four years after Nicaea, has a similar thought when he draws attention to the different way the Council of Nicaea spoke when it was making laws about ecclesiastical discipline and when it was facing the problem of Arius. "The fathers at Nicaea speaking of the Easter feast say 'We have decided as follows.' But about the faith they do not say 'We have decided,' but 'This is what the Catholic Church believes.' And immediately they proclaim how they believe, in order to declare, not some novelty, but that their belief is apostolic, and that what they write down is not something they have discovered, but those very things which the Apostles taught."[10]

This little book of mine—"little," surely, for it surveys twenty General Councils and fifteen hundred years of history—has no

[7] *Definiens subscripsi*. The passage I have translated is in Prümmer, *Manuale Theologiae Moralis*, 5th ed., 1928, I, 119.

[8] Testing token.

[9] *Apostolical Tradition*, an article in the *British Critic*, July 1836, reprinted (1871, and many times since) in *Essays, Critical and Historical*, vol. I, 125.

[10] *Epistola de Synodis*, par. 5, in Rouet de Journel, S.J., *Enchiridion Patristicum*, no. 785.

claim on the reader's notice beyond its purpose to say how each of these councils came to be, and what each achieved. Many questions about General Councils as such, and about particular General Councils, are inevitably not even alluded to. I have no ambition to write a survey course in which everything is mentioned and nothing taught. Nevertheless there are some serious matters that cannot be omitted, and yet can only be dealt with summarily—the new theories which became heresies, for example, and the orthodox statements of the truth which the theories perverted. In summary accounts of such things the impression is easily conveyed that these disputes are a mere war of words. Actually, what any study of the voluminous writings on both sides reveals is that the conflicting minds are of the first order, that the points at issue are the fundamentals of revealed truth, and (a very important circumstance that often has escaped the historian's notice) that the contestants are passionately in earnest, not as rivals in scholarship or philosophy, but as pastoral-minded bishops, anxious about the salvation of men's souls. A master mind, reviewing a situation we shall shortly be studying, affords an illustration of this.

"Cyril, it may be, was overharsh in the words he used, words used without enough reflexion. Deep within him his passionate attachment to the truth that Christ is a single being was intertwined with the innermost strands of the mysticism of the East. For the disciple of Theodore of Mopsuestia, as for the disciple of Pelagius, the question of the relations between man and God is, above all, a question of merit and no-merit. In the great book of deserts each man's account is kept in two columns, debit and credit. As a man's merits pile up, as he lessens his faults, so does his situation improve. At the end God balances the account, and places us according to the excess of credit over debit. Moralism pure and simple, this way of looking at things, and not religion at all. Where, in such a system, does the Incarnation come in? or the cross of Christ? Here, Jesus Christ is our model, nothing more. Here we never meet our true *saviour*, our *redeemer*, He who by His divine presence purifies everything, lifts all to a higher plane, consecrates all, makes divine beings of us so far as the limits of our nature allow this communication of divinity.

"Very, very different is the spirit that gives life to the theology

18

of St. Cyril. Here, Jesus Christ is truly God-within-us. The Christian makes a direct contact with Him, by a union of natures, a mysterious union indeed, under the sacramental veil of the Eucharist. Through this body and this blood he comes to make the contact with God, for these have, in Jesus Christ, a union (equally a union of natures) with divinity. . . . To the poor peasant working in the fields of the Delta, to the dock labourer at the port of Pharos, Cyril gives the message that, in this world, he can touch God. And that through this contact, whence springs a mystical kinship, he can receive an assurance about the life hereafter; not only the guarantee that he is immortal, but that he will be immortal joined with God."[11] Such can be the practical importance of "abstract theological thought."

And, with reference to the stormy history of the first eight councils, events of a thousand to sixteen hundred years ago, we may remind ourselves that the actors here are Greeks, Egyptians, Syrians; their natural temperament and sense of nationality was not a whit less ardent than it can show itself to be in their descendants of this mid-twentieth century.

And now, to bring these introductory remarks to an end, it will perhaps be helpful to draw attention to one feature particularly of the history of the first seven councils. This is not so much the serious differences of opinion as to the interpretation of the basic mysteries of the Christian religion, which is their main concern, but rather the way these differences, at times, seem to turn so largely on different ways of understanding the terms used to express or explain the doctrine. Since all this is likely to be unfamiliar to the general reader, to him I would say some words of the great authority I have already made use of, a writer who all his life was ever conscious that the course of true historical study is strewn with difficulties.

"First of all," says Newman, "and in as few words as possible, and *ex abundanti cautela*: Every Catholic holds that the Christian dogmas were in the Church from the time of the Apostles; that they were ever in their substance what they are now; that they ex-

---

[11] Monseigneur Louis Duchesne, *Les Églises séparées*, 38–40. I came across this passage in Bardy, *Les Luttes Christologiques après le Concile de Chalcédoine*, i.e., Fliche and Martin, vol. 5, 273, n. 1.

isted before the formulas were publicly adopted, in which, as time went on, they were defined and recorded, and that such formulas, when sanctioned by the due ecclesiastical acts, are binding on the faith of Catholics, and have a dogmatic authority. . . .

"Even before we take into account the effect which would naturally be produced on the first Christians by the novelty and mysteriousness of doctrines which depend for their reception simply upon Revelation, we have reason to anticipate that there would be difficulties and mistakes in expressing them, when they first came to be set forth by unauthoritative writers. Even in secular sciences, inaccuracy of thought and language is but gradually corrected; that is, in proportion as their subject-matter is thoroughly scrutinized and mastered by the co-operation of many independent intellects, successively engaged upon it. Thus, for instance, the word *Person* requires the rejection of various popular senses, and a careful definition, before it can serve for philosophical uses. We sometimes use it for an *individual* as contrasted with a class or multitude, as when we speak of having 'personal objections' to another; sometimes for the *body*, in contrast to the soul, as when we speak of 'beauty of person.' We sometimes use it in the abstract, as when we speak of another as 'insignificant in person.' How divergent in meaning are the derivatives, *personable, personalities, personify, personation, personage, parsonage!* This variety arises partly from our own carelessness, partly from the necessary developments of language, partly from the defects of our vernacular tongue.

"Language then requires to be refashioned even for sciences which are based on the senses and the reason; but much more will this be the case, when we are concerned with subject-matters, of which, in our present state, we cannot possibly form any complete or consistent conception, such as the Catholic doctrines of the Trinity and Incarnation. Since they are from the nature of the case above our intellectual reach, and were unknown till the preaching of Christianity, they required on their first promulgation new words, or words used in new senses, for their due enunciation; and, since these were not definitely supplied by Scripture or by tradition, nor for centuries by ecclesiastical authority, variety in the use, and confusion in the apprehension of them, were unavoidable in the interval. . . . Not only had the words to be adjusted and explained which were peculiar to different schools or traditional in different places, but there was the formidable necessity of creating a common measure between two, or rather three languages—Latin, Greek, and Syriac."[12]

[12] J. H. Newman, *On St. Cyril's Formula* (1858), reprinted in *Tracts, Theological and Ecclesiastical* (1874), pp. 287–90.

1. *The First General Council of Nicaea, 325*

It is more than sixteen hundred years since the first of the General Councils of the Church met. This is so long ago that the very names of the places connected with its history have quite disappeared from common knowledge and the atlases. They have about them an air of the fabulous; Nicaea, Bithynia, Nicomedia, and the rest. The very unfamiliarity of the sounds is a reminder that even for the purpose of the slight consideration which is all that these pages allow, a considerable adjustment of the mind is called for. We must, somehow, revive the memory of a world that has wholly passed away, that had disappeared, indeed, well nigh a thousand years already when Columbus and his ships first sighted the coasts of the new continent.

The business that brought the three hundred or so bishops to Nicaea in 325 from all over the Christian world was to find a remedy for the disturbances that had seriously troubled the East for now nearly two years. The cause of these disturbances was a new teaching about the basic mystery of the Christian religion.

Let our expert summarise the position, and say what it was that the new leader, Arius by name, had lately been popularising, through sermons, writings, and popular hymns and songs. "It was the doctrine of Arianism that our Lord was a pure creature, made out of nothing, liable to fall, the Son of God by adoption, not by nature, and called God in Scripture, not as being really such, but only in name. At the same time [Arius] would not have denied that the Son and the Holy Ghost were creatures transcendently near to God, and immeasurably distant from the rest of creation.

"Now, by contrast, how does the teaching of the Fathers who preceded Arius, stand relatively to such a representation of the Christian Creed? Is it such, or how far is it such, as to bear Arius out in so representing it? This is the first point to inquire about.

"First of all, the teaching of the Fathers was necessarily directed by the form of Baptism, as given by our Lord Himself to His disciples after His resurrection. To become one of His disciples was, according to His own words, to be baptized 'into the Name of the Father, and of the Son, and of the Holy Ghost'; that is, into the profession, into the service, of a Triad. Such was our Lord's injunction: and ever since, before Arianism and after, down to this day, the initial lesson in religion taught to every Christian, on his being made a Christian, is that he thereby belongs to a certain Three, whatever more, or whether anything more, is revealed to us in Christianity about that Three.

"The doctrine then of a Supreme Triad is the elementary truth of Christianity; and accordingly, as might have been expected, its recognition is a sort of key-note, on which centre the thoughts and language of all theologians, from which they start, with which they end."[1]

Examination of a chain of pre-Arian writers, from every part of Christendom, reveals that "there was during the second and third centuries a profession and teaching concerning the Holy Trinity, not vague and cloudy, but of a certain determinate character," and that this teaching "was contradictory and destructive of the Arian hypothesis."[2] And from all this literature the fact emerges that, from the beginning, "some doctrine or other of a Trinity lies at the very root of the Christian conception of the Supreme Being, and of his worship and service": and that "it is impossible to view historical Christianity apart from the doctrine of the Trinity."[3]

It was round about the year 323 that the Arian crisis developed. The struggle between the advocates of the new theory and the Church authorities who stood by the tradition was to continue thence onward for a good fifty years and more. And now, for the first time in the history of the Church, the State intervened in what was, of itself, a dispute about belief. A second point to note is that

[1] Newman, *Causes of the Rise and Successes of Arianism* (February 1872), in *Tracts, Theological and Ecclesiastical*, pp. 103–4.
[2] Ibid., 116. For Newman's "examination," 103–11.
[3] Ibid., 112.

the State, on the whole, sided with the innovators, and was hostile to the defenders of the traditional truth.

The history of those fifty-six years (325–81), that followed the Council of Nicaea and closed with the next General Council (Constantinople I), is part of the history of both these councils. And its complexity defies any summary simplification. If we turn to Newman for a clue to the meaning of it all, he will tell us that this long and stubborn struggle is nothing else than a particular passage in the conflict that never ceases between the Church and the secular power. "The same principle of government which led the emperors to denounce Christianity while they were pagans, led them to dictate to its bishops, when they had become Christians." Such an idea as that "religion should be independent of state authority" was, in the eyes of all these princes, contrary to the nature of things. And not only was this conflict "inevitable," but, Newman continues, it might have been foreseen as probable that the occasion of the conflict would be a controversy within the Church about some fundamental doctrine. Newman's last remarkable words may usefully warn us that in Church History things are not always so simple as we expect.[4]

Even the full history of a General (i.e., world-wide) Council called in such circumstances, the first council of its kind—which had no precedents to guide its procedure, or to instruct the generality about the special value attaching to its decisions—even this would inevitably present difficulties to minds sixteen hundred years later; minds bred in a detailed, centuries-old tradition about the kind of thing General Councils are, and furnished with definite ideas about their nature, procedure, and authority.

But we are very far from possessing anything like a full history of this first Council of Nicaea. Of any official record of the day-to-day proceedings—the *acta* of the council—there is no trace. The earliest historians, from whose accounts our knowledge must derive, were in large measure partisan writers. And of the two writers who were present at the council, the one who was a historian[5] was an ally of the heretics and the quasi-official panegyrist of the emperor Constantine who called the council; and the other,[6] though he has

---

[4] Ibid., 96, 97 for the passages quoted.
[5] Eusebius, bishop of Caesarea (?265–338).
[6] St. Athanasius, bishop of Alexandria (328–73); born ?295.

24

much indeed to say about the council, does not anywhere profess to be writing a record of its acts.

Nowhere, of course, is our knowledge of the history of these first centuries of the Church anything like so complete as is our knowledge of, let us say, any part of it during the last eight or nine hundred years. In the matter of Nicaea, as in other questions, scholars are still disputing—and not on religious grounds—whether, for example, certain key documents were really written by the personages whose names they bear. About the details of the history of all these early councils, because of the insufficiency of our information, there is inevitably much confusion, great obscurity. Yet there are compensations for those who study it. "History does not bring clearly upon the canvas the details which were familiar to the ten thousand minds of whose combined movements and fortunes it treats. Such is it from its very nature; nor can the defect ever fully be remedied. This must be admitted . . . still no one can mistake its general teaching in this matter, whether he accept it or stumble at it. Bold outlines, which cannot be disregarded, rise out of the records of the past, when we look to see what it will give up to us: they may be dim, they may be incomplete, but they are definite; there is that which they are not, which they cannot be."[7]

The state, or political society, in which the Arian troubles arose and developed was that which we know as the Roman Empire. This state, for its inhabitants, was one and the same thing as civilisation, and not surprisingly. As the accession of Constantine to the sole rulership, in 324, found the empire, so it had endured for three hundred years and more. History does not record any political achievement even remotely parallel to this. For the empire took in, besides Italy, the whole of Europe west of the Rhine and south of the Danube and also the southern half of the island of Britain. In the east it included the whole of the modern state we call Turkey, with Syria also, Palestine, and Egypt, and the lands on the southern shore of the Mediterranean westward thence to the Atlantic.

Races as varied as the peoples who today inhabit these lands, with just as little to unite them naturally, lived then for some four hundred years under the rule of the emperors, with a minimum of in-

[7] Newman, *The Development of Christian Doctrine*, 1st ed., 1845, pp. 7, 5; with one sentence ("Still no one," etc.) from ibid., rev. ed., p. 7.

ternal disturbance and in almost entire freedom from foreign war. The stresses and strains of the internal life of the empire were, of course, a constant menace to this marvellous unity. The supreme ruler, with whom lay the fullness of legislative power, who was the final judge in all lawsuits, and the head of the national religion, was the ruler because he was the commander in chief of the army: his very title *imperator*, which we translate "emperor," means just this.[8] And for the *imperator*, it was one of the chief problems of government to maintain his military prestige with the vast armies. No man could long rule the Roman world who did not first hold the legions true to himself by his own professional worth. All the great rulers who, in the course of these four centuries, developed and adapted and reformed the complex life of the state, its finances, its law, its administration, were in the first place great soldiers, highly successful generals: Trajan, for example, Hadrian, Septimius Severus, Decius, Diocletian.

And Constantine, the first emperor to abandon the pagan religion and to profess himself a Christian, stood out to his own generation primarily as a highly successful soldier, triumphant in a series of contests with rivals for the supreme place. Such wars, fights between rival generals for the imperial throne, were the chief curse of Roman political life, and especially so in what we reckon as the third century, the century in the last quarter of which Constantine himself was born. He would have been a little boy of nine or ten when the great Diocletian became emperor in 284, who, to put an end to these suicidal wars, immediately associated another soldier with himself, as joint emperor, the one to rule the East, the other the West. In 293 Diocletian took this devolution of power a step further. With each emperor there was now associated a kind of assistant emperor, with the title of Caesar, the actual ruler of allotted territories and destined to be, in time, his principal's successor. The soldier chosen in 293 as the first western Caesar was Constantine's father, Constantius, commonly called Chlorus (the Pale) from his complexion. His territory was the modern countries of Portugal, Spain, France, Belgium, and England.

These details of political reorganisation have a direct connection with our story. The reader knows—who does not?—that one feature

---

[8] A standard Latin dictionary will give as a first basic equivalent, "commander in chief."

of the history of this Roman state was its hostility to the Christian religion. Scarcely a generation went by without some serious persecution. And Diocletian ended his reign with the most dreadful persecution of all (303). This was largely due to the influence of his colleague, the Caesar, Galerius who, in 305, was to succeed him as emperor in the East. And of all the territories, it was Egypt that provided most of the victims in the eight years the terror lasted— Egypt which was to be the principal scene of the Arian troubles and, par excellence, of the Catholic resistance to them. In the West the persecution was, by comparison, mild, and in the domains of Constantius Chlorus there was no persecution at all. This emperor's personal religious history, and his attitude towards the Christian religion, is full of interest. His views were also the views of his son Constantine, and they perhaps provide a clue to the strange and baffling story, not only of the long successful Arian defiance of the decisions of the Council of Nicaea, but of that first Christian emperor's seeming unawareness of the defiance.

Constantine's own character is, of course, an element of the first importance in the history of the council he convoked; and so also is the kind of thing which his "conversion" to Christianity was, some twelve years before the Arian problem arose. At the time of the council he was nearing his fiftieth year, and he had been emperor for almost twenty. History seems to reveal him as intelligent indeed, but passionate and headstrong; a bold campaigner and, as an administrator, "magnificent" in the Aristotelian sense. That is to say, he loved great schemes, supported them always with princely generosity, improvised readily, and delighted to dazzle by the scale of his successes. It was a natural part of the character that he was ambitious, confident of success, and—a less obvious trait—his ambition was linked with a "mystical" belief that he was destined to succeed, and a sure, if confused, notion that the heavenly powers were on his side. Be it remembered here, once more, that this man was omnipotent in public affairs, as no ruler has been even in the recent revolutions of our own time; for the Roman emperor's omnipotence was universally accepted by his millions of subjects as his right, as something belonging to the very nature of things.

It is less easy to say exactly what Constantine knew or believed about the religion of Christ, twelve years after he had, as emperor, publicly made it his own. Certainly it would be a gross error to consider the business of his mystical dream on the eve of his victory at the Milvian Bridge (312), that made him supreme master of the West, as parallel to what happened to St. Paul on the road to Damascus. His own personal religion at the time was that of his pagan father, the cult suddenly promoted to the supreme place as the official religion about the time that Constantine was born, by the then emperor, Aurelian (269–75). This was the cult of *Sol Invictus* (the Unconquered Sun), the worship of the divine spirit by whom the whole universe is ruled, the spirit whose symbol is the sun; a symbol in which this spirit in some way specially manifests itself. Under Aurelian this cult was organised with great splendour. The temple of the Sun which he built at Rome must have been one of the wonders of the world. Aurelian's coins bear the inscription *The Sun is the Lord of the Roman Empire*. The whole cult is penetrated with the idea that there is a single spirit who is supreme, with the idea of an overruling divine monarchy. Moreover, the cult was in harmony with a philosophical religion steadily growing, in the high places of the administration, throughout this same century, the cult of *Summus Deus*—the God who is supreme.

Constantine's father remained faithful to this cult of *Sol Invictus* even when his seniors, Diocletian and Maximian, reverted to the old cults of Jupiter and Hercules. And once Constantine—no more than Caesar on his father's death (306)—felt himself really master in the West, Hercules and Jupiter disappeared from his coinage, and *Sol Invictus* was restored, while the official panegyrics laud "that divine spirit which governs this whole world." This in 311.

What Constantine gathered from his famous dream in September 312 was that this supreme divinity was promising him salvation in this military crisis, had despatched a messenger to assure him of it and to tell him how to act, and that this messenger was Christ, the God whom the Christians worshipped, and that the badge his soldiers must wear was the sign of Christ, the cross. He did not, on the morrow of his victory, ask for baptism, nor even to be enrolled as a catechumen. Constantine was never so much as even this. And not until he lay dying, twenty-five years later, was he baptised.

It was, then, an all but uninstructed, if enthusiastic, convert who now, with all the caution of an experienced politician, set his name to the Edict of Milan (313), set up the Christian religion as a thing legally permissible, endowed its chief shrines with regal munificence, showered civic privileges, honours, and jurisdiction on its bishops, and even began the delicate task of introducing Christian ideas into the fabric of the law. It was an all but uninstructed convert who, also, in these next ten years—and in the turbulent province of Africa—plunged boldly into the heat of a religious war, the Donatist Schism, with the instinctive confidence that his mere intervention would settle all problems. Between the truce with the Donatists, 321, and the appearance of Arius in Egypt the interval is short indeed. What had Constantine learned from the Donatist experience? What had it taught him about the kind of thing the divine society was in which he so truly believed? Very little, it would seem.

The great see of Alexandria in Egypt, of which Arius was a priest, had for many years before his appearance as a heretic been troubled by schism. One of the suffragan bishops—Meletius by name—had accused his principal of giving way during the persecution; and, declaring all the bishop of Alexandria's acts invalid, had proceeded to consecrate bishops in one place after another, in opposition to him. Nor did Meletius cease his activities when this particular bishop of Alexandria died. In many places there were soon two sets of Catholic clergy, the traditional line and the "Meletian"; the confusion was great and the contest bitter everywhere, the faithful people as active as their pastors. "It was out of the Meletian schism that Arianism was born and developed," one historian[9] will tell us. Arius had been a "Meletian" in his time, but the new bishop, Alexander, had received him back and had promoted him to an important church. And here his learned eloquence and ascetic life soon gave his novel teaching as wide publicity as he could desire.

The bishop's first act, as the news spread, was to arrange a public disputation. In this Arius was worsted. He next disobeyed the bishop's natural injunction to be silent, and began to look for support outside Egypt. Meanwhile the bishop called a council of the hundred bishops subject to his see; ninety-eight voted to condemn Arius; and his two supporters, along with a handful of other clerics, were deposed. Arius fled to Palestine, to an old friend generally re-

---

[9] J. Lebreton, S.J., *Histoire de l'Église*, edited by A. Fliche and Msgr. V. Martin (henceforward referred to as F. and M.), vol. 2, p. 343.

garded as the greatest scholar of the day, Eusebius, the bishop of Caesarea. And from Caesarea the two began a vast correspondence to engage the support of bishops expected to be friendly to the cause, as far away as the imperial capital, Nicomedia.

Already there was a bond between Arius and many of those to whom he wrote. They like himself were pupils of the same famous teacher of the last generation, Lucian of Antioch, whose school—and not Alexandria—was the real birthplace of this new theological development. And Arius could address such prelates as "Dear Fellow-Lucianist." Of all those to whom he now wrote, none was so important as a second Eusebius, the bishop of the imperial city itself, and a possible power with the emperor through his friendship with Constantine's sister, the empress Constantia, consort of the eastern emperor, Licinius. The Lucianist bishop of Nicomedia rose to the occasion, "as though upon him the whole fate of the Church depended," the bishop of Alexandria complained. For Eusebius, too, circularised the episcopate generally and summoned a council of bishops, and they voted that Arius should be reinstated, and wrote to beg this of the bishop of Alexandria.

Arius' bishop, meanwhile, had been active also. We know of seventy letters which he wrote to bishops all over the Christian world; amongst others to whom he wrote was the pope. And since all these episcopal letters were copied and passed round, made up into collections and, as we should say, published, the whole of the East was soon aflame, fighting and rioting in one city after another. Few indeed of these enthusiasts could have understood the discussions of the theologians, but all grasped that what Arius was saying was that Christ was not God. And if this were so, what about the saving death on the Cross? And what was sinful man to hope for when he died? When the bishop of Alexandria stigmatised his rebellious priest as *Christomachos* (fighter against Christ), he clinched the matter in such a way that all, from the Christian emperor to the meanest dock hand in the port, must be personally interested, and passionately.

During these first months of agitation Constantine had, however, other matters to occupy him, and, to begin with, the agitation was none of his business. At the moment when the great movement began, none of the lands affected came under his jurisdiction. But in that same year, 323, war broke out between himself and his eastern colleague, his brother-in-law, Licinius. In July 324 Constantine, invader of Licinius' territory, defeated him heavily at Adrianople, and in September he gained a second victory at Chrysopolis.[10] Later Licinius was put to death. When the victor entered his new capital in the ensuing weeks, there was in his household a Spanish prelate who had dwelt with Constantine for some years now, Hosius, bishop of Cordova. It was to him that Constantine, with the new Arian crisis confronting him, now turned.

Arius, by now, had returned to Alexandria, fortified with the vote of the council at Nicomedia and of a second (more peremptory) council at Caesarea, to demand the decreed reinstatement. His arrival, and the campaign of propaganda now launched, set the whole city ablaze. And Constantine despatched Hosius to make a personal investigation of the affair. When he returned to make his report, Alexander and Arius soon followed. The crisis next moved to the third great city of the empire, Antioch. The bishop there had recently died, and when the fifty-six bishops subject to Antioch came in from Palestine, Arabia, Syria, and elsewhere to elect a successor (January 325, probably), they took the opportunity to notice the Arian development. All but unanimously (53-3) they condemned the new teaching, and excommunicated—provisionally—the three dissidents. One of these was the bishop of Caesarea.

And now, sometime in the early spring of 325, it was decided to summon a council representative of all the bishops in the world. Who was it that first put out this grandiose, if simple, plan? We do not know. Within a matter of months—not indeed simultaneously, but with impressive nearness in time—councils had been held at Alexandria, Antioch, Caesarea, Nicomedia, in which a good half of the bishops of the East must have taken part, i.e., a good proportion of the vastly more numerous half of the entire episcopate. Whoever it was to whom the idea of a council of the Christian universe first occurred, it was Constantine who decided it should be held, and who chose the place and sent out the invitations to the bishops, offering to all free passage in the imperial transportation service.

The council opened, in the imperial summer palace at Nicaea,[11] May 20, 325, with something over three hundred bishops present,

[10] The modern Scutari, on the Asiatic shore of the Bosporus.

[11] A city 60 to 70 miles from Constantinople, on the Asiatic shore of the Bosporus, at the head of Lake Iznik. It was about 25 miles south from the then capital, Nicomedia.

the vast bulk of them from the Greek-speaking lands where the trouble was raging, Egypt, Palestine, Syria, and Asia Minor. But there were bishops also from Persia and the Caucasus, from the lands between the Danube and the Aegean, and from Greece. There was one from Africa and one from Spain, one from Gaul and one from Italy, and since the great age of the Bishop of Rome forbade his making the journey he was represented by two of his priests.

Eusebius of Caesarea who has described the great moments of the council was evidently moved, as we too may be, by his recollection of the scene when, the bishops all assembled in the great hall of the palace, some of them lame and blind from the tortures undergone in the persecutions, the Christian master of the whole Roman world entered, robed in scarlet and gold, and before taking his place at the throne, bade them be seated. Constantine came with a minimum of pomp, and in his brief address he did no more than welcome the bishops, exhort them to peaceful conference, and admit that the spectacle of "sedition" within the Church caused him more anxiety than any battle.

The little we know of the actual history of the council is soon told. The theology of Arius was condemned unanimously—though he is said to have had twenty-two supporters among the bishops. But if it was a simple matter for the episcopate to testify to its belief that the Divine Word was truly God, it was less easy to agree about the best way to phrase a declaration of this faith, i.e., to construct a statement to which no subtlety could give a heretical Arian meaning also. One section of the bishops was anxious that no terms should be used which were not already used in Scripture. But the Scriptures had not been written for the purpose of confuting philosophically minded heretics. It was now necessary to say that the accepted Scripture meant just "this" and not "that" as well. And if this were to be accomplished, the technique must be adopted of coining a special word for the purpose.

The statement as the council finally passed it—the creed of the council of Nicaea—states: "We believe . . . in one Lord Jesus Christ, the son of God, born of the Father, the sole-begotten; that is to say, of the substance of the Father, God from God, Light from Light, true God from true God; born, not made, *consubstantial* with the Father [in the Greek original, *homo-oúsion toi patrí*],

32

through whom all things were made, which are in heaven and on earth . . ."[11a] The word *homo-oúsion* is the special non-Scriptural word which the council adopted to characterise the true, traditional belief, a word it was impossible to square with any kind of Arian theory, a test word that would always make it clear that any Arian theory was incompatible with the Christian tradition, and which would serve the practical purpose of preventing any further infil- tration of these enemies of Christ within the Church, and defeat any endeavour to change the belief from within.

Who it was that proposed to the council this precise word, we do not know. An Arian historian says it was the bishop of Alexan- dria and Hosius of Cordova. St. Athanasius, who was present at the council, says it was Hosius. What seems clearer is that the bishops, solidly determined that the heresy should be rooted out, were yet by no means happy about the means chosen. The word *homo- oúsion* was known to them already. Since long before the time of Arius and Lucian it had a bad history in the East, as will be ex- plained. But Constantine definitely declared himself in favour of the uniquely useful instrument, and the council accepted it, each bishop rising in his place and giving his vote. Two bishops only refused their assent. With Arius, and a few priest supporters, they were promptly sent into exile by the emperor's command.

The bishops then passed to other problems. In the first place the twenty-year-old Meletian schism. Its leaders had appealed to Con- stantine, and the emperor left it to the council to judge. The bishops supported their brother of Alexandria, but offered the schismatics very easy terms, restoring Meletius himself to his see of Lycopolis. But he was not, ever again, to confer Holy Orders, and all those whom he had unlawfully ordained were to be reordained before again officiating. Moreover they were to be subject hence- forward to the true, i.e., Catholic, bishop of the place. Those whom Meletius had made bishops might be elected to sees in the future, as vacancies arose—always with the consent of the bishop of Alex- andria, the traditional head of this extensive episcopate.

A second practical problem, that had teased the eastern churches for generations, was now finally solved, viz., how the date of the Easter feast should be calculated. "All our good brothers of the

---

[11a] Denzinger, *Enchiridion*, no. 54, prints the Greek text; Barry, *Readings in Church History*, p. 85, gives a translation.

East[12] who until now have been used to keep Easter at the Jewish Passover, will henceforward keep it at the same time as the Romans and you," so the bishops of Egypt announced in a letter to their people.

Finally the bishops promulgated twenty laws—canons—for general observance. Like the solution proposed for the Meletians they are notable for a new mildness of tone, a quality more Roman than Oriental, it may be said. They are, in great part, a repetition of measures enacted eleven years earlier in the Latin council held at Arles, in Gaul.[13] Five canons deal with those who fell away in the recent persecution. If any such have since been admitted to ordination they are to be deposed. Those who apostatised freely—that is, without the compulsion of fear—are to do twelve years' penance before being admitted to Holy Communion. If, before the penance is completed, they fall sick and are in danger of death they may receive Holy Viaticum. Should they then recover they are to take place with the highest class of the penitents—those who are allowed to hear mass, though not to receive Holy Communion. Catechumens who fell away—i.e., Christians not yet baptised—are to do three years' penance and then resume their place as catechumens. Finally, the Christians who, having once left the army, had re-enlisted in the army of the persecutor, the lately destroyed emperor Licinius, are to do thirteen years' penance, or less if the bishop is satisfied of the reality of their repentance, but always three years' penance at least.

There are two canons about the readmission of heretical schismatics. First of all there are the remnants of the schism begun in Rome by the antipope Novatian, some seventy-five years before the council. Novatian was one of that fairly numerous class for whom the rulers of the Church deal far too mildly with repentant sinners. He ended by denying that the Church had the power to absolve those who fell away in times of persecution; and his followers, self-styled "the Pure," extended this disability to all sins of idolatry, sex

[12] The word has here a special meaning as the name of the (civil) diocese of which Antioch was the chief city, *Oriens:* the modern Lebanon, Israel, Jordan, Syria, the coast of Turkey thence north and west for a good 200 miles with a vast territory in the interior that went beyond the Euphrates.

[13] Schroeder, *Disciplinary Decrees of the General Councils* (1937), prints the text and a translation. This note serves for all the councils down to the Fifth Lateran of 1512–17. Barry, no. 16, gives a translation.

sins, and murder. They also regarded second marriage as a sex sin. At this time there were many Novatians in Asia Minor, and the council offered generous terms to those who wished to be reconciled, recognising the orders of their clergy, and the dignity of their bishops, but exacting written declarations that they will regard as fellow Catholics those who have contracted a second marriage and those doing penance for apostasy.

To a second class of schismatics the same generosity was shown. These were the sect that descended from the notorious bishop of Antioch, Paul of Samosata, deposed in 268 by a council of bishops, for various crimes and for his heretical teaching that there is no distinction between the three persons of the Holy Trinity. But these "Paulinians," so to call them, are to be rebaptised. Those who had functioned as clergy may be reordained if the Catholic bishop to whom they are now subject thinks fit.

On various aspects of clerical life there are as many as ten canons. No one is to be ordained who has had himself castrated, nor anyone only recently converted to the faith. "Yesterday a catechumen, today a bishop," says St. Jerome; "in the evening at the circus and next morning at the altar; just lately a patron of comedians, now busy consecrating virgins." It is the canon itself which speaks of ordination, and episcopal consecration, following immediately on baptism. Bishops are not to ordain another bishop's subject without his consent. No clerics—bishops, priests, or deacons—are to move from one diocese to another. Clerics are forbidden to take interest for money loans, and for this offence they must be deposed.

Finally there are two canons regarding three famous sees: Alexandria, Antioch, Jerusalem. The council confirms the ancient custom that gives the bishop of Alexandria jurisdiction over the bishops of the civil provinces of Egypt, Libya, and Pentapolis. And likewise the ancient privileges of the see of Antioch and of [the chief sees] of the other provinces. Jerusalem is a city apart, the Holy City par excellence, and although its bishop remains as much as ever the subject of the metropolitan bishop at Caesarea, he is allowed what canon 7 calls a precedence of honour, without a hint to say in what this consists.

All this variety of business was rapidly despatched, for the council held its final session barely four weeks after it opened, June 19, 325.

35

As the date all but coincided with the celebrations that marked the twentieth year of Constantine's reign, the emperor entertained the prelates at a banquet in full imperial style, and as they passed before the guards, presenting arms in salute, they asked themselves, says Eusebius, if the Kingdom of Heaven on earth had not finally come to pass.

Save for the letter of the bishops of Egypt, mentioned already, and two letters of the emperor, the one general, announcing the new rule about Easter, the other telling the people of Egypt that the bishops had confirmed the traditional belief and that Arius was the tool of the devil, we know nought of what might be called "the promulgation" of the council's decisions. But the breakup of the great gathering was by no means followed by the silence that accompanies peace perfectly attained. The real troubles had not yet begun.

2. The First General Council of Constantinople, 381

The second General Council of the Church, which met at Constantinople in the year 381, was summoned primarily as a solemn demonstration of the unshaken loyalty of the eastern bishops to the faith as set forth at Nicaea, a demonstration that the church of the East had never gone over to Arianism, that the Arians were no more than a heretical faction—had never been anything more, despite their power—and were now finally discredited. Why was such a declaration necessary, fifty-six years after the bishops of the East, with the enthusiastic support of the all-powerful emperor, had condemned Arius as a falsifier of the truth and had provided, in the *homo-oúsion,* a sure touchstone to test the orthodoxy of future bishops? The answer to this question is one of the strangest and most involved chapters in all Church History. The simplest way, perhaps, to set out as much of it as is essential to the story of the General Council of 381, will be to list the turning points of the story, and then attempt some explanation of the "why" of it all.

On the morrow of the Council of Nicaea three bishops revoked their signatures to the condemnation of Arius—the bishops of the neighbouring sees of Nicaea, Nicomedia, and Chalcedon. They were promptly banished by the emperor, and others elected in their stead (325). In 328 the bishop of Alexandria died, and the young deacon Athanasius, who had been his main advisor at the great council, was chosen to succeed him, and despite the active hostility of the Meletian faction, he was consecrated. That same year Constantine recalled the exiled bishops and reinstated them—why, we do not know; it may have been for personal reasons only. From this moment, until his death in 341, the ex-Lucianist, Eusebius of Nicomedia, becomes the leading figure in the movement to undo the work of Nicaea. After the emperor founded his new capital city, Constantinople, Eusebius became its bishop.

Eusebius never openly attacked the achievement of 325. His line was to work for the destruction of the leading bishops who had supported the *homo-oúsion*, on the plea that they were heretics, but of a different kind, i.e., men who did not really believe in the Trinity, who by the word *homo-oúsion* meant that the Father and the Logos were one. The first victim of this campaign was the second greatest prelate in the empire of the East, the bishop of Antioch, Eustathius by name. It was, possibly, he who had presided at Nicaea. A carefully chosen council of bishops now met at Antioch, condemned and deposed him. And, once again, the emperor followed up the ecclesiastical judgment by a sentence of exile. Nine other leading bishops were similarly removed in the course of the next year or so (330–32). In 332 the intrigue to remove Athanasius began. The agents of this were the Meletians of Alexandria. The point of attack was not the orthodoxy of his belief but his loyalty to the emperor. Athanasius was summoned to the court, and cleared himself easily, returning home with a letter of high commendation from Constantine. Two further attempts to disgrace him, in the next two years, also failed.

Then, in 334, Constantine did the most astonishing thing of all —astonishing to us who know, really, so very little of the day-to-day history of these events. He recalled Arius from banishment, and received him at court. And while a council was ordered to "investigate" what we may call "the Athanasius problem"—why it was that the greatest city of the eastern world had never known peace since this young prelate had been its bishop—Arius persuaded the emperor that he was as orthodox as the best, and on the strength of a formula drawn up by himself (in which the *homo-oúsion* did not appear) he was received back into the church, 335. As to the council, it was held at Tyre, and it deposed Athanasius; and the emperor, after a personal hearing, banished him to Trier, in Germany, as far almost as a man could travel from Alexandria and still be in the emperor's territory. It was now ten years since the farewell ceremonies at Nicaea.

In 336 Arius died, on the eve of a solemn ceremony of rehabilitation prepared in the cathedral of Constantinople, and in 337 Constantine, too, died.

Constantine's death brought the Arian party a still greater freedom of action. He was succeeded by his three young sons as joint emperors, and to none of these could the upholding of Nicaea be the matter of personal prestige it was to him. Certain it is that it is from this time that the party begins to propose alternatives to, or substitutes for, the Nicaean formula; more or less innocuous substitutes in the first years—had they not been put out by known opponents of the *homo-oúsion*, and by men who were the declared foes of the bishop, Athanasius, who had become the very symbol of all that the categorical test word stood for.

And here it needs to be said that there were many bishops, as little Arian as Athanasius himself, who, nevertheless, had no love for the famous Nicaean word—as there had been many such bishops at Nicaea. These Catholic bishops, supporting the various alternatives of the kind described, played the Arian game of course, albeit unconsciously. Their dislike of the test word arose from the fact that, in the East, as has been said already, the word *homo-oúsion* had a bad history. Its first use, by Clement of Alexandria and by Origen too (around 230–50), was seemingly in the Nicaean sense; and when a bishop of Alexandria, answering heretics, seemed to critics so to defend the distinction of persons in the Holy Trinity that he obscured the truth that there is only one God, it was made a point against him that he had not explicitly said the Logos was *homo-oúsion* with the Father. And this bishop, Denis, explains to his namesake, the pope, in his defence, why he had not used the useful word: it was a word nowhere found in Holy Scripture. This was about the year 257, nearly seventy years earlier than Nicaea. But eleven years only after this interchange between the two Denises, when the bishop of Antioch, Paul of Samosata, was condemned (268) for the heresy of teaching that the Father and the Logos are one person, he actually used the word *homo-oúsion* to express this oneness, and so his condemnation gave the word an ill sound in the East.

Whoever first proposed the use of the term at Nicaea, it was surely not any bishop from the East. To these it stank of heresy, ever since the council of 268, even when it had, so to speak, been disinfected by the Council of Nicaea, and given an undoubtedly orthodox employment. Sabellianism, the denial that there is a Trinity, was the great scare heresy of the East to the generation upon which Arianism came, and *homo-oúsion* had been the heresy's shibboleth, in eastern ears.[1]

Again, there is latent a first-class difficulty in the Nicaean council's formal condemnation[2] of those "who say that the Son is of another hypostasis or *ousia* [*substantia*, in Latin] than the Father"; and this was fully exploited in the troublous years after Constantine's death. The latent difficulty is that to Greeks these two terms did not necessarily and always mean exactly the same thing, as they did to Latins. Hypostasis to the Greeks came to mean what the Latins call "person"; *ousia* meant "nature" rather. The sentence "The Son is not of another hypostasis than the Father," a Greek might take to mean, "Father and Son are one person"; while the Latin understood by it, "are of the same nature."

All this is set down to convey something of the causes that held quite orthodox minds in doubt about their practical action during these controversies—a state of doubt which for years played into the hands of the radically unorthodox. This was an especially dangerous condition of things, seeing that it was these radicals—the real Arians—who had the ear of the court, and who stood to the world of officials and administrators for the ideal type of Christian believer, the kind that should be officially supported. For in this first generation that followed the personal conversion of Constantine, the official world was very far from being Christianised in belief. Though the emperor, especially after he had become sole emperor, turned his back very definitely on the pagan rites, these were by no means forbidden. The whole life of official paganism went on as before. And the cult of *Sol Invictus* and *Summus Deus* still held very many of its adherents. To these enlightened monotheistic foes of polytheism, the Arian version of the Christian idea of God naturally appealed. On a first view it was simpler, more logical—terms meaning just what they appeared to mean—its language nonmysterious, rational.[3]

[1] Cf. Newman, *Tracts* (as before), p. 100: "We cannot be surprised then that the *homoousion*, which perplexed the Western bishops, should have irritated the Orientals; the only wonder is, that East and West had concurred in accepting it at Nicea."

[2] As a conclusion to the creed.

[3] See Newman, *Tracts* (as before), p. 102: "It must be added that to statesmen, lawyers and military chiefs, who had lately been Pagans, a religious teaching such as Arianism, which was clear and intelligible, was more acceptable than doctrines which described the Divine Being in language, self-contradictory

It is not, of course, suggested that there was a carefully worked out plan, in all this, on the part of high officials. But the two tendencies existed side by side in these years, and it was this accidental coincidence that did much, so it is suggested,[4] to make Arianism the highly dangerous threat it proved to be, and to give it a toughness out of all proportion to the number of its real adherents.

As to its quality as a danger to Catholicism, let Harnack's judgment be recalled, that Arianism, had it been victorious, must have ruined Christianity completely, emptying it of all religious content, leaving it a mere system of cosmology and ethics. It was, in the circumstances, one of the greatest dangers that true religion has ever had to face, and this despite the fact that, in the critical fourth century, Arianism was never a popular thing. "The laity, as a whole, revolted from it in every part of Christendom. It was an epidemic of the schools and of theologians, and to them it was mainly confined. . . . The classes which had furnished martyrs in the persecutions were in no sense the seat of the heresy."[5]

The only one of Constantine's sons who really favoured the anti-Nicaean party was Constantius II, and once he became sole master of the empire (350) the Radicals really threw off the mask, and Arianism proper—the explicit renunciation of the doctrine that the Logos is truly God—was now propounded in councils and, with great violence and persecution, imposed by the emperor. And it was in these years (350–61) that the heresy was first thrust upon the bishops of the still largely pagan West, of Illyricum, Italy, and Gaul. In council after council, in the west and in the east, whether perplexed by the confusion of the issues, whether terrified by the threats of the emperor and the knowledge that bishops had been murdered who opposed him, whether overcome by the specious argument that it was all, in reality, a matter of ridding the Church of Athanasius, "whom they were taught to consider a restless, violent, party-spirited man, and of his arbitrary formula"[6]—in council after council the bishops gave way wholesale, at Arles (353), Milan (355), Sirmium (357), and, most spectacularly, at the simultaneous

---

in its letter, and which exacted a belief in truths which were absolutely above their comprehension."

[4] See Msgr. Pierre Batiffol, *La Paix Constantinienne et le Catholicisme* (1914), p. 310.

[5] Newman, as before, pp. 97–98.

[6] Newman, as before, p. 100.

councils of Rimini-Seleucia[7] (359) about the morrow of which St. Jerome wrote a celebrated phrase, that the whole world woke up one morning, lamenting and marvelling to find itself Arian.

In 361 Constantius disappeared, baptised (just in time) by an Arian. He was followed by Julian the Apostate, who set about a systematic revival of Paganism. Then came Jovian, a Catholic, and after him Valentinian, a "liberal," with Valens, his brother, co-emperor for the East. Valens (365–78) a true Arian, of the political type, returned to the policy of Constantius, and a real persecution of Catholics followed. But the cloudiness of the early period had been dissipated. The issue was now clear to the bishops, that only by insistence on the *homo-oúsion* could the Church rid itself of the crypto-Arians whose influence meant death. And when to Valens, killed in a war with the Goths (378), a Catholic general, from Spain, succeeded—Theodosius—the way was at last open to a real restoration of the traditional belief. Nicaea, for the first time in fifty years, was to come into full operation in all the sees of the East.

The General Council of 381 is an epilogue to a drama just concluded. It does little more than register a *fait accompli*, and its essential importance is its demonstration to the world that the Christians of the "East," after more than fifty years of continuous disturbance and of oppression on the part of their rulers, remain Catholics, are not Arians; it is a demonstration that the council of Nicaea was no mere ecclesiastical pageant, but a source of strong and unfailing leadership.

No two general councils follow the same historical pattern—not even when a bare fifty years separates them, and when the matter of their discussions is the same. In this council Rome, the West, was not represented at all—was not so much as invited. The same problems had for years now vexed the churches of the West. The same political revolution—the appearance of sovereigns who were wholeheartedly Catholic—was to be their salvation also. And they, too, demanded a council, and it took place, at Aquileia some weeks after the council we are dealing with. And why the council which met at Constantinople came, in after years, to be regarded as a Gen-

[7] Rimini, on the Adriatic coast of Italy, for the bishops of the West; Seleucia, then the chief city of Isauria, is the modern Turkish port of Silifke on the Mediterranean.

eral Council is something that may puzzle the legists and the theologians.[8]

The bishops who sat in the council were 150 in all. There were none from Egypt, only half of them from Thrace and Asia. Almost one half of the bishops came from the vast (civil) diocese called the East, *Oriens,* whose chief see was Antioch. And it was the bishop of Antioch, Meletius, who presided at the council.

Once again the crosscurrents and misunderstandings of these much troubled years had borne strange fruit. At Antioch there was a rival claimant to the see, Paulinus. And it was Paulinus whom Rome (and Alexandria also) recognised as the lawful bishop. But the Catholic East was solidly behind Meletius, and this meant the support (among others) of the three great Cappadocian bishops, St. Basil, St. Gregory of Nyssa, his brother, and St. Gregory of Nazianzen, the greatest theologian of the day and one of the greatest preachers of all time.[8a]

Meletius died before the council had been long in session, and it was the last named Gregory who was elected president in his place. The actual business before the council was slight, and now, with the see of Antioch vacant and seventy-one bishops of its "jurisdiction" already assembled (to say nothing of the no less interested eighty bishops from other provinces), it is not surprising that the question of the successor of Meletius took the first place in the minds of all. The president of the council had the happy idea that the bishop whom Rome and Alexandria recognised, Paulinus, should be chosen, and so the schism be ended. But of this the bishops would not hear. And then there arrived the bishop of Alexandria himself, the successor of Athanasius, with some of his suffragans, and he made such a bitter attack on the president because he had consented, being already bishop of Sasima, to become bishop of Constantinople,[9] that Gregory, already discouraged by the revelation of what ecclesiastical politics could be at a high level, resigned both his see and his presidency.

[8] The first stage in the development of its recognition as oecumenical was the unanimous vote of the General Council of Chalcedon, 4th session (451), taking as the rule of faith, "that fixed by the council of Nicaea, and which the 150 bishops of the council assembled at Constantinople by Theodosius the Great confirmed."

[8a] Barry, no. 17, prints a translation of his speech to the council.

[9] A breach of the law enacted at Nicaea.

The council closed on July 9. What it had accomplished was, first, to issue a statement of belief which explicitly renewed the *homo-oúsion* definition of Nicaea, and then, naming the many varieties of Arianism, to condemn each and every one of them as heretical. The bishops next published (what has long been lost) a detailed statement of their faith in the consubstantiality of the Divine Logos with the Father, in the distinctness of the three Persons of the Holy Trinity, and in the reality of the Incarnation of the Second Person. These statements about belief involved the condemnation of two other theories related to Arianism, namely, the denial, by Macedonius and his followers, that the Holy Ghost is really God, and the theory of Apollinaris, bishop of Laodicaea, that in the Logos Incarnate—in the God-man, Jesus Christ—the Divine Logos functions in place of a human soul: Christ, who is truly God, is not truly a man. This last heresy was to have a famous history in the next seventy years, to be the occasion of two later General Councils, and, ultimately, in one form or another, so to divide the Catholics of the East as to paralyse their resistance to the assault of Islam.

There are four canons enacted by this council.[10] The first is the declaration renewing the work of Nicaea, and condemning these various heresies. The second, between the lines of which can be read much of the history since that council, forbids bishops to cross the frontiers of another [civil] diocese, or to interfere in another bishop's administration. The bishop of Alexandria, it is explicitly laid down, is to confine himself to Egypt; the bishops of the East (i.e., *Oriens*) shall confine their joint action to the East, with the reservation that the bishop of Antioch keeps the rights acknowledged at Nicaea; and statements no less explicit restrict the bishops of Asia, Pontus, and Thrace to those three [civil] dioceses, respectively. The bishops are reminded of the Nicaean rule that the affairs of the sees of any given province are to be regulated by a twice-yearly meeting of the bishops.

About the time that St. Gregory Nazianzen was invited to become bishop of Constantinople, the efforts of the bishop of Alexandria, Peter II, had brought about the "election" of an Alexandrian philosopher, Maximus, and his unlawful, clandestine consecration. The council (canon 4) now declared that Maximus was not a

10 Schroeder, op. cit., prints the text and a translation.

bishop, and that whatever ordinations he had ever performed were worthless, and the candidates "in truth not ordained at all."

There remains the third canon, the most famous action, in its historical effects, of this council: "The bishop of Constantinople shall have the primacy of honour after the bishop of Rome, because [Constantinople] is New Rome."

3. The General Council of Ephesus, 431

One of the minor activities of the General Council of 381 was to provide a new bishop for the see it thought worthy of the second place in the Church, in place of Gregory of Nazianzen who had been forced out. The bishops chose an old retired veteran of the high places of the imperial administration—Nectarius. He ruled for sixteen years, and gave general satisfaction. And it is recorded that, in his quiet and peaceful way, this practiced administrator began to turn the new primacy of honour into something very like a primacy of fact. It gradually became the fashion to send appeals of various kinds to Constantinople, and for the bishop there to deal with them as though to do so were part of his jurisdiction. When Nectarius died, in 397, the question who should succeed him was, then, something to interest the whole East.

The personage who moved immediately was the bishop of Alexandria, Theophilus. He had a candidate, one of his own priests, one of his chief confidants in fact. But the court had a candidate also—the court being no longer the emperor who had called the council in 381, Theodosius,[1] but the minister Eutropius who governed in the name of Theodosius' youthful successor, Arcadius. The court had its way, and brought from Antioch an ascetic personage, the monk John, famed as the great preacher of the day, known to later ages thereby as Chrysostom, the man with the tongue of gold. He was consecrated, by Theophilus, in February 398. But Theophilus went home bitter, it is thought. Alexandria had failed to place its man in 397, as it had failed on the like occasion in 381, in the time of its late bishop Timothy; and it was only the threats of Eutropius —that there were serious charges on file against Theophilus—that

---

[1] He had died January 17, 395, the last man to rule the whole Roman world as sole emperor; and he died a man in the prime of life.

had brought that bishop to accept the appointment of the monk from Antioch.

A few words about the actual power of the bishop of Alexandria will revive some of the faded colour of the tragic history that is to follow. He was, first of all, more absolutely lord, in all matters of daily life, of the bishops dependent on him than was, at that time, any other bishop in the Church; and of these dependent bishops there were something like one hundred. He chose them all, and he personally consecrated them, the metropolitans no less than their suffragans. He was also, whether himself a monk or not, a kind of supreme patriarch of the monks, in this country where the monastic life had begun—and he thereby enjoyed unique prestige in the whole monastic world. He was immensely wealthy, with revenues coming from such extraordinary sources as his see's monopoly of the right to sell salt, and nitrates and papyrus, and all the various lugubrious paraphernalia needed in funerals. Alexandria, until Constantinople rose to the fullness of its promise, was the wonder city of the whole Roman world, the greatest of all trade centres, the queen of the Mediterranean. And of nothing was the great city prouder than of its see. The bishop of Alexandria moved in an habitual popularity and power that made of him a kind of native king, with mobs willing to demonstrate in his favour at a moment's notice. For forty-five years the see had had in Athanasius a saint for its bishop, a saint whose endless contests with the never much loved imperial government, whose many exiles, and inflexible fidelity to Nicaea, had achieved for his successors a position the like of which has probably never been known. This, in the hands of a saint! But Theophilus was far from being a saint. The saint, now, was at Constantinople, and in a world of Theophilus' kind he was soon to be hopelessly lost.

These considerations, the space given to them, rather—and to the story of St. John Chrysostom—in a study of the councils of Ephesus and Chalcedon, is due to the simple facts that rivalry between the two sees, Alexandria and Constantinople, ceaseless after 381, mattered very greatly in the history of these councils; that Alexandria sought endlessly to control Constantinople; that at Ephesus in 431 and again in 449 a bishop of Alexandria was the very willing agent of the deposition and excommunication of a bishop of Constantinople; and that at Chalcedon, in 451, the all but impossible happened and a bishop of Alexandria was deposed and excommunicated; and Alexandria—civic, popular Alexandria no less than the clerical world and the monks—never forgot this, and never forgave it. And it being the fifth century and not the twentieth, the more human side of these grave ecclesiastical contentions ultimately brought down to ruin the wealthiest province of the empire.

Chrysostom, as he is commonly called, the first effective bishop his see had known for many years, found abundance of employment for his zeal, and inevitably made as many enemies as friends; wealthy enemies and highly placed, clergy among them, and even the young empress. The first occasion of his clash with the bishop of Alexandria was the kind reception he gave to alleged victims of Theophilus' harsh rule. This was some three years after his appointment. On the heels of these fugitives there came other monks, sent by Theophilus, with counter-accusations of heresy. But they failed to prove their case, before the emperor, and were themselves condemned. And the fugitives brought it about that Theophilus was summoned to answer their charges in person. He arrived (403) with a cohort of twenty-nine of his bishops in attendance, blaming Chrysostom for all that had happened, and swearing openly that he had come to the capital "to depose John."

And this is what his familiarity with the great world, his political skill and his lavish expenditure, actually achieved. John, when bidden by the emperor to summon a council for the trial of Theophilus had refused: Alexandria lay outside his jurisdiction. He now, in turn, was bidden by the emperor to take his trial, Theophilus his judge with his twenty-nine suffragans and a chance half-dozen visiting bishops picked up in the capital—the group called the "Synod of The Oak," from the country seat at Chalcedon where these bishops met.

John again refused to acknowledge an uncanonical jurisdiction. Whereupon, for his refusal to appear, he was condemned and deposed. The ultimate outcome of these proceedings was his exile to the farthest limits of the empire; and his treatment was so harsh that he died of it (407). Theophilus celebrated his victory by composing a book against John filled, it would seem, with all manner of hideous calumnies. And in John's place there ruled one of the priests of Constantinople whom the saint had had to censure.

These bare facts, which seemingly all writers accept, are sufficient witness to the existence of malevolence at Alexandria, and to the corruption of life at the court of a Christian emperor. The other feature of this story is the action of the pope,[2] when the full account of these deeds reached him—letters from Theophilus (wholly misleading), from John (a full account, down to the day he wrote) and the minutes of the Synod of The Oak. This last the pope refused to accept as a council at all. Its sentence on John was mere words. He took John to be still the lawful bishop of Constantinople, and when he was asked to recognise Atticus, put in John's place, he refused, and broke off relations with both Alexandria and Antioch who had recognised him.

Theophilus was still out of communion when he died (412). His successor, a nephew, Cyril, began his long career as bishop equally under the ban. Antioch was the first see to surrender and make the symbolic submission, by restoring John's name "to the diptychs"—placing him in the list of deceased bishops officially prayed for. Then Atticus did the same, explaining fearfully to Alexandria that he really had no choice but to do this. Cyril, very young, as self-confident and absolute as was ever his uncle, stubbornly —even passionately?—refused. "You might as well ask to put Judas back in the company of the Apostles," he wrote. Cyril had been with his uncle at The Oak. But in the end, he too restored John's name. It was fifteen years or so since these terrible scenes of episcopal vindictiveness. But the saint's body had now been brought back with honour to his cathedral, and in a kind of public *amende* for the crime of the emperor Arcadius in banishing him, his son, Theodosius II, knelt before the coffin and kissed it. And between Rome and all the major sees of the East there was communion and peace.

The new troubles came then, as it were, out of a blue sky. Alexandria and Constantinople had long made their peace with Rome. And when Atticus died in 424 the new bishop, an elderly civil servant, managed the affairs of the turbulent capital so as to please all parties, his clergy, the monks, and the court. But with the appointment of Nestorius as his successor, in April 428, the peace was suddenly, and very rudely, broken. Like St. John Chrysostom the new bishop was a monk from Antioch. There he, too, had been a famous

[2] St. Innocent I, 402–17.

preacher, whose appointed task was the public explanation of the Scriptures. And he began his new career with a great oration, in which he called on the emperor to root out the remnants of the many heresies, pockets of which still existed in Constantinople.

In the new controversy which this sermon heralded, the natural characters of Nestorius and of Cyril of Alexandria play a great part —not more so perhaps than the personalities of such chiefs always play, but for once we are well supplied with evidence about this. As to the precise point on which Nestorius soon fell foul of all his world, he is himself our earliest witness—in two letters to the pope, Celestine I (422–31), written in the early months of his administration. He is explaining to the pope the difficulties he has to face in his war against the heretics, and he proceeds to say that one very serious matter is the unconscious heresy of good Catholics, of monks and even some of his clergy, about the meaning of the belief that Christ is God. They are confused in their minds about the great mystery that Christ is both God and man, and they speak as though what is human in Christ was divine. They talk, for example, of God having been born, and of God being buried, and invoke the most holy virgin Mary as the "God-bringing-forth," the mother of God (using the Greek word that expresses this so succinctly, *Theotókos*). They should, of course, be more careful in their speech, and say she is *Christotókos*—the one who brought forth Christ, the mother of Christ. "The Virgin," he told the pope, "is certainly *Christotókos*: she is not *Theotókos*." In speaking and acting as they do these Catholics are reviving, says Nestorius, "the corruption of Arius and Apollinaris," heretics notoriously condemned long ago. And Nestorius speaks feelingly of "the fight which I have to put up over this."[3]

By the time Nestorius had written these letters, his public support of preachers whom he brought in to "correct" his ignorant clergy, and his own sermons, his prohibition of the use of the word *Theotókos* and the punishments he meted out to the disobedient, had set the capital in an uproar. And the trouble was crossing the seas. For the news of his ill treatment of the monks had spread to the land which was the centre of the monastic movement, Egypt, and when the Egyptian monks laid the theological problem before their bishop, Cyril—the accusation that the traditional Catholic

[3] Batiffol, Msgr. Pierre, *Le Siège Apostolique*, 359–451, 343.

piety towards the God-man and his mother was heretical—there entered the field the very unusual combination of a first-rate theologian who was also a finished man of affairs and an experienced politician. Cyril wrote, for his monks, a theological defence of the tradition which was necessarily a severe denunciation of Nestorius.[4] This was sometime after the Easter of 429, and the "reply" was presently circulating in Constantinople. And Cyril also wrote to Nestorius.

In the events of the next two years the natural man in Cyril was to reveal itself fairly often. What of the same in Nestorius? What was it that so suddenly moved him to attack what was not a local piety peculiar to the city where he had just begun to live but, as the event showed (and as Nestorius must have known), a general, traditional way of regarding this doctrine? His own first letters on the subject are a curious mixture of orthodoxy and of novel statements, "startling to pious ears," as a later day would have said; statements capable indeed of being explained as in harmony with the tradition, but until so explained, and especially when set out in criticism of current practice, justifiably causing real suspicion that the speaker was himself a heretic—a man, that is to say, out to propagate a new, personal, antitraditional version of fundamental belief. What prompted all this? The vanity of the learned man who has found out something the generality do not know? the possession of key-knowledge that will "make all the difference"? the desire of a gifted man, promoted suddenly from obscurity to one of the highest places in the world of his time, to make his mark, to set all things right? For his point that, although *Theotókos*, rightly understood, is perfectly orthodox, it is better to use his own new word *Christotókos*, the suitable place to air this—a first time—might have been a conference of theologians or bishops. But Nestorius chose to do it in sermons to the multitudes that filled his cathedral, and not in terms of learned, anxious speculation, but in blood-and-thunder denunciation of universally practiced piety. There is a levity about the action which, given the gravity of the issue, is itself surely scandalous. And was Nestorius a really honest, straightforward type? In his first correspondence with the pope, when he tells of his problem with Pelagian refugees from Italy, he is even naïvely devious, and the pope in his reply points this out very bluntly. And

[4] Whom, however, Cyril does not name.

once the major forces had been brought in against him, Cyril of Alexandria and the verdict of Rome, he certainly shows himself, in his manoeuvres with the court, a twister of the first order: *Trop habile Nestorius*.[5]

When Cyril wrote directly to Nestorius, in February 430, seemingly, he said how surprised he was that he should disturb the peace of mind of the faithful by such very controvertible statements. Nestorius in return attacked the explanation Cyril had given the monks, called it untraditional, and said explicitly that it was the Apollinarian heresy all over again. Cyril had given him the news that Rome considered his views scandalous, and Nestorius ended his letter with a hint that the court was on his side. Cyril was not unaware that at Constantinople there were clerics from Egypt, gone there with a case against their chief bishop, and that Nestorius was taking care of these enemies. It was with reference to this situation that Cyril wrote to his agents in the capital, about this time: "This poor fellow does not imagine, surely, that I am going to allow myself to be judged by him, whoever the accusers are that he can stir up against me! It will be the other way round. I shall know well enough how to force him back to the defensive."[6] The temperature is rising rapidly, on both shores of the Mediterranean.

It was now that Cyril first approached the court on the matter of Nestorius, sending explanations of the point at issue to the emperor, his wife and sisters.

The next move was a council in Egypt, sometime after Easter 430, and an elaborate report to the pope on the part of Cyril—his answer to the Roman query whether certain sermons that have come to the pope were really Nestorius' sermons.[7] Cyril's reply was a "skilfully written letter"[8] describing the situation at Constantinople, saying that all the bishops of the East are united in their anxiety about these errors of Nestorius. He is quite isolated in his denial that the Virgin is *Theotókos*, but flatters himself that he will bring the rest round, "so greatly has the power[9] of his see in-

[5] Batiffol, as before, 361; also, 343.
[6] Batiffol, as before, 348, n. 5. St. Cyril's *Letters*, no. X. Also quoted Bardy, *Les débuts du Nestorianisme*, F. and M., vol. 4, p. 172, n. 2.
[7] Batiffol, as before, 349, n. 1.
[8] Bardy, 172, *fort habilement redigée*.
[9] The word translated by "power" is *dunameis*. When the pope passes to state his decision to the clergy and faithful of Constantinople (August 11,

fatuated him." The bishops will not publicly break off relations with Nestorius without consulting the pope. "Deign then to make known to us what seems good to you, and whether we ought either to remain in communion with him or to declare publicly that no one should remain in communion with a man who thinks and teaches so erroneously." The pope's reply, Cyril recommends, should be sent to all the bishops of the East.

With this letter went copies of Nestorius' sermons (and a Latin translation of them), then the Cyril-Nestorius correspondence, then a list drawn up by Cyril of the errors said to be taught by Nestorius, and a compendium of texts from the classic theologians of the past on the doctrine called in question.

When this dossier reached Rome, Pope Celestine set it before a specially summoned gathering of bishops, and on August 11, 430, he wrote his judgment. This he sent, in the first place, to Cyril. In this letter the pope speaks of Cyril's communication as a consolation amid his grief at the sermons Nestorius had been preaching. Already, that is, before receiving Cyril's letter, the pope had handed over these sermons to one of the great scholars of the day, the bilingual John Cassian, to be the basis of a book against Nestorius. But Cyril's letter, the pope continues, suggests how to cure this terrible evil. To the question about remaining in communion with the bishop of Constantinople, the pope replies that those whom Nestorius had excommunicated because they opposed him remain, nevertheless, in full communion, and those who obstinately follow the path that leads away from the apostolic teaching cannot be "in communion with us," i.e., the pope. Nestorius, he instructs Cyril, is to be summoned to make a written recantation of his errors, and to declare that his belief about the birth of Christ is what the church of Rome believes, the church of Alexandria, and the universal church. And Cyril is charged with the execution of this decision. He is to act in the pope's place, and, speaking with all the authority of the pope's see, is to demand this retraction of Nestorius, to be made in writing, within ten days of the notice given. If within this time Nestorius has not complied he is to be declared expelled from the church.

---

430) and says, "The authority of our see has decided," the noun used is *authentia*—i.e., supreme authority, where the other term *dunameis* is "high rank," or "resources."

To the bishops of Antioch, Jerusalem, Thessalonica, and Phi-lippi[10] the pope also wrote letters which follow the same line as that to Cyril, but make no mention of the commission to act which the pope had sent him. The pope merely says, with great gravity, "The sentence we pronounce, which is even more the sentence of our master Christ who is God, is . . ." and so on, as in the letter to Cyril.

We possess, besides the letter to Cyril, the letter which the pope wrote, that same day, to Nestorius. In this Celestine explains that lack of scholars who could translate the bishop's letters and sermons had delayed his reply, then came the dossier sent from Alexandria, which has been studied. The pope tells the bishop of Constantinople that his letters are "full of evident blasphemies." The sermons, for all their obscurity, plainly teach heresy. What a dreadful mistake it was to make Nestorius a bishop! The sheep have, indeed, been handed over to the wolf. And now, those whose lack of foresight brought this about are calling on the pope to help them out of the difficulty. The pope does not point out to Nestorius the particular places where he has gone astray, list any of "your many impious declarations, which the whole church rejects." But, as he tells him, this present letter is a final warning. The bishop of Alexandria is in the right, in this controversy. "Brother, if you wish to be with us . . . openly show that you think as we think." "Our sentence is this," and the letter ends with a demand for a written declaration that Nestorius believes the very thing he has repudiated, with a notice of the ten days allowed, and a warning that noncompliance means his immediate excommunication. Celestine then tells him that all the papers concerning the process have been sent to Alexandria, and that he has commissioned Cyril to act in his name and to inform him, Nestorius, and the other bishops what the pope has decided.

A letter, in much the same terms, also went from the pope to the clergy and faithful people of the capital. But the pope did not write to the emperor.

What the normal time was for a public letter to go from Rome to Alexandria, in the fifth century, and thence on to Constantinople,

[10] In the province of Macedonia (and therefore directly subject to the Holy See), 70 miles east of Thessalonica, 240 due west of Constantinople.

a business involving sea-journeys of something like a thousand miles, it is not easy to say. But it is surprising that not until December 7 was Nestorius officially summoned by Cyril to recant. And the bishop of Alexandria did not carry out his task in person—as, presumably, the pope designed. He sent the ultimatum by four of his suffragan bishops. Nor did he content himself with sending the pope's letters of commission, his own credentials in the matter. Before moving, he had called a synod of the bishops of Egypt, and he now sent on to Nestorius their synodal letter condemning his teaching. Finally, to make the expected retractation doubly sure, Cyril had drafted twelve statements about the heresies Nestorius was alleged to support, statements all of which ended: "Whoever believes this, may he be anathema," i.e., accursed.[10a] These Nestorius was to sign.

But in the long interval between August 11 and December 7 much had happened at Constantinople and elsewhere. Nestorius had had a correspondence with the bishop of Antioch, who urged him, in very plain language, to do as he was asked, and not to cause trouble merely about a word he disliked (*Theotókos*) but which he admitted could bear an orthodox meaning, and to which many saints and doctors of the past had given sanction by themselves using it. "Don't lose your head," wrote the Antiochean. Ten days! "It will not take you twenty-four hours to give the needed answer. . . . Ask advice of men you can trust. Ask them to tell you the facts, not just what they think will please you. . . . You have the whole of the East against you, as well as Egypt." Nestorius, in his reply to this surely good friend, hedged. He gave no explicit answer, merely saying he had not been rightly understood, that if his book forbade the use of the famous word it was because heretics were using it, with an heretical meaning. And that now he will just wait for the council,[11] which will settle this, and all other problems. As to Cyril, it is he who is the troublemaker. "As to the Egyptian's insolence, it will scarcely surprise you, for you have many evidences of it, old and new."[12]

On November 19, the emperor had summoned a General Coun-

[10a] Barry, no. 18, prints a translation of the synodal letter and the anathemas.
[11] Announced since John of Antioch's letter.
[12] For this correspondence, Batiffol, as before, 361–62.

cil of the Church, for certain vaguely described purposes, the summons said, but actually, no one doubted, to settle this controversy between Constantinople and Alexandria and—in the expectation of Nestorius—to be the scene of the trial for heresy (Apollinarianism) of Cyril. The council was to meet at Ephesus, at Pentecost (June 7) 431.

When Cyril's four bishops reached Constantinople, December 7, Nestorius refused to receive them. John of Antioch, in the letter just mentioned, had passed on to Nestorius copies of the pope's letter condemning him, and also of a letter he (John) had received from Cyril. Long before Cyril's four bishops walked into the sanctuary of the cathedral at Constantinople, that December Sunday, to hand over the ultimatum, Nestorius had known all about it. And he had not been idle. It was from Nestorius, it is often said, that the council idea had come. And in the emperor's letter inviting Cyril to the council there was much to make it evident that the glorification of Alexandria was no part of the programme. Cyril's writing separate letters to the emperor, the empress, and the princesses was here declared to be an attempt to divide the imperial family, and the bishop was ordered—not invited—to attend the council, under severe penalties.[13] On the other hand, the emperor's act had changed the whole situation for Nestorius. In summoning the council Theodosius had forbidden all and every ecclesiastical change, no matter by whom, until the council had concluded. And when Nestorius now wrote to the pope of the crimes that were to be brought against Cyril when the council met, he made light of the theological controversy, gave not a hint that he knew of the pope's judgment, but wrote that Cyril, he hears, is preparing a "Faith in danger" campaign, in the hope of distracting the council from his own anxieties.

The pope made no difficulty about the emperor's plan to call a council, nor about the prohibition which—in fact—had called a halt to the summons to Nestorius. And when Cyril wrote to ask whether Nestorius was now to be treated as excommunicated, for the ten days had long since gone by, the pope in reply quoted the Scripture

[13] Cf. Newman on the emperor, "distrustful of Cyril": "Theodosius disliked Cyril; he thought him proud and overbearing, a restless agitator and an intriguer; and he told him so in a letter that has come down to us." *Trials of Theodoret*, in *Historical Sketches*, II, 348. It seems safe to date this essay, first printed in 1873, in the 1860s.

that God wills not the death of a sinner, but rather that he be converted and live. And Cyril is exhorted to work for peace with the rest of the bishops.

The date of this letter is May 7, 431—one month before the day appointed for the council, five months from the day Cyril's deputation tried to deliver the ultimatum to Nestorius. And in those five months the twelve anathemas of Cyril, so to call them, had time to circulate; and—in the vast territories where the influence of Antioch was strong—they had raised issues which now quite overshadowed the differences between Cyril and Nestorius, or between Rome and Nestorius even. In the eyes of these Antiochean theologians the language in which the bishop of Alexandria had framed his statements revealed him as a pure Apollinarian. And John of Antioch had organised a party to make this clear at the council, and had in the meantime induced two bishops—one of them held to be Cyril's equal as a scholarly writer, Theodoret of Cyrrhus[14]—to come out with public refutations of the Alexandrian's "heresies." And this group wrote to the bishops of the West for support, to Milan, for example, to Aquileia, and to Ravenna.

How much of this was known to Pope Celestine, when he wrote his letter of May 7, we do not know. But he surely knew that minds were inflamed, and as he gave Cyril the news that he was not himself able to make the journey to Ephesus, he urged "the Egyptian" to be moderate, to remember that what the pope wanted was that Nestorius should be won back. We must not, said the pope, again scripturally, be of those "swift to shed blood."

The day after this letter was written the pope signed the instructions for the three legates who were to represent him at the council. They were told to act throughout with Cyril and to watch carefully that the authority of the Apostolic See was duly respected. And, finally, the pope sent a letter to the council. It is a moving document, in which Celestine reminds the bishops of the beloved apostle St. John, whose remains lie in the church at Ephesus where they are meeting, and reminds them that they are the successors of the twelve apostles, privileged to preserve what their labours had established. The pope speaks plainly about the Nestorian novelties: they are treason to the faith. He exhorts the bishops to unanimity,

---

[14] Whom John had already called in to induce Nestorius to admit the orthodoxy of the use of the word *Theotókos*.

and to be courageous in act. Then he presents his legates, who will take part in the council and will tell the bishops, "the things which we decided at Rome were to be done." "Nor do we doubt your assent to all this," the pope goes on, "when it is seen how all that is done has been ordered for the security of the whole church."[14a]

To the legates the pope entrusted a letter for the emperor, announcing that he would be represented at the council by legates, and praying he would give no encouragement to these novel ideas now causing such trouble, the work of men who would reduce the idea of God to the limits of what a finite intelligence could explore. The pope leaves it in no doubt, in this as in the other letter, that Nestorius is already condemned; if the pope consents to the case being discussed once more, this is in the hope that the unfortunate man will retract.

The emperor had not convoked every single bishop of the empire to the council, but only a certain number from each of the fifty-nine provinces of his own jurisdiction, the choice being left to the metropolitans. In all, something like 230 or 250 ultimately arrived at Ephesus. Cyril came in a few days before the appointed date. He found Nestorius already established. He had been at Ephesus since Easter, with a small group of sympathetic prelates. Cyril had brought with him fifty Egyptian bishops. Sometime after Pentecost the (anti-Nestorius) bishop of Jerusalem arrived with fifteen supporters, and later came news from the Antiocheans, forty-six in all, that they had been delayed by accidents. This last group had chosen to travel by the land route, a thousand miles and more of difficult and—as it happened—famine-stricken country.

The most numerous group at the council was the bishops of what we, today, call Asia Minor, the nineteen provinces that then made up the (civil) dioceses of Asia and Pontus, and the district called Proconsular Asia which was subject to the emperor's direct rule. It was in this last that Ephesus itself was situated. In Asia Minor there were, in all, something like three hundred sees. It was the most Catholicized territory of all the empire. Something like a hundred of these bishops came to the council. The bishop of Ephesus, Memnon, acted as their leader, and they were to a man anti-Constantinople—the question of the *Theotókos* apart. The repeated attempts

14a These three letters are in Jaffé, nos. 377, 378, 379.

of successive bishops of the capital city, since 381, to turn the primacy of honour then voted it into an effective hold on the only territory not already dominated by Antioch or Alexandria, made the bishops of Ephesus allies of the foe of Constantinople in all these disputes.

Meanwhile the Antiocheans did not arrive, and the bishops waited, for a good two weeks after the appointed day, June 7, in the great city, two hundred of them nearly, each with his retinue, in the scorching latitude of 38 degrees north. Disputes were frequent, fights and riots with the Nestorian minority, in which the town naturally took an interested part.[15] But Cyril made no attempt to meet Nestorius. The two prelates avoided each other. Each, to the other, was a wicked heretic, awaiting his trial and deserved condemnation. And while the bishop of Ephesus forbade the churches of the city to Nestorius, Cyril was free to preach on Nestorius as the enemy of truth, the outcast already condemned by the pope.[16]

On June 21 the long wait was broken. Cyril announced that the next day the council would hold its opening session. Immediately there were protests. From the imperial commissioner, in the first place, Count Candidian, who was charged with the safety of the council, under orders to prevent any but the bishops from entering the church where the meetings would take place,[17] and with keeping order in the council itself, i.e., to see that every bishop who wished to speak was allowed to speak, and to reply to attacks made on him; also to see that no bishop left Ephesus until the council had ended its business. Candidian demanded a delay until the Antiocheans arrived. So did no fewer than sixty-eight bishops, in a written protestation. And Nestorius, with his party, made their protest too, saying the council was no council until all the bishops were assembled. But Cyril stood to his announcement, and on June 22 the council opened—a memorable first session in which much was enacted, and in which still more lay mischievously latent, *suppositos cineri doloso* indeed.[18]

---

[15] The leading prelates brought each his own bodyguard; Cyril, sailors from Alexandria, Nestorius, gladiators from the circus.

[16] Newman, as before, 349–50.

[17] The great church called Maria Theotókos.

[18] "Beneath ashes deceptively cool." The reference is to Horace's famous warning to historians, *Odes*, II, 1.

The question has been raised by what authority Cyril thus opened the council, acting as though he was its acknowledged president. That the mass of the bishops at the time accepted the *fait accompli*, without any sign of protest—even the sixty-eight signatories—is certain. It was also traditional that Alexandria was the first see of the East. Its bishop being present at a General Council, and neither pope nor emperor having named another to preside, he was surely its inevitable president. Nestorius, in the memoirs he wrote, many years later, says: "We expected that he who exercised authority (the emperor, through Candidian) would have chosen the president. No one thought you would have taken it for yourself." But from the 159[19] bishops who were in the church as the day's work began there was not a sign of objection to Cyril.

The first, unallowed-for incident was a protestation, to the council this time, not to Cyril, from Candidian. It was the emperor's will, he said, that there should not be any "fragmentary councils."[20] He was asked to show his instructions and did so. But the bishops stood firm, and begged him to leave, which he did, after a final plea to wait for the absentees, upon whose arrival Nestorius and his party would join the council.

The council then settled down to its business. A notary read a summary of the case against Nestorius, told how Cyril had intervened at Constantinople, and then at Rome, and how "the most holy bishop of the church of Rome, Celestine, has written what it behoved." And the notary announced that all the documents were here and at the disposition of the bishops.

Nestorius was then sent for. Three times—as the Law demanded —he was officially and personally summoned, a deputation going from the council to the place where he lived. He ignored all three citations, and the council passed to the study of his case.

The next act was the reading of the creed of Nicaea, and then of Cyril's letter to Nestorius. Cyril then rose, acknowledging the letter, and to put it to the bishops to vote whether the theology of his letter was in accord with the creed of Nicaea; 125 of the bishops followed him, each making profession of the Nicene faith, and affirming that the letter accorded with Nicaea. A demand was made

[19] "Round about 160," says Bardy, F. and M., 4, 180. The exact figure is a matter of dispute.

[20] *Nolle particulares quasdam synodos fieri.* Batiffol, as before, 371.

for Nestorius' reply to the letter. When it was read, and the question put as to its accord with Nicaea, thirty-four bishops had individually answered in the negative when the patience of the assembly gave out. There was a call for a mass vote, and without a dissentient they shouted their views in a series of acclamations: "Whoever does not anathematize Nestorius, let him be anathema. Curses on him. The true faith curses him. The holy council curses him. We all say anathema, to his letter and his views. We all say anathema to the heretic Nestorius. . . . The whole universal church says anathema to the wicked religion taught by Nestorius."

The bishop of Jerusalem now asked that the pope's letter to Nestorius be read. So far not a word had come from the president to say that Rome had condemned Nestorius already, and looked to the council to ratify this. It was in the name of Nicaea that Nestorius had been condemned. The council—or Cyril—had not merely begun the business before the Antiocheans had come in, but before the arrival of the pope's representatives also. The Jerusalem proposal, so to speak, was adopted and the pope's letter was read —and listened to as a matter of routine, one would say, without a single acclamation. Next was read the letter delivered to Nestorius by the four bishops, the letter of the Egyptian synod. But not the now famous twelve anathemas which Cyril had composed in order to stop every retreat for his wily opponent—or perhaps they were read? Historians do not agree. Then, after an account by one of the four bishops of their mission to Nestorius, the notary read out a long collection of texts from all the classic theologians of past days justifying the orthodoxy of the term *Theotókos;* and followed this with a long selection of passages from Nestorius that were evidence of his errors. Finally, in a solemn resounding sentence, the council deprived Nestorius of his bishopric of Constantinople and ejected him from the ranks of the episcopate; 198 signatures of bishops were attached to the sentence.

In all the day's proceedings not a single voice had been raised to say that the views of Nestorius were what the faith really was. All that long day crowds had stood round outside the great church, while the interminable routine had slowly worked to its inevitable end, echoes from within making their way to the streets, no doubt, in the more lively moments. When the result was known there were scenes of the wildest joy, and Cyril, in a pastoral letter written on his return to Alexandria, has left a vivid picture of it all.

"The whole population of the city, from earliest dawn until the evening stood around, in expectation of the council's decision. And when they heard that the author of the blasphemies had been stripped of his rank, they all began with one voice to praise and glorify God, as for the overthrow of an enemy of the faith. And as we [the bishops] came forth from the Church, they led us with torches to our lodgings, for it was now evening. Throughout the city there was great rejoicing, and many lighted lanterns, and women who walked before us swinging thuribles."[21]

The Council of Ephesus was now over? No, its history had hardly begun, although, without a shadow of opposition, it had carried out the task for which, in the eyes of all, it had been summoned; and although the justice of what it had done was not questioned, and no move was ever made to reverse the decision. These strange words promise a complicated story. There were to be six more sessions of the council, spread through the month of July, and then, for the mass of the bishops, a long dreary wait of weeks, while, at the capital, rival delegations argued before the emperor about the orthodoxy of Cyril. It was late September, three months after this night of triumph, before the council was dissolved, and the bishops free to begin the long journey back to their sees.

The morrow of the celebrations was taken up with the task of notifying the decision to all the interested parties: letters from Cyril and his bishops to the emperor, and to the clergy and people of Constantinople; a report from Candidian to the emperor; and from Nestorius (who had been officially told his sentence at the conclusion of the session) a complaint about the way his friends had been dealt with.

The next day, June 24, the Antiocheans arrived. They speedily learnt all that had happened, and were soon officially notified of the sentence against Nestorius and ordered, by Cyril, not to communicate with him in any way. Their immediate reaction was to form themselves into a council—along with some of the bishops

<hr>

[21] The text of this letter, Greek and Latin, is printed in Kirch, *Enchiridion Fontium Hist. Ecclesiasticae Antiquae*, pp. 461–62.

who had held aloof from the great session of the twenty-second. They gave Count Candidian audience and he, as well as protesting against what was then done, gave a full account of all the events of the week. It was then the turn of those bishops to speak, against whom Memnon had closed all his churches, shutting them out in this way from the liturgy at the great feast of Pentecost. There was speech of Cyril's autocratic conduct, of the heresy which his twelve anathemas contained and, finally, John of Antioch who presided over the gathering proposed a sentence that Cyril and Memnon be deposed as the authors of the heresies contained in the anathemas, the heresies of Arius and Apollinaris, and all the bishops be excommunicated who had allowed themselves to be led away by these chiefs. Notice of this sentence was served on all concerned, and once more the elaborate business gone through of officially informing the emperor and all the ecclesiastical world of the capital.

When these letters were despatched, whether June 26 or 28, the previous despatches to the emperor can hardly yet have reached Constantinople. His answer to Candidian's report on the session of June 22 is, in fact, dated June 29. It is a severe condemnation of all Cyril's proceedings. The emperor regards all that was done as of no effect, and orders the bishops to meet again, in accord, this time, with the instructions given to the count. None is to leave until this new discussion has taken place. And one of the highest officials of the court, it is announced, is on his way to regulate matters.

By the time this communication had reached Ephesus, something else had happened: the three Roman legates had arrived, the two bishops Arcadius and Projectus, and the priest Philip. In accord with the instructions given them, ten or eleven weeks before, they joined themselves to Cyril. On July 10, all the bishops who had taken part in the act of June 22 came together once more in session. The difference in the procedure is evident, notable, significant. Cyril presided,[22] and the session opened with a demand from the legates that the pope's letter to the council, which they had brought with them, should be read. This was done, and one of the legates then said, "We have satisfied what custom demands, namely, that first of all, the letters from the Apostolic See be read in Latin."

[22] And the official record of the proceedings notes that he does so "taking the place of Celestine, the most holy and most reverend chief-bishop of the church of the Romans."

They were next read in Greek—a translation brought by the legates.[23]

And now there were acclamations from the council. The papal sentence had anticipated the bishops' own vote. The counteraction of John of Antioch against themselves for their support of Cyril, the emperor's gesture of repudiation, were, perhaps, the lighter for this wholehearted confirmation. "Celestine," they called, "is the new Paul. Cyril is the new Paul. Celestine is the guardian of the faith. Celestine agrees with the council. There is one Celestine, one Cyril, one faith of the council, one faith of the world-wide church." And then one of the papal legates intervened to point out that what Celestine's letter had said was that it was the council's business to carry out what he at Rome had decided should be done. And another legate, acknowledging the acclamations, said in a terse phrase, "The members have joined themselves to the head, for your beatitude is not ignorant that the head of the whole faith, and furthermore of the Apostles, is the blessed apostle Peter." And then this legate, the priest Philip, asked for the official record of what had been done on June 22, so as to be able to confirm the sentence passed, according to the instructions of "our blessed pope."

At the session of the following day the same legate pronounced that the judgment of June 22 had been made "canonically and in accordance with ecclesiastical learning"; and, "conformably with the instructions of the most holy pope, Celestine," the judgment was confirmed. Whereupon the minutes of the session and the sentence against Nestorius were read, following which the legate Philip made a speech in which occurs this passage, that has never ceased to be quoted since: "No one doubts, nay it is a thing known now for centuries, that the holy and most blessed Peter, the prince and head of the Apostles, the pillar of the faith and the foundation on which the Catholic Church is built, received from Our Lord, Jesus Christ, the saviour and redeemer of the human race, the keys of the kingdom, and that to him there was given the power of binding and of loosing from sin; who, down to this day, and for evermore, lives and exercises judgment in his successors."[24]

In the report of these last proceedings made by the bishops to

---

[23] The term used by the legate for his native Latin tongue is interesting—*Romana oratio*. Mansi, IV, p. 1288.

[24] Text, Greek and Latin, in Denzinger, no. 112.

the emperor, the principal part which the Roman see has played in the condemnation of Nestorius, "before the present council was summoned," is stressed, and the fact that Cyril had been charged by the pope to act in his place. But the bishops do not excuse themselves for—once more—ignoring the emperor's commands as to what they shall do and how. In their letter notifying again to the clergy of Constantinople the deposition of their bishop, the next signature, after Cyril's is that of Philip, "priest of the church of the Apostles,"[25] then comes that of the bishop of Jerusalem, and next of the other two Roman legates.

It remained to resolve the council's situation vis-à-vis the Antioch group who, now nearly three weeks since, had declared these two hundred or so bishops excommunicated, and no council. John of Antioch and his adherents were now, three times, formally summoned to appear before the council, and upon their final refusal they were all solemnly excommunicated (July 17). And, once again, pope and emperor were formally notified of all that had been done.

At Constantinople there were general rejoicings at the news that Nestorius' reign was over. But the emperor still refused to recognise the work done as it had been done. He did not reprove the bishops for ignoring his orders of June 29, and he wrote as though all the bishops then at Ephesus were one body—a single letter addressed to all.[26] But he confirmed all three depositions, i.e., of Nestorius and of Cyril and of the bishop of Ephesus. All the other acts he condemned. The faith as defined at Nicaea sufficed, he said. His new envoy, Count John, who brought the letter, would further instruct the bishops about "our divinity's plan for the faith." And the bishops were bidden return to their sees.

When the count arrived, with this somewhat confused, and confusing, decree, it must have been the beginning of August. He had all the bishops brought together in a single assembly to hear his news, their leaders with them. The effect was a general riot, Nestorius and Cyril had to be removed before order was restored. That evening they, with Memnon of Ephesus, were placed under arrest. "If I see the pious bishops to be irritable and irreconcilable (though

---

[25] The Roman basilica of this title.

[26] To fifty-three, rather, by name, belonging to all parties; to the pope and the bishop of Thessalonica, also, who did not attend the council; and to St. Augustine, dead now eleven months.

what causes their rage and exasperation is a mystery to me), and if I find it necessary to take other measures, I shall as soon as possible give your majesty news of this"; so the count reported to Theodosius.

There were, of course, protestations to the court from the council. And Cyril, who knew well the world of Constantinople, made immediate use of the vast wealth of his see. "At the court every man had his price, and Cyril did not stop to count the price."[27] We have a list of the valuable presents that flowed in, carpets (of various sizes), furnishings, valuable silks, jewels, ivory chairs, ostriches, and good plain golden coin. Of this last, one group of fifteen high personages "touched," between them, the equivalent of nearly a million dollars. *"Il est certain que Cyrille a payé très cher."*[28] No less effectively, he influenced the monks, and an abbot who in forty-eight years had never left his cell headed a great demonstration, that all the town turned out to cheer as it made its way to the palace. And the abbot solemnly warned Theodosius of the sin he committed when he interfered with the council's action.

What the emperor decided was to hold a conference, which both sides would attend. Eight delegates from each party came to the palace at Chalcedon, the town directly across the Bosporus from the capital. The legate Philip went with the party of the council. John of Antioch led the other group. Cyril was still under arrest; nor did any pleas on his behalf at Chalcedon overcome the emperor's determination not to see him. The conference began on September 4.[29] There were five meetings in all, and we have no record of what took place except what has survived of letters to the bishops still kicking their heels at Ephesus from their friends in the delegations—or rather in the delegation of John of Antioch's party, one of whom was the great Theodoret. The emperor's decision— presuming it was his office to decide—was sensible enough. He refused to condemn Cyril for his twelve anathemas, would not even have them examined; refused to accept the Antioch policy that no more needed to be said than to repeat the definition of Nicaea; and he utterly refused to reconsider the personal question of Nestorius. "Don't talk to me of that fellow," he said. "He has shown the sort

[27] Batiffol, Msgr. Pierre, *Le Siège Apostolique, 359–451*, p. 388.
[28] Ibid., p. 389. *See also* Bardy, p. 188.
[29] Bardy says September 11, p. 190.

he is." As to the excommunicated John of Antioch and his party, "Never so long as I live will I condemn them," said the emperor in his edict. "When they appeared before me none were able to prove anything against them." Cyril and Memnon were tacitly allowed to keep their sees. The bishops were allowed to go home. The great council was over.

4. *The General Council of Chalcedon, 451*

"What Nestorius had endangered by his rash sermons and his erroneous formulae . . . was the central doctrine of the Christian religion. This fact is enough to explain the intensity of St. Cyril."[1] And the bishop's belief about the Antiocheans, as he made his way home to Alexandria, was that they still stood by Nestorius. Their excommunication by the great council the pope did not, however, confirm, despite an increasing severity of tone towards Nestorius himself, and despite a real uneasiness about the situation at Antioch. So long as there was hope that John of Antioch would conform, the Apostolic See would follow its practice of careful patience. "In cases of this kind," the pope wrote to the bishops who had assembled at Constantinople for the consecration of Nestorius' successor, "there are many things to be taken into consideration, which the Apostolic See always has had regard to."[2] And the policy—the traditional Roman habit, *parcere subiectis*—brought its reward, though not in Celestine's time, for on July 27, 432, he died, a bare four months after this letter.

How to reconcile John and Cyril? John no less fervently believing that Cyril was a heretic, an Apollinarian, who had striven, in his twelve theses, to insinuate, or impose, on the Church a heresy as grave as that which Nestorius had patronised. Both parties, luckily, really desired an understanding. And there was an intermediary whom both could trust, whom all the world venerated, the aged bishop of Boerea, Acacius. To him both sides had recourse. The emperor also begged him to undertake the peacemaker's part,

[1] Bardy, 196.
[2] Batiffol, 397; the letter, dated March 15, 432, is in Jaffé, no. 385. A more familiar fact, to most of us, about St. Celestine I is that he was the pope who commissioned St. Patrick for the conversion of Ireland.

and the new pope, Sixtus III, sent him a letter of encouragement. John and Cyril interchanged letters whose tone revealed to each the truly apostolic spirit of the other, and on April 12, 433, eighteen months nearly after the dissolution of the council, the accord was complete. John made an explicit declaration that Nestorius was a heretic, and that he had been rightly deposed and was no longer bishop of Constantinople. He also signed a statement of his belief in the Incarnation of Christ the Divine Logos, an explanation in which he used the terms traditional in the region dominated by his see of Antioch. And Cyril accepted the statement as wholly orthodox, as the belief of the Catholic Church. John was not asked to make a similar statement about Cyril's twelve anathemas. They were never so much as mentioned, by either side. And why should they have been? In the intention of the theologian who had framed them they had never been meant as a public statement of doctrine. They were merely a special formula, drawn up for a special occasion, the testing of the meaning of phrases used by a notoriously slippery controversialist.

To the agreement of 433 Theodoret of Cyrrhus sent in his adhesion in the following year; and, after much hesitation, he too consented to anathematize Nestorius and to admit that he was rightly and lawfully deposed. And now once again, after six years of tumult, there was peace—among the chiefs, at any rate. The bickering did not however cease altogether, and one incident calls particularly for notice because it was the beginning of a dispute that was seriously to harass the Church in later years, and to be the occasion of the summoning of the strangest of all the General Councils, that which met at Constantinople in 553. This skirmish arose from the fact that, in the schools of the kingdom of Armenia, there had developed a keen interest in the teaching of two Antiochean theologians—both of them now dead—who had been the (unconscious) first-begetters of the Nestorian heresy. These were the bishops Diodore of Tarsus (378–?92) and Theodore of Mopsuestia (392–428). Their works were now translated into Syriac, and a certain amount of enthusiasm was growing for their ideas, when two neighbouring bishops, of an Alexandrian cast of mind, intervened. The Armenians sought counsel at Constantinople and the bishop, Proclus, after some study of the texts of Theodore, condemned his (undoubtedly) erroneous teaching, but set out his own exposition

of the orthodox teaching in a terminology that threatened to undo
the work of the Union of 433. Moreover, Proclus sent round a letter
for the bishops of the East to sign, in which they explicitly, by
name, condemned the dead Theodore, and he, furthermore, procured from the emperor a letter which transformed this into an
imperial order. John of Antioch, in return, flatly refused to condemn
as a heretic a man who had died in the peace of the Church. This
was a thing never done before. And the flames would, no doubt,
have spread as rapidly as in 428 but for the intervention of Cyril,
who pointed out to Proclus that the Council of Ephesus had left
the memory of Theodore of Mopsuestia in peace, never so much
as mentioning his name although it had condemned a creed at-
tributed to him. Proclus ceased to urge his demands, and now there
was really peace (437).

John of Antioch died in 440, Cyril in 444, Proclus in 446. Of
the great figures of the council of Ephesus, Theodoret survived—
with Nestorius; and with one who had played his part behind the
scenes at Rome, Celestine I's deacon, Leo, who was now, since 441,
pope. Theodosius II was still emperor. Such was the personal setting when, in 448, the theological controversy about the true meaning of the mystery we call the Incarnation broke out afresh, and
more violently than ever. It was this crisis that led to the General
Council of Chalcedon, held in 451.

The protagonists in the new controversy were a monk of Constantinople, Eutyches by name; the bishop of the capital, Flavian;
and the bishop of Alexandria, Cyril's one-time deacon, Dioscoros.
The disputes arising from the theories now to be brought before
the judgment of the bishops were destined not only to survive the
condemnation of the next council, Chalcedon, but to be the occasion of the most serious defection from Christian unity which
the Church had yet experienced, a defection that still endures in
organised form after fifteen hundred years. The history of this,
and other defections, is in no way the subject of this present book.
But the account of the council would be untrue as to the facts if
it were told without reference to this history. It must also again
be said that the theological questions raised were far from simple,
hardly to be understood without some training in technical theology. Finally, truth demands that we make clear that the human

beings on the orthodox side, in the course of their fight to protect the traditional faith against the new errors, made mistakes in their attitude to the innovators.

From the beginning, to instance one major theological complication, the party of Eutyches claimed to be nothing more than loyal disciples of St. Cyril, one of whose favourite theological dicta became, as it were, their watchword and (for them) the touchstone of orthodox belief about the Incarnation of the Divine Word—"There is only one *physis*, since the Incarnation, of God the Word"; where (for St. Cyril) the Greek word italicised stands for what the Latins call "person"; but, the old trouble all over again, to a vast number of the Greek-speaking theologians of this time, the word meant not "person" but "nature." Cyril himself, in the settlement of 433, had recognised that the Antiochean way of expressing the doctrine—that spoke of two *physes*—seemingly the contradictory of his own, was just as orthodox as his: that the other side was using the same word to mean something else. But, to the men who claimed to be carrying on Cyril's work, the Antiocheans held the heresy that there were two *persons* in the Word Incarnate.

What now began, within two or three years after Cyril's death, was a movement, at Constantinople, on the part of a highly influential monk, of great austerity of life, to spread a doctrine—seemingly based on the Cyrillian formula—that made heretics of all but the Alexandrian party, the one-*physis* (Monophysite) party as they came, eventually, to be called. Popular sermons on any of these fundamental doctrines, that condemned as heresy other ways of expressing them, could very soon (as the events of twenty years before had shown) bring great cities to a state of chronic disorder. And so it was to prove yet once again.

The pope, St. Leo, was to say that Eutyches went wrong from his lack of skill in these matters rather than from malice.[3] Newman notes[4] that the early writings of the party "display . . . unction," rather than logic; that the Eutychians "write devotionally, rather than controversially," and that "Eutyches in particular refused to argue, out of reverence, as he said, towards our Lord. Whenever his

---

[3] *Epistles*, no. 31.
[4] *The Heresy of Apollinaris* (1835), printed in *Tracts, Theological and Ecclesiastical* (1874), p. 260. The notes in square brackets to this "tract" were seemingly added in the 1870s.

inconsistencies were urged upon him, he said the subject was beyond him." His first leading idea, it would seem, was that Christ was not, as man, man in the fullness of what we mean when we use the word of the rest of the human creation. Christ, he said, was not of the same substance (*homo-oúsion*) as we are. What made Him different was that He had not a human soul (i.e., a spiritual, intellectual soul; a human mind). In Christ our Lord it was the Divine which functioned, where, in us, it is the mind.[5]

Eutyches was an old man, close on ninety, but very influential—he was the head of a monastery of three hundred monks, the leading personage, after the bishop, in the religious life of the capital; he was friendly with, and in constant touch with, like-minded followers of St. Cyril in Asia, in Syria, and in Egypt; the emperor venerated him for his long ascetic life, and the emperor's chief minister, Chrysaphios, was his godson. Eutyches saw himself as fighting a revival of Nestorianism, and he said this, in so many words, in a letter to the pope, some time in the spring of 448.

As the new teaching spread, opposition grew among those who saw this activity as an attack on the settlement of 433. Soon, from the bishops of Antioch, there came complaints to the emperor, and from Theodoret, in 447, a popular kind of dialogue called *The Beggarman* (Eranistes), between a "Eutychian" and a Catholic, in which, however, Eutyches was never mentioned by name. The emperor's reaction to the accusations was an edict (February 16, 448) which renewed all the laws enacted against the Nestorians, and a law against all books which did not conform to the faith of Nicaea, and Ephesus, and of Cyril's twelve anathemas. As to Theodoret, he was bidden never to leave his diocese for the future, not even to come to the council which the emperor had it in mind to summon. The appeals against such bishops as Theodoret had also gone to Alexandria as well as to Constantinople, and a bitter correspondence passed between the two bishops. Then in November, there came an unexpected flash of lightning to clear the sultry atmosphere. A synod of bishops, at Constantinople, was considering some

[5] To quote Newman once again, this was equivalent to saying that for the sacred purpose of the Incarnation of the Divine Word, there was brought into existence a unique creature, a human body animated with an animal soul: "That He had united Himself to what, viewed apart from His presence in it, was a brute animal." *Tracts*, as before, p. 270.

local problem when one of them, Eusebius, bishop of Dorylaeum,[6] producing a dossier of evidence, denounced Eutyches as a heretic, and demanded that he be summoned before the synod to explain himself.

The bishop of the capital city, Flavian, was very reluctant to credit the accusation. In the end, however, the accuser carried the day, and a summons was duly sent. It was fourteen days before it was obeyed—fourteen days spent in arguments and *pourparlers*. Meanwhile the synod put out a declaration of belief—a repetition of that of 433—accompanied by such works of St. Cyril as the letter to Nestorius demolishing his heretical theses, and the letter of 433 making his peace with John of Antioch. The declaration stated that since the Incarnation there are two natures [of the Divine Word] in one single person, the one only Christ, one only Son, one only Lord.

When Eutyches finally consented to appear, he arrived with a high official of the court, sent by the emperor, as his protector, and with an escort of hundreds of monks. He was heard, there was a vast amount of argument, and even the court dignitary did his best to win the old man over. But he would not agree that there are two *physes* in God incarnate. The synod proclaimed him a heretic, deposed him from his post in the monastery, forbade him to exercise his priesthood, and ordered that none should have any access to him for the future. Thirty-two bishops put their names to this sentence, and twenty-three heads of monasteries endorsed it.

There were two highly placed personages, however, who did not accept the synod's deposition of Eutyches—the emperor, and the bishop of Alexandria. When the monk appealed to Rome against his sentence, the emperor sent a letter supporting him. Dioscoros, to whom also an appeal had been sent, called a synod of his own and annulled the deposition. The pope's reply (February 18, 449) was a complaint that from the bishop of Constantinople he had not yet had a word about these proceedings, regarding which he ought, long since, to have notified the Apostolic See. And, as well as to Theodosius, Leo wrote that same day to the bishop, saying he was astonished that no information about the Eutychean affair had

---

[6] It was he who, in 429, had made the first open move, at Constantinople, against Nestorius.

been sent, whereas Rome should have been the first to be told. "We desire to know the reasons for your action, and that all the documents should be sent. . . . Would you then, beloved brother, hasten to tell us the whole story as fully and as lucidly as possible, as you ought to have done already . . . to say what this new thing is that contradicts the old belief, and which you have seen fit to punish with so severe a sentence."[7]

Sometime after this—we do not know exactly when—Flavian's report arrived at Rome. It left the pope in no doubt that Eutyches was in the wrong, and he confirmed the sentence passed on him. Then, on March 30, the emperor summoned a council—in his intent a General Council of all his own states[8]—to meet, once again, at Ephesus, on August 1. The pope was invited to be present. He agreed to be represented by three legates (as Celestine had been represented in 431), and in this reply to the emperor, he stated his view that Eutyches had been justly condemned, and said that in a letter to Flavian, written that same day,[9] he had set out "that which the Catholic Church universally believes and teaches about the mystery of the Incarnation of our Lord."

This letter to Flavian[10] is a different kind of production altogether from the writings whether of Cyril or Theodoret, or any of the contending theologians. It is not, in tone or form, a work of theology at all, but a judgment, a decision, an authoritative statement that "this is the Catholic faith." Incidentally it is a model of Latin style, of the way the Latin language can be used to set out Christian doctrine. The pope also wrote to the council itself, accrediting his legates, a letter which makes it clear (while he left it to the council to decide the fate of Eutyches) that the doctrinal issue has been decided in his letter to Flavian, and that he expects the council to accept this. From this last letter it would seem that the pope expected Eutyches to submit, and he urges that he be treated mercifully. Leo, nevertheless, had no great hopes that the council would bring peace, nor had Theodoret, safely locked up at Cyrrhus, seven hundred miles away. But neither can ever have anticipated what actually was to take place, proceedings such that the pope was

[7] Batiffol, 503–4, quoting Jaffé-Wattenbach, no. 420.
[8] I.e., not of all the bishops of the Church.
[9] June 13, 449.
[10] Always known by its Greek name, the *Tome* of St. Leo (*tomos*, i.e., "volume"). Barry, no. 19, prints a translation of it.

moved to say, in a phrase that has stuck, *non iudicium sed latro-cinium.*[11]

The council opened on August 8, with some 130 bishops[12] present, Dioscoros (by the emperor's command) presiding. After the edict summoning the council had been read, the legates called for the pope's letter to the council, but Dioscoros passed to the emperor's letters authorising the presence of the monk Barsumas. Eutyches then appeared, to read his appeal against the sentence of the synod of the previous November, and the legates made a second effort to have Leo's letter read. They were again ignored, and after Eutyches had read a statement of his belief, the votes were taken amid great uproar. The name of his accuser, Eusebius of Dorylaeum, was greeted with cries of "Burn him alive," "Cut him in two, the man who wants to divide Christ," "Anathema," and so forth, while 114 bishops agreed that Eutyches' theory was good Christian doctrine. By the emperor's orders no bishop who had taken part in the condemnation of Eutyches was allowed to vote. This decision of the council was thus quasi-unanimous, of those with votes.

Dioscoros had already done what little needed to be done to excite his brethren, and now he passed to propose the punishment of Flavian and Eusebius—deposition. After an inflammatory harangue, which provoked reprisals from the supporters of these two, with Flavian interjecting an appeal and the Roman legate Hilarius protesting also, Dioscoros cried out that his life was in danger, and on his appeal the imperial officials threw open the doors of the church, and a mob of soldiers, seamen, monks, and the general rabble poured in. Flavian took refuge in the sanctuary, and clung to the pillars of the altar. In the end he was dragged away, and taken to prison. The bishops then voted his condemnation, 135 of them signing the decree, many of them through sheer fear, and unable to escape.

Flavian was exiled, and after three days on the road he died, apparently from shock or from injuries received in the dreadful

[11] "Not a council at all, but a 'get together' of bandits."
[12] As so often, authorities are not agreed as to the figures.

scene.[13] But he managed to draft an appeal to the pope, and to get this into the hands of the all but helpless legates.

Two weeks went by, while the emperor considered the reports sent him and then, August 22, the second, final session of the council took place—the papal legates not present: they had, by this time, made their escape. The business was simple enough, the deposition of a number of bishops, leading members of the Antiochean party, some of whom had been under fire since the first stirrings of Eutyches. They were Ibas of Edessa, Irenaeus of Tyre (the close personal friend of Nestorius), Domnus of Antioch (who had been pliability itself in this *latrocinium*), and Theodoret. The bishops solemnly accepted the twelve anathemas of Cyril, and then, with acclamations that should be remembered—"Hail Dioscoros," "God has spoken through Dioscoros," "the Holy Ghost has spoken through Dioscoros"—the council of 449 came to an end.

Between the end of the *Latrocinium* and the meeting of the General Council of Chalcedon there is an interval of two years and two months nearly. The period is fairly evenly divided by the death of Theodosius II, and because his successor, Marcian, a man who knew his own mind, was a loyal Catholic also, the religious history of the two halves of the period is as unlike as may be.

The situation could not have been more serious than the scandal of Ephesus left it. Except that Dioscoros had not excommunicated the pope, he had all but arrayed the East in open opposition to Rome and the West, the dividing line being the principle that the only true exposition of the Christian faith was not Leo's *Tome*, but the Alexandrian formula of Cyril *as used by Dioscoros*. A faction of bishops, powerful because it had the full support of the state, dominated all the churches of the East, as, one hundred years earlier, in the worst days of the Arian terror.

To Rome the inevitable appeals came in, as soon as the victims found a means to make contact; very moving letters from the now dead Flavian, from Eusebius, and from Theodoret, who, fifteen

[13] The accounts of what happened in the church are conflicting. According to one story Flavian was set upon by Dioscoros himself and the monk Barsumas. At the ensuing Council of Chalcedon, Dioscoros was greeted with shouts of "Murderer!"

hundred miles away from Rome, managed to send two of his priests to support his case. And the pope had the story from his legates also. He now wrote a protest to the emperor, saying that what had happened at Ephesus was "an insult to the faith, an injury to all the churches of the world." A more authoritative council was needed, to which the bishops of the whole church should be invited, and it should meet in Italy. The fact of Flavian's appeal to Rome, made at Ephesus and brushed aside, is the basis of this demand, and brings from Leo a strong reminder that the right of bishops to appeal to Rome is something fundamental in the church; recognised by Nicaea and by a decree of the whole body of the bishops, it is a custom of the church universal.

From the emperor there came not a word of reply, and he left unanswered also the letters sent by the pope on December 25, in which the request for a new council was repeated, and in which the emperor was warned not to allow himself to be the tool of intriguers, a reference to the corrupt régime of Chrysaphios, the real patron of Eutyches. In February 450 the emperor's western partner, Valentinian III, left Ravenna to reside in Rome. With him came his mother, the empress Galla Placidia, and his wife Eudoxia, the daughter of Theodosius. The pope promptly enlisted the prestige of these imperial personages, and once more letters went to Constantinople. All three stress the same point: this is a case (i.e., Flavian's appeal, which is the foundation of the pope's demand for a new council) where all law and all precedent demand that the pope shall be judge. Is he not Peter's successor? they say, tenant of the see in which he to whom the heavenly keys were given set up the supreme episcopal authority? The pope also wrote to the sister of Theodosius, Pulcheria (driven from the court these ten years by Chrysaphios), and to the clergy of Constantinople, encouraging them to stand firm despite the manoeuvres of the wicked minister.

To his imperial equals Theodosius had no choice but to reply. In April he blandly explained that the excellent work done at Ephesus, and especially the deposition of Flavian, had brought peace at last to the religious world. What need was there of another council?

Meanwhile, Theodosius had appointed new bishops in place of those deposed. The successor of Flavian was Anatolios, who had been the agent of Dioscoros in the capital. This appointment was the occasion of the pope's last letter to Theodosius. It is an explanation that he has not yet acknowledged the new bishop, because he is not sure of his orthodoxy. In order to remove all doubts, Anatolios is to make a written acceptance, in the presence of his clergy and the people, of the decrees of Ephesus 431, and of Leo's own doctrinal letter to Flavian, the *Tome*. It was on July 16, 450, that this was written. The letter crossed the news from Constantinople that Theodosius had died (July 28) after an accident with his horse, that Pulcheria had taken the throne, and that her first act had been the execution of the wicked Chrysaphios. She also offered her hand to the senator, Marcian, and on August 24 had him proclaimed emperor. Overnight, as it were, a new world came into being, a world in which religion could again breathe freely, and the private fancies of "mystics" and the feuds of theologians no longer tyrannise over the ordinary believer.

It was, then, Marcian who replied—towards the end of August—to the last of Leo's letters to Theodosius, announcing now his own elevation. It was fitting, he said, that he should begin his reign by writing to the man who "held the supreme place [*principatus*] in the episcopate of the divine law"—the writer knows well what principate means, he is the holder of that principate in the temporal order to describe which this term was first coined, centuries before. As to the council Leo has asked for in Italy, Marcian[14] would prefer it in the East, with Leo presiding in person. Should the distance seem too great, let the pope suggest some other place, and Marcian will summon to it all the bishops of the East, of Thrace and Illyricum.[15] Other news from Constantinople strengthened the good impression thus created. At the new emperor's command the body of Flavian had been brought back to the capital and buried alongside his predecessors in the church of the Holy Apostles. Anatolius had duly signed his acceptance of the *Tome*. The bishops exiled after the *Latrocinium* had been recalled.

What of the bishops who, through sheer fear, had submitted to the usurpation of Dioscoros, and voted all this iniquity? They now desire to be readmitted to the communion of Rome. At Constantinople, with the approval of St. Leo's legates,[16] a partial recon-

[14] This is his letter of November 22.
[15] Three of the civil dioceses that make up Marcian's imperial jurisdiction.
[16] Sent June 16, 450.

ciliation has been allowed, to be followed by a restoration to full communion later. This the pope confirms (April 13, 451). But he excepts from this boon Dioscoros, and also the bishop of Jerusalem.

And now (June 9) the pope announced a change of plan. Sending a new delegation to the emperor, with powers to settle finally, in consultation with the bishop of Constantinople, the fate of the repentant bishops, he writes that these measures will, he thinks, suffice. The council asked for is not really necessary. But the pope was too late.[17] Already by the time he had come to this conclusion, the emperor had acted, and sent out the summonses for the council (May 17). It was to meet on September 1, and at Nicaea. On June 26 the pope wrote accepting the arrangement. He asked one thing only, that none should be allowed "to call in question the belief which our fathers received from the Apostles, as if there were any doubt what this is." The pope will not come to the council, but be represented by his legates; and of these, Paschasinus, bishop of Lilybaeum,[18] in Sicily, "it is fitting, shall preside over the council in my place."

The pope also wrote to the council,[19] a blend of good wishes, information, and authoritative instructions. The emperor has called the council but "with due regard to the rights and honour of St. Peter," as shown by his invitation "to us also to lend our presence" to the venerable assembly. But neither the critical situation at the moment,[20] nor precedent allows us to accept. The presence of the legates will be a reminder that it is really the pope who is presiding. Passing to the business before the bishops the pope reminds them that he has already stated, in his letter to Flavian, what is to be believed about our Lord's Incarnation. As to the question of reconciling, and reinstating, the repentant bishops, the pope leaves this entirely to the council, and the question also about restoring the exiled bishops to their sees, now provided (thanks to the late emperor) with "successors." But—no bishop is to be degraded from his episcopal character. It is in this letter that the famous phrase is

---

[17] Letter sent June 16, 450.

[18] The modern Marsala.

[19] As in 431 and 449. This is the third time we see the system at work. Did the legates to Nicaea in 325 go uninstructed? and without any word for the council? No record survives certainly.

[20] It is the year, of course, of Attila's famous invasion of the West.

found that has for fifteen centuries blasted the council of 449 as the *Latrocinium*.[21]

By the appointed September 1 the bishops had assembled at Nicaea, but matters of state kept the emperor occupied, and he finally decided that it would be more convenient if the council took place, not at Nicaea, forty miles away, but at Chalcedon just across the Bosporus from the capital. And it was there that on October 8 the opening session was held. The delay at Nicaea, with the papal legates still at Constantinople—they did not leave until the emperor left[22]—gave Dioscoros his last opportunity to manoeuvre, and he used it to arrange an excommunication of the pope—his last fling, as it turned out. Something like five hundred bishops had come to the council, an attendance never seen again at one of these assemblies for another seven hundred years. To keep order during the debates, to see fair play, and to be the emperor's channel of communication generally, Marcian had appointed a body of no less than eighteen commissioners, various high officers of state. The council met in the great church of St. Euphemia, the commissioners and the legates and such principal figures as the bishops of Alexandria and Constantinople sitting in line before the sanctuary balustrade, the bishops placed on either side of the nave, probably in two blocks facing each other, as in the English parliament.

It was the pope's senior legate, the bishop Paschasinus for whom Leo had demanded the actual presidency of the council, who opened the proceedings, explaining as he said, the instructions sent to the council by "him who is the head of all the churches." And, in the first place, Dioscoros was not to be given a place among the bishops. If he resists this ruling he must be expelled. Such are our instructions, and if Dioscoros is allowed to sit as a bishop, we leave. Dioscoros, said the second legate, is here only to be judged. To treat him as a father of the council would be to insult the rest. Dioscoros then left his seat and was given a place in the nave of the church. And another bishop with him, Eusebius of Dorylaeum, to whom fell the rôle of formally reciting the Alexandrian's alleged

[21] *In illo Ephesino non iudicio sed latrocinio* are the pope's actual words. Jaffé-Wattenbach, 473.

[22] For his palace at Chalcedon.

offences. Next the commissioners demanded that Theodoret—freed by the new emperor from his confinement—should be given a place, and his entry was the occasion of the first "scene" at the council, the "Orientals" and the bishops from Asia Minor applauding and crying, "Out with Dioscoros the murderer," the Egyptians shouting anathemas to Theodoret and acclaiming the emperor who had destroyed Nestorius. It was a storm that only the lay commissioners could have controlled, with their guards in support. At their suggestion, Theodoret, for the sake of peace, also took his seat in the nave, but as a member of the council. The commissioners had already made clear his rights, "because the most holy chief-bishop Leo has restored his episcopal rank, and the most divine emperor has commanded that he take part in the council."

Eusebius then opened the case against Dioscoros, by readings from the minutes of the *Latrocinium*, and of Flavian's synod that had condemned Eutyches in 448, in Greek and again in Latin. Dioscoros interrupted to say that it was at the command of Theodosius II that he had presided at Ephesus, and to name the two other bishops who had shared the responsibility with him. At Ephesus, he said, the bishops had unanimously agreed to all that was done, and the emperor had confirmed their decisions. Whereupon tumult again, reminders from all sides of the violence used to extort consenting votes, and a strong intervention from the commissioners.

The day ended before the readers had got through to the full tale of the doings at Ephesus. It was concluded two days later. And then a message from the emperor interrupted the business. Marcian, hoping to end, once and for all, the theological conflict, proposed to the council that it should put out a solemn definition of the church's belief about the Incarnation, something that both Alexandrians and Antiocheans would accept. The council, however, thought another creed unnecessary. In the earlier session they had acclaimed Flavian's statement of 448 as orthodoxy itself. Not a voice had protested that the truth lay with Eutyches.[23] And now, when one bishop said, "The pope has given us a ruling about Eutyches, we follow the pope, we have signed the letter," the rest called out in agreement. And to clinch the matter the classic documents were again read out, the bishops applauding each: the creeds

[23] Nor any, one may add, had cried, "Cyril rather than Flavian."

of Nicaea and of the council of 381,[24] the letters of Cyril to Nestorius (on his heresy) and to Antioch at the conclusion of the peace of 433, and (this time) the letter of Leo to Flavian, the *Tome*. And at this last the bishops called out, "It is Peter who says this through Leo. This is what we all of us believe. This is the faith of the Apostles. Leo and Cyril teach the same thing." And so went by the second day of the council.

On October 13 the bishops returned to the case of Dioscoros. He did not, this day, come to the council. Though three times formally summoned he kept away. He was judged contumacious, and the council asked Paschasinus to pronounce the sentence.[25] And this he did, saying explicitly that he was acting in the place of the pope. What Dioscoros had done was recalled: the reinstatement of the heretical Eutyches, despite the just sentence of the monk's own bishop and his persistence in the condemned belief; the holding up at the *Latrocinium* of the *Tome* of Leo; the excommunication of Leo; the refusal to stand his trial. Wherefore the pope, "through us and through this holy council, in accord with the thrice blessed apostle Peter, who is the foundation stone on which the Catholic Church is built, the foundation of the orthodox faith, has stripped him of his rank of bishop and of all his episcopal functions." Then the bishops began, turn by turn, to stand up and deliver their judgment. They had got as far as the 187th, each of them declaring his agreement, in a variety of phrases, when (seemingly) a block vote was taken. Not a bishop opposed the sentence, not even the terrified Egyptians (who were, however, to make a great scene a few days later).

Dioscoros was immediately notified of his fate, and the reports went off to Rome and to the emperor, not an hour's distance from the scene. Marcian confirmed the sentence and promptly banished the Egyptian to Gangra, a town 250 miles away[26] in the mountainous country of southern Paphlagonia.

On October 17, the council took up the case of the five bishops who had been the principal aides of Dioscoros at the *Latrocinium*.

[24] It is now, at Chalcedon, that we first hear this council spoken of as though regarded as of the same class as Nicaea and Ephesus, 431.

[25] From this session, whose business was the trial of a bishop, the commissioners were absent.

[26] That is, as the crow flies. It is the modern Cankiri, fifty miles N.E. of Ankara (Turkey).

It was decided, unanimously, to reinstate them in their sees. Then the commissioners revived the emperor's demand for a creed. Paschasinus replied. He went once more through the classic list, Nicaea—Leo's *Tome*, and said, once more, nothing need be added to this; and, once again, the council unanimously agreed—or all but unanimously. For a group of thirteen Egyptian bishops now demanded to be allowed to say no more than that they accepted "their traditional faith," meaning by this "the faith of St. Mark, of Nicaea, of Athanasius and Cyril." The bishops shouted them down. "It's a trick," they cried. "Let them sign Leo's letter." But the Egyptians threw themselves on their knees. "When we get home we'll be murdered," they protested, "if we have done anything else than be faithful to our own chief bishop. It is our custom that we obey the bishop of Alexandria, as Anatolios knows well.[27] And at this moment we have no chief bishop. We do not want to seem to disobey the council. But kill us here if you like. We are willing; rather than to return to be killed at home, for betraying the chief see of Egypt."

The council persisted in its demands that the Egyptians sign. The Egyptians persisted in their refusal. It was the commissioners who solved the problem. The Egyptians should wait at Chalcedon until the successor to Dioscoros was appointed. *"C'est une comédie!"* is a modern historian's comment.[28] But was it not rather a foresign of the bloody scenes presently to be enacted at Alexandria, once the council had broken up?

In the next session, October 20, various disputes between bishops and metropolitans, appeals from sentences, were heard and settled, and the useful principle was voted that no imperial interference with the canons regulating episcopal elections was valid. It was the new emperor himself who was the cause of this unlooked-for bold independence among the bishops. "The emperor's will," said the commissioners, "is that in all business between bishops, the pronouncements of the court shall have no force if they are contrary to the canons laid down by the councils."

And then, two days later, quite unexpectedly it would seem, the plan for a new statement of belief made its appearance yet a third time. In the interval since its rejection on October 17, there had been busy work behind the scenes, the centre of which was the

---

[27] This successor to Flavian being himself an Alexandrian cleric.
[28] Batiffol, as before, p. 546, n. 1.

(Alexandrian) bishop of Constantinople, Anatolios. The commissioners, this time, came forward with a creed already prepared. What it contained we can only surmise from the ensuing dispute, for the text did not survive. It seems to have been yet another attempt to state the doctrine in terms that would offend neither of the extreme parties, terms that (experience surely shows) will not have sinned through any excessively clear meaning. When the formula was read, the majority of the bishops were in favour, a minority (Antiocheans) were opposed, and the papal legates would have nothing to do with it. Their instructions were simple. The *Tome* of Leo had been set for the council's acceptance as the official teaching about the Incarnation, the final word for Alexandrians and Antiocheans alike, the Catholic Faith. And now Paschasinus said, "If you will not accept the letter of the blessed pope, Leo, make out our passports, that we may return to Italy and the General Council be held there."

Here was a crisis indeed, before an ultimatum evidently meant.

The commissioners proposed that a committee be chosen to revise the formulary. "No! down with Nestorians," from the bishops. "Mary is *Theotókos*, Christ is God." Then the commissioners, "Do you accept Leo's letter?" "All of us; we have signed it." "Then add to the formulary what Leo has written." "No! no change in the formulary. The formulary is sufficient; it confirms the letter. Leo says what Cyril says. Celestine, Sixtus, agree with Cyril." And the baffled officials sent for direction to the emperor.

Marcian came down on their side—and the side of the legates. If the bishops refused to have the formula amended, the council should go forward in Italy. Even now a nucleus still clung to the text as it stood. "Those who don't like it can go back to Rome," bishops from Illyricum cried; "they are Nestorians." The commissioners cut to the root of the matter, asking point-blank, "Do you follow Leo, or Dioscoros?" "We believe what Leo believes" was the answer. "Then add to the formula what Leo says, namely [we believe] that, according to the decision of our most holy Leo, in Christ there are two natures united, inconvertible [natures], inseparable [natures]." The bishops agreed. The committee was chosen. A new formulary was written.

It is a lengthy statement, for, acknowledging belief in the teaching of Nicaea and the council of 381 it repeats these two creeds verbatim; it passes to the two famous letters of Cyril, and then to the *Tome*, which it greets with a world of compliment enshrining the statement that the letter "is in harmony with the confession of the great apostle Peter,[29] and is for all of us a landmark against ill thinkers, a protection for orthodox teaching." And then the formulary comes to the point, a statement of faith on the point in dispute. It is written in the terminology of Leo's *Tome*.[30]

To the next session (October 25) the emperor himself came. He spoke words of praise to the bishops. Thanks to them all the peoples of his empire would henceforth have no other belief about the Incarnation but what the Holy Apostles had taught, the faith of Nicaea and of Leo, beloved of God, who rules the Apostolic See. And the bishops applauded, and then all set their names to the formulary, the three legates in the first place.

What remained to be done, in the week that followed, was the enactment of twenty-eight canons, or disciplinary laws.[31] The first of these is very important for it gives universal force to an existing collection of 104 canons, the work of five previous councils, of which only Nicaea was a General Council.[32] Bishops, clerics, and monks are the chief objects of the new legislation. One only of the new canons has reference to the laity—prescribing penalties for all those concerned in abductions.

Bishops are given authority over all the monks of their diocese, and their permission is needed for new foundations. They are not to receive clerics who have left the diocese to which they belong. They are to appoint a priest to administer the temporalities of their sees. Disputes between bishops are to be decided by the synod of the bishops of the province—which synod, they are reminded, is to meet twice a year; this last rule is too often neglected, says the canon. Disputes between a bishop and his metropolitan are to be settled either by the exarch,[33] i.e., by the bishop of the chief city

---

[29] "Thou art the Christ, the son of the living God." Matt. 16:16.

[30] For the text, Greek and Latin, see Denzinger, no. 148. Barry, no. 20, prints a translation.

[31] For the text and a translation of these, see Schroeder.

[32] The others were Ancyra (Ankara) 314, New Caesarea 315, Gangra 340, and Antioch 341; all Eastern councils, it will be noted.

[33] The exarchs for the three (civil) dioceses concerned, Thrace, Asia, and Pontus, were the bishops of Heraclea, Ephesus, and Caesarea.

in the (civil) diocese, or by the bishop of Constantinople. Bishops are to be consecrated within three months of their election, and those who ordain for money are to be deposed. Bishops must not ordain candidates not provided with a livelihood.

As to the clergy: they can belong to one diocese only, and must not leave it on their own authority; they are not to take up any secular employment, or join the army; in those places where certain orders of clergy are allowed to marry they must not marry heretics, nor give their children in marriage to heretics, Jews, or pagans; strange clergy who arrive without appropriate introductions are not to be allowed to officiate; in disputes between themselves clerics are not to seek remedies in the civil courts without first consulting the bishop; accusations brought against the clergy are not to be listened to until the bishop is satisfied of the accuser's good character; clerics fall under the penalty of deposition if they have any part in an abduction.

Monks are warned that they are not to wander about outside their monasteries, nor are they to marry—both classes of offenders are to be severely punished. Like the clergy, secular employments are forbidden them, and they must not become soldiers—or they risk excommunication. About both the monks and the clergy it is stated that far too many of them drift to Constantinople, and spend their lives there in disedifying idleness. To end this, such *désoeuvrés* are now handed over to the officials of the see of Constantinople, who are to arrange their expulsion from the city.

No woman is to be accepted as a deaconess before the age of forty. And if, later, she marries she is to be deposed from her office. If a nun marries she, too, is to be excommunicated.

In canon 12 there is an indirect reference to the state. Some bishops desiring to achieve metropolitan status have gone so far as to induce the state to divide the civil province where they live, so that their see-city is now the metropolis of the new province. The civic authority treats the bishop now as metropolitan and he acts as such towards the other bishops of the province. Such successful adventurers on the high seas of clerical ambition are now reduced to their real status, although allowed to keep the honorific title they have procured.

Much more serious than the nonsense thus proscribed in canon 12 is the new place in the ecclesiastical firmament contrived at

Chalcedon for the bishop of the capital. At Nicaea when, for the first time known to us, the bishops faced the situation that not all sees were equal in dignity or powers, there is reference to two eastern sees by name, Alexandria and Antioch. Nicaea does not add anything to whatever it is that distinguishes these sees. It records —and records as traditional, as "the ancient custom"—their present status, as super-sees; their bishops have rights over the other bishops of the (civil) diocese of which these two cities are the capitals. By the time of the second of these General Councils, 381, the eastern bishops had before them the experience of half a century of trouble caused largely by bishops of every rank crossing the frontiers of their neighbour's jurisdiction. Moreover, a new city had come into existence in 330. The small town of Byzantium had been transformed into the imperial capital, Constantinople—a town which, from its unique geographical position in the empire and its wonderful harbour, was as inevitably destined to outstrip all other cities, as ever, from its foundation, was New York. And the bishops of this eastern council of 381 were determined to give the new city a kind of practical blessing, an ecclesiastical recognition of the marvellous place it had already become after a mere fifty years' existence. Constantinople, they said explicitly, is New Rome; and, in the church, it shall have the second place, shall come next after Rome, with a "primacy of honour." Now, after another seventy years, the bishops at Chalcedon take up the matter once more.

There are two incidental references to the capital in these canons, and one canon deals with nothing else. In the new law about disputes between a bishop and his metropolitan, and in that about disputes as to which see rural parishes belong, it is said that the case must go for judgment to the exarch of the (civil) diocese *or* to the bishop of Constantinople. Was this meant to the detriment of the jurisdiction of Alexandria and Antioch? Apparently not. The bishops whom it concerned are those of the two (civil) dioceses, Asia and Pontus, that took in the whole of Asia Minor, and that called Thrace,[34] in Europe.

If the option to choose Constantinople were usually taken, it

[34] Thrace meant, roughly, European Turkey, Bulgaria, and the strip of Greek territory to the east of the island of Thasos. The bishops of Greece (the civil diocese of Achaia) and of the western Balkan lands (the civil diocese of Macedonia) were still *directly* subject to Rome. The pope's local agent for these sees was the bishop of Thessalonica.

would mean that this bishop now enjoyed (as a judge of appeals) a jurisdiction akin to Alexandria and Antioch, but over a still larger territory, over four (civil) dioceses, whereas theirs extended, in each case, over one alone.

The 28th canon of the council carries the matter much further. And all this seemingly petty squabbling for place between prelates, in the excited atmosphere of a General Council in 451, fifteen hundred years ago, still matters. What we are considering is, in fact, one of the fundamental acts from which derive the divisions to consider which the coming General Council seems principally summoned. Here is one beginning of troubles that have lasted for a thousand years or so, to the great detriment of religion, and of our common civilisation.

In this 28th canon the bishops begin by recalling the act of the council of 381, and they confirm it. They then speak of the see of Rome, and of how "the Fathers" always recognised its special privileges, as something due to that city's imperial state. "We therefore define and declare the same about the privileges of the see of Constantinople, New Rome. The city now honoured with the presence of the emperor and the senate, and which enjoys the same [state] privileges as the old royal Rome, should be as great as she in what relates to the church, and rank second to her." And for the future, all the (26) metropolitans of the three (civil) dioceses of Thrace, Asia, and Pontus are to be consecrated by the bishop of Constantinople—he is to be definitely their overlord. And likewise it is he who will consecrate the bishops of the churches among the barbarian peoples beyond the frontier.

The legates were not present at the session of October 31 when this canon was voted, nor the imperial commissioners. But the next day, Paschasinus protested strongly. He was answered that these were domestic affairs, in which it was thought the legates were not interested. Another of the legates said that the bishops had voted the canon under duress. But they denied this violently. He then said—it was the bishop of Ascoli, Lucentius—the canon went contrary to the relevant law of Nicaea. Upon which he was asked whether this matter came within the legates' mandate. To which the third legate replied trenchantly, by reading out the passage that bade the legates not to allow anything that violated what the holy fathers decreed (i.e., Nicaea) or that lessened the dignity of the

Roman See. Should any bishop, relying on the importance of the capital, attempt any usurpation, he was to be opposed.

The commissioners decided that the previous declarations now in conflict should be produced. Paschasinus read the canon of Nicaea—in a text which opens with the words "That the Roman See has always held the first place." It was then read in Greek by one of the emperor's officials, and with it the canon of 381. The bishops were formally asked by the commissioners whether their votes had been forced. They unanimously answered they had been free, and various speakers explained that the new arrangement about the consecration of bishops merely stated in law what had been the practice now for some years. Eusebius of Dorylaeum—the "prosecutor" of Dioscoros, it will be remembered—then told of how he had read the canon of 381 to Leo when he was a refugee at the papal court, and that the pope had assented to it. (And, of course, in this very council Paschasinus had given the first place after the legates to Anatolios of Constantinople.) When the commissioners turned to the bishops who had not voted for the new canon, to ask their views, the metropolitan of Ancyra said that not wanting to do any more consecrations he had left it to the bishop of Constantinople to consecrate his suffragan the bishop of Gangra, but for himself he suspected that money played too great a part in consecrations done at the capital. Whereupon, as may be guessed, there was a really hot discussion, which the commissioners broke up by declaring the canon carried. The rights of the bishop of old Rome, they said, have been safeguarded, but it is only right that the bishop of New Rome should have the same rights and honours, and also these rights to consecrate in the three civil dioceses mentioned. And the bishops again applauded.

But the last word fell to the legates. "The Holy See," said Lucentius, "ought not to be basely treated while we look on. And therefore, all that was done yesterday, in our absence, to the prejudice of the canons and laws, we demand of your highnesses [this to the commissioners] to order that it be annulled. Otherwise, let this our appeal in law against the canon be attached to the minutes, that we may know what it is we must report to the apostolic bishop who is the first personage in the whole church, so that he may be able to pronounce sentence on the unjust act against his see, and on this overthrowing of the canon law." One of the bishops called out to the presiding officials, "We still agree with you." And they said, "The whole council approves our position." And with this rupture between the bishops and the pope the council came to an end.

And the end of the story?

The bishops, before they separated, addressed a letter to the pope. They were grateful, they said, that he had been faithful to the command given to the Apostles, "Teach ye all nations . . . to observe all things whatsoever I have commanded you."[35] Five hundred and twenty of us were at the council, "and you led us as the head guides the limbs of the body." Dioscoros has been punished as a man deserved who in his madness had struck at him to whom the Lord had confided the care of His vineyard, the one whose mission it is to give unity to the church. They make the smoothest of references to their "confirmation of the canon" of 381; enacting their new canon, they say, in the persuasion that "since in you the apostolic light shines in all its splendour, you will often, with your customary care, see that Constantinople benefits from that brightness." They beg the pope to confirm this arrangement which they have presumed to think would please him, being confident that the head will allow to his children what is for their good.

The bishops, in this letter, have dropped the language about the imperial importance of the new city, and about recognition of the pope's primacy as related to the like importance of Rome. It is to him as primate because Peter's successor that they address their plea—the one sure concrete reality beneath their wealth of insinuating compliment.[35a] And with their letter they send the minutes of the council's proceedings. The legates also brought with them letters from the emperor and the bishop of Constantinople—a somewhat uneasy production, this last, from "the see of Constantinople to its father, your own Apostolic See."[36]

Leo's reply to Anatolios is grave. This council called to strengthen the faith seemed to you, he says, a useful opportunity to cause Alexandria the loss of its traditional second place, and Antioch its rank as third, so that, these put below you, all metropolitan

[35] Matt. 28:19.
[35a] The bishops' letter is no. 98 in the collection of St. Leo's letters.
[36] Anatolios' own words in this letter.

bishops would lose their special privileges. As to the canon of 381, "this vote of some bishops or other, given (as you brag) sixty years ago now, and never notified to the Apostolic See by your predecessors—this affords no support to what you are doing." . . . Dioscoros may have disgraced Alexandria, "but the bishops of a see are one thing, the see itself another."[37]

The emperor, congratulated on his share in bringing about this triumph of the true belief, is told of the sorrow felt at the news of Anatolios' usurpation. How prosperity has fanned his ambition! That the sacred guarantees of Nicaea should be jettisoned, and this new rank created, all to increase the importance of a single see, and that not an apostolic see. Let Anatolios be content with his see's imperial importance, for it is not possible to turn it into an apostolic see. Let him not covet more than his predecessors enjoyed. And let him keep to the rules,[38] if he does not wish to find himself cut off from the church universal. Everything done in contravention of the Nicaean rules "we dismiss as without legal effect. . . . By the authority of the blessed apostle Peter we quash it utterly by a general sentence."[39]

Finally the pope replied to the council, March 21, 453. He renews, by this letter, the approbation already given by the legates to the council's execution of the task for which it was called—the case concerning the faith, the case for which alone the council, he reminds them, was called. As to the work which the bishops then took it upon themselves to do—the reorganisation of sees—the pope says he prefers not to know anything about it. For it violates "the inviolable canons of Nicaea." Whatever is not according to these is null and void.[40]

The emperor, distressed at the evident breach between the pope and the bishop of his capital, wrote to Rome, some months later, pleading for Anatolios (? November or December 453). Leo replied, and Marcian read the reply to the bishop. The pope's letter

[37] *Aliud enim sunt sedes, aliud praesidentes.* For the letter, Jaffé, no. 483. The date is May 22, 452.

[38] An allusion to the fact that Anatolios had gone so far as to consecrate one who is his superior in rank, the new bishop of apostolic Antioch, the third see in the church.

[39] These last two quotations are from Leo's letter, of the same date, to the empress Pulcheria, joint ruler with Marcian, her husband. Ibid., 482.

[40] Ibid., 490.

said that a reconciliation would be welcome, but that Anatolios must first "make satisfaction to the canons."[41] The only way to a peace and charity that are genuine is "by keeping to the Catholic faith and the canons of Nicaea." And Anatolios, after his interview with Marcian, wrote his submission to the pope (April 454). He declines all responsibility for the new canon which has exalted his see. He himself is a lover of peace and lowliness of life. It was the zeal of the clergy of Constantinople, it was the eastern bishops who worked this for their own profit. And, he goes on to say, "Whatever was thus done, all its worth and the confirmation of it was reserved to the authority of your holiness."[42] All this is so much hot air until you choose to ratify it!

The pope took the reply as made in good faith, and the matter closed with his writing to Anatolios that he looked to find in him a worthy successor of his great predecessors, and to find him a useful guardian against all attempts against the Catholic faith or the laws of Nicaea (May 29, 454). This was two years and seven months almost since, at Chalcedon, the bishops had voted the canon in the teeth of the legates' protests. The crisis was really closed that opened with the speech of Eusebius of Dorylaeum at the synod of November 448.

[41] *Satisfaciat canonibus*, Jaffé, 504.
[42] The letter of Anatolios is in the collection of St. Leo's letters, no. 132 (April 454). For the whole of this see Batiffol, as last, 562–81.

5. *The Second General Council of Constantinople, 553*

I. THE DELICATE SITUATION

The fifth of the General Councils met at Constantinople, in May, 553—just one hundred years after the date of St. Leo's final letter to the fathers of Chalcedon (March 21, 453). To the minds of many contemporaries this council of 553 was to seem a flat repudiation of Chalcedon, and it was to be the occasion of numerous schisms in the Latin sees of the church, the most widespread (nondoctrinal) revolt which the papacy has ever had to face. It was a council whose strange history was very closely related to the hundred tense years of controversy that preceded it, controversy partly theological, partly political, partly nationalistic.

More particularly, this council was the crowning effort of a Catholic emperor's policy to reconcile the Monophysites; an emperor who came in after some fifty years of Monophysite domination, and at the end of a period of thirty-five years when even the pro-Chalcedon party had been out of communion with Rome; thirty-five years when, in law, there had been no Catholics at all within this empire of the East. That emperor was Justinian (527–65), the restorer par excellence, the ruler who set himself to halt disintegration everywhere, and by no means unsuccessfully; who brought back under imperial control Italy and Africa and even part of Spain, the last great emperor who can be called Roman. His leading idea, in this stage of his religious activities, was to make it clear beyond clear to the Monophysites that the Catholics, faithful to the Council of Chalcedon, were as orthodox as themselves, that there was no difference, in fact, between what each party believed. It was the policy of a sincerely religious Catholic that had nothing in common with the attempts of his predecessors, through the previous fifty years, to heal the breach through dishonest, ambiguous formulae which each party could sign with its own meaning in mind as it did so.

The differences that separated Monophysite from Catholic were undoubtedly as subtle as they were real. The Church has never used any other form of expressing the doctrine of the Incarnation than that of St. Leo's *Tome*. It has, on the other hand, never condemned the formula of St. Cyril—which, as he used it, is a wholly Catholic formula; and that he used it in a Catholic sense is shown by the whole body of his writing on this great truth. Nor did the Monophysite leaders—the bishops and theologians—understand the formula in any other sense.[1] None, at Chalcedon, supported the views of Eutyches, or asserted that Eutyches and St. Cyril were at one in their belief. And this loyalty to the real St. Cyril characterises the main body of the party throughout the next hundred years and more after Chalcedon. Where the party and such of its great leaders as the patriarch of Antioch, Severus, went wrong, and put themselves outside the communion of the church, was in their constant assertion that the language of St. Leo's *Tome* did not have a Catholic meaning, could not have a Catholic meaning; that it showed, on the contrary, that he was a Nestorian. And Chalcedon, they persisted, was a council to be held accursed, for, according to them, it had reversed the decision of the truly Catholic Ephesian Council of 431 where St. Cyril had triumphed.

If this seems now merely a tale "of old forgotten far-off things" —an especially pitiful tale of violent disputes between people substantially in agreement—let it be remembered that in the next eighty years after 553 the differences had so undermined the stability of a good half of the empire in the East, as to lose forever to the emperors the loyalty of Egypt and Syria, and reduce the numbers of the Catholics there to a handful, and the jurisdictions of Alexandria, Antioch, and Jerusalem to all but nought. These lands were the original strongholds of the Catholic faith, Egypt, Syria, and the rest, names which whatever they now bring to mind do not suggest the triumph of the religion of Christ our Lord. Islam, of course, has

---

[1] ". . . the great Monophysites who claimed that their doctrine was his [Cyril's] were Monophysite in language, rather than doctrine." Tixeront, *Histoire des Dogmes*, III, 75 (72) (the figures in parentheses refer to the English translation). It has to be added that there were soon divisions in the party, and many of these were certainly heretical in their theories about the Incarnation.

for a thousand years and more dominated them. But the break with the Catholic Church, and its destruction in these lands, goes back earlier still, to long before Mahomet was born, to the Monophysite reaction following the Council of Chalcedon. The emperors who, in the two hundred years after Chalcedon, showed such a passionate anxiety over the various pacts by which they sought to end the division, and who treated the opponents of their endeavours with such ferocity, were by no means despots, half-crazy through their determination that all men should believe as they believed about these high mysteries. What prompted them was their realisation that a continuation of the division meant the end of their empire and, as we should say now, of civilisation.

As to the great council itself, taken as a whole it has never inspired historians with any excessive affection. *Le malentendu de Chalcédoine* is, with many of them, the impression they seem to retain most vividly. The reason for this is, perhaps, that "The Council of Chalcedon had drawn up a doctrinal formula: it had not produced a union of minds or of hearts."[2] It was a council occasioned by a serious and long-standing theological quarrel about the interpretation of technical keywords. That this initial misunderstanding survived the council is the tragedy of its history. What the council needed to have done, it was impossible that it could have done— given the passions of the disputants; given, especially, the feelings engendered on all sides by what had happened at the *Latrocinium*. Given, what all knew, the fact of these two quasi-permanent theological factions, Cyrillian and anti-Cyrillian, and their mutual ferocity, there ought, ideally, to have been some specific act of the council showing that its statement of the faith did not conflict with the decisions of Ephesus (431) nor condemn Cyril's theology of the Incarnation; saying plainly what it was that the Antioch party found faulty in the Alexandrian's terms and why[3]; showing how there was yet no conflict between these last and the formula in which St. Leo had expressed the doctrine. But could such a reasonableness in these actual bishops of 451 have been expected?

[2] Tixeront, *Histoire des Dogmes*, III, 104 (99).
[3] Of the saint's classic formula that "Christ is the unique incarnated nature of God the Word," the last named theologian can say, "It is true . . . that if one looked only to the words, Cyril is a Monophysite." Ibid., 73 (70).

One thing alone seems to have controlled them, the words of him whom, whether joyfully or reluctantly, they acknowledged to be a peculiarly privileged authentic witness to the truth. In this acknowledgment by these passionate, mutually hostile men, there lies whatever is glorious in the conciliar action of 451. These Greeks, Syrians, Egyptians may not like to yield their minds to the papal authority as a concrete factor of life; they may with all possible ingenuity avoid and evade it; and once returned to their sees they may disregard and flatly disobey; but their homage at Chalcedon to what is greater in the papacy than any pope is indeed *"L'apogée en Orient, du principatus du Siège Apostolique."*[4] And it is this that has survived in the popular memory as the great glory of the council—its acceptance, that is to say, of a statement of the true belief about the Incarnation on the authority of the bishop who, so they believe, is Peter's successor and heir.

From these simplicities we turn to the jungle of events. The opposition to the Council of Chalcedon's acceptance of St. Leo's teaching showed itself as soon as this was known. A Syrian monk, present at the council, made his way home, to Jerusalem, and began a campaign of violent preaching on the theme, "Chalcedon has betrayed Cyril." He speedily had the city aflame, and the empress-dowager heading a plot to bar out the bishop—not yet returned—and set another in his place: a successful plot, for the bishop fled before the insurrection. In town after town in Palestine and Syria the same thing happened. It took the whole force of an army to get the lawful bishop of Jerusalem back into his see.

Egypt received the news of Chalcedon's deposition of Dioscoros —and its new chief bishop, Proterius—no less badly. Troops had to be used to get him safely through the streets of Alexandria. The vast mobs then turned on the soldiery, and when these took refuge in the great temple of Serapis, burned it down and the troops with it. The government reprisals were, of course, terrible—but efficient, and it was amid a military occupation that Proterius ruled. Until 457; when the emperor Marcian died, and without awaiting the news of his successor's policy the Alexandrians rose again. The bishop was murdered, and his naked, mutilated corpse dragged

[4] Batiffol, *Le Siège Apostolique* (1924), 543.

through the streets in triumph. In his place a leading Monophysite, Timothy, was elected.[5]

The new emperor, Leo I, was so impressed by all this that his first thought was to call a council that should repudiate Chalcedon. Those bishops he consulted gave no support to his plan, and advised that Timothy should be banished. The strong arm once more operated, and as long as Leo reigned, another sixteen years, the surface calm was unbroken. It was after Leo's death (474) that the real trouble began, not the mere matter of rioting mobs and fanatical clerics, but of the state proposing its own official solution of the great dilemma, to which every bishop had to set his signature. It was a usurper, Basiliscus, hoping thus (it may be) to make his throne safe, who inaugurated the new policy: the policy that reached the heights of its mischievous possibilities eighty years later, when the General Council we are now about to deal with (the fifth) was summoned, for no other purpose than to accredit an imperial reconciliation scheme. Basiliscus sent to all the bishops of the empire an encyclical letter, setting forth what that faith is which "is the basis and foundation of mankind's happiness." It is, he states, the faith of Nicaea, of the council of 381, and of the Council of Ephesus that condemned Nestorius. But "we decree that all the bishops of the world shall anathematize, and give to the flames, the *Tome* of Leo, and all that was done at Chalcedon in the matter of defining the faith."[6] Every bishop was ordered to set his signature to the letter, as testimony of submission. It was an eventful twenty months[7] in which Basiliscus reigned. Throughout Egypt, Palestine, and Syria, especially, the bishops signed by hundreds. Then the lawful emperor, Zeno, managed to regain the throne.

Zeno was a crude type, from the mountains of Isauria, the first Asiatic to rule at Constantinople, a soldier, and notoriously one of the great blackguards of his day. Religious affairs he handed over to the bishop of Constantinople, Acacius, almost the only bishop who had stood firm against the Encyclical. This Acacius had done, apparently, from policy—Zeno might soon be back; and Acacius had a Monophysite past. He was the real author, it seems, of the next attempt to settle the problem by imperial edict.

[5] Called, from his elegant figure and dainty carriage, *Ailouros*, the Cat.
[6] Kirch, *Enchiridion*, prints extracts from this document, 542–46.
[7] January 475–September 476.

The problem had not, in fact, diminished as the years went by, and it was a practical problem; for example, every time a new bishop was appointed in Egypt or Syria the chances were that there would be a miniature civil war for some days or weeks or for longer still. Zeno had closed his eyes to the fact that Timothy had returned to Alexandria during the usurpation, and after Timothy's death he recognised a second leading Monophysite as bishop.[8] The new edict, called the *Henoticon*,[9] was, in form, Zeno's letter to this personage, Peter Mongos (i.e., the hoarse). It was to have the most disastrous consequences. Once already, a bare twenty years after Chalcedon, the all but entire episcopate of the empire had repudiated the council at the bidding of the state. Now, six years later, it was to repeat the performance and, in doing so, to fall foul of the Apostolic See.

The *Henoticon* of 482 was more subtly contrived than the short-lived edict of Basiliscus. It spoke of the traditional faith in which alone all Christians are baptised, and upon which the preservation of the state depends, and proceeded to say that this faith was that of the councils of Nicaea, of Constantinople (381), and Ephesus. It anathematized, by name, Nestorius and Eutyches also, and it accepted the twelve anathemas which St. Cyril had drawn up against Nestorius. Then came a summary of the doctrine of the Incarnation to which no Catholic could object, and, in the closing words, a casual back-kick at Chalcedon which ruined all: "Whoever believes, or has believed, otherwise, now or at any time, whether at the council of Chalcedon or at any other council, him we anathematize." The implication of this is clear enough. But the rest was orthodox, and so Catholic bishops signed it freely. The last clause dispenses from any need to reverence Chalcedon those who thought the council accursed, and so gave the Monophysite all the freedom he desired. There was no mention of Leo's *Tome*, nor of his terminology, "two natures."

The mass of the bishops rallied to the new formula, those who were Monophysites having trouble with their own extremists. The pope—Felix III—excommunicated Acacius for accepting the *Henoticon*, and deposed him from his see, and with him excommunicated all who remained in communion with him (484). Acacius in

[8] June 482.
[9] I.e., Act of Union. Kirch, as before, prints extracts, 546–48.

return struck off the pope's name from the diptychs of the church of Constantinople. For the first time, there was now open schism, separating the whole Catholic East from the Roman See. It was to continue for thirty-five years.

Acacius died five years after his condemnation, still bishop and still unsubmissive. His successors made as full profession of faith in Chalcedon as could be desired. But they would not retract their signatures from the *Henoticon,* nor recognise the excommunication of Acacius. A new emperor came to the throne in 491, an elderly official, Anastasius. He was himself a Monophysite. Once he had completed his careful reorganisation of the state he, too, turned to solve the great problem, and called in leading Monophysites as his advisors—two very notable personages, Philoxene bishop of Mabboug[10] and the monk Severus whom, in 512, the emperor made patriarch of Antioch.

It was during this period of the reign of Anastasius that the first signs were given of what was to be the storm centre—the whole business indeed—of the General Council of 553. This was a Monophysite crusade against three bishops—writers all of them—now long since dead, who had once been friends and associates of Nestorius: the bishop of Mopsuestia, Theodore; the bishop of Cyrrhus, Theodoret; the bishop of Edessa, Ibas. These three personages and their writings, a trinity of subjects for controversy henceforward inseparable, the three topics, items (*kephalaia* in Greek; *capitula* in Latin), headings; the Three Chapters, of the English-speaking historians.

It was Philoxene who, around 506–7, began this campaign against them, denouncing them as heretics, Nestorians, at Antioch, the metropolis with which all three were associated. Five years later, in the same city, he again raised the question of their orthodoxy, in his endeavour to bring about the deposition of his superior, the bishop, Flavian—a strong anti-Monophysite. Monophysites traditionally detested Theodoret and Ibas as leading critics, in their own day, of St. Cyril's theology of the Incarnation. Catholics, on the other hand, stood by them as victims of the Alexandria-managed *Latrocinium,* who later were restored and pronounced wholly orthodox at Chalcedon. From now on, with both Catholics and Mo-

[10] Hierapolis, in Greek; a town 50 miles east of Cyrrhus, 100 miles from Antioch.

nophysites, to be against or for their condemnation was a sure way of proclaiming oneself for or against the Council of Chalcedon. "The Three Chapters" was, for the next hundred years, to be a watchword and a battle cry through all the churches from Spain to Arabia.

Severus ruled Antioch for a brief six years. In 518 his emperor died, and the general to whom the throne now came, Justin, was a convinced Catholic, a Latin, whose first thought was peace with the Apostolic See. Once again Roman legates appeared in the capital and, as the condition *sine qua non* of restoration to communion, the emperor and the bishop—and all the bishops of the empire—signed the formulary drawn up by the pope, Hormisdas.[11] No discussion of the terms was allowed, the pope was as firm as St. Leo at Chalcedon. The signatories admitted that the first rule of salvation was to keep the rule of belief, with regard to which the promise of Christ to St. Peter[12] had been marvellously fruitful since, "in the Apostolic See the Catholic faith has ever been kept spotless." They therefore, desiring and hoping never to be separated from this faith, anathematize all heresies, and, by name, "Nestorius, once bishop of Constantinople and condemned by Celestine pope of Rome and Cyril bishop of Alexandria." Likewise they anathematize Eutyches and Dioscoros, "condemned by the holy council of Chalcedon which we follow and embrace," a council which, "following the council of Nicaea, taught the apostolic faith." The bishops declare their detestation of the "murderous Timothy the Cat" and his successor Peter; and they also condemn with these "Acacius, the bishop of Constantinople whom the Apostolic See condemned," and all who had remained in communion with Acacius. Returning to Chalcedon, the signatories accept the *Tome* of Leo, because "in all things we follow the Apostolic See and preach as it has decided." Here, "in this See," is to be found "the whole, true, perfect strength of the religion of Christ." And, for the future, they promise never to recite in the sacred mysteries the names of those who "have been cut off from the communion of the Catholic Church, that is of those who are not one in thought with the Apostolic See."[13] "If I

[11] It is printed in Denzinger, nos. 171–72.
[12] The formula quotes Matt. 16:18, "Thou art Peter and upon this rock I will build my church, and the gates of hell shall not prevail against it."
[13] *Id est non consentientes Sedi Apostolicae.*

attempt to vary from this my profession, I acknowledge I should make myself the accomplice of those whom I have condemned."

This root and branch condemnation of Acacius and the hundreds of his episcopal accomplices, all now deceased, was a stiff draught to swallow. But if the bishops were serious in their statements about the unique privilege of the Apostolic See as the standard of belief, what choice had they but to drink it down?

But it was a long generation since, in these lands, the pope's name had, publicly, been allowed to matter. At Thessalonica there were riots when the commissioners arrived to reconcile the bishop, riots which he organised. In Thrace generally the changeover went through fairly peaceably, and in Asia Minor too. But in Syria there was violent opposition in many places. The recusant bishops were ejected and, as of old, troops were needed to secure the installation of their successors. Egypt the emperor let alone.

And in Syria, in some places where the anti-Monophysites came into their own again, the Three Chapters made an ominous reappearance. At Cyrrhus there were feasts in honour of Theodoret, and at Mopsuestia in honour of Theodore and his master Diodore of Tarsus—and, also, of "St. Nestorius."[14] Pro-Chalcedon enthusiasm of this sort augured ill for the new emperor's hopes of a real peace. Was it now that the first seeds were sown in the mind of his nephew Justinian, soon to succeed to the throne, of a deep aversion for these Syrian heroes as symbols of strife, and bound to provoke it everlastingly?

In April 527, at the age of forty-five Justinian began his reign— or, to speak according to the realities, what began was the joint reign of Justinian and his accomplished and really capable wife Theodora. And Theodora was a Monophysite. While, for the greater misery of the years to come, her husband was, among many other things, a talented amateur theologian, who studied under the best masters of the day.[15] Justinian regarded himself as personally

---

[14] Following this there was a government inquiry, and the bishop was deposed.

[15] For example, Leontius of Byzantium (485–543), called the first of the Scholastics, because one of the first to give his books a rigorous demonstrative pattern; one of the first to use, in the exposition of theology, Aristotle's logic; he had a deep knowledge of the theologians who had preceded him, was the principal antagonist of the great Monophysite, Severus, and it was his life's work to show the perfect harmony of the definitions of Ephesus and Chalcedon.

responsible to God for the well-being of his empire, and in nothing more awfully responsible than for the maintenance of the Church. Hence the constant support his laws gave to bishops in their disciplinary tasks, the care to provide good bishops and a determined, never ceasing war on the enemies of the Church—the pagans, the Jews, the heretics. But the austere emperor did not, ever, think of the Monophysites as heretics. These were, to him, victims of a profound misunderstanding, and it was one of his most rooted convictions that he had a mission to reconcile them to the Church.

II. THE QUESTION OF THE THREE CHAPTERS, 527–44

The reign began, then, with overtures to the Monophysites. The exiles were recalled, preachers of the party were heard once again in the churches, and the empress set up a monastery of five hundred of their monks in one of the imperial palaces. In 533 Justinian called a conference of Catholic and Monophysite bishops and theologians to discuss the vital questions. He himself presided. And at this conference the question of the Three Chapters came up. According to one account the Monophysites accepted the Catholic explanation of their relation to Chalcedon and Ephesus. But another story relates that the conference broke down on this very point.

This same year also witnessed the emperor's first attempts to make official declarations about Christian doctrine; an edict, for example, which settled the orthodoxy of the latest attempt to state Catholic belief in language usually held by the other side. This was the statement, "It was one of the Trinity who, in the flesh, suffered for us"—a mode of speech no Nestorian heretic could possibly use, and therefore useful on Catholic lips as convincing evidence that the pro-Chalcedon party were not Nestorians. The statement however grieved the most Chalcedonian of all the Catholics of the capital, the monks called Akoimetoi,[16] and thereupon Justinian appealed to the pope, John II. Back came an assurance (March 534) that the formula was wholly orthodox, and also, among other

---

[16] The Unsleeping; so called because in their church the service of prayer went on ceaselessly, day and night, the community being divided into relays for this purpose.

testimonies in its favour, the pope cited the anathemas of St. Cyril[17]—the first time in a hundred years of controversy that a Roman document had quoted them. If Leo, through John, was now quoting Cyril, what became of the Monophysite case against Chalcedon? But, of course, men (even ecclesiastical men) are not purely rational animals. And there was always the empress, whom no one has claimed as a theologian.

On February 8, 535, the patriarch of Alexandria died, and on June 8, the patriarch of Constantinople. Between these deaths came that of Pope John II, May 8. Through Theodora's activity both the new patriarchs were Monophysites—after street fighting in Alexandria, where the rival candidate was also a Monophysite, of the straiter sort. And now the emperor thought the moment opportune to invite to Constantinople the arch-Monophysite of the day, Severus, whom he had been, in part, responsible for depriving of the see of Antioch, sixteen years before, and who, in all these years, had been a proscribed exile. The ex-patriarch was now lodged in the emperor's palace, and no doubt Justinian fully enjoyed his unique opportunity of talking over these questions with the monk who, to all seeming, must be counted one of the really great theologians. One effect of the presence of Severus in the capital was to confirm the new patriarch—Anthimos was his name—in a resolute anti-Chalcedon spirit.

Such was the position when political events in Italy—the threat to the Gothic king of Justinian's army, now master of Sicily—brought to Constantinople the unlikeliest person of all, the new pope, Agapitus I. He arrived on February 2, 536, and was given a stupendous reception by the imperial court. At the thought of the other guest lodged with the emperor, the Catholics recalled the story of St. Peter and Simon Magus.[18]

The pope had come on a political errand, to plead for the Gothic king. But he had first to settle the problem of his own relations with Anthimos—whom he must meet at every turn, at the court no doubt, and above all at the sacred liturgies. It was a weak point in the patriarch's position that he had previously been bishop

---

[17] Denzinger, nos. 201–2, prints the relevant part of the letter. It is the twelfth of the propositions of St. Cyril that is quoted.

[18] "*Naturellement les Monophysites les voyaient tout autrement.*" Duchesne, *L'Église au VIme Siècle* (1925), p. 95.

of Trebizond, in an age when translations were most stringently forbidden. The pope opened with this objection, and when the emperor overruled it, he asked whether Anthimos admitted the two natures in the incarnate Son. Anthimos saw the game was up. His only reply was to cast off his patriarchal robes and disappear. He was an extremely pious ascetic, still the monk through and through, happy to be back in his cell, and his "cell" the empress provided for him—in the upper stories of the vast palace; and he occupied it peacefully for the next twelve years or so, when he died.

At a lower level, the election of his successor went forward, whom the pope, assured this was truly a Catholic, consecrated on March 13.

The Catholics, heartened by this great demonstration of power, petitioned that all this world of important Monophysites should now disappear. The pope was already negotiating this with the emperor when, April 22, he suddenly died. But the council he had asked for was held, and all the excommunications and expulsions of the leading Monophysites were renewed and carried out. It was the beginning of a general purge throughout the empire, and the beginning of a new chapter in Justinian's religious policy, of a change that lasted for seven years or so.

The defeated empress turned to explore the chances offered by the vacancy of the papal see. From Rome the late pope had brought with him an elderly official of the Curia, Vigilius, who once already had all but been pope—had been appointed pope, in fact, five years before by the reigning pope, Boniface II; a strange innovation which public opinion caused the innovator to renounce very speedily. It is Vigilius—who, very soon, will really be pope—who is the pope of the fifth General Council. Here is the leading actor in the incredible, stormy scenes of the year 553.

At this moment Vigilius is the confidant of the empress, and she is promising him the papacy, on condition that once elected he will . . . what? The stories, and the guesses, of the details of this intrigue are as difficult to summarise as they are to reconcile one with another. But in some way Theodora thought she had bought Vigilius, and he ultimately became pope through her influence—this seems certain.

His present task was to go with all speed to Rome. When he

arrived, however, it was to find the election over. The new pope, Silverius, had been chosen, June 1 (or 8).

In Italy the armies of Justinian slowly made their way north from the toe of the peninsula. They were besieging Naples while Silverius was being elected pope, and next it was the turn of Rome. On December 10, 536, the ancient capital was once more really in the power of the Roman emperor, after eighty years' subjection to "Barbarians." But the Goths rid themselves of their incompetent king, and the imperialists soon found themselves, in turn, defending Rome. And it was now that Vigilius acted, Theodora's other instrument being the great commander of the armies, Belisarius. What it was that Silverius, supposedly, refused to do for the empress, though warned of the retribution this would bring, we know not. The pope was summoned to the palace of Belisarius, accused of intrigues to deliver the city to the Goths, declared to be deposed, stripped of his insignia and, clad in a monk's dress, hurried off to Greece. A few days later, March 29, 537, Vigilius was elected in place of the man who, it was announced, had abdicated in order to become a monk.

Silverius found a protector in his exile, the bishop of Patara,[19] who made a most indignant protest to Justinian. Whereupon Silverius was taken back to Italy and an enquiry there ordered—despite the protestations of the empress, and the endeavours of yet another cleric of the Roman Curia, a friend of Vigilius, the deacon Pelagius. His, too, will be a curiously ambiguous rôle in the events of 553; and, succeeding Vigilius as pope, he will have to face the storm which his predecessor's tergiversations had raised. Meanwhile the enquiry went against Silverius—thanks to the machinations of the new pope; and, despite the commands of Justinian that he should be allowed to live, as a bishop, in some other city than Rome, Silverius was hurried off to the tiny island of Palmaria,[20] and there perished miserably, of starvation, some months later.[21]

Pelagius acted in Constantinople as the pope's permanent legate

[19] The town in Lycia (Asia Minor) to which the pope had been taken. The nearest approximation to its position on a modern map is the coast of Asia Minor (in modern Turkey) due east of the southern tip of the island of Rhodes.

[20] It lies in the Mediterranean, some 70 miles west of Naples. It is now called Palmarola.

[21] November 11, 537. The church keeps his feast as a martyr-pope, June 20.

at the court, *apocrisiarius* was the title. He was an extremely able personage, an experienced diplomatist, and well skilled in theology. In the next few years he was, perhaps, Justinian's chief advisor in the difficult business of keeping the peace in these eastern churches.

But he had a rival, an eastern monk, Theodore Askidas, whom the empress had procured in 536 to be bishop of one of the greatest sees in the church, Caesarea in Cappadocia, once the see of St. Basil. Theodore belonged to Palestine, really. What had brought him to the court was an appeal arising out of clamour caused among the monks by a revival of interest in the often condemned theories of Origen, belief in the transmigration of souls for example, and the final return of all things to the Creator. Askidas had been a leading Origenist, and from the court, which continued to be his residence, he lent his new prestige, secretly, to his erstwhile associates.

Next when, in 540 or so, matters wholly unconnected with this dispute took Pelagius to the Holy Land, as commissioner for the pope, the Roman legate could not be indifferent to these new noisy troubles that were the scandal of the day in Jerusalem and elsewhere. He returned to Constantinople the natural ally of the anti-Origenists, and induced the emperor (in 543) to put forth as an edict what was, in fact, a tract on the errors of Origen. All bishops were required to sign their adherence to this, and it was sent to Rome for the approval of the pope. There was no resistance anywhere among the bishops—were any but a handful of them, at any time, adepts of this semi-pantheism?

Among the adepts, in 543, was Askidas of course, but he signed. And to be revenged on Pelagius he revived the idea of a condemnation of the Three Chapters, the three reputations whose rehabilitation in 451 had been for so long a striking witness in the East to the Roman primacy. It was Rome again, in Pelagius, that had brought down Origen. To bring down Rome's prestige in the East, through the condemnation of the Three Chapters, would be an appropriate riposte. Does this sound too childishly fanciful? It was apparently thus that the mind of Askidas worked. And he won Justinian round to the plan—most probably because, of all moves to reconcile the Monophysites, this public condemnation of leading "Antiocheans" seemed the one most likely to succeed. And the move was heavily backed by a more powerful counsellor than Askidas, the empress. Also Pelagius had, by this time, been recalled to Rome, and the deacon Stephen sent in his place. The new edict appeared in 544.[22]

The trouble began when, as with the edict against Origen, this condemnation was sent for signature to the patriarchs and the pope. The legate Stephen immediately refused to sign and, impressed by this, the patriarch of Constantinople hesitated. When, finally, he signed, the legate broke off relations with him. At Antioch, also, the patriarch at first refused but then yielded to threats. It was the same story at Jerusalem and at Alexandria. Though all signed they did so against their judgment and, even so, only conditionally. The officials who brought the edict explained that, by the emperor's orders, the pope was going to be consulted. At Constantinople the patriarch, as he signed, reserved his right to withdraw his signature should the pope refuse to sign. None of these bishops was willing to seem to reverse Chalcedon and St. Leo. In view of the coming debacle in the eastern episcopate this initial attitude is of high importance.

Meanwhile it was Vigilius who was cast for the spectacular part. All these signatures were provisional. They would not have any value until Vigilius had signed.

Vigilius it seems, was not a popular figure in Rome. The stories current about him might be guessed even if, in all their improbability, they had not come down to us. Some of them cast doubts on his faith. He was said to be leagued with the Monophysite chiefs, for example. But Vigilius by no means gave in to the request that he sign the emperor's edict. It was the expressed belief of Pelagius, now in Rome as his chief advisor, that the aim of those who had inspired the condemnation was simply to destroy the dogmatic effect of Chalcedon.

The pope's delays provoked the emperor to a singular act of violence. As Vigilius was celebrating the feast of St. Cecilia, November 22, 545, in the church that is her shrine, he was kidnapped, hurried the few yards down to the Tiber and a waiting ship, thence to Ostia and the open sea, and so to Sicily. As the ship made its way down the river the crowds who lined the banks called out, some of them, insulting remarks, and others were encouragingly indig-

---

[22] The date is an approximation. The text of the edict no one knows; it has long since disappeared, and no writer of the time quotes it in any work that has survived.

nant; and others shouted, "Don't condemn the Three Chapters." What none realised, of course, was that what they were witnessing was the beginning of a ten years' captivity. Vigilius never saw Rome again.

The pope remained in Sicily until the end of the year 546. Then new orders came, and he was once more embarked, his destination Constantinople, where he arrived January 25, 547.

Once again, as in 535, there was a pompous ceremonial, and vast external deference, under cover of which there began a theological siege of the pope. He steadfastly refused to lend his authority to a dogmatic pronouncement put out by the state, and he broke off relations with the patriarch who refused to withdraw his support. Then, after months of harassing discussions to prove that the Three could be condemned and Chalcedon not involved, Vigilius pledged himself, in a secret writing given personally to Justinian and to Theodora, to condemn the Three Chapters, June 29, 547. It was his first defeat, and almost the only one in the six years of continuous warfare that now began.

Nine months after this promise, the pope sent his judgment to the emperor; it is known as the *Iudicatum* (April 11, 548). The text has only survived in fragments, quoted in the ensuing controversies, but it was a condemnation so written as to make clear that it in no way involved Chalcedon. It suited the emperor, seemingly, and all the professional clerics who surrounded him. But the whole of the West, all the Latins, spontaneously rose in rebellion as the news reached them. That the Latins were fairly solid against the plan to condemn the Three, Vigilius had already learned during his stay in Sicily. Scarcely any Latin bishop had signed the emperor's edict. But the *Iudicatum*, the pope had expected—had taken for granted?—would win them round. This first revolt of the Latins against Rome was a fearful surprise, and it did not die down for nearly fifty years. And so from Illyricum, Dalmatia, Italy, and Gaul came news of councils and protestations, but nowhere more violent news than from Africa, where a council at Carthage excommunicated the pope. And at Constantinople his own curial staff, so to call it, boycotted him.

The letters that came in, the controversial exchanges, showed that many of the indignant prelates in these distant lands did not really know what the famous dispute was about—they were in no condition to take sides, far too ill-informed to see that it was possible to condemn certain things in the three Syrian bishops and yet cast not a shadow of blame on the great council of 451. And the idea developed, at Constantinople, of a General Council where the whole thing could be made clear, and a universal condemnation be achieved more readily than by sending officers all round the Roman world, to each individual bishop. So the emperor consented that the pope withdraw the *Iudicatum,* the council plan was accepted by both, and both agreed to keep silent on the whole question until the council met. And Justinian wrung from the pope a most solemn oath that he would really condemn the Three Chapters and do nothing that would work against their condemnation; all this in August 550.

The preparations for the council now began, on the part of the emperor. One important item was to see that only well-trusted bishops should be sent from such places as Africa. From this desire to be certain before the council met how the verdict would go came the idea of another imperial edict making the theological problem clear. All would be thus instructed by the time the council met, and at the council could accept the edict or, as the emperor entitled it, the Confession or Declaration of Faith.

To this plan the pope, immediately, gave a firm refusal, and spoke of excommunicating all who set their signature to the Declaration. Then, as the air grew sultry with threats he took sanctuary in the neighbouring church of St. Peter. On August 14 the emperor ordered his arrest, and the church became a battleground, soldiers fighting their way through the mob that fought to protect the pope, who clung to the altar while soldiers took him by the feet. Vigilius was an old man, by this time, but tall, well built, and forceful. He resisted manfully, and finally, as the columns of the altar fell in under the strain of the conflict the crowd began to prevail, and the soldiers fled.

The pope returned to his home in the palace of Placidia which, now filled with spies, became a close prison. After some months, in the week before Christmas, he made his escape, clambering over the roofs of neighbouring buildings, and so to the shore where a waiting boat conveyed him to Chalcedon, and in the very church where the council had sat, just one hundred years before, he found a refuge (December 551).

In the basilica at Chalcedon the pope remained for the next eight months—to the fury of Justinian, as well aware as any ruler of the prodigious "loss of face" all this entailed, and of serious possibilities that any day the mob might rise against him with "religion" as its war cry. The emperor began negotiations.

It was now six years since Justinian had kidnapped the pope, and how much nearer was he to his goal?

The pope busied himself with an encyclical letter in which he related the full story of Justinian's outrages and deceptions. To the deputation of high officials who came across the Bosporus from the emperor, Vigilius, ignoring the new wonderful promises, made only one request, the restoration to the church of the freedom of action it had once enjoyed; and he bade them beg Justinian to avoid the company of the excommunicated. This brought threats of new violence from the tyrant, and the pope replied with a copy of his encyclical. The letter, February 5, 552, ended with a profession of faith, as explicit as a pope's should be. It declared his fidelity to Chalcedon and made no mention of the Three Chapters.

The emperor now arrested all those who had joined the pope at Chalcedon. Some of the Italian bishops he put to the torture; Pelagius (the pope's chief intelligence officer, as ever) he threw into prison. Vigilius retorted with strength, by publishing the deposition of Theodore Askidas from his see, and an excommunication of all who had signed the emperor's Declaration of Faith, the patriarch of Constantinople notably. And he contrived to have these sentences posted in various places of the capital. It was a bold act that, once more, rallied the city to his side. Justinian bade his bishops make their submission, and in the basilica at Chalcedon they did so, very fully if something less than sincerely. And the pope returned to Constantinople (August 552).

III. THE GENERAL COUNCIL OF 553

And now the summonses to the General Council were sent out. It was to meet not, as Vigilius had desired, in Italy or Sicily, but at Constantinople, and while the bishops assembled, indeed when most of them had already arrived, the conflict with the emperor took up again.

As the months had gone by and almost no bishops from the
Latin sees were arriving, the pope's anxieties grew. He was willing
to condemn the Three Chapters, but in his own way—the way of
the *Iudicatum*—in a way that would not lose the Latin west to the
unity of the church. And so, while his Latin advisors were strong
that he should refuse utterly to have any part in the council, the
pope wavered, now of their opinion, now hoping against hope,
through the council to keep the East and not lose the West. At
last he announced that the council should go its own way. He would
not be present, nor be represented, but would let the council know
his decision. Justinian replied that his decision would be ignored.
And with affairs in this state the council, 145 bishops in all, held
its first meeting, May 5, 553.

Almost all these bishops were Greeks. There were none from
Gaul or Spain. The dozen or so Italians who had been with the
pope these last eight years were there, but no bishops from the Latin
provinces of Dalmatia and Illyricum. The only bishops from Africa
—six—were a chosen few already engaged to follow the emperor's
lead.

The council lasted four weeks (May 5–June 2). There were eight
sessions. On the first day the emperor sent a long message about
the historic rôle of the emperor as defender of the faith, noting how
the decisions of the great councils had been enrolled among the
laws of the state. His criticised Declaration of Faith had been simply an imperial consultation of the bishops of the empire, its purpose to root out what remained of the heresy of Nestorius. Hence
his questions about the Three Chapters. The bishops had unanimously condemned these, but since there were yet some who defended them, he had thought it good that the bishops should be
given the chance to express their views as a council. As to "the most
religious pope of Old Rome," he too had been consulted, and had
condemned the Three Chapters. His definitive judgment, he had
told the emperor, would shortly be forthcoming.

The council voted that the pope be asked to preside, and on
May 6 an imposing deputation waited on him with the invitation,
the three patriarchs of Constantinople, Antioch, and Jerusalem
leading. The pope pleaded his present sickness—he was now a
chronic sufferer from stone—as a reason for not deciding. The deputation came a second time, on May 7, with one of Justinian's chief

officers of state in attendance. Vigilius now boldly said he would
not appear at the council until more Italian bishops had been
brought over. The next day the report of this was made to the
council—its second session. The third session was taken up with
the council's formal declaration of its orthodoxy—it held to the faith
of the previous "four holy councils" of the Fathers.

The next three sessions, May 12, 17, 19, dealt with the case
against the Three Chapters, the reading out loud of the writings
held against the three bishops, in full or in extracts. There were
seventy-one passages from Theodore of Mopsuestia, for example,
and also the creed he had drawn up, which already had been condemned at Ephesus in 431. About the letter from Ibas, bishop of
Edessa, to the Persian bishop Maris, there were differences of opinion. The point was raised that at Chalcedon this particular document had been definitely declared to be orthodox. It was Askidas
who steered the majority around this formidable obstacle, and the
day ended with the condemnation voted.

Meanwhile, May 14, the pope had made his own judgment about
the Three Chapters. It had been sent to the emperor, who had refused to receive it. What he thought of the judgment his action
twelve days later, at the seventh session of the council, was to show.
In the interval the text of the document, known to us as *The Constitutum of Pope Vigilius about the Three Chapters*,[23] was no doubt
known all over the town. It is a very lengthy piece, a good hundred
pages such as this, and "one of the finest works, as literature, that
have survived from the fifth century."[24] Upon the emperor's careful arrangements by which the council was to be all and the pope
a nullity, it fell like an unexpected bomb. We shall see the unheard-
of violence it drove Justinian to enact. Meanwhile, here is the
pope's decision.[25]

The message falls into three sections. In the first he gives the
profession of faith made to him by Theodore Askidas and by the
patriarch of Constantinople, Mennas, at Chalcedon in 552, and
also the profession lately made by Mennas' successor, Eutychius,

[23] The text is in Mansi, IX, cols. 61–106; also in Migne, *Patrologia Latina*,
vol. 69, cols. 67–114.
[24] Tixeront, as cited, III, 143 (137).
[25] This résumé follows very closely the account in Tixeront, III, 143–45
(137–39).

January 6, 553. There follows a résumé of what has happened down to the council's first meeting. The main part of the *Constitutum* is the pope's examination of the three accused bishops—for that was, in fact, their status at this moment.

As to Theodore of Mopsuestia, the pope had before him the list of seventy-one extracts from his writings that was to be put before the council, a list supplied by the emperor. He accepted that twelve of these were certainly heretical and added a thirteenth—against all these he placed the mark anathema. But, pointing out that Theodore's case had never been before the councils of Ephesus and Chalcedon, and that it is not the Church's custom to condemn the dead, the pope, while condemning the errors in the writings, refused to cast a stigma on their author. And he forbade that others should stigmatise him.

As to Theodoret, the pope refused to condemn him too. He had been received as orthodox at Chalcedon, and as a test he had there been asked to anathematize Nestorius, and had solemnly done so before the whole assembly. As to the insulting language about St. Cyril with which he was charged, in part he had denied that he was the author of these words, and St. Cyril had never raised this against him. This had satisfied St. Cyril and the council, why should men now be demanding more than they? Wherefore the pope strictly forbade anyone to condemn now any work or writing of Theodoret's, or any writing as though it were his. At the same time, he solemnly condemned all propositions contrary to the faith whether found in Theodoret's writings or in any other author. To strengthen this, the pope quoted four Nestorian theses, and to each fixed the note anathema.

As to Ibas of Edessa, the *Constitutum* recalls, first of all, that at Chalcedon the papal legates said, "The letter of Ibas having been read we have decided that he is orthodox," that the then patriarch of Constantinople agreed that he was clear of heresy, and the patriarch of Antioch too. Other bishops there had spoken in a like sense. None, at Chalcedon, rose to denounce him as a heretic. Not that the bishops had approved of the insults he had lavished on St. Cyril, but when Ibas accepted to be in communion with Cyril, recognised solemnly, that is to say, that Cyril's teaching was the orthodox faith, he, as it were, recalled and withdrew these insults [e.g., that St. Cyril was an Apollinarian heretic]. With the warning to the council of 553, that to go back on the judgment of Chalcedon was dangerous, the pope came to his conclusion: the verdict that Ibas was orthodox should stand, and stand so far as the letter to Maris was concerned, a verdict, Vigilius said, based in part on this letter exactly and rightly interpreted.

Wherefore, summing up his decision, the pope forbade any cleric to make any change whatever in what Chalcedon had decided, and —no matter what the rank of the cleric—to write or teach anything against what this *Constitutum* laid down, or, in the face of this decisive sentence, ever again to raise the question of the Three Chapters. The document was signed by the pope, and counter-signed by the sixteen bishops with him and six clerics of his house-hold, one of them Pelagius. It was probably he who was the actual author of the piece.

The emperor showed his hand at the next, seventh, session of the council, May 26. His representative, the *quaestor* of the imperial palace, appeared with the dossier of all the pope's iniquities, and to the council he read out document after document. There were letters of Vigilius going back four years, when he defended his earlier judgment against the Three Chapters, the so-called *Iudicatum*, and there were the two written promises given to Justinian and Theodora that he would condemn the Three Chapters; and there was the signed statement made on oath, August 15, 550, to the same effect, the pope pledging that he would not act against the emperor's wishes, and would do nothing to defend the incriminated three. Vigilius, then, was a perjured liar, and his name should be struck off the diptychs. Not, the emperor craftily argued, that any wickedness of a particular pope could blemish the Apostolic See. This was not a breach with Rome, but only with Vigilius. For seven years he had condemned the Three Chapters, and now he had repudiated obligations of the most solemn kind. In defending the Three Chapters he shares in the wickedness of Nestorius, and has put himself out of the Church.

The council listened, and it did as the emperor intended, declaring the pope's name should be put out of the sacred liturgy; but not decreeing a sentence of excommunication, and using Justinian's distinction between the *sedes* and *sedens*—the chair of Peter and the one now sitting in it. "The council, sitting so far despite the pope, was now in session against him. It was in full schism."[26]

One week later to the day the council held its final session. The task before it was to put in form its condemnation of Theodore of Mopsuestia and his writings, of Theodoret's writings against St. Cyril, and of the letter of Ibas of Edessa. The decree took the form, first, of a résumé of the council's proceedings, and then, fourteen statements calling down a curse on whoever did not accept the council's judgment regarding various heresies and their authors, and supporters.

These fourteen sentences reflect, very clearly, the mind of a disciple of Leontius—they are evidently the work of an author very concerned to show that the decisions of Ephesus and Chalcedon are not contradictory. In the first, the doctrine of the Trinity is set out, in the second the two births (in eternity and in time) of the Divine Word. The third declares the identity of the Word and Jesus Christ, one person, God and man at the same time; it was the one same person who both wrought the miracles and suffered death. In these last two sentences the student will recognise echoes of the theological conflict of the previous hundred and fifty years, the flames of which, of course, were still flickering brightly in 553.

Theodore of Mopsuestia makes a first appearance in sentence 4 of the series, described as a maniac for his particular theory of the manner of union between the divine and human in the Incarnate Word, and condemned along with the Nestorians, Apollinarians, and the followers of Eutyches. He is again the subject of a condemnation in sentence 5, and Nestorius with him, for saying that the union is but a moral union that unites two persons. Supporters of these theories now calumniate the Council of Chalcedon when they interpret its decree of the unity of person to mean just this, and this travesty is met by another condemnation. This sentence 5, in part, is repeating the sentence of Ephesus on the Nestorians, and 6 also repeats the same council when it condemns those who say that the ever-virgin Mary is not truly *Theotókos*, but only the mother of a human being. And once again the later heretics are condemned who falsely say that this heresy was allowed by Chalcedon—this, the heresy "invented by the detestable Theodore." Sentence 7 condemns those who, when they distinguish the two

[26] Tixeront, III, 146 (140).

natures, do so in such a way as to convey that these are two persons —again the repetition of the old condemnation of Nestorius.

With the eighth sentence the council comes to grips with the Monophysites, for it quotes verbatim the much controverted formula of St. Cyril,[27] and determines the, Catholic, sense in which he used it, a sense that fits with Ephesus as well as with Chalcedon. This formula, it is now said, should not be understood to mean that the unity by which Christ is one being is the effect of a fusion between the divine and the human natures; the two natures remain two natures in the union, and the union is a union in a single person. Those who thus fuse the natures are as erroneous as those who speak of them as separate beings. Both are condemned by this sentence 8. It is the turn of the Nestorians again in 9—their practical direction is condemned, that Christ should be worshipped with a double worship simultaneously directed, first to the divine in Him, and then to the human. To balance this the single adoration of Christ in the sense of Eutyches—i.e., as though before the adorer there were present God alone and this being, neither man nor God, who cannot be adored—is also condemned. The doctrinal decision of Pope John II, twenty years ago now, is repeated in sentence 10; it is correct to say, "One of the Trinity suffered in the flesh for us." The eleventh sentence strings together a list of heresiarchs from Origen to Eutyches, and with all others condemned already "by the four holy synods"[28] condemns them and their supporters anew. We then come to the explicit condemnation of the Three Chapters, sentences 12, 13, 14.

"If anyone defends the wicked Theodore of Mopsuestia," so the twelfth sentence is framed, "who said . . . and also . . . and what is worse still . . . If therefore anyone defends the aforesaid wicked Theodore and his wicked writings . . . and does not anathematize him and his wicked writings . . . let him be anathema." The errors of his teaching—unmistakable Nestorianism—as set out run to a good page of print.

The judgment on Theodoret is somewhat different. Nowhere is he himself anathematized, or the good Catholic ordered to anathematize him. It is "the writings of Theodoret, against the true belief, against the council of Ephesus, and against St. Cyril and his twelve

---

[27] *There is* [but] *one incarnate nature of God the Word.*
[28] Nicaea, Constantinople 381, Ephesus, Chalcedon.

chapters" that are the target; and "all that he wrote on behalf of the wicked Theodore and Nestorius and of others who smacked of the same [ideas] as these two aforesaid—writings defending them and their wickedness and, to this end, stigmatising as wicked men those ecclesiastical teachers who professed" the true doctrine about the oneness of God the Word. All, therefore, who do not anathematize these writings and those who savour of the like ideas, "and especially all those who have written against the true faith, or against St. Cyril and his twelve chapters, and who remained to the end in this wickedness," let them be anathema.

The condemnation, in the case of the third of these bishops, is even more circumscribed. "If anyone defend the letter which Ibas is said to have written to the Persian heretic Maris . . ." The letter is said to deny that God the Word took flesh of the ever-virgin Mary and was born of her, so that God the Word was one thing, the man the other. It says also that St. Cyril, who set out the true Christian belief, was a heretic of the sect of the wicked Apollinaris, and it blames the first (*sic!*) council of Ephesus because it condemned Nestorius without a hearing. The letter also is said to stigmatise St. Cyril's twelve chapters against Nestorius as "impious and contrary to the true belief," and to defend Theodore and Nestorius and all their wicked doctrines and writings. So then, all who defend this wicked letter, and do not anathematize it and those who defend it, who say it is right, or part of it, those who defend either the letter or the wickedness it contains in the name of the Council of Chalcedon, and persist to the end in this, let them be anathema.

Nowhere is it said that Theodoret or Ibas is a heretic, nor are those who have defended "the aforesaid wicked Three Chapters" denounced or threatened as heretics. To this final act of the council, June 2, 553, 164 bishops set their names.

The council over, Justinian ordered that every bishop in the empire should endorse the condemnations. In the East there were no difficulties about this, but the Latins everywhere resisted. At Constantinople the pope's chief counsellors were arrested; some were exiled to the depths of the Egyptian deserts, Pelagius (the real force behind Vigilius) was once more thrown into prison. Was the pope, too, imprisoned? It is not certainly known. But whether in prison (in the technical sense) or not, he was the emperor's captive still. What it was that, as the months went by, brought him to change his mind no one knows. But by December 8, 553, the pope had accepted the council's condemnation of the Three Chapters.[29] And we possess a second document, dated February 23, 554, in which the pope argues at great length that the condemnation is justified, and that it in no way conflicts with Chalcedon. This document, generally known as the second *Constitutum* of Vigilius,[30] was possibly meant to persuade the Latin bishops.

The pope was now allowed to make his journey homeward—it was all but ten years since he had been carried off—but when he reached Sicily he fell ill, and at Syracuse he died, June 7, 555.

Chalcedon was not in conflict with Ephesus. The fourteen "chapters" of the council just dissolved seem to have established this clearly, with, if anything, a little more favour for the Alexandrian way of speech than that of Antioch. But had one alleged conflict been extinguished only for another to spring from its ashes? Was the council just dissolved at cross purposes with Chalcedon? The West seems to have thought so, and the action of those who for years deprecated the condemnation of the Three Chapters had been compromised by this fear that Chalcedon must, thereby, be compromised inevitably. And certainly Askidas and his party—the crypto-Monophysites of the court—hoped that Chalcedon must, thereby, be so compromised. But this was never any part of the emperor's plan. How could he have intended such a wholesale surrender? Nor, among the great majority of the eastern bishops— better equipped to deal with these matters than their Latin brethren —did the name of Chalcedon suffer. As to the Monophysites, they already, and for a hundred years, had the worst possible opinion of Chalcedon. Moreover—as we, with what is called "hindsight," can so easily see—the Monophysites had by now washed their hands of the Catholic Church, and what its councils decided would no longer have any interest for them.

The subsidiary questions apart—for example, should councils

[29] The letter to Eutychius, patriarch of Constantinople. It is printed in Mansi, IX, cols. 414–19, and Migne, *P.L.*, vol. 69, cols. 122–28.

[30] "The *Constitutum* of Pope Vigilius for the Condemnation of the Three Chapters"; such is its title. The text is in Mansi, IX, cols. 457–88, and Migne, *P.L.*, vol. 69, 143–78.

condemn men dead long ago, who died in the peace of the Church? —what had the bishops of 553 done, in their list of reprobations, except condemn yet once again the Nestorian theology (as Vigilius had condemned it in his own message to the council) whether this heresy showed—as it certainly did—in the writings of Theodore, or of Theodoret and Ibas? The last two had, of course, corrected themselves long before they died. Even their controversial language about St. Cyril had been, as it were, apologised for and the *amende* accepted, in the reconciliation of 433. This did not, of course, alter the fact that they had, once upon a time, written erroneously. But the condemnations of 553, in so far as it touched these writings, was little better than spite. And the spirit that so moved the bishops in 553 was, obviously, not that of the bishops who at Chalcedon had welcomed Theodoret and Ibas back to their sees. Other conflict than this, between the councils of 553 and 451, there was none.[31]

Vigilius and Justinian had had a grave difference about an important policy. The emperor's tyranny, and the shiftiness of the pope had no doubt aggravated it—but nowhere had they differed as to what had been defined about the Incarnation by the councils of Ephesus and Chalcedon, or denied that what these councils had defined was the divinely given truth of the matter.

[31] I do not forget the difficulty that, at Chalcedon, the papal legates explicitly said the letter of Ibas was orthodox.

6. *The Third General Council of Constantinople, 680–81*

What this sixth of the General Councils achieved was to reconcile the churches of the East with the Roman See, and to condemn a heresy. And yet again was the adage warranted that once a General Council meets the unlikeliest things may happen—for this sixth council was to treat a pope as the fifth had treated the Three Chapters. The sixth General Council was, in the intention of the emperor who called it, a "peace conference" that terminated sixty years of grave disorders. And, yet once again, those responsible for the beginnings of the disorder had been conscious rebels in part only. As had happened with Justinian, what had moved a seventh-century emperor to act as a theologian—and had he not so acted the heresy would never have had any importance outside the schools of theology—was the hope of uniting his people to fight, this time, for the empire's very life against an all-victorious enemy, the Persians.

This seventh-century heresy is traditionally called Monothelism: the heresy that Christ our Lord did not possess a human will, or ever act with a force—an "operation"—that was human, but that, in Him, all that in us comes from our wills came from His being God. If this were true, then Christ was not really a man. It was the Monophysite claim all over again, and the theory was the outcome of the strongly felt need to tempt the Monophysites back to the spiritual unity from which they had been separated now nearly two hundred years. The practical plan to restore religious unity in the harassed state along these lines had for its authors the emperor Heraclius (610–41) and Sergius, the patriarch of Constantinople.

Heraclius was a man of Armenian extraction—that is to say, sprung of a family from Monophysite territory—but born in Africa, where his father, another Heraclius, was commander in chief of the imperial army in the opening years of the seventh century. The ruling emperor, Phocas, was a barbarous and incompetent tyrant, under whom the state seemed about to disintegrate, at the time the Persians, led by a very able king, Chosroes II, were executing a successful invasion of the Roman East. The elder Heraclius declared against Phocas, and set his son in command of the armament he sent from Africa against the capital. The rebels were victorious, and the younger Heraclius was crowned emperor, by Sergius the patriarch, October 5, 610. He was thirty-five years of age, and was to rule for thirty years.

Nothing could have been more desperate than the situation the new emperor faced: an empty treasury, a nation impoverished and embittered, hardly any army, and the Persians advancing without any hope for some years of checking them. The list of their uninterrupted victories recalls the events of 1939–41. In 611 they took Antioch, in 613 Damascus, in 614 Jerusalem, and in 617 Alexandria. Meanwhile Heraclius, ably assisted by the patriarch, kept his people from despair and slowly prepared for the offensive. A holy war was preached, for the invaders had taken the Holy Land and had defiled the sacred places; they had captured the most sacred of all possessions, the very Cross on which Christ died. As to military plans, Heraclius proposed to fight his way through Asia Minor and Armenia to the Euphrates, and then down the rivers and across to the heart of Persia. Once the Persian monarchy was destroyed, the recovery of the provinces Rome had lost would not be difficult. The task occupied the emperor a good six years (622–28). But the day came when he dictated terms to the Persians in the heart of their own land, and he had the happiness of escorting the Cross to Jerusalem in 629.

In all these years Heraclius had been busy with theological conferences, binding to the imperial cause—as he hoped—some of his most embittered subjects, the Monophysites of Armenia (622) and the Caucasus (626) very notably, and of Syria (631). At Phasis, a city on the shores of the Black Sea, the modern Poti, he had a long conference with the bishop, Cyrus, whom he found it difficult to persuade that the new point he was urging, about the "unity" of action in the Divine Saviour,[1] was in harmony with the teaching of

[1] I.e., that there is only one "action" or "operation" in Him.

St. Leo and Chalcedon, that was still, of course, the religion of the State. The emperor advised him to consult Sergius of Constantinople. Cyrus received, in reply, a dossier of literature to support the orthodoxy of the new idea. It included a letter—later proved spurious—of a former patriarch of Constantinople to Pope Vigilius. Cyrus was won over. When, five years later, the see of Alexandria fell vacant the emperor thought of the able bishop he had met in fabled Colchis, and Cyrus was brought the thousand miles or so to sit in the seat of St. Cyril and St. Athanasius (631). And, as patriarch he brought about, in Egypt of all places, a reunion of Catholics and Monophysites—all on the strength of the new point that since Catholics believed there was but a single source of the acts done by the saving Christ, there was no reason why Monophysites should anathematize them as though they were really Nestorians. The date of this union was 633.[2] Monothelism was now, as a fact of public life, some ten years old.

It is a curious thing to us, perhaps, that the new system had lived as long as this and never attracted any comment from the Roman See. But in that far-off seventh century, "the Roman See, well-established as was its supremacy, did not in fact . . . exercise within the [four] Eastern patriarchates . . . that authority which today it exercises everywhere. Then it was only rarely that it intervened in the affairs of these other churches, in moments of crisis; and even so, Rome usually did not intervene until appealed to."[3]

At the time of the Act of Union of 633 there happened to be living at Alexandria a monk, Sophronius, learned and reputed a saint, who from a lifetime spent in scholarly travel, was well known throughout the East, and at Rome also. His trained mind saw at once that Cyrus had brought peace at the cost of truth. The treaty with the Monophysites had concluded with a number of agreed doctrinal statements, and the seventh of these has been described as the very definition of the new heresy. It condemned and anathematized whoever denied that "there is but a single Christ

---

[2] "If this is really Catholicism," Duchesne represents the Monophysites as saying in their hearts, "Chalcedon and Leo will soon be going the way of the Three Chapters." *L'Église au VIᵐᵉ Siècle*, p. 401.

[3] Ibid., 268–69.

and Son, whose divine acts and whose human acts are done by a single divine-human operation, as St. Denis[4] says."

While Cyrus and the patriarch of Constantinople were exchanging messages of joyous satisfaction—Sergius going out of his way to say (with a deft touching up of the quoted text) that this is the very teaching of St. Leo[5]—Sophronius prepared his criticisms. But Cyrus referred the monk to Constantinople, and Constantinople bade him be silent, and not start a new controversy, viz., whether in the Word Incarnate there were two "operations" or only one, but keep to the acknowledged teaching that the single person Jesus Christ works acts that are divine and also acts that are human. And with this command laid upon him, the monk returned to Palestine, his home—to find the patriarchal see vacant, and himself, presently, elected. Commands to be silent lost all their authority, of course, by the fact. In the official notification of his election, sent to the pope and to the patriarchs, Sophronius exposed the new heresy, with a wealth of learning[6] and an abundance of strong language about shepherds who were really wolves.

And now Rome comes into the action, through a letter from Sergius of Constantinople to the pope, Honorius I (625–38). This letter will, nearly sixty years later, figure in the proceedings of the sixth General Council, and with it the pope's reply; and for this reply that council will anathematize the pope. Had Sergius guessed what line the new patriarch of Jerusalem would take, whom he had so lately dismissed with a certain bland insincerity? Did he hope to put himself right with Rome before Rome heard from Sophronius? or was he not that kind of man at all, but just honestly puzzled by the criticism which a professional theologian had made of his move for peace, and anxious to know what Rome thought of it? Both "interpretations" have found favour with the historians. Whatever the truth, the certain thing is that at the highest level there was not too much understanding of what was afoot in the East, and that the pope's professional advisor was incompetent—the

---

[4] "St. Denis" being the sixth-century theologian who passed (and for many centuries to come) as St. Paul's disciple, Denis the Areopagite, Acts 17:34.

[5] Tixeront, III, 163, who gives the passage.

[6] This synodal letter runs to 24 folio columns, Mansi, XI, 461–509, Migne, P.G., vol. 87, pt. 3, 3148–3200.

man who put the pope's reply into appropriate form. What happened was this.

Sergius, in his letter to the pope, described his interview with the monk, and his command not to make trouble by starting a new controversy, and said that he had written to Alexandria, in the same sense, i.e., not to use the expression "one operation" because there were people whom it would startle, for all that some of the Fathers had used it already; and not to use the expression "two operations," because this was a novel way of speaking and would scandalize very many. This last phrase might suggest that in the Divine Saviour there were two wills, which could be contrary the one to the other—an outrageously wicked idea, said the patriarch. After some further argument, Sergius comes to the point. All this discussion, he says, we have determined to set aside, and to keep to the traditional way of speaking. Sophronius has agreed to this, and so has the emperor, to whom our advice has been to keep away from either of the controverted phrases. He concludes by asking the pope, "if there be anything wanting in what has been said . . . with your holy syllables and with your desirable assistance to signify your opinion on the matter."[7]

The letter sent in reply to this by Honorius is something unique in the vast series of papal letters. The reader will have noticed that in Sergius' letter a second term has now come into controversy—there is question of "one or two wills," as well as of "one or two operations." The pope begins by saying, you tell us about "certain discussions, and new controversies about words begun by one Sophronius, a monk (who now, so we hear, has been made bishop of Jerusalem), against our brother Cyrus the bishop of Alexandria, for preaching to those converted from heresy 'the one operation of Jesus Christ, our Lord.'" He repeats Sergius' summary of his own action and says of the reply he gave to Sophronius that it was prudent enough and careful,[8] adding, "We praise your doing away with this novel vocabulary which could be a scandal to the uninstructed." Then follows a correct statement about the way in which the Divine Saviour works divine acts and human acts, a statement innocent of any reference to the new dispute "how" this happens, about which

---

[7] Abbot John Chapman, *The Condemnation of Pope Honorius*, 15.

[8] *Satis provide circumspecteque fraternitatem vestram scripsisse.* The letter is printed, in part, in Denzinger, nos. 1057–64.

the pope's advice is asked. From this the pope passes to the statement that in our Lord there is one will. This, he says, is what we
believe; and in his exposition of the reason for the belief the pope
reveals that he and the patriarch are not talking about the same
thing. Our Lord's nature, Honorius says, being free from the taint
of original sin, there can never have been in Him that conflict which
all of us experience between the two wills, the will to execute the
law of the spirit and the will to serve the law of the members. Sergius' "two wills," on the other hand, were not these human con-
trarieties experienced by sinful man, but (*i*) a divine will, said to be
the source of the operations that are divine, and (*ii*) a human will,
the source, likewise, of the operations that were human. The pope
has missed the point, the point which is the centre of the whole
controversy. The answer he gives to Sergius, his decision, is in regard to something altogether different. After this came some
healthy generalities about avoiding the pitfalls and traps of heresy,
and then a warning to "certain babblers" (who, to win over their
hearers, give themselves the airs of doctors) that they are not to set
forth their theories as though these were the teaching of the Church
—theories on subjects which no council or lawful authority has seen
fit so to explain that men have the right to teach that there are
either one or two operations in the Lord Christ. The Scriptures tell
us plainly that He worked both human and divine things. The question whether, because He so worked, we are to understand He did
it through one or through two "operations" is no concern of ours.
It is a question we may leave to grammarians and to tutors who earn
their living by drilling schoolboys in quibbles of this sort. As for
ourselves, we (that is the pope) discover that our Lord and His
Holy Spirit worked not "one operation nor two . . . but a great
variety."

The pope ends by a warning that the new controversy will revive
the old, and that the contending parties will be taken to be either
Eutychians or Nestorians, and the faith of ordinary simple people
be disturbed. Let Sergius follow the pope's example and impose
silence about these matters on all, keeping to the old way, the truth
about the one person and two natures of the Incarnate Word.

"The result of the pope's letter was the so-called heresy of Monothelism, which up to this point can scarcely be said to have ex-

isted, except as an opinion under discussion."[9] Was Honorius indeed the begetter, albeit unwittingly, of the new trouble? Certainly it is not in the pope's letter that we first meet the topic "one or two wills," and since this was a logical next point in discussions about "one or two operations"—the will being the source of operations—it could only be a matter of time before the controversy shifted to the question of the wills. And this now happened. Again, as to Honorius' personal responsibility, the General Council that later dealt so drastically with him—and the pope, Leo II—condemn him, the council only because "in all things he followed the mind of Sergius,"[10] and the pope because Honorius "by his negligence blew up the flame of heresy,"[11] and because he "consented that the spotless tradition of Rome should be soiled."[12]

All this was fifty years or so later. To complete the story of Pope Honorius, it needs to be said that he wrote to Sergius, a second letter of which a few fragments only are known. There is nothing retracted from, or added to, the statements in the first letter. Silence is recommended on the thorny question—the foolish question, Honorius now says, almost violently. The letter relates that the pope has written to Alexandria and to Jerusalem in the same sense,[13] and that the priests who have brought the synodal letter of Sophronius have promised that he will say no more about "two operations" if Cyrus will engage to cease to speak of "one operation."

The next news of the affair to survive is that Sergius now prepared an imperial edict in which the policy of silence should be made obligatory for all. The emperor, once more, was away with his armies in the East, and Sergius, as so often before, was acting as regent. Only when Heraclius returned, three or four years later, was the edict published (638). It is known as the *Ecthesis*, or Declaration about the Faith.[14] What it does is to give force of law to the policy of "prudent silence" devised by Sergius once the reaction had begun against the reconciliation movement, the policy for which

[9] Chapman, 17.

[10] Kirch, no. 1084.

[11] Ibid., no. 1087, letter to the bishops of Spain.

[12] Ibid., no. 1085, letter to the emperor, Constantine IV.

[13] These two letters have not survived.

[14] The text is in Mansi, X, 992–97. Kirch, nos. 1070–73, publishes extracts from it.

he had ingeniously secured the patronage of Honorius. Silence on the whole dispute about "operations," lest the reunited Monophysites take fright and race off once again, silence and oblivion. But the *Ecthesis* took a different line about the question, "will" or "wills." To avoid the danger of people thinking that in the Incarnate Word there could be strife between the divine and the human, said the Declaration, "we profess that there is but a single will."

Sophronius had died before the *Ecthesis* was published, Honorius also (October 12, 638). Sergius lived long enough to give it the solemn approval of a synod, and then he too died (December 638).

Throughout the East the bishops signed the new creed, so to call it, without difficulty. As to the West, after the death of Honorius the action of the Holy See was sterilised for a good eighteen months by the fact that the pope-elect, Severinus, could not obtain confirmation of his election from the emperor—a formality without which (since the time of Justinian) he could not be consecrated. Then, four months after his consecration, the new pope died. With the election of his successor, John IV (December 24, 640) the Roman See reverts to its traditional ways, for John's first act was to hold a council and condemn as heresy the new theory that in the Incarnate Word there is but a single will. This decision he sent to the emperor. Heraclius replied that he was not the author of the *Ecthesis*, he had but signed it, and the Declaration had been the cause of troubles innumerable. This must have been one of the emperor's last acts, for on February 11, 641, he died.

His eldest son and successor, Constantine III, a young man in his twenties, was already dying of consumption, and a dispute about the succession lay ahead when John IV's letter arrived, acknowledging him as emperor, and dealing with the slanders already in circulation that charged Honorius with heresy. The letter ended with a demand that the *Ecthesis* be withdrawn. To this the emperor replied that already the text had been taken down from its place in the church of St. Sophia. Then, May 25, Constantine III died, and for the rest of the year the rival factions within the imperial family fought it out. By November the faction that supported the heir of Constantine III had won, and his eldest son reigned as Constans II, a child of eleven. It was in his name that an answer was now sent to John IV's last letter to Constantine III[15]—a resolute statement of the emperor's resolve to defend the new Monothelism *and* the Council of Chalcedon. Whereupon the pope—not John IV but his successor, Theodore[16]—condemned the *Ecthesis*, and expressed his surprise that the promises of Constantine III had not been kept.

The pope had changed, the policy remained firm.

The new pope had the unusual experience of receiving the patriarch of Constantinople, come to Rome to abjure his heresy and seek reconciliation. This was Pyrrhus, successor to Sergius and part author of the *Ecthesis*. It was by a strange route that Pyrrhus had come to Rome. He had, in 641, been deposed by the new emperor for political reasons. When his successor, Paul, applied for recognition to the pope, Theodore explained that since Pyrrhus had been uncanonically thrust out he could not recognise Paul. Meanwhile he would be obliged if the emperor would despatch Pyrrhus to Rome, to clear himself of the charge of heresy. At this stage Pyrrhus fled from Constantinople to Africa. This province was a boiling hot centre of opposition to the new heresies, the heart of which was the Greek abbot honoured today as St. Maximus the Confessor.[17] He immediately engaged the fugitive patriarch in controversy, and converted him. So it was that Pyrrhus made his way to Rome and Pope Theodore (645 or 6).

[15] This letter of John IV did not reach Constantinople until the summer of 642. The emperor to whom it was addressed had been then dead a year or so. When the official correspondence of popes and emperors could suffer such delays, misunderstanding was likely to be a permanent factor of life, and the action of any central authority ineffective. Another fact to be borne in mind is the short reign of the average pope, in these sixth and seventh centuries. In the 182 years from 526 to 708, there were 34 popes. Eight of these had "long" reigns, the other 26 averaged three years each.

[16] John had died, October 12, 642. Theodore was consecrated November 24 following, without awaiting any imperial approval of his election. He was a Greek, born in Jerusalem. Theodore (642–49) is one of the "long-reigned" popes of the period.

[17] This great saint, one day to pay with his life for his defence of true doctrine, had many years before this been a secretary of the emperor Heraclius. He was personally acquainted with the two chiefs, Sergius and Pyrrhus, and had been keenly critical of the "one operation" theory since its first appearance. The sack of his monastery, in the Persian invasion, had driven him to Africa, and here he met Sophronius, his senior by a good forty years perhaps. For his high place as a theological writer, cf. Tixeront, III, 188–92 (180–84). It was the publication of the *Ecthesis* that brought Maximus into open opposition.

Councils of bishops began to be held in various parts of Africa, denouncing the heresy, begging the patriarch Paul to return to the traditional faith, and the emperor to suppress the *Ecthesis,* and calling on the pope to make use of his great authority vis-à-vis the patriarch, who, if he will not submit, they say, should be cut off from the Church by the pope, "like a diseased limb." To the pope's summons, sent to Constantinople by a solemn embassy, the patriarch replied with a renewal of his heresy, in which he claimed Honorius as one of his patrons! Whereupon Theodore excommunicated him.

And now, once again, the emperor intervened with an edict—not this time a mere statement, but a rule, imposed under severe penalties for the disobedient, varying from deposition for bishops to fines and floggings for the ordinary public. The rule (*typos* is the Greek word, so that historians call this edict the *Type* of Constans II) was a simple prohibition of all discussions, lectures, sermons, writings on both the question of the "operations" and that of the "wills." This appeared in the last months of 648.

On the part of the emperor or his advisors (Constans II was now a youth of 18) it would seem to have been a police measure pure and simple, behind which was the fear of what such movements as the Catholic reaction in Africa, for example, might bring about. Already there had been in that province a widespread revolt, led by the emperor's commander in chief, the exarch. Only the accident that he was killed in a battle with the Arabs had halted its progress. It was not yet forty years since the hero of a similar revolt in that province had won through to the imperial crown—the present young emperor's grandfather, Heraclius. As it was, Africa was to be quasi-independent for the next ten years or so.

To the pope the new law initiated a persecution, the drastic punishment of all who protested that it was vital that Christians be taught and believe the truth about who and what the Divine Saviour was; or that error had not the same rights as truth; or who objected to the official government thesis that the difference between truth and error, in this fundamental belief, was of no importance. The truth was to be stifled, because Caesar had so willed. And Caesar had so willed—to placate the Monophysites? Hardly, for except for the fashionables, the intellectual mystics, the self-segregated elect who shunned the vulgarity of being as the rest, except for these the Monophysite had disappeared. Rather the lands where he dwelt by the million and flourished, Egypt, Palestine, Syria, Armenia, had now, finally and forever, been wrenched from the imperial rule; had lapsed, after a thousand years, from Hellenism too. Barely recovered by Heraclius in 628–29, these countries had become, in the next ten years after his triumph, the spoil of a power whose very name the victor of 629 had never heard— Islam. Once again a brief list of dates and places with the note "lost irrevocably," will show the world of the emperor at Constantinople as remodelled more drastically than any internal revolution could have changed it.

Mahomet died June 8, 632—three years or so after Heraclius had triumphantly restored the Cross to Jerusalem. In 634 his Arabs began to raid Syria. Damascus fell to them in 635. The next year the last imperial forces capable of containing them were wiped out. In 637 they took Jerusalem, in 638 Antioch, in 639 Caesarea. Other Arabian forces, in 637, overthrew the Sassanid empire of Persia. In 639 they began their drive towards Egypt—the economic heart of the Roman Empire for centuries. Babylon fell to them in 641 and, in 642, Alexandria. By 651 other Arab armies had reached the frontiers of India.

It was a new pope who had to meet the new edict, Martin I (649–55). He was thoroughly versed in the controversy, and knew well the personalities opposed to him, for he had spent several years as the pope's representative at the imperial court. His reaction to the appearance of the *Type* was immediate and vigorous. Within a few weeks of his election—for which no confirmation was asked at Constantinople—the pope sent out summonses to a council to be held at Rome, under his own presidency, that should definitively sum up all that the various local councils throughout the West had been declaring. This Lateran Council of 649, to which 105 bishops came, is the most spectacular demonstration of the Roman *principatus* since the *Tome* of St. Leo, just two hundred years before. And it was staged with the State already arrayed in opposition. This pope was to pay for his boldness with his life.

The council sat for three weeks (October 5–26) and the results of its deliberations were twenty canons,[18] which yet once again

[18] Denzinger, nos. 254–74 for the text. Chapman, as quoted, gives a good general account of the pope's speeches at the council.

state, point by point, with great clarity, the fundamentals of the faith regarding the mystery of the Incarnation, as tradition and the five General Councils set it out, introducing, in its proper place, a condemnation of the novelties about "one operation" and "one will" (canons 10–20). Those who have propagated the new ideas are in each case stigmatised as, "the wicked heretics." In the canon (no. 18)[19] that lists the heretics whom the various general councils have condemned, a place is found—"rightly, since they are similar to all these"—for Cyrus of Alexandria, for Sergius of Constantinople and his two successors, Pyrrhus and Paul (all by name), and for all others who hold what they held or hold; condemned also is "the most wicked *Ecthesis* which the emperor Heraclius put out against the orthodox faith, at the persuasion of Sergius." Along with all these the canon condemns also "the most wicked Typos, lately published by the *serenissimus* emperor Constans, [a law] hostile to the Catholic Church, namely by promulgating that a like silence and refusal shall bind [all], in respect, both of what the holy Fathers have preached and what the heretics are wickedly venerating —thus deciding that the wicked heretics shall, against all justice, be freed from blame and condemnation; which is as much as to cut away from the Catholic Church its definitions and its rules."

The decision of the council, addressed in its final letter to "all our spiritual brethren, bishops, priests, monks . . . and to the entire sacred fullness of the Catholic Church," was sent broadcast over the West by the pope's orders, to places as various as Africa and Holland. The news of what was afoot reached the emperor, of course, and orders were sent to his chief officer in Italy, the exarch at Ravenna, to march on Rome, seize the pope, and force the bishops to accept the *Type*. But the exarch arrived with his army to find the council in session, and the feeling in Rome so strong against the emperor that he conceived the idea of setting himself up as ruler of an independent state. It was to be charged later against the pope that he had a hand in this scheme. Actually he gave the pretender less than no encouragement, and the exarch passed on to try his fate in Sicily, where the plague eventually carried him off.

But in the year 653 the emperor struck again. This time the pope was kidnapped, carried bodily from before the high altar of St.

[19] Denzinger, no. 271.

Peter's, loaded with chains and shipped as a common criminal to Constantinople. When the ship arrived Martin was thrown on the deck, half starved, in rags, and exposed for some days to the derision of the scum of the town. After three months in a dungeon he was brought to trial—not for anything done or spoken in the council, but for high treason, for plotting to deprive the emperor of his Italian lands. He was condemned, and then unceremoniously degraded of his rank by the public executioners, the young emperor looking on from behind a lattice. The pope was not executed, but thrown into the gaol, chained with the murderers and the rest. Meanwhile the emperor went to relate his triumph to the patriarch Paul, then seriously ill. The terrified prelate begged him to cease the persecution. "I am so soon to answer for so much," he said. And the pope was exiled to the wilds of the Crimea. There, worn out by his sufferings, he died September 16, 655.

Simultaneously with the pope's ordeal, Constans II had ordered the arrest of Maximus and two of his associates. They, too, were brought to the capital to face the like accusations, but at one stage the true reason for the trial was forced from the court by the abbot. In the end they were sentenced to be flogged, have their hands cut off and their tongues torn out, and to be imprisoned till they died.

Constans II had exceeded the worst of his predecessors.

Between the martyrdom of St. Martin I[20] and the sixth General Council there lies a more or less uneventful quarter of a century—for the Church. For the empire, these were years of continuous crisis before the ever closer menace of the now Mohammedan Arabs, culminating in the famous siege—or succession of sieges—of Constantinople, for the Arab fleets returned every spring for five successive years. Constans II was by this time no more. Wearied of life, and of a capital that hated him for his morbid cruelty, he spent his last years in Italy and Sicily, and here in 668 he had met his death, murdered by one of his officers while he took a bath. His successor was his eldest son, Constantine IV (668–85), who at the time of the first siege was twenty.

Between the court and the Holy See there had never been any

---

[20] Both the Catholics and the Orthodox keep his feast on the same date, November 12.

formal reconciliation. Both seem tacitly to have agreed to say nothing about the past. The long-lived pope Vitalian (657–72) did not open his reign by condemning the *Type* anew. And with the new emperor it seemed banished to the attic. The patriarch Paul was long since dead, and Pyrrhus his rival also. Their successors had ceased to mention Monothelism in their inaugural letters. Constantine IV, admittedly grateful for the pope's support in the first years of his reign, when Sicily seemed about to be lost to the empire, was no sooner free of the terrible menace from the Arab fleets than he turned to Rome with proposals to end the long misunderstanding (August 12, 678).

It was from this letter that the sixth General Council developed. There ensued first, of course, one of the incredible delays of those times. The pope to whom the letter was addressed had died four months to the day before it was written. His successor, Agatho, had been reigning since June 27. He was a Greek, born in Sicily. And before he accepted the emperor's invitation—to send representatives to a kind of conference which should work out a reconciliation between Constantinople and Rome—Agatho proposed to consult the whole Latin episcopate, much as had been done before the Lateran Council of 649. At his bidding councils were held in various places—one we know at Hatfield, under the presidency of the Archbishop of Canterbury—and their findings were studied and put into the shape of a reply to the emperor, at a gathering of bishops at Rome at Easter (March 25) 680; a year and a half since the emperor had written, considerably less, perhaps, since his letter had reached the pope. The delay had caused some anxiety at Constantinople and, on the part of the patriarch, Theodore, a revival of antipapal feeling, for he took the opportunity of removing from the diptychs the name of the last pope who figured there, Vitalian, dead seven years now. For this the emperor deposed him.

The final results of Pope Agatho's consultation of the bishops, and of the work done in Rome, was a profession of faith signed by the pope and 125 bishops,[21] and a letter to the emperor from the pope accrediting his representatives to the conference, three bishops, two priests, and a deacon—specialists from the Curia Romana, these last three, and sent as legates personally representing the pope

---

[21] One of these was St. Wilfrid, bishop of York.

—and four Greek monks from Greek monasteries in Sicily and Rome (the emperor having especially asked for this).

This convoy reached Constantinople in September, and the emperor forthwith ordered his new patriarch to summon all the metropolitans and bishops subject to him to attend a conference where the theory of "one operation" and "one will" would be examined. This conference, which held its first session on November 7, in the emperor's palace, developed insensibly into the sixth General Council.

The council held, in all, eighteen sessions, concluding its work September 16, 681. The number of bishops present varied. At the first session there were only forty-three present, at the last 174. The young emperor presided, in person, at the first eleven sessions, with the pope's personal representatives in the place of honour, on his left.

It was the legates who opened the proceedings. Beginning with a reference to the dissensions of the last forty-six years—since the time when Sergius wrote for advice to Pope Honorius—all these, they said, had been due to the acts of various patriarchs of Constantinople. They asked therefore what justification, it was thought, these prelates had had for the novel views whence all the troubles had come.

It was the patriarch of Antioch, Macarius, who replied. "We did not publish any new expressions," he said. All they had had to say was what they had been taught by the General Councils of the past, and by saintly bishops like Sergius, and Cyrus, "and also Honorius, who was Pope of Old Rome." Whereupon the emperor asked for proofs of this, from the synods and the Fathers; and from now the council hall became something of a university classroom. The official records of all the proceedings at Ephesus, Chalcedon, and at the council of 553, with all the documentation—letters of popes and so forth—were read out, a business that occupied the bishops for some days. During the reading of the *acta* of Justinian's council of 553 the papal legates interrupted. Three of the documents read out did not figure in the official proceedings, they objected; they were forgeries interpolated many years later. These three documents were an alleged letter from Mennas, patriarch in 553, to Pope Vigilius, and letters from Vigilius to Justinian and to

Theodora, in all three of which there was mention of "the one will," and a recommendation of this as orthodox teaching, i.e., plain Monothelism, eighty years before Sergius. Archivists and palaeographers were brought in, the actual originals of the proceedings of 553 were taken from the library of the see of Constantinople and examined. It was discovered that, in these authentic originals, the sheets on which the three letters were written were indeed of later date than the council, and had at some time been surreptitiously slipped into the genuine *acta*.

At this stage (November 15, the fourth session) the patriarch of Constantinople asked that the letter of Pope Agatho to the emperor be read, and the profession of faith which the 125 bishops had signed. This was assented to, these bulky treatises[22] were read out, and Agatho's authoritative statement of the traditional faith, modelled on the *Tome* of St. Leo, was greeted with shouts that recall the triumphs of 451: "It is Peter who is speaking through Agatho."[23]

The unanimous, spontaneous applause with which the bishops—halfway through Macarius' defence—hailed this statement of the belief which the Monothelites had laboured for fifty years to destroy, may have been discouraging, but in the next two sessions (December 7 and February 12) Macarius took up his task again of proving, this time from the Fathers, that the primitive belief of the church was indeed "one operation" and "one will." Again the legates interrupted. His quotations were not what the originals said. The texts had been altered to make them prove the Monothelite theories. Passages were quoted as applying to the Incarnate Word which, in the originals, referred to something else altogether. When Macarius had finished, the emperor ordered all his papers to be locked up and sealed. And he made the same order the next day (February 13) about the dossier read out by the legates, from the councils and the Fathers and from the Monothelite writers also. All these papers were then taken away to be compared with the originals, or the standard copies in the Patriarchal Library.[24]

This task took time. It is not surprising that it was three weeks before the council met for the next—eighth—session, March 7. The

---

[22] For the texts, the letter of Agatho to Constantine IV, Mansi, XI, 234–86, the profession of faith of the 125 bishops, ibid., 286–315.

[23] Something more must be said of Agatho's letter later.

[24] As were the letters of Agatho and the western bishops which the legates had brought.

emperor, on this day, put the question point-blank to the patriarch of Constantinople, whether the doctrine of the passages, as actually found in the Fathers and in the General Councils, tallied with the letter of Agatho and the profession of faith of the western bishops. The patriarch answered that all this mass of testimony did indeed bear out that what Agatho taught was the truth of the matter, "and so I profess and believe," he said. And all the bishops present, save a handful, assented likewise. The pope's name was then restored to the diptychs. The schism of recent years—whatever that had amounted to—was ended.

When the other patriarch present, Macarius, was asked whether he now agreed that Agatho's teaching was that of the councils and the Fathers, he bluntly declared himself a Monothelite. "I do not say two wills or operations in the mysterious Incarnation of our Lord, Jesus Christ, but one will and a single divine-human[25] operation." The council then demanded that Macarius justify himself. He thereupon read a declaration which asserted that those who held to the two wills, revealed themselves thereby as Nestorians; and to the list of the heretics of the past whom he anathematized he added the name of Maximus, for "his dogma of division" of the Incarnate Word, a dogma, he said, "rejected before our time by our blessed Fathers, I mean Honorius and Sergius and Cyrus . . . and [to the emperor] by Heraclius of pious memory, your own great-grandfather." Never, he said, would he acknowledge there were two wills or two operations, not even if he were to be torn limb from limb, and cast into the sea. It was next proved against Macarius that he had garbled the testimonies he was quoting, upon which he admitted he had quoted them in this way in order to prove his own belief. At which bold defiance the bishops shouted him down, with cries of "Dioscoros again," "Another Apollinaris." He was immediately stripped of the badge of his patriarchal rank, and placed standing in the midst of the council—for trial. And the following day, March 8, the council deposed him.

Two weeks later, at the twelfth session, yet more of the documents put in by Macarius under seal were examined and read out. Among them was the fatal reply of Honorius to Sergius. On March 28 (thirteenth session) judgment was given on the letters read on

[25] Theandric.

March 22, and on the writers. The letters of Sergius were condemned as against the true faith and heretical, and, as though they were still alive, the council voted that "the names of those whose wicked teaching we execrate shall be cast out of the holy church of God, that is, Sergius, Cyrus of Alexandria, Pyrrhus, Paul and Peter, patriarchs of Constantinople . . . persons, all of them, mentioned by Agatho in his letter and cast out by him." Then came one whom Agatho had not named. "And in addition to these we decide that Honorius also, who was Pope of the Older Rome, be with them cast out of the holy church of God, and be anathematized with them, because we have found by his letter to Sergius that he followed his opinion in all things and confirmed his wicked teaching." Grim moment in the history of the councils when the presiding Roman legates put this sentence to the bishops! At a later stage of the council (sixteenth session, August 9) a group of bishops, led by the patriarch of Constantinople, made a move to annul the anathematizing of the dead patriarchs Sergius, Pyrrhus, Paul, and Peter. This, if accepted, would have saved the name of Honorius too. We do not read that the legates welcomed the opportunity thus given. The council voted that the sentences stand, and the legates made no objection.

The session which followed the stern business of these condemnations saw a strange sight indeed, when the bishops transferred themselves into one of the public places of the town for the spectacle of a leading Monothelite essaying a miracle in proof that the doctrine was true. This was a priest, Polychronius, who claimed that the Monothelite profession of faith would raise the dead to life. A corpse was procured, and the Monothelite, in the presence of an immense crowd, laid the document upon it. For two hours he was allowed to pray, and to whisper in the dead man's ear, but nothing happened except the jeers of the spectators—not even the recantation of the would-be wonder worker, and the bishops added him *nominatim* to the list of the condemned. This was on April 26.

At the seventeenth session, September 11, the text of the council's profession of faith was settled: "We teach that in our Lord, Jesus Christ, there are two natural wills, and two natural operations, indivisibly, inconvertibly, inseparably, without any fusion, as the holy fathers have taught, and that these two natural wills are not contrary, as wicked heretics have said."[26] On September 16 it was solemnly voted and signed by 174 bishops. The sixth General Council was over.

It had been a novel feature, in this particular council, that at the initiative of the papal legates, the heresy, to condemn which the council had been called, had been given a full hearing. This was new. No Arian expounded his theories at Nicaea, no one spoke for Nestorius at Ephesus, or for Eutyches at Chalcedon. At each of these councils the bishops, before they came together, were all but unanimously opposed to the new theories and set on their condemnation. And so it was at Constantinople in 680. It was to an audience in no need of being persuaded that Pope Agatho's letter was read out—a letter not indeed addressed to the council, for at the time it was written there had been no thought of more than a small conference of bishops. It was to the emperor that the pope addressed his statement of the true doctrine, and his message that this was the doctrine of salvation, and that this is what the patriarch of Constantinople must profess, if there is to be peace. Whether or not the pope understood the realities of the eastern situation, this teaching was in fact what all already believed, there also; it was what, if untroubled by imperial interference or the manoeuvres of the patriarchal diplomacy vis-à-vis the Monophysites, all the bishops had always professed, as well after the fatal year 634 as before. Whence the spontaneity of the applause that greeted Agatho's categoric statements and his strikingly phrased reminder of the special privilege of his own see, the privilege now in very evident operation.

Something of what the pope said to the bishops, and of the words they used in their gratitude to him, ought to find a place here, not because this is a history of Catholic doctrine—for it is not that of course—but for the reason that this particular interchange is an important event in the gradual development of that new, "post-Persecutions" institution of the Church of Christ, the General Council.

It is today a thousand years and more since a General Council last met at the summons of an emperor, since any emperor played

---

[26] Denzinger (nos. 289–93) prints a six-page extract from the decree, the Greek text and the Latin. It is from this, no. 291, that my quotation is taken.

any part in the conduct of a council. The emperors have gone, the empires too, and the very conception of empire which then gave cohesion to the state; all this has gone. And in that thousand years twelve General Councils have been held. The very term suggests to us an institution whose life derives from some pope's *fiat*, an institution where the pope's action is all-important, and the suggestion that an emperor has, or ever had, a rôle to play is incredible, save to the ecclesiastical archaeologist. But the pope was always all-important in the General Council, from the beginning. From the time of the first council whose history is at all really known to us in detail—Ephesus—although the emperor may call the council, and the pope assent to and support his initiative, it is the pope who, before the council meets, decides the point of belief, who directs the bishops of the council that this is the truth, and that it is not to be called into question: Celestine I in 431, Leo I in 451, Agatho in 680. So instinctive is this papal action, with regard to the General Council facing a revolt against the traditional belief, that were it one day to be discovered that Silvester I sent with his legates to Nicaea the famous phrase *homo-oúsion toi patri* for the council's acceptance, we should scarcely be surprised at the news—it would be so perfectly in keeping with the rest of the history.

Never, so far, had this doctrine of the rôle of the pope been set forth, to a council itself, so completely and so explicitly, by the pope himself as in the letter of Pope Agatho. It is thereby a main landmark in the history of the development of the General Council, and since (from lack of translations) this vital documentary source is all but unknown, outside ecclesiastical circles, I make no apology for the extensive quotations that follow.[27]

In the first place, to show exactly how the letter of Agatho was received, here are quotations from letters of the council of 680, and of the emperor Constantine IV. There is, first, the letter of the bishops to the emperor, written at the close of the council, congratulating him on the victory of the true faith. In this victory the pope's action was all-important, they proceed to explain: "Assenting to the letter of our most blessed father, and most high pope, Agatho . . . we have followed his teaching, and he the Apostolic and Patristic tradition, and we have found nothing that was not consonant with

[27] The translation is taken from Chapman, op. cit., whose language I have occasionally simplified.

what they have laid down. . . . Who has ever beheld such wondrous things? The spiritual lists were arrayed, and the champion of the false teaching was disarmed beforehand, [i.e., by the pope's letter], and he knew not that he would not obtain the crown of victory, but be stripped of the sacerdotal crown. But with us fought the Prince of the Apostles, for to assist us we had his imitator and the successor to his chair, who exhibited to us the mystery of theology in his letter. The ancient city of Rome proffered to you a divinely written confession and caused the daylight of dogmas to rise by the Western parchment.[28] And the ink shone, and through Agatho it was Peter who was speaking."[29]

The bishops also wrote to the pope. Their letter makes clear what these Easterns believed his place in the universal church to be: "The greatest diseases demand the greatest remedies, as you know, most blessed one. Wherefore, Christ, our true God, has revealed your Holiness as a wise physician, mightily driving away the disease of heresy by the medicine of orthodoxy, and bestowing health on the members of the Church. We therefore leave to you what is to be done,[30] since you occupy the first see of the universal Church, and stand on the firm rock of the faith, after we have dwelt with pleasure upon the writings of the true confession sent from your fatherly blessedness to the most pious emperor, which also we recognize as pronounced by the chiefest head of the Apostles, and by which we have put to flight the dangerous opinion of the heresy which lately arose. . . ."[31]

The same ideas about the unique rôle of the Papacy in the Church, with regard to disputes concerning doctrine, are found in the edict by which the emperor published to all his people the findings of the council: "These are the teachings of the voices of the Gospels and Apostles, these the doctrines of the holy Synods, and of the elect and patristic tongues; these have been preserved untainted by Peter, the rock of the faith, the head of the Apostles; in this faith we live and reign. . . ."[32] And again the emperor says, in

---

[28] The profession of faith, signed by Agatho and the 125 bishops of the West.
[29] Chapman, 100–1.
[30] With Macarius and other heretics left to the pope's discretion.
[31] Ibid., 102.
[32] Ibid., 104.

his letter to the pope,[33] describing the events of the council: "We ordered the letter of Pope Agatho . . . to our majesty . . . to be read in the hearing of all . . . we perceived in it the word of the true confession [i.e., of Peter] unaltered. And with the eyes of our understanding we saw it as if it were the very ruler of the Apostolic choir, the first chair, Peter himself, declaring the mystery of the whole dispensation, and addressing Christ by this letter: 'Thou art the Christ, the Son of the living God'; for his holy letter described in word for us the whole Christ. We all received it willingly and sincerely, and embraced it, as though the letter were Peter himself . . . Glory be to God, who does wondrous things, Who has kept safe the faith among you unharmed. For how should He not do so [with regard to] that rock on which He founded His church, and prophesied that the gates of hell, all the ambushes of heretics, should not prevail against it? From it, as from the vault of heaven, the word of the true confession flashed forth, and . . . brought warmth to frozen orthodoxy."

And in his letter to the 125 western bishops, the emperor wrote, "We admired the writing of Agatho as the voice of St. Peter, for nobody disagreed save one."

And now, what was the message of Pope Agatho[34] which aroused so much enthusiasm in the churches of the East? As what did the pope propose himself to them? and take for granted that he would be listened to?

Let it first be recalled that Agatho is writing not to Constantine IV proposing a General Council to celebrate union and peace, but to Constantine IV proposing a conference on the present situation, a discussion of differences with a view to peace. Agatho's letter is, in itself, a reply to this invitation of the emperor. His first business is to explain the long delay in answering and to accredit those whom he has sent as his representatives. In doing this, Agatho tells the emperor that the function of his legates is to explain what the Roman Church teaches. They do not come as learned theologians, but as bringing testimony of what is believed, charged to state "the

---

[33] To Leo II, successor to Agatho, who died before the council ended. The translation is Chapman, 105–6.

[34] For the text see Mansi, XI, 286–315; the extracts here are Chapman, 77–82.

tradition of this Apostolic See, as it has been taught by our apostolic predecessors." And they have been commanded not to presume to add or take away or change anything. It is in a plain statement, a kind of creed, that the pope sets out the traditon, "We believe one, holy, undivided Trinity", and so forth. At the appropriate point he sets down as part of the belief the doctrine of the two wills and the two "operations," and then proceeds to say: "This is the true and undefiled profession of the Christian religion, which no human cleverness invented, but which the Holy Ghost taught by the Prince of the Apostles. This is the firm and irreprehensible doctrine of the apostles. . . .

"And therefore, I beseech you, deign to stretch forth the right hand of your clemency to the apostolic doctrine which Peter the Apostle has handed down, that it be proclaimed more loudly than by a trumpet in the whole world: because Peter's true confession was revealed from heaven by the Father, and for it Peter was pronounced blessed by the Lord of all[35]; and he received also, from the Redeemer of us all, by a threefold commendation, the spiritual sheep of the Church that he might feed them. Resting on his protection, this Apostolic Church of his has never turned aside from the way of truth to any part of error, and her authority has always been faithfully followed and embraced as that of the Prince of the Apostles, by the whole Catholic Church and all Councils, and by all the venerable Fathers who embraced her doctrine, by which they have shone as most approved lights of the Church of Christ, and has been venerated and followed by all orthodox doctors, while the heretics have attacked it [i.e., the authority of Peter's Apostolic Church] with false accusations and hatred. This is the living tradition of the apostles of Christ, which His Church holds everywhere, which is to be loved and cherished above all things and faithfully preached. . . .

"This is the rule of the true faith, which in prosperity and adversity this spiritual Mother of your most serene Empire, the Apostolic Church of Christ, has ever held, and defends; and she, by the grace of Almighty God, will be proved never to have wandered

[35] He said to them, "But whom do you say that I am?" Simon Peter answered and said, "Thou art the Christ, the Son of the living God." Then Jesus answered and said, "Blessed art thou, Simon Bar-Jona, for flesh and blood has not revealed this to thee, but my Father in heaven." Matt. 16:15–17.

from the path of the apostolic tradition, nor to have succumbed to the novelties of heretics; but even as, in the beginning of the Christian faith, she received it from her founders, the princes of the apostles of Christ, so she remains unspotted to the end, according to the divine promise of our Lord and Saviour Himself, which He spake to the prince of His disciples in the holy Gospels: 'Peter, Peter,' saith He, 'behold, Satan hath desired to have you, that he may sift you as wheat; but I have prayed for thee, that thy faith fail not, and thou being once converted, strengthen thy brethren.'[36] Let your clemency therefore consider that the Lord and Saviour of all, to whom faith belongs, who promised that the faith of Peter should not fail, admonished him to strengthen his brethren; and it is known to all men that the apostolic pontiffs, the predecessors of my littleness, have always done this with confidence.

"Woe is me, if I cover the truth in silence, when I am bidden . . . to instruct the Christian folk therewith. . . . Wherefore also my predecessors, of apostolic memory, being furnished with the teachings of the Lord, never neglected to exhort the prelates of the Church of Constantinople, who tried to introduce heretical novelties into the immaculate Church of Christ, and to warn them with entreaties to desist from the heretical error of teaching falsehood at least by their silence.

"Consequently, the holy Church of God, the Mother of your most Christian Empire, must be freed from the errors of teachers like these, and in order to please God and save their souls, the whole number of prelates and priests, and clergy and people must confess with us the formula of truth and Apostolic tradition, the evangelical and Apostolic rule of faith, which is founded upon the firm rock of blessed Peter, the Prince of the Apostles, which by his favour remains free from all error."

The pope concludes by declaring that "if the prelate of the Church of Constantinople shall elect to hold with us, and to preach this irreprehensible rule of the Apostolic teaching of the Holy Scriptures, of the venerable Synods, of the spiritual Fathers, according to their evangelical interpretations, by which the formula of the truth has been shown to us through the revelation of the Holy Ghost," then there will indeed be peace. But if he should refuse,

[36] Luke 22:31.

"let him know that of such contempt he will have to make satisfaction to the divine judgment of Christ before the Judge of all, who is in heaven, to whom we ourselves shall give an account, when He shall come to judgment, for the ministry we have received."

7. The Second General Council of Nicaea, 787

The seventh General Council, the Second Council of Nicaea, was summoned in order to settle a controversy which "to a great extent was a domestic controversy of the church of Constantinople and its immediate dependencies."[1] And the subject of this controversy was a matter "in which the peculiar character of all the nations concerned played a large part."[2] It was a controversy about the lawfulness of venerating holy images and relics, and about prayer to the saints. Why these controversies arose, towards the year 725, historians still can only make guesses, as they can also only guess what it was that led the emperor, Leo III (717–40), to lead the anti-image party, so to call it.[3]

Leo III was one of the great emperors, a ruler under whose government "the empire not only ceased to decline, but even began to regain much of its early vigour."[4] Yet at the time he was proclaimed emperor, the empire was threatened with immediate ruin. "Six emperors had been dethroned within the space of twenty-one years. Four perished by the hand of the public executioner, one died in obscurity, after being deprived of sight, and the other was only allowed to end his days peacefully in a monastery, because Leo felt the imperial sceptre firmly fixed in his own grasp. Every army assembled to encounter the Saracens had broken out into rebellion. The Bulgarians and Sclavonians wasted Europe up to the walls of Constantinople; the Saracens ravaged the whole of Asia Minor to the shores of the Bosporus."[5]

[1] Jalland, 370.
[2] Tixeront, III, 482 (467).
[3] More formally, and, by a universal convention for centuries now, the Iconoclastic Movement.
[4] Finlay, *The Byzantine Empire* (Everyman's edition), 3.
[5] Finlay, 14.

The new emperor's first task was to save his capital. He was crowned on March 25, 717, and just four months later the siege of Constantinople began; huge armies of Mohammedans on the land side, and a vast fleet in the sea of Marmora and the Black Sea. The siege lasted just a year. In the end it was the besiegers who starved, and little by little their fleet was destroyed. For the next twenty years the empire had nothing to fear from the Saracens, and the prestige of the great defence was perhaps Leo's main resource in his unexpected career as a religious reformer.

"Unexpected" would seem to be accurate. For while we can fix the date when the emperor first published his views on these religious practices, the years 726 and 727, none can say whence these ideas came to him. But one of the historians best versed in the story gives him credit for a sincere desire to purify religion from an ever increasing superstition.[6] Images—paintings, that is, mosaics, reliefs, statues—are in part the decorative furniture of a church; they are reminders of holy personages now no longer in this world, or of past incidents of religious history, and they are a means by which the devout can pay honour to Christ and the saints, honouring these by honouring their images; by using precious woods, ivories, gold, and silver, out of which to make the image; by clothing it in costly silks, ornamenting the figure with jewels and so forth; most of all by a certain ceremonious use of the image, burning lights in front of it, offering incense to it, and especially by kneeling before the image when one is praying to the personage it represents. According to the personal taste or temperament of the believer, these practices can vary indefinitely from what seems mere gesture to what, no less certainly, can seem the very extravagance of passion. But, even at the very extreme, devotion to the image for the sake of the saint represented is, of course, a different kind of thing altogether from the act of the ancient heathen who thought the image itself a god, itself actually able to reward the devotee or work him harm, and who addressed his prayer to the image itself for the image's own sake—the image thus being, in his case, what we call an idol.

[6] Louis Brehier, whose *La Quérelle des Images* (1904) is still a classic text. The quotation is from the similarly titled Chapter XIII of his *Grégoire le Grand, les États barbares et l'Invasion Arabe* (590–757), p. 441, n. 1. This book is vol. 5 of the *Histoire de l'Église*, ed. A. Fliche and Msgr. V. Martin (1947).

What exactly the mentality was that underlay Leo III's anti-image policy we shall probably never know. That he was a great reorganiser of the whole machinery of the state is certain. Inevitably, in this particular state, the Byzantine Empire, this meant a deep interest in the welfare of religion. Was it as part of the very necessary regeneration of the state that the question of the religious exercises of the ordinary man came under the emperor's notice? somewhat as (just one thousand years later) they seem to have fascinated another emperor, Joseph II?

The historians of the religious arts will tell us that round about the time when Leo III grew up, religious art was passing from a state where the pictures were repetitions of "typical" figures (saints in hieratic postures, symbolised according to a rigid convention), to a very different condition of things, where the pictures were more like those of ordinary human beings. They speak of a new, naïve, crude realism, especially in the pictures of the martyrs, where the artist's imagination revelled in the delineation of horrific tortures. And once the taste for pictures of the saints in action grew, there began to appear, as well as their authentic deeds, pictures of what they had never done except in pious fairy tales—miracles and other wonders that had, in fact, never taken place at all; and this even in the pictures of the Blessed Virgin and of her Divine Son. In other words, legend was being given the same credence as truth—which is one of the most direct routes, of course, to superstition. There seems to be no doubt of these developments, particularly in the matter of icons properly so called—that is, the pictures, in metal, wood, ivory, or painted, made for private devotion. We read of icons alleged to have worked miracles, and held especially sacred or valuable because of this reputation, and of others not made by human hands, miraculously conveyed to this earth. And all this with little or no supervision from the authorities in the church. In a word, grave abuses, long tolerated.

We do hear of bishops who protested against these developments —it was with three bishops of sees in Asia Minor[7] that the movement began which Leo III was to take up. But we have not any-

[7] Constantine of Nacolia, Thomas of Claudiopolis, Theodosius of Ephesus. From a letter of the patriarch of Constantinople, Germanos, whom Constantine had consulted, we learn that the bishop's difficulty was the explicit prohibition in Exodus, 20:4, 5.

thing like sufficient detail about episcopal action in general to judge the bishops as a whole. Later, the emperors—Leo's son and successor, Constantine V, at least—were to take up the position that image-veneration is simple idolatry. But was this the original position? Or was it something like this: "Too many people pay reverence to images in such a way as to make it seem that they are actually idolaters"? Or did anyone assert: "Too many people have become idolaters through the custom of venerating images"? Even today, strange to say, one occasionally finds educated men, whom the Catholic use of images repels, hard to convince that Catholics do not believe the actual wood or plaster statue is a being capable of doing what is asked. I have never had reason to think these non-Catholic friends of mine thought myself an idolater, but every time they see a seemingly less educated Catholic (whom they presume, of course, to be a less intelligent being than themselves) kneeling in prayer before a statue, or lighting a candle to burn before it, their suspicion is aroused that here is idolatry. Given the fact of the never ceasing war of the Church on superstition in all its forms, the unanimous violence of theologians and preachers, at all times, against even the quasi-superstitions of social life,[8] the presumption is dead against the accusation. The American Catholic can be just as startled as his non-Catholic friend, at the spectacles he sometimes sees in the churches of latitudes far to the south, at the way statues are dressed, bedizened with jewellery, paraded around and apparently treated, at times, as though they were the central feature of religion. A little experience shows that this is but an instance of that general truth upon which Montaigne so loved to dwell: "It is the common weakness, not of the lower classes only but of all mankind almost, to form their judgments and their plans according to the way of life where they were born."[9] Who will ever persuade the image-loving Italian or Spaniard that the teen-age maidens of the United States do not suffer from the freedom with which their parents allow them to run around with the boys of their choice?

[8] For example, belief that it is dangerous to sit 13 at table, or to spill salt, general belief in "charms, omens, dreams and such like foolery."

[9] *Essays*, Book I, Chap. 49, "The Customs of the Ancient World." The reader will recall the half-contemptuous amusement with which Newman compares his Protestant conviction of Catholic abuses with his Catholic knowledge of the facts in later years.

The point where the Iconoclasts roused against themselves the general feeling of the Church was not that they said, "There is too much of this image devotion in the religious life of the day," or "This if not checked will lead to superstition,"[10] but the openly expressed principle of the whole campaign: "Image devotion is idolatry." And, at a later stage in the controversy, they protested that all prayer to the saints is superstitious and sinful.

Leo III's first "iconoclastic" act of which we have certain knowledge was the removal of the image of Christ from over the principal gate of the palace at Constantinople. This caused a riot and there were some deaths, and arrests, and punishments. Next there were mutinies in the armed forces as the orders went round that images were to be destroyed. The emperor endeavoured to win over the patriarch, Germanos, to approve the new policy, and he also wrote to the pope, Gregory II. These letters are lost, but we do possess the pope's replies, and we can learn that the correspondence was an interchange of doctrinal treatises, the pope explaining to the emperor that the Old Testament prohibition was about *idol* worship, and explaining how idols and the Catholic images are different kinds of things. The emperor's threat that unless the pope submitted he would be deposed had no effect except to cause a revolt in the Italian provinces, and then, February 11, 731, the pope died.

Gregory II died without knowing that on January 17 the emperor had called together his senators and chief officers of state and the patriarch to put before them an imperial declaration that whoever refused to destroy any images he possessed, or whoever paid honour to images, was a rebel against the state. The patriarch refused to put his name to the declaration. He took off his badge of office and went away, not to the official palace he had occupied for so long, but to the family home. The emperor appointed one of his officials to succeed him, who signed willingly; the declaration (thus fortified with the approval of the Church) was published, and the first persecution began.

It was the newly elected Gregory III[11] who received the new patriarch's demand for recognition as lawful bishop of Constantinople in a profession of faith, made up, in part, of the edict or

---

[10] Giving to created things what is due to God alone.
[11] Elected March 18, 731.

manifesto he had just signed. This pope, like the emperor, was a Syrian by birth. He replied by refusing the recognition asked for, and threatened the petitioner that unless he returned to orthodox ways he would be cast out of the priesthood. Gregory III was a man of great determination, and his "reaction" to the emperor's violence was to call a council that sat at Rome from November 1 to the end of the year—very much as Martin I had acted in 649. As many as ninety-three bishops attended. The pope published a sentence of excommunication against all who, "despising the ancient practice of the church," set themselves against the veneration of images, destroyed or profaned them. The emperor, on receipt of this news, prepared an expedition to punish the Italian bishops and to arrest the pope. But the fleet was wrecked by storms. Only the remnant of it reached Sicily. All that Leo could do was to confiscate the vast papal domains in Sicily, upon whose revenues the popes had depended for their administration of Rome and for their traditional care of the poor.

Leo III died in June 740. His son, who succeeded as Constantine V, was to reign for thirty-five years, and to show himself as capable as his father had been. Such a succession—nearly sixty years of continuous, good, strong government—was without precedent. The great event of the new reign, from the point of view of religion, was the council called by Constantine in 753, for the purpose of solemnly condemning the cult of images. For this emperor was much more of an Iconoclast than Leo III. In a treatise which he wrote, and circulated to the bishops on the eve of the council, he explained that all images of Christ were heretical, since they must portray Him as merely human, i.e., as though He had but one nature. At the same time that he thus, indirectly, seemed to reprobate the ancient Monophysite heresy, he used its terminology to explain himself; and as well as this, by refusing to the Blessed Virgin the name of *Theotókos*, by asserting her to be no more than *Christotókos*, he aligned himself with the Nestorians. It was at the first real breathing space of his reign—which had begun with a civil war, in which the rebels held Constantinople—that Constantine V held this council.

It met in the emperor's palace called Hieria, near Chalcedon, February 10, 753, and it sat for as long as seven months, with 338 bishops attending. So far as numbers went, this was one of the greatest of all the councils so far. The pope was not invited to it; the see of Constantinople was vacant; Alexandria, Antioch, and Jerusalem were now well and truly sees *in partibus infidelium*. The president was that archbishop of Ephesus who, nearly thirty years before, had been one of the first promoters of iconoclasm. What took up the time of so many bishops for so many months was not the proposal to forbid the veneration of images. Here all were agreed. But the bishops resisted the emperor steadfastly when he proposed to go back on the earlier, acknowledged General Councils. They refused to endorse his heresies about the nature of Christ, the *Theotókos*, and her rôle of intercessor for mankind, the practice of prayer to the saints, the veneration due to their relics. So that the final summing up of the council does no more than speak of the images as being idolatrous and heretical, a temptation to the faith that originated with the devil. No one is to possess or venerate an image, even in the secrecy of his home. All who disobey are to be excommunicated, and also to be punished by the law of the emperor, for their disobedience is also a crime against the state.

It is now that the real persecution began. The names of several illustrious martyrs have survived, some of them beheaded, others flogged till they died. Especially did the emperor rage against the monks, against whom as a class he organised a campaign of slander, whose dress and celibacy he ridiculed in pageantry and shows. At one moment a law enacted that all the emperor's subjects should swear never again to venerate an image, and the first to take this oath was the patriarch of Constantinople, publicly, holding up the relic of the true Cross, in the pulpit of St. Sophia. The minority who refused suffered cruelly. And now the emperor went beyond his council of 753. All prayer to the saints was forbidden, and all veneration of their relics. These were to be destroyed. From the great basilica at Chalcedon the body of the martyr to honour whom it was built, St. Euphemia, was thrown into the sea. And so the reign of terror continued until Constantine V died, the feast of Holy Cross, 775.

His son, Leo IV, lasted only five years, and then, as regent for the child Constantine VI, Leo's widow, Irene, ruled. She was a devout Catholic; that is to say, she had always been opposed to the whole iconoclastic business; and once the winter was over (Leo IV died in September, 780) a Byzantine embassy once more appeared in Italy. It was bound for the court of Charlemagne, to negotiate a marriage for the young emperor. And it was an augury of coming recovery, the first sign of the future seventh General Council of 787.

In May 784 the patriarch Paul of Constantinople, without a word even to the sovereign, suddenly went into retirement. Death was coming, he explained, and he must repent, and make reparation for his bad oath to work for the destruction of the cult of images. To the empress, he said, further, that the church of Constantinople was in schism, and that the only remedy for the evil was a General Council. Nothing but the unsettled state of the empire after her husband's death had delayed Irene's plans to reverse the policy of the last sixty years, and now she acted with decision. On August 29 the empress wrote to the pope (Adrian I, 772–95) that she had decided to summon a General Council and, inviting him to take part in it, she said, "It is God Himself, wishing to lead us to the truth, Who asks you to come in person, in order to confirm the ancient tradition about the veneration of images."[12] If Adrian could not come himself would he send worthy men to represent him?

Shortly after the despatch of this letter the patriarch Paul died (September 784). To fill the vacancy the empress chose a layman, one of the highest officers of the state, Tarasios. To a great meeting of bishops and state officials, he made a speech explaining exactly the present position in law and fact of the see of Constantinople and the hundreds of sees dependent on it. Ever since the time of Pope Gregory III, fifty-three years before, all these had been cut off from the universal church. This state of things could not be borne any longer. A General Council was the only way out of the complex difficulty. If the assembly agreed and would support him, Tarasios would accept the empress' nomination and consent to be patriarch. There were some objections and a discussion, but in the end the meeting pledged its support. On Christmas Day, Tarasios was consecrated.

His first act was to send to the pope the official notice of his election, which, as was the usual form, took the shape of a detailed

[12] There is a dispute among historians whether this letter was sent in 784 or 785.

profession of faith. Tarasios also frankly explained how he came to acquiesce in the unusual (not to say irregular) business that he, a layman, had been chosen to be the new bishop. With this so-called synodical letter, there went the official announcement of the election and consecration from the empress.

It was many months before these letters reached the distant pope. His replies are dated October 29, 785. Adrian was ready, he said, to be represented at the council, if such a council was the only way to bring about the restoration of the images. But, even so, on conditions: the coming council was to anathematize the gathering at the Hieria of 753, and this in the presence of the papal legates,[13] the empress was to guarantee full freedom of action to the council, and that the legates would be allowed to return to Rome. Adrian's conditions were accepted and so, from the outset, by virtue of this initiatory letter, the pope's position vis-à-vis the council is that of Agatho in 680 and of St. Leo in 451.

The summonses for the council—ordered to meet at Constantinople—went out in the summer of 786, and on August 1 the bishops assembled in the basilica of the Holy Apostles. But the proceedings had scarcely begun when the church was invaded by a regiment of soldiers, and despite the presence of the empress and her son, Constantine VI, the bishops were put out of the church. The army was, notoriously, one of the chief strongholds of the Iconoclasts—loyalty to the religious peculiarities of the great soldier-emperors, Leo III and Constantine V, was a thing seriously to be reckoned with. Irene resigned herself, sent the bishops home to their sees, and turned to the task of securing for the garrison of the capital troops on whom she could rely.

This took time, and it was May 787 before the call to the council was again issued. This time the bishops were not convoked to the capital, but to Nicaea, fifty miles away, and separated from the turbulent city by the waters of the Bosporus. There, on September 24, with memories no doubt of the other council held there cen-

---

[13] "That pseudo-council which took place without the Apostolic See is to be anathematized, in the presence of our legates . . . that the words of our Lord, Jesus Christ, may be fulfilled, 'The gates of hell shall not prevail against it' [the Apostolic See] and again, 'Thou art Peter' [Peter] whose see, holding the first place, gives light to the whole world, and is the head of all the churches of God." This passage Denzinger quotes, no. 298.

turies before,[14] the seventh General Council held its first session, with something like three hundred bishops in attendance.

The council opened with an address by Tarasios. Then the letter of the empress was read, guaranteeing freedom of speech to all, and ordering that the pope's letter to her should be read. The remainder of the session was taken up with the question of reconciling the handful of iconoclastic bishops who appeared—and a discussion whether they should then be allowed a place in the council. It was made a condition *sine qua non* that each should renounce and anathematize the council of 753.

At the second session (September 26) the pope's letter was read. It began with the statement of the powers divinely given to St. Peter to bind and to loose, and that this power was the inheritance of his successors. Now Peter's successors had never wavered, in this matter of the devotion to images, and with regard to the controversy of the last sixty years, the pope recalled all that had been done since the reign of Gregory II in protest against the innovations, and what the popes had done to defend this pious practice from the charge of idolatry. Adrian cited such well-known Biblical facts as the figures of the cherubim in the Holy of Holies, and the brazen serpent. He quoted the long line of authority for the practices as it is found in the Greek Fathers of the Church. And then he passed on to matters of a different kind, where the late emperors had grievously wronged the Roman See, matters where he demanded that injustices should be righted. This part of the pope's letter was not read out to the council. Were the legates aware of the omission? It is hardly likely. The matter of complaint was Leo III's confiscation of the papal properties in Sicily, and, what mattered still more, his adding to the jurisdiction of the see of Constantinople the sees of Calabria[15] and Sicily. Adrian also reproved the elevation of a layman—Tarasios—to the patriarchal see.

When the letter was read the legates rose and demanded that

[14] The space of years between the two councils of Nicaea is roughly what separates us from the discovery of America by Columbus, or the death of Savonarola. The second council of Nicaea took place just a thousand years before the fall of the Bastille. These are staggering distances of time, in the record of an institution still as active as it was in 787 and 325, with Pope John XXIII, at this moment, preparing exactly as Pope Adrian I was preparing in 785.

[15] Southern Italy.

the patriarch declare his acceptance of the doctrine as there stated. Tarasios did this, and the legates next asked that each bishop should rise and personally make the same declaration. This also was done, and the monks present also professed this as their faith.

It was after this act of submissive faith that the council, in its fourth and fifth sessions (October 1 and 4), went into the theological case for the practice of venerating images and praying to the saints. For two days long extracts were read from Scripture and the Fathers and explained and commented by various speakers, and stories were told of marvellous happenings in one diocese after another that proved the duty of honouring the saints through their images. The writers who had taught otherwise were condemned, among them such leading Monophysites of bygone years as Severus of Antioch and Philoxene of Mabboug. The fifth session closed with the solemn enthronement of an image, in the church where the council was held; this at the proposition of the legates.

Two days later, at the sixth session, the prescribed condemnation of the council of 753 took place. The decree of that assembly was read out, and after each clause there was read a lengthy refutation of what it stated, a reprobation worded, as to the bishops of 753, in language too coarse to reproduce. It is more interesting that one reason given for denying that council's claim to be oecumenical was that the pope was not represented at it; and it was boldly stated that it was just not possible that the Church of Christ should ever fall away into idolatry.

At the seventh session the final dogmatic profession of the council was drawn up. It followed the now traditional fashion of a declaration of faith, beginning with the creed of Nicaea and anathematizing all past heretics—Pope Honorius among them, but not (curiously) the Three Chapters. Coming to the crucial point, "We define," the decree states, "that, as with the priceless, life-giving cross,[16] so with the venerable and holy images, they may be set up in their various forms in the churches, on the sacred vessels and vestments, on the walls; likewise in private houses, and along the wayside. . . . The more often we look upon them, the more vividly are our minds turned to the memory of those whom they represent . . . to give to them, the images, an *adoration of honour*, but not,

[16] From all the teaching and proscriptions of the Iconoclasts images of the cross and its relics had been carefully excepted.

however, the true *latria*, which, as our faith teaches, is to be given only to the divine nature . . . so that, like the holy cross, the gospels, and the relics of the saints, to these images offerings of incense and lights may be made, as was the pious custom of our ancestors. For the honour rendered to the image passes to that which the image represents, and whoever adores[17] an image adores the person it depicts. For in this way, is the teaching of the holy Fathers strengthened, that is to say, the tradition of the holy catholic church, receiving the gospel, from one end of the world to the other. . . . Those, therefore, who dare to think or to teach otherwise, or, as the wicked heretics do, to spurn these traditions of the church . . . if they are priests or bishops, let them be deposed; if monks or laymen, let them be excommunicated."[18] And the decree ends with words of praise for the two bishops who had been leading opponents of the heresy, Germanos of Constantinople and George of Cyprus, and for the great theologian whose writings had been the heart of the resistance, John Mansour, John of Damascus, our St. John Damascene.

With regard to the words here italicised in the decree, it may be noted that *Honorariam adorationem* is the Latin translation given of the original Greek *timētikēn proskýnēsin*, where the second word, a noun, means literally "a paying obeisance to," "a prostrating oneself before"—a gesture of great respect, obviously; the degree, or kind, of respect intended being something in the mind of the doer, primarily; and the significance, as it is done, a thing known only to himself. A Christian in front of an image, and an idolater in front of an idol, each gives the same salute—with a wholly different meaning in each case. The newly appointed Anglican bishop (in England), clad in his robes, kneels before Queen Elizabeth II, his hands joined—he is not adoring her, nor praying to her, but taking an oath of allegiance. It is folly to judge by appearance what we have never experienced personally, or have studied in the declarations of those who have had the experience. Which said, we may be allowed to regret that, from so early a time, the one Latin word *adoratio* was used officially to mean acts wholly

[17] *Adorat* in the Latin translation, *proskynêi* in the Greek original. For this difference see the explanation about to follow.
[18] From the text printed (with Latin translation) in Denzinger, nos. 302, 303, 304.

different in kind. It is only in our own time that it has ceased to be used for the veneration of the Cross in the liturgy of Good Friday.

As to *latria:* the Latin does not here translate, but takes over bodily the actual Greek word, whose original meaning "hired service, servitude," came to be restricted to the special meaning "the service of the gods," and so to "worship," the act by which we publicly recognise that God is the creator and sovereign lord of all that is—the uniqueness of His being, and of the dependence of all upon Him. As a technical term in theology, *latria* denotes the reverence especial to God, reserved to God—what the English word "worship" nowadays usually means and only means; although, a survival of other ages, the mayor of an English town is still "Your worship"; the bridegroom in the marriage service still says to the bride, "With my body I thee worship"; and in recent English translations of papal documents, the pope's address to the bishops, *Venerabiles fratres* has been rendered "Worshipful brethren." But neither mayors, nor brides, nor bishops are therefore regarded as divine!

In addition to this definition of faith, the council also enacted twenty-two disciplinary canons. They are of a routine character, reminders to the bishops and clergy of existing laws; a reminder to the modern reader that the council marks the beginning of the restoration of order, after sixty years of persecution and a régime of emergencies.[19]

The fathers of this General Council of 787 did not ask the pope to confirm its decrees, nor did the pope ever do so of his own initiative. Indeed, seven years later Adrian took great pains to explain to Charlemagne that he had not done so, and why. Here we are brought up against another of those strange sequels that would suggest that not every one of these twenty councils was, at the time it took place, regarded by all concerned as what we understand as a General Council.

But first of all, the appearance of the great name of Charlemagne suggests the usefulness of recalling to the reader the revolutionary changes in the "political" state of Italy and France which the hundred years had witnessed that separated the council against the

---

[19] The canons are listed fully in Mansi. Schroeder, somewhat routed by their verbosity, offers only a summary in his translation, pp. 144–56.

Iconoclasts from the council against the Monothelites. These changes had a great influence upon the relations of the popes with the emperors at Constantinople in the eighth century (715–95); and they were to influence powerfully these same relations for the hundred years that followed, the century in which the eighth General Council (869–70) took place, the council conventionally regarded as marking the beginning of the breakaway of Constantinople from Rome that still endures.

Briefly, within a matter of months after the death of Justinian (565), the emperor who at such a cost had restored the imperial authority in Italy, there came into that much ravaged land, from the north, the last and least civilised of all its invaders, the Arian Lombards (568). Throughout the century of the Monothelite troubles, of Pope Honorius and St. Martin I, there was constant petty warfare between the various Lombard chiefs and the imperial officials at Naples and Ravenna—this last being the central city of the new Byzantine-governed Italy. Very slowly, but very surely, in the course of 150 years the invaders established themselves, and in that time they gradually gave up their heresy and became Catholics. By the time of Pope Gregory II (715–31), whom we have seen threatened with deposition by the Iconoclast emperor Leo III, the real bulwark of the empire in Italy was no longer the exarch at Ravenna and his little army, but the prestige of the pope as the heir of St. Peter. Time and time again, armed only with this, the popes of the eighth century persuaded the Lombards to retreat from new conquests—this in the time of the persecuting Iconoclasts, Leo III and Constantine V. The day was to come, however, when a Lombard king grew tired of thus "obeying St. Peter as his son" for the benefit of the distant Byzantine czar. And the popes then turned for help to the Catholic barbarians north of the Alps, to the Franks. How their appeals were finally heeded, the pilgrimage of Pope Stephen II to the court of Pepin in the winter of 753–54 (the winter following Constantine V's pseudo-council at the Hieria), how Pepin agreed to expel the Lombards from the territories around Rome and to convey the conquest to St. Peter in sovereignty, and how the pope ratified Pepin's hold on the Frankish crown by anointing him king with the holy oils, Pepin and his two sons, Carloman and the future Charlemagne—this is what every textbook tells at length.

Pepin was a great ruler (741–68) as his father Charles Martel (716–41) had been before him, and as Charlemagne was to be after him (768–814). Pepin not only defeated the Lombards, and mocked the demand of Constantine V that he reinstate Byzantium, but he watched with care over the apprenticeship of the popes as temporal sovereigns. And Charlemagne was no less interested, that they should be firmly established and rule in peace the far from peaceful lay lords who, all but independent each in his own fortress, resented the notion that priests were now their masters; and who, if the chance offered of seizing the supreme place, would make light of sacrilegiously going through the ritual formality of ordination and consecration in order to attain it.

All which is recalled to explain the harsh statement that the first twenty years of the new papal state were a bloody chapter indeed of Italian history. The election of Adrian I in 772, the pope of this seventh General Council that is our subject, brought a beginning of statesmanship. He ruled for all but twenty-four years—the longest-reigned pope hitherto—wisely and firmly and humanely, with the young Charlemagne as his protector and counsellor, and yet without subservience to him: for all that Charlemagne, in a rather attractively naïve way, made it ever evident that if it were his duty to protect the pope, it was the pope's duty to accept that protection, e.g., to hearken to the protector's advice, and carry it out. The two great men, however, managed together marvellously. The findings of the General Council of 787 were the greatest test to which their relations were put.

Charlemagne, by this time, had utterly destroyed the Lombard kingdom. It was he who was now, in title and in fact, King of the Lombards, the ruler of all Italy to the north of the little papal state as well as of the whole of what we call France, and over the Pyrenees to the Ebro, and east as far as the Rhine. The Holy See, not yet realising it, is now facing a pattern of potential dangers from the powerful protector which will be repeated century after century for the next thousand years—which, however, is none of our business just now. But the pope and his protector met in what promised to be a head-on collision *à propos* the decrees of this Second Council of Nicaea.

What we would first like to know, as we study this crisis, is how much information Charlemagne had about the council of 787 at the time it took place. This may seem an odd remark, seeing who Charlemagne was, and what his relations with the pope were, and given the undoubted fact that Charlemagne was in Italy from January to Easter of that year. But the suggestion is that the pope took care not to inform Charlemagne of the new *rapprochement* with Constantinople, and its sequel the council. And that politics were the reason for Adrian's deliberate silence: Byzantium (still in 787 master of Sicily and southern Italy) being the secret sustainer of resistance to the Franks of certain Lombard "pockets" in central Italy. And in the spring of that same year Charlemagne broke off the long-drawn-out negotiation for the marriage of his daughter to Irene's son, Constantine VI.[20]

Such was the situation, ominous for the papal state, in the weeks while the bishops of Asia Minor were journeying to Constantinople and there convening with Adrian's legates, under the aegis of Irene. Charlemagne, in this same autumn, was occupied with the business of destroying a treacherous vassal, the duke of Bavaria. On October 3 the rebel surrendered—the council was now busy examining the dossier of Scriptural authority for the cult of images. In the spring of 788 Charlemagne's diplomacy won the Lombards from their alliance with Constantinople. Irene's countermove was a command to her generals in Italy to destroy the Lombard duchy of Benevento. But the Lombard had now the Franks on his side, and it was Irene's forces that were destroyed, and the Byzantine frontier pushed back to the south.

These few details are set down to show the reality of the Charlemagne versus Constantinople animosity in these years, its importance to the great papal problem of political security as the protection of the independence of religion. The pope, needing the Frank most urgently, was walking on thin ice when, in these years of war, he had to be friendly with the Byzantines. Which is why not too much was said—if anything was said—to Charlemagne about the negotiations that produced the council. This may also raise the question whether the council was, in Adrian's mind, anything more than a council of the bishops of the Byzantine empire which, under his direction, was re-establishing Catholic belief and practice after sixty years of disorder.

[20] Or Byzantium broke them off; crisis and unpleasantness in either case, whichever story is the truth.

Charlemagne's first news about what had been happening elsewhere while he dealt with Bavaria was the arrival of a Latin translation of the *acta* of the council of 787. The date of his receipt of this we do not know[21]—most likely it was around 791. This translation—an incredibly bad one, by all accounts, and to judge from what has survived—perished long ago. When the scholars in Charlemagne's council came to examine it they were seriously disturbed, and by the king's command they prepared a lengthy systematic refutation of the council's decrees—the so-called *Caroline Books*.[22] The essence of what so moved the Frankish world was a statement that images are to be given the very same veneration that we give to the Trinity itself—the arch-mistranslation of the whole masterpiece of illiteracy. Now what historians have, for centuries, called the *Caroline Books*, was, in form and fact, an official state paper, a law of the King of the Franks. In this Charlemagne reviews the history of the two councils, of 753 and 787, and he condemns both, criticising in detail, and with biting sarcasm, the evidence for the lawfulness of image-veneration officially set forth by the council of 787, a council convoked and animated by a woman, over which a woman had presided. And such a body as this is to impose its erroneous ideas on all the churches of the world, the bulk of whom have never even heard there has been such a council? Are these Greeks orthodox, even on the fundamental doctrine of the Trinity? Do they not believe that the Son proceeds from the Father alone? No wonder they blunder about the right and duty to venerate images. And so the long indictment rolls on.

But there is in it not a word of criticism for the pope. The document is written as though he had had no share in the council at all, and it contains the remonstrance that "Whenever a dispute arises about matters of belief, we must consult the holy, roman, catholic and apostolic church, which is set in authority over the other churches"[23]; understand, perhaps, "and not a synod of Greek

[21] Historians have had to tax their brains to set these events in a chronological order that is also logical. For a comparison of results cf. Amann, *L'Époque Carolingienne*, 1947 (F. and M., vol. 6), 127, n. 2. It is Amann's "solution" that I am following.

[22] The piece takes up some 120 pages of the *Patrology* of Migne (*P.L.*, vol. 98, cols. 991–1248).

[23] *Quod sancta romana catholica et apostolica ecclesia caeteris ecclesiis praelata, pro causis fidei cum quaestio surgit omnino sit consulenda.* Book I, Chap. 6; quoted Amann, 123, n. 2.

bishops." For the note that sounds through all this polemic "is not so much one of hostility to the doctrine set out at Nicaea, as to the fact of these Greeks sitting in council and giving forth as though they were the infallible rulers of Christendom."[24] The trouble is that there is now a second empire in Christendom, although its chief as yet only calls himself king—and this chief is a genius, and as passionately interested in culture and religion as in politics and war; and this new western potentate will not tolerate that questions of doctrine shall be decided for the whole church by a council of those churches where his Byzantine rival is lord. That the force behind the *Caroline Books* and the law called the Capitulary *About Images*, and behind the action, regarding the council of 787, of the council about to meet in 794 at Frankfurt, is a political force is what no man can easily deny.[25]

The great council which met at Frankfurt in the summer of 794 was not called merely in order to deal with the situation just summarily described, but with a serious heresy about the Trinity that had arisen in Spain. There had been appeals about this matter to the pope, an intervention from Rome, and a refusal to accept this; then a council at Ratisbon, and the trial of a leading Spanish bishop for heresy. It was to a council whose task was to settle this Spanish affair that Adrian agreed to send legates, and a dogmatic letter stating the true belief on the point at issue.[26] It was an imposing assembly, three hundred Latin bishops from every part of the West, the equal, in this material sense, of any of the General Councils, save the exceptionally large gathering at Chalcedon three hundred years before.[27] All that concerns our present subject is that the criticism of the council of 787, as made in the *Caroline Books*, was

[24] Amann, as quoted, p. 123.

[25] So Amann, 123, "*On n'en saurait disconvenir.*" It also needs to be said, with Tixeront, III, 474 (459), that "in Gaul, not only was it denied that images should be given adoration, in the proper sense of the word [the adoration with which we adore God as an act recognising He is God] but denied also that images could be given a relative honour [i.e., that the image could be honoured for the sake of the being it represented, an honour related to the living original]. This was an error in no way fostered by mistakes in the Latin translation sent by the pope."

[26] Once again, the reader must be warned, there are problems about dates and the true sequence of events.

[27] The official record of the proceedings—the *acta*—has not been preserved. We know nothing at all of the debates. Only the decrees of the council have survived.

now put before the three hundred bishops at Frankfurt, and that they thereupon condemned the idea that images were the lawful object of adoration *properly so-called*, and that they condemned the council of 787 for encouraging this heretical notion. The evidence, for this last serious charge, upon which the Latin bishops acted is explicitly stated—it is the mistranslated extract from a speech made at the council by one of the Greek bishops.[28] It is worth noting, first, that to these Latins the council they are rebuking is merely "the recent Greek synod at Constantinople," and next, that none of the wild language of the *Caroline Books* and nothing of the erroneous teaching just noted[29] appear in the proceedings of the council.

To strengthen the impression which the council of 794 might make upon Adrian, Charlemagne now sent to him the famous Capitulary *About Images*, eighty-five extracts from the *Caroline Books*. The pope examined the indictment, and patiently refuted the eighty-five, point by point, patiently and with studied moderation, correcting the vast series of misunderstandings and ignoring the impudence and malice.[30] As to the alleged difference in belief between the two councils, of 787 and 794, the pope says very simply, "With regard to images, the belief of St. Gregory [the Great][31] and our belief are the same; and so the Greek bishops themselves, in this very synod, accepted the definition, [namely] to reverence images with salutations of honour, but by no means to give to them that true worship which, according to our faith, we give to the divine nature alone. . . . And therefore it is that we have accepted this said synod."[32] This, so far as the pope was concerned, was the last word. A few months later he died, December 25, 795.

[28] See before, p. 161.

[29] See before, ibid.

[30] "Answers as subtle as the objections are futile," Tixeront, III, 477 (461). The text of the Capitulary has perished, Adrian's answer, in 50 columns of close print, is in Migne, *P.L.*, vol. 98, cc. 1247–92, a text "crawling with mistakes," says Tixeront.

[31] The reference is to a letter from this pope to Secundinus, saying what is and what is not lawful in the veneration given to images—a classic text in these controversies, and one now cited against the second council of Nicaea's misunderstood teaching.

[32] Mansi, XIII, 808; *P.L.*, vol. 98, c. 1291.

8. *The Fourth General Council of Constantinople, 869–70*

The empress Irene came to a bad end. She could not bring herself to step aside as her son came to man's estate. She so lusted for power that she organised a plot against him—he was now approaching thirty—overthrew him, and had him blinded in the very room where she had given birth to him.[1] For four years Irene ruled supreme, then she also was overthrown, banished, and died miserably. Charlemagne, meanwhile, had become an emperor, created such (if this is the right term) by Pope Adrian's successor, Leo III, on Christmas Day, 800—one of the dates that every schoolboy is expected to know. He was then fifty-eight, and he lasted another fourteen years. Then came the first weak ruler the family had produced, his son Louis, called the Pious; and an affectionate partitioning of power with *his* sons, and presently chronic civil war, and the destruction of Charlemagne's achievement.

The Byzantines were not so unlucky as this, but generals fought one another for the supreme place, and one emperor was dethroned and another murdered before stability was attained.

With the accession of Leo the Armenian in 813, the Iconoclastic trouble revived, for the new ruler was himself a passionate Iconoclast, and in a great campaign of more or less learned propaganda he strove to put the clock back sixty years and restore the régime of the council of 753. In the debates which the emperor arranged in order to give some prestige to his jejune ideals, the Catholics were easily victorious, and one of them, Theodore, abbot of the Stoudion monastery, carried the argument well beyond all hairsplitting about the meaning of Old Testament quotations, by asserting that these religious questions lay wholly outside the em-

[1] Finlay, 79.

peror's sphere of authority. The patriarch of Constantinople was forced out, for standing by the tradition, and in his place a married layman was installed—an unheard-of novelty. He faithfully carried out the emperor's orders, and called a council of bishops to sanctify the revolution. Here there were bloody scenes, when the Iconoclasts battered their Catholic opponents into insensibility. From the church the victims were taken off to the emperor's prisons or banished, and it was announced that the council had quashed the decrees of the General Council of 787.

In the persecution that now began, there appeared this novelty of a Catholic leader, Theodore, who strove to unite the Catholics around the twin ideas that the state has no rights in questions of belief, and that the survival of the true tradition of Christian belief lies in the union of Catholics with the Apostolic See of Rome. Never before had these truths been stated so explicitly by a cleric subject to the Byzantine power. Theodore now became the chief target of the emperor's fury, but everywhere bishops, priests, monks were arrested, tortured, banished. As so often happens in persecutions that are systematic and ruthless, thousands gave way—a shocking fact, of course, to the pious whose safety has never been threatened, and who see themselves as instinctively resisting tyrants to the bitter last. Then in 820 the Iconoclast emperor, Leo V, was murdered, and the general who (to save his own life) had organised the deed, took his place; this was Michael II (820–29).

There did not now follow a general reversal of religious policy, but the active persecution was halted. The new ruler hoped for a compromise that would satisfy both the Iconoclasts and their victims. And he strove to enlist, as his ally in the task of winning over the pope to these views, the man whom he now acknowledged as "Emperor of the Franks and the Lombards," Louis the Pious. The imagination easily takes fire as to what might have been the history of the papacy in the next two centuries, striving to maintain its authority in a world where there were now two such blocs of imperial authority—had they both endured—and where the Mediterranean sea was a Saracen lake.

Michael II died in 829, his problem unsolved, and the empire heaving uneasily with religious conflict. He was succeeded by his son Theophilus, a conscientious Iconoclast, under whom, for the best part of twelve years, the business of arrests, imprisonments, floggings and exiles took up once again. All to no real purpose—the mass of his subjects remained at heart faithful to the tradition. Among these were the emperor's wife and all the womenfolk among his kinsmen.

When Theophilus died, prematurely in 842, leaving a child of three to succeed him, the great men of state—realising that Iconoclasm was a chronic irritant that no empire endlessly troubled by hostile neighbours could, during a long regency, endure—made common cause with the empress-mother. Together they got rid of the main obstacle to internal peace, the Iconoclast patriarch, John the Grammarian; a council saw to all the formalities of a restoration of the General Council of 787; and in a great new liturgical feast—the Feast of Orthodoxy[2]—March 11, 843, the restoration of the cult of the images and of the saints was solemnly inaugurated. Never again did Iconoclasm lift its head.

The imperial church was now just a quarter of a century away from the eighth General Council, and in those twenty-five or six years no new heresy disturbed its peace. Crisis, when it came, would be largely a matter of personal rivalries, conflicting jurisdictions, and resentment at subordination; no longer a matter of self-willed imperial theologians, but of "turbulent priests"—and tactless handling of the situation generally, to say nothing of misunderstandings that were inevitable in an age when means of communication had all but disappeared, and Rome might wait twelve months before it received replies from Constantinople.[3]

The eighth General Council, Constantinople 869–70, was about the consequences of the expulsion of an intruded patriarch, Photius, and the restoration of the rightful patriarch, his predecessor, Ignatius. The situation, as the legates left the papal chancellery in the summer of 869, was complicated by the fact that the intruder had been in undisturbed possession for nine years; that, in a council called by him, in 867, he had excommunicated the pope, anathematized him and declared him deposed from his see; that he had had on his hands a serious quarrel with Rome of another sort alto-

---

[2] Still one of great annual feast days in the church presided over by the patriarch of Constantinople, and its daughter churches.

[3] Cf. Amann, 475, n. 4, on "la lenteur des communications entre Rome et Constantinople. Cette lenteur explique bien des choses."

gether, about missionary activities among the Bulgarians; and, final complication, that the rightful patriarch, Ignatius, agreed with the usurper Photius about this last matter.

Ignatius, a man of seventy at the time of the council, was the youngest son of the emperor Michael I, dethroned in 813 by Leo the Armenian. He was then forced into a monastery, professed, ordained and as an abbot was a champion of the faith in the days of the Iconoclastic reaction. In 847 he became patriarch of Constantinople. It is regrettable to say it, but he was something of an episcopal czar, and he presently fell foul of the Roman See through his highhanded deposition of the Archbishop of Syracuse, for Rome refused to confirm this until it had heard the archbishop's side of the story. Then, while Ignatius was still making his stand, a palace revolution swept him away. The child successor of Theophilus the Iconoclast was now a young man of 19, Michael III (soon to be known as Michael the Drunkard), and he had just succeeded in getting rid of the chief counsellor of his regency days, by murder, and of promoting in his place his own uncle, Bardas, a capable man but of foul morals, whom Ignatius had to forbid to receive Holy Communion until he amended his notorious life. It was this offence, and a refusal to force the empress-mother and her daughters into a convent, that was punished when, in November 858, Ignatius was summarily arrested and deported, and the announcement was made that he had returned to the monastic life.

Photius, who was now promoted to be patriarch, has a high place in the history of culture as a miraculously learned man, a scholar, one of the great bibliophiles, through whose works a great deal of the bygone classical antiquity has been preserved. He was, at this time, in his forties (perhaps), and in the service of the emperors he had climbed very high, as administrator and diplomatist. Between this accomplished statesman, whose life was a model of decorum, and the joint rulers of the empire there was nothing in common, of course, but Bardas (among other feats) had personally re-created the University of Constantinople, and could really appreciate the rare quality of the man he now set on the patriarch's throne.

Was he really the lawful patriarch? It is not certain that he was not. Ignatius resigned, but did he do so freely? These are questions still discussed, but the general verdict is that Ignatius executed an abdication that was valid, and it was not until this was done that Photius was consecrated—by that Archbishop of Syracuse whom Ignatius had endeavoured to depose.

Whatever the sentiments of Ignatius, his friends in the episcopate organised against Photius, declaring his election null and void, and drawing upon themselves the inevitable reprisals. At a council in 859 Ignatius was declared deposed, and others also; bishop after bishop was soon toppling from his see. The great monasteries were divided.

Photius notified Rome of his election and consecration, in the customary manner, not hiding, of course, the fact that his predecessor's reign had been ended by an act of state. The letter found at Rome a newly elected pope, Nicholas I—who was soon to show himself, in event after event, one of the greatest popes of all. He was the last man ever to take such a story as the whole truth of the matter, without asking many pertinent questions. And so, inevitably, between these two first-class intelligences, there was conflict. Nicholas would not send the expected, due recognition until he had a report from Constantinople made by his own men. He sent two Italian bishops to find out the facts. The legation made the long journey, delivered the apostolic letters, to Photius and to the emperor, and then forgetting they had been sent as mere observers, joined with Photius at a second council before which Ignatius was brought to be judged (and deposed) once again—by (as it now seemed) the papal authority also. This was in April 861. The prisoner put his finger on the weak place in this parade. "I cannot be judged by you," he said to the legates, "for you are not sent here in order to judge me." And when the legates returned with their story of these events the pope broke them, and at a council of his own he quashed the proceedings of April 861. This was just one year later, and the pope dismissed Photius' plea that in the East the rule forbidding laymen to be elected to sees was a dead letter, by reminding him that what the pope decides, in the exercise of the primacy he has inherited from St. Peter, is final; even in matters of discipline there is no appeal possible from it. And then, some months later, there came in at last to Rome the appeal of Ignatius against his deposition—the whole story of events, from the disciplinary admonition about Holy Communion made to Bardas.

The sequel to this was yet another council at Rome, April 863, in possession, at last, of the whole tale. There was a general deposition of Photius and his friends, Gregory of Syracuse, the legates he had seduced from their duty, all those he had ordained or consecrated. Ignatius was proclaimed the lawful patriarch, and Photius ordered to surrender his see to him. All those bishops deprived and exiled in 859 for their loyalty to Ignatius were likewise restored. No more spectacular sentence had ever been laid upon the life of the splendid capital from this backwoods village in Italy that somehow managed to survive amid the ruins of the great days of long ago. And the pope turned from the problems of Byzantium to the conflict with the Carolingian king, Lothair II, who had taken to himself a second wife while the first was still living, "divorced," on his behalf, by complacent local bishops.

Upon this mighty sentence of Nicholas I there fell a long silence. Our next date, indeed, that of the Roman letter that answers Michael III's reply, is two and a half years later, September 28, 865. The emperor's reply is described in this as "a mass of blasphemies." What else it contained we do not know, for it has not been preserved. But something there was that brought about a change in the pope's line of action, for he now, as it were, reopened what he had settled, and again invited Photius (turned back into a layman in 863) and Ignatius to appear in Rome, personally or by proxy, to put their case. It was a deliberate gesture of conciliation: "We have moderated our sentence," the pope wrote, "and we have promised peace, and to restore him to communion with the church."

And now follows another long silence, not a word that has come down to us from Constantinople, or from Rome, for more than a year. It is broken—i.e., for us—by the fierce blast of Pope Nicholas' letters of November 13, 866. Evidently he has received no reply to his previous letter. The emperor is again severely castigated for the letter "full of blasphemies," and told that unless he makes amends by burning it publicly, the pope will do so "in the presence of all the bishops of the west." Did the emperor, and the patriarch, ever receive these last letters? We know nothing, except that the legates who brought them were stopped at the Byzantine frontier, whence they made their way to another band of legates sent by Nicholas to the court of the Bulgarian king, Boris. And with the mention of this personage we touch the hidden conflict between Rome and

Constantinople which burned more fiercely than all the disputes about Photius and Ignatius.

This race of warlike barbarians had been, for a hundred and fifty years now, the great standing menace of the empire on its European side, as the Saracens were by sea and in Asia. The Bulgarians had long ago possessed themselves of the territory still called by their name—the ancient Roman province of Thrace—and they commanded what is now the southern part of Yugoslavia, well nigh to the Adriatic. At some undetermined date during these controversies of which Photius was the centre, Michael III had offered to make peace with the Bulgarians, on condition that their king, Boris, become a Christian. He agreed, and was baptised, the emperor standing godfather, and giving him his own name, Michael. Whereupon, from Constantinople, a flood of missionaries set out to convert the Bulgarians. How, it may be asked, could all this have offended the pope?

Very simply—too simply, perhaps—it may be stated that much of this territory had, in times gone by, been under the *direct* control of the popes, i.e., its bishops supervised as those in Italy, let us say, and not as in Syria or in Asia Minor. When the emperors, at various times, drew the line that marked where the western and eastern empires divided, they cut across territories directly controlled in spirituals by Rome. Thessalonica, for example, which had stood to Rome as Ravenna or Milan, was now a city that belonged to the empire whose capital was Constantinople. Would it not be logical that it one day passed to the direct spiritual control also of Constantinople? All through the fifth and sixth centuries this question sputtered continually between the two great ecclesiastical points—the question of eastern Illyricum, to speak technically. Then, as has been told, the Iconoclast emperor, Leo III, had formally annexed all these lands to the domain of the patriarch of Constantinople, as well as Sicily and Calabria. To the popes—whose rights never die, especially when they are seen in relation to the maintenance of their vital, divinely given primacy—the appearance of Byzantine missionaries in their own ancient Illyricum, was an affront, and much more than an affront. And while Nicholas I observed what was going on, there was suddenly a break between Boris and his new spiritual guide, Photius. And Boris turned to Rome. How tempting here, to wander away in the reverie that the Balkans never change, to speak of attraction to St. Petersburg or Vienna, to Moscow or London!

What Boris really wanted was a church under his own control —his own patriarch. Photius, of course, could not oblige him here, and he seems to have said his "No" without any of those pleasant accommodating offers that sometimes soften such inevitable refusals. Rome, also, could only say "No," but it offered him an archbishop. Rome too, Boris *may* have thought, was farther away than Byzantium—a good year or more away, once embarrassing questions developed.

More important than this kind of speculation is the fact that the neo-Catholic king now was made aware that, in the Catholic Church, there are indeed many mansions; and that life in the Latin mansions differed considerably from life with the Byzantines. And the new Latin missionaries, now despatched by Nicholas I under one of his leading men—the cardinals of later centuries—namely Formosus, bishop of Porto,[4] were only too happy to point out where the superiority lay. Boris, thereupon, sent back the Greek missionaries to their chief, the patriarch Photius. As to the time when all this happened, Formosus and his band had formed part of the same cavalcade as the legates who took to Constantinople the strong threats of November 866 and, when stopped at the frontier, as has been told, it had been to Formosus at the court of Boris, that these legates betook themselves.

Need it be asked how the happenings in Bulgaria might seem— or be said to seem—to Photius and his emperor? The patriarch certainly rose to the occasion. In an encyclical letter to the bishops of the East, he set out all the points where Latin ways differed, and condemned them all roundly; and in one point he denounced the Latins for heresy—they believed that the Holy Ghost proceeded from the Father *and the Son*, and they had corrupted the ancient creed by adding these last words to it.[5] Therefore a council would shortly be held at Constantinople to discuss these matters, to publish the joint condemnation of the churches of Constantinople, Alexandria, Antioch, and Jerusalem. This sentence would have its

---

[4] This is the Formosus who will, thirty years later, be pope, and the subject (after death) of the most revolting action of all these barbarous centuries, fished out of his tomb, robed and enthroned while a council sat in judgment on him.

[5] In Latin, *Filioque.*

effect in the West also, for said Photius, people were getting tired of the tyranny "of him who now, at Rome, is in power."[5a]

The promised council met in the summer of 867, with a great attendance of bishops, and it assented to Photius' sentence of deposition and excommunication against the pope. Also it called on the emperor in the West to carry out the sentence and expel the pope from Rome. This is the high-water mark of the centuries-old restiveness of New Rome. But, whatever the impudence, or even malice, it is not a denunciation or denial of the Roman claim to be, by divine appointment, the head of all the churches.

Nicholas I never knew to what lengths Photius had gone. The pope had been ailing throughout the summer of 867, and on November 13 he died—long before the news about the sentence came to Rome.

And somewhere about the time the pope died, Photius had ceased to be patriarch. For a good two years now the young emperor had been fostering a mightier personality than himself, Basil, called the Macedonian. In April 866 this man had brought about the murder of the all powerful Bardas—the creator of Photius. Now, on September 24, 867, he had Michael III murdered too, and took his place. In the general sweep-out of the old régime, Photius went with the rest, November 867. And since Ignatius was still available, and willing, he now reappeared on the patriarch's throne in St. Sophia. The new emperor wrote to inform the pope of these changes, and in this letter (December 11, 867 or 868) is the suggestion which developed into the General Council of 869–70.

As so often before, to solve the problems by a council was the emperor's idea, in the first place, and his solutions were not what was in the mind of the pope. Basil I, the successful murderer of his predecessor, meant to unite all parties, to do away with all possible reasons for "lawful" discontent, and in the ecclesiastical sphere to unite the rival parties of Ignatians and Photians. Hence, to say nothing at all about the council which, on the very eve of the fall of Photius, had presumed to depose a pope. If in the new council these "old issues" could be passed over, and in the blessed presence of the Roman legates the factions be reconciled, how happy it would be for all.

[5a] Barry, no. 59A, prints a translation of Photius' letter.

But although the new pope, Adrian II, was not in stature a second Nicholas, he was none the less a pope. And, preparatory to the council proposed by the emperor, he did as Adrian I had done in 787 and Agatho in 680. He called his own council in Rome, June 10, 869, and the sole subject of the debates was precisely the Byzantine council of 867 that had anathematized his predecessor. The *acta* of this council were produced and ordered to be burned. The proceedings of the earlier Photius councils of 861 and 859 were likewise condemned. Photius himself was cast out of the church once more, with the special proviso that even should he repent he was never more to be anything but a lay member. The bishops who, at his impious council, had assisted in the excommunication of Pope Nicholas were to be forgiven upon repentance, but those consecrated by Photius were never again to perform any of the sacred rites. Finally the legates were appointed to represent Adrian II at the coming restoration council, and given their instructions, and letters of credence.

The question of Photius *v.* Ignatius had been solved, it will be seen, without any reference to their mutual rights and wrongs. The unprecedented outrage to the papacy had overshadowed all else. The legates' task was simple. The council was not to reopen past questions, but simply to confirm the decisions expressed by the pope in this council of June 869. In this coming council at Constantinople no bishop consecrated by Photius was to have a seat. Those consecrated previous to his usurpation in 858 were to be allowed a place, provided they signed the retractation brought by the legates—it was the formula drawn up by Pope Hormisdas three hundred and fifty years before,[6] for the reconciliation of the bishops after the schism of the patriarch Acacius. These were Adrian's express orders to Ignatius.

It is evidence how general had been the support of Photius that it was scarcely possible, on the arrival of the legates, to collect enough bishops to make up a council—bishops qualified, according to the orders of the pope, to sit in the council. Nor did the situation greatly improve in the six months the council lasted. At the first session, October 5, 869, there were present, besides the legates and Ignatius, no more than eighteen bishops. This and the next

[6] See p. 100 supra. Amann, 485, n. 3, notes that in all this the Roman Curia followed very carefully the precedent of 519.

three sessions were spent in examining whether bishops who came were excluded altogether, because ordained by Photius or, if reconcilable, were willing to sign the formula of Hormisdas. By the eighth session (November 8) the numbers had crept up to 38, by the ninth (February 12, 870) to 65. At the final session (February 28) 102 were present, 37 of them metropolitans, i.e., archbishops, to whom other bishops were subject. There were ten sessions in all, and between the eighth and ninth a mysterious interval of three months.

The main event of the council was the trial, so to miscall it, of Photius and his associates for the crime of 867—the council, in the mind of the pope, had been called for nothing else. It occupied the fifth, sixth, and seventh sessions (October 5 to November 7). Despite the high officers of state whom, in accordance with the practice since 431, the emperor had sent to keep order in the council, the legates of the pope had their way: this was not to be a trial, but an acceptance of the decisions already reached at Rome. There was to be no debate on the rights and wrongs of Photius, or on the value of the arguments he had used to persuade the bishops to join him in his excommunication of the pope. Whatever Photius might have said, in other circumstances, as things were he made no attempt to defend himself or to explain. Still less was there, from him, a single sign of regret or repentance. He appeared on October 5, to hear the charges made against him, and on November 8 to be sentenced. And he said never a word. Others of his party tried a defence that greatly interested the emperor. Popes, they said, were not above the canon law, and history showed that some of their decisions had later been revoked. But the legates objected to these dissertations. What the bishop who spoke was summoned for, they said, was to say whether or not he would sign the formula—repudiate, that is to say, his schismatical conduct—and acknowledge he had done wrong. The legates held firm, and they had their way. And just a week after the condemnation of Photius, there was a solemn bonfire—as the pope had ordered—of all his antipapal writings and of the proceedings of his council of 867.

The real business of the eighth General Council was now over. All that remained was to put its achievement into shape for the record—to formulate it in twenty-seven canons.

There are two versions of these canons, the Greek and the Latin, of which the Latin set contains thirteen canons not included in the Greek. Ten of these thirteen deal with duties of metropolitans and bishops; their right to dispose of church property by sale or lease, for example; that metropolitans must not burden their suffragans with taxes, nor, giving themselves to public affairs, leave to their suffragans their spiritual tasks. Three canons deal with the choice of bishops. First, promotions in the see of Constantinople are to go to those already eminent by their long service to it, and not to outsiders, to men brought in after a great career as laymen. There is no mention of Photius in the canons, nor any need to mention him. Bishops appointed through intrigues, or imposed by arbitrary action of princes, are to be deposed, as men who have willed to receive the gift of God through human acts. No prince or lay authority is to have any part in the election of bishops, metropolitans, or patriarchs. The choice of these is the exclusive business of the college of bishops, who may, however, invite the ruler to assist in the choice of a suitable successor to the late occupant. Rulers who thrust themselves in uninvited fall under the anathema of the council.

There is a canon restating the right of appeal from the judgment of lower courts to higher, and another to the effect that it is sacrilege for any authority to take away property once given to the church and in its possession for thirty years. A lengthy canon speaks of the sacrilegious debauches of the late emperor, Michael III. Michael is not indeed named, but the phrases, "Certain laymen of senatorial rank, in the time of him who lately reigned," and "If any emperor," in the clause about punishment for future offenders of this sort leave no doubt who the chief culprit was. If, in the future, a patriarch of Constantinople does not suitably correct such offenders he is to be deposed.

Finally, there are two canons where Photius is named. The first recounts how, in the days before he was patriarch, presumably when he was the extremely successful university professor, Photius had gathered written promises of fidelity from these disciples, then learning from him the wisdom which in God's sight is folly. The council declares that these pledges are null, that they are to be collected and burned, that those who hold any such are to surrender them. The second canon declares that all those ordained or consecrated by Photius' two predecessors, Ignatius (847–58) and Methodius (843–47), and who have taken Photius' part, and who have not joined with "this holy and universal council," are deposed, and suspended from all their priestly functions, "as, not long before, the most blessed pope Nicholas[7] decided." Nor are they ever to be restored to the catalogue of clergy even when they repent; no more is to be allowed them than to receive Holy Communion, and this as a most merciful concession on our part, say the bishops. For they do not deserve to be restored to their former state, even though they do penance, even though they plead with tears. They are like the detestable Esau.

Of the fourteen canons common to both texts, one is a general renewal of previous laws, one repeats the teaching about images of the council of 787, and a second dogmatic pronouncement condemns a new heretical theory, viz., that man has two souls. Three canons deal with bishops and their affairs: they are rigorously to observe the law about the intervals between ordination to the various ecclesiastical degrees, i.e., one year to be spent as lector, two as subdeacon, three as deacon, and four as priest. No one is to be made a bishop until at least ten years after his first step in the clerical life. The decree speaks plainly of some who, being of senatorial rank and after a career as laymen, become clerics solely to qualify for appointment as patriarch. "Especially do we forbid," say the bishops, the practice of ordaining without observance of these intervals, in cases where the person to be ordained is being promoted by the authority of the emperor. Plainly enough the circumstances of Photius' election are censured here, and his condemnation on this account by Pope Nicholas is endorsed. Lay princes, says another canon, are to give bishops the honour due to their office, and a third canon regulates the wearing of various episcopal insignia.

Next there is a group of canons that deal with the rights of the patriarchs—the first time this term occurs in the laws made by a general council. They are forbidden to exact from the clergy, or from the bishops subject to them, written pledges of fidelity. This has been the practice of orthodox and legitimate patriarchs of Constantinople, as well as of usurpers. It must now cease: and the canon states a severe penalty for the disobedient—deposition from their dignity. Patriarchs have the right to compel their metropolitans to

---

[7] *Vere*, Adrian II (867–72), whose command to the council this was.

attend the synods which they summon. It is not a valid reason for staying away that the metropolitan has held his own synod, nor that the patriarch's synod cannot be held unless the emperor is present. Temporal princes have no place in any synod, except in the General Councils of the Church. A further confirmation of the patriarch's position is the canon which declares that no one, not even a bishop, is to withdraw his obedience from his patriarch or cease to make public prayer for him (even though he thinks he knows the patriarch is guilty of some serious crime) until the case has been judged by a council and a sentence given against the patriarch.

Finally, with regard to patriarchs, the council enacts that no lay authority is to depose a patriarch, "and especially the most holy pope of the older Rome . . . nor to get up movements against the pope, and to set in circulation writings that suggest he is guilty of serious misconduct, as Photius did recently, and as Dioscoros did long ago. Whoever shall again treat the pope with the impudent arrogance of a Photius or Dioscoros, heaping insults (whether in writing or otherwise) upon the see of Peter, prince of the Apostles, let him receive the same punishment as was given to them." If any lay prince "attempts to drive out the aforesaid Pope of the Apostolic See, or any other patriarch, let him be anathema." And if, in any General Council, there is a dispute about the holy, Roman Church, the matter must be discussed with all the respect and reverence due to it, and some solution found and put forth, "but let none presumptuously give sentence against the supreme pontiffs of the elder Rome."

Photius' name has at last appeared, in this summary. It may end with reference to the three canons directed explicitly against him. First we have a canon which enacts that, for all time, the sentences are to be observed which "the most blessed Pope Nicholas, whom we hold as the instrument of the Holy Spirit, and the most holy Pope Adrian his successor" have in their synods decreed for the preservation of the see of Constantinople, namely, about its "most holy patriarch Ignatius, and about the expulsion and condemnation of the latecomer[8] and usurper Photius." Secondly, it is decreed that

---

[8] Neophyte, is the exact word used, whose literal meaning is "newly enlightened," a common expression in ecclesiastical literature for the newly baptised. The reference here is not to baptism, but holy orders—the rapid translation, at so late a time in life, of the Secretary of State into the Patriarch.

Photius was never a bishop, is not now a bishop, and that none of those whom he ordained or consecrated are what he promoted them to be. The churches which he, or they, consecrated are to be reconsecrated. Finally, since it has appeared that Photius (after his just condemnation by Pope Nicholas for his wicked usurpation of the see of Constantinople, and for other wicked acts), picking up from the streets of the capital certain evil flatterers, whom he put forth as vicars of the three other patriarchs, began an action against Pope Nicholas and declared him to be anathema, the council now anathematizes the said Photius, as the man responsible for all this wickedness, and with him all his helpers and collaborators, according to the synodal law of that most courageous champion of true piety, the most holy Martin, pope of Rome.

The eighth General Council was now over. But the legates' troubles were not at an end. To the final meeting, the ceremonial closing of the great affair, there had been admitted as spectators an embassy from the Bulgarian king, that had just arrived in the capital. Boris had once more changed his mind. When the pope promised him an archbishop of his own, he asked that the legate Formosus should be appointed, and when it was answered that this could not be, for to translate a bishop from one see to another was unlawful, Boris' brief affection for Latin ways ended. The embassy had come to ask the emperor and Ignatius to take over the Bulgarian mission. The last act of the legates was to warn the restored Ignatius, under the most serious penalties, that he must do nothing of the kind, and to hand him a letter from the pope, which, in anticipation of this precise situation, had been sent with them. Ignatius, it is recorded, put the letter aside without opening it, and replied with an evasion. The legates set off on their journey to Rome, and the next news was that Ignatius had consecrated ten bishops for Bulgaria.

That the eighth General Council should leave a critical situation in its wake was nothing new in the history of these institutions, but the sequel, this time, was the strangest of all the series. More strangely still, it is only within the last thirty years—more than a thousand years after the events—that the true story of what happened has been discovered.

The legates of Pope Adrian II had a most adventurous return journey, in which they were shipwrecked, captured by pirates, and lost most of their papers. It was not until the June or July of 871 that they reached Rome. They found the pope already prepared for what they had to report, for the most cosmopolitan figure of the time, Anastasius (called the Librarian), who had been at Constantinople as ambassador for the emperor Louis II, had got to Rome months before, and he had brought with him a full report of the council's proceedings. On November 10, after hearing the legates, the pope wrote to the emperor a letter which was, in a way, an approbation of the work the council had done, but principally it was a list of complaints about the negligent way the legates had been treated, the attitude of Ignatius to the Bulgarians (with threats about this), and an excommunication for the Bulgarian king. As to the emperor's plan to reconcile "Photians" and "Ignatians," the pope declared that, unless an enquiry held at Rome brought out some new evidence, the decisions already arrived at must stand. And there the matter remained for the next four or five years.

Meanwhile (December 14, 872) Adrian II died, and was succeeded by a still more resolute personage, John VIII, whose first care was to renew the demands about Bulgaria, and to remind Ignatius that it was only on his promise to withdraw the Greek missionaries that the pope had restored him to his see. Unless he now made good his promises, he would be deposed. John VIII's mind was very clear about this problem. It was not the matter of prestige that moved him, but the obvious danger that if the new convert nation was so closely related to the Byzantine patriarch, it would be everlastingly in danger of schism and heresy. The pope said this explicitly.

Finally, in April 878, the patience of the pope gave out before the endless delays of Ignatius, and two legates were despatched to Constantinople to give him a final admonition. If within thirty days of this he had not acted, the legates were to excommunicate him, and next to depose him. When the legates arrived, some time in the summer of that same year, they learnt that Ignatius had been dead nearly a year, dead six months already when John VIII was drafting this sentence against him. Such are the hazards of international relations, in the centuries when no letter goes more quickly than a post horse can run, and when, with the winter, all transport ceases on the stormy Adriatic. What, no doubt, astonished the legates even more than the news about Ignatius was that it was to Photius that they were presented. Without the least trouble in the world, as though indeed he had been *coadjutor cum iure successionis*,[9] Photius had immediately taken Ignatius' place—to the almost entire satisfaction of the whole patriarchate.

It seems that, for some years now, Ignatius and he had been on the best of terms, both collaborating wholeheartedly with the policy of the emperor Basil, "No religious faction fighting, at all costs." The legates just did not know what to do, save to report these strange events to their distant master and await what new instructions he chose to send.

In the framing of these papal directions, political considerations played an important part. One of the tasks for which the legates were sent, as well as the Bulgarian trouble, was to put to Basil the pope's urgent plea that he would do something to halt the seemingly impending Mohammedan conquest of Italy. Already the Saracens were masters of Sicily and of various places on the mainland. The wretched remnants of the house of Charlemagne, the potentates whom all mankind mocked as Charles the Fat, and Charles the Bald, "transient embarrassed phantoms" indeed, could do nothing but hasten the steady political and social decomposition. Constantinople, or so the pope thought, was the only hope. When Basil's embassy of the spring of 879 arrived in Rome to negotiate the peaceful recognition of the *fait accompli* of Photius, they were certainly in a strong position.

The outcome was a second council at Constantinople, to which 383 bishops came, with Photius as the central figure—but where he presided, and to which the presence of three papal legates gave the full outward sign of the pope's approval. John VIII had accepted the *fait accompli*, and also the emperor's plea that "bygones be bygones." Photius was to acknowledge his great crime, the excommunication of the pope in 867, and at the new council express his sorrow. And the pope agreed to quash all that the eighth General Council had enacted against Photius. The remnants of anti-Photians, at Constantinople and elsewhere, were now told by

[9] A happy *mot* I steal from the great work of Father Francis Dvorník. See Appendix.

the pope that he was their lawful patriarch, and that they were not to oppose him in the name of the council of 869, for the former things had passed away. All things were, indeed, made new; for, said the pope, the Apostolic See that can impose such sentences can also remove them. And this it had done. And to mark the pope's satisfaction, the legates at the council presented the patriarch with a magnificent set of patriarchal insignia, the gift of John VIII.

Of what happened in the next ten years or so this is not the place to write. This is no more than the story of the eighth General Council, and with a reference to the papal act cancelling the council's principal work, a bare ten years after it had been achieved, the story may end. The reader will notice that it ends as it began—a matter of personalities in conflict, and not ideas, still less doctrines.

9. *The First General Council of the Lateran, 1123*

In the five hundred and fifty or so years between the first of the General Councils and that whose history has just been told, there has never been more than 130 years without a General Council being summoned.[1] But between this eighth of 869–70 and that we are now to consider, there stretches an interval almost twice as long —time enough for some revolution to have called a new world into being, and for this new world to have forgotten that the old had ever been; an interval slightly greater than that which separates Luther from Napoleon, or Elizabeth II from Queen Anne. In that long space, 870–1123, revolution there had been, and the Catholic Church greatly affected thereby. The General Council of 1123 is, in fact, a kind of victory celebration, proclaiming unmistakably that the Church has survived the revolution, has pulled itself clear of the all but fatal dangers inseparable from the long generations of social crisis. It is as part of the history of this age when "the Church was at the mercy of the lay lords,"[2] that the First General Council of the Lateran must be described, or we shall be left wondering what there was, in its achievement of a score of routine legal enactments, to cause its memory to survive where so much else has perished.

First, the political system that historians call the empire of Charlemagne had crashed—it was all but over by 870—leaving Italy, France, and Germany a welter of petty states with the strongest man's will everywhere law. From the north there had then descended upon this Christendom in ruins the fierce pirate pagans of

[1] Second Council of Constantinople, 553—Third Council of Constantinople, 680.

[2] Cf. the title of Monseigneur Amann's classic work, *L'Église au pouvoir des Laiques,* 888–1057 (1945), pp. 544. This is volume 7 of F. and M.

Scandinavia; from the east came the no less aggressive pagan Slavs and Magyars; to the south the Mohammedans were all-powerful and the Mediterranean sea a Saracen lake. The siege lasted through a good hundred years and more, that "century of iron" (888–987) when it really seemed as though the last remnants of civilised ways must be engulfed in these brutal and barbaric tides. A great warrior king emerges in Germany, Otto I (936–72), around whom the resistance begins to make a permanent gain, and the anarchy subsides; and a generation later the same good fortune comes in the West with the appearance of Hugh Capet, king of the French from 987.

In these afflicted generations nothing suffers so horribly as religion—the delicate, barely adolescent Christianity of the still semi-barbarous Carolingian times. Here, too, the will of the local strong man—the chieftain of the local *résistance* in the long fight with invaders, and the most powerful of the local petty kinglets—is law. The church system, above all the appointments to abbeys and sees, these potentates, half-hero, half-scoundrel, take to themselves. Pillage, murder, general brutality of living—the prelates appointed by such princes are too often indistinguishable from the baronage whence they are taken.

And, of all the sees of Christendom, it is Rome that provides the most spectacular of the horrors, where for a hundred years and more the savage barons of the surrounding countryside intermittently make themselves master, and elect, depose, restore, depose again, and murder the popes according to their own political plans. And some of these popes are as wicked as their masters. These are the classic "bad popes" indeed, and even stripped of the customary rhetorical decoration the story of what they did is truly terrible.

But the tide of goodness that had gone so far out that it seemed to have gone forever turned at last. The northmen were gradually converted, and the Magyars and the Slavs. The chaos of petty rulers began to give way to the better ordered rule of a dozen or so greater lords, dukes, and what not, vassals of the new kings of France and Germany—and the German king being, since Otto I, the emperor, the Roman Emperor, either in lawful claim or by the accomplished fact of papal acceptance and coronation, the better day had arrived for Italy too.

It was through German kings who were the Roman Emperor that

the Roman See was delivered from its tyrants; on two occasions very notably, in 963 and again in 1046. But the good German who appointed good bishops and abbots wherever he really was master, and who now, 1046–56,[3] himself appointed a succession of good German popes—this good emperor was for the good popes the beginning of a new problem, and good men, at Rome too, were divided by it: the problem how the Church could profit by the unlooked-for phenomenon of emperors and kings who were good men and yet manage to be independent of them in the control of church life, especially in the vital business of the choice of its rulers, the bishops, and of its supreme ruler the pope.

The solution of that problem took years to work out. It took still longer to win acceptance for it from the Catholic kings. The ninth General Council, with which this chapter is concerned, has been described very truly as "the conclusion and the synthesis of what a whole half century of hard struggle had brought about."[4]

The two most flagrant, universally visible evils that afflicted religious life as these new-style popes began their great task were simony and clerical immorality. The kings and princes were taking money (or lands or property) as the price of appointing a man to be bishop or abbot; the bishop or abbot was taking money, etc., from men who wished to be ordained, and from priests who wanted parishes, canonries, and so forth; the priests, in their turn, were only ministering for a price; such is simony, and church life, by the testimony of every writer, every reformer, every saint of these times, was saturated with the poison, and had been so for generations. Clerical immorality: it had been, from very early times indeed, the rule in the Latin church (though not in the East) that no married man could receive Holy Orders, and that no man in Holy Orders could marry, i.e., no subdeacon, deacon, priest. This ancient rule had suffered heavily in the transformation of social life from a system where cities dominated, with systematic education, easy supervision, and a good tradition of manners, to a rural economy—the life of the backwoods—where "civilisation" went little further than the individual man's ability to fend for himself. With bishops more baron than Father-in-God, and priests as rude as the illiterate serfs

---

[3] The emperor, Henry III.

[4] Fliche, in *La Réforme Grégorienne et la Reconquête Chrétien*, 1057–1123, 1950, i.e., F. and M., vol. 8, 394.

to whom they ministered, such a refinement of ecclesiastical discipline as the mystic celibacy was exposed to altogether unheard-of losses.

From the time when the first "Barbarian" kings became Catholics, the sixth century Franks, semi-Catholics in all but their good intentions, church life suffered an increasing brutalisation. St. Gregory of Tours, who saw it all, has described it in pages that are a classic collection of horror stories. Gradually, through the seventh and eighth centuries, matters improved. The genius of Charlemagne offered, for a brief space, the illusion that the bad times had gone forever. With the breakup of his system, and the new most terrible invasion of all, the devils returned—but sevenfold. One of the devils was the bad-living priest. And here we need to distinguish, as we look at the problem before the reforming pope or bishop. It was the law that the man in Holy Orders must not marry. But if he did so—and if there was no impediment, say of kinship— the marriage was a real marriage. He did wrong in marrying, for marriage was most strictly forbidden him. But he and the woman he married were man and wife. There was also the matter of the priest living with someone to whom he was not married. And who was to say whether the pair living in the church house were of one kind or the other—clerical marriages being, inevitably, clandestine affairs, as often as not without a witness? The scandal to the faithful people was as bad in the one case as in the other—where scandal was given.

That the scandal was less, in these backwoods, than we might at first suppose seems to be suggested from the incredibly violent language which the reformers used with regard to these unfortunates, lurid and horrific to a degree; from the universality of the evil in every country of Christendom; and from the long campaign of a century and more, when so many good men needed to give so much of their lives to the restoration of the Church's normal ideal of clerical continency. That it was precisely this restoration of an ideal that moved them, their very exhortations show; but there was, too, a relation between clerical marriage and the appointments system —another main object of the reformers' zeal—which must be mentioned, that is to say, the tendency for the priest's son to become a priest, forming a clerical caste within the Church; and for the ordained son to take over his father's benefice, church property becoming a family endowment—never, of course, promising such a crop of evil as when the benefice was a see. And there were efforts in these tenth and eleventh centuries to make some of the greatest sees hereditary.

The third of the chronic evils which the reformers fought—lay investiture, as it was called—was not, at first, seen by all of them as a thing evil in itself, or even as the main reason why the other evils had been impossible to reform. "Investiture," the word, signifies pretty much what we who have been to college or who belong to a fraternal order of one kind or another mean by "initiation"—the becoming something one was not before; the acquirement of a new status, with its rights and duties, together with the ritual by which this is acquired, and which symbolises what is acquired. The feudal lord proposes to make over his manor of Beauseigneur—land, buildings, village, mill, serfs, woods, streams, fish, game, hunting—to one Smith, or Le Maréchal. Smith agrees and, kneeling before his benefactor, becomes his "man," i.e., swears to be faithful to him, to be at his side in all disputes, and to render the customary services of a vassal. The lord, in visible sign of the grant, then hands Smith maybe a piece of turf, or a stick. Smith is now possessed of his fief —the manor aforesaid—and has become a lord in his turn, by virtue of the ceremony of investiture. Such pacts, their oaths and their investitures, were going on daily in hundreds of places throughout western Europe, for centuries before the grace of God raised up our ecclesiastical reformers and for centuries after they had passed away. Here was the basis of all social organisation—the sworn relation of lord and vassal.

By the time our reformers were born, this was also, pretty universally, the relation of the ecclesiastical ruler to the temporal prince—to the state, we should like to say, except for the risk of a score of misunderstandings generated by the anachronistic term. New bishops and abbots, before any ceremony took place regarding them in church, knelt before their prince, made their oath, and were then invested—the prince putting on a finger of their right hand the episcopal ring, and into their left hand the episcopal crozier. Smith was now bishop, of Chartres, or of Mainz, or of Winchester. And then he went into his cathedral where his metropolitan, or some other bishop, performed the sacred rite of consecration, the final step in the sacrament called Order. And the original, and permanently influential, reason for this royal investiture was the same reason as of all such—these prelates held, "of the king," vast lordships, and it was vital to the stability of the country that the king be assured of the competence and the loyalty of the prelates to whom they were granted. And it had come to be, by long practice, a matter of course that it was the king who actually chose, with finality, who should be bishop or abbot—and, by long abuse, how much the cleric should pay for the favour. Not all kings were bad men—Henry III, the father of the emperor whom Gregory VII fought so hard, was an excellent man, an appointer of good bishops (and popes); so too was William the Conqueror, held almost in veneration *apud Curiam Romanam* if only for this, that he never in Normandy or in England sold an ecclesiastical appointment, in all his forty years of rule. In lay investiture, however, the stricter school of the reformers discerned the root of all the evils. They decreed its abolition, a root and branch extirpation. The ninth General Council was the confirmation of their victory.

The great reform began at Rome itself, and the primary agent was the emperor Henry III (1039–56). At the Council of Sutri (1046) he despatched all three rival "popes," and appointed one of his own good German bishops, Clement II. This pope soon died, and his successor also, and then in 1049 came the emperor's third nomination, Bruno, bishop of Toul, who took the name Leo IX, and became in his life, his outlook and methods, the pattern for all the good men that were to follow.

The method was simplicity itself, the summoning in place after place of councils of the local bishops, presided over by a trusted ecclesiastic sent from Rome, clad with all the fullness of the pope's powers. At these councils all that was wrong locally was investigated, the bishops were reminded of the kind of men they were supposed to be, indeed obliged to be by God's law, the old regulations about simony and clerical continency were renewed, incorrigible prelates were deposed, and a general revival of religious life inaugurated. And, most prominently, the appeal of the legate was constant to the reality that he spoke with the authority of him who was the successor of Blessed Peter, and must therefore be obeyed unquestioningly. Unpalatable as the reminder must have been to the recalcitrant, unwelcome as the resurrection of this too long ignored fundamental fact of life may have been—and miserable the mere lip service rendered it—nowhere was it challenged. With Leo IX it was the pope himself who thus "went on circuit," through Italy and in France and in Germany. And other popes were no less constantly "on the road" through the seventy years that followed, very notably Alexander II, Urban II, Pascal II, Honorius II, all of whom had been previously active for years in this conciliar movement as papal legates in one country or another.

This is indeed the true age of the councils—the church council in its traditional sense, viz., a gathering of the local bishops to plan a common action in furtherance of religious life; the tradition that went back, through the Eastern churches, so much older in organisation than the West, to the days of Constantine and even before then. That three generations of such constant, and successful, conciliar action should give rise sooner or later to a revival of the idea of a General Council, and then to the practice of summoning these fairly regularly, was very natural. The break of 250 years between the eighth and the ninth of the General Councils is followed by a similar period in which there are no fewer than six General Councils.

To restore the past in black and white—which is what all historical summaries must do—is to risk, at every step, not only serious misrepresentation, but also an unintelligible puzzle for the reader where, continually, the second chapter seems either to be about a different subject from the first, or to be based on the assumption that there never was a first. The story of the investiture controversy is extremely complicated, and the increasing attention given in the last fifty years to the vast polemical literature of the time, to the developing Canon Law treatises, and then to restudy the official documents and the correspondence in the light of the new knowledge, all this has led to a new representation of the story —to say nothing of the effect of the new type of scholar who is only interested in the event for its own sake.

It has always been known that the Concordat of Worms of 1122, in which pope and emperor finally came to an agreement, was a compromise. And those of us whose initiation into these mysteries antedates the arrival on the scene of the re-creating genius of Augustin Fliche, can recall the miserable figure poor Calixtus II was made to cut (for his "signing" the concordat), by the side of such stalwarts as Gregory VII and the Cardinal Humbert. *Nous avons changé tout cela.* The reformers started out united in zeal, devoted, to the very last, to ends that were purely spiritual, men of prayer all the time. But not all were equally clearheaded as to the theology they made use of, or the implication of the sacred party cries. Not all had, in the requisite degree, what is called a political sense, the gift to do the right thing in the right way, to distinguish the essential from the rest, and to avoid stressing equally the essential and nonessential in their thesis. The first pioneers of the ideas that finally triumphed at Worms were not always welcome to the chiefs of staff. The war was on, and against bad men, and it was the cause of Christ against these, and after twenty years of suffering and loss it was no doubt hard to be asked to reconsider any part of one's case!

The war against the princes' control of ecclesiastical appointments began in the principal see of all, at Rome itself. It was the emperor who had put an end to the bad popes, and now the Roman clergy themselves put an end to the emperor's hold on papal elections. When Pope Victor II died, in 1057, their leaders did not wait for any news of what the German overlord proposed, but straightway, within four days, elected a pope, the cardinal who was abbot of Monte Cassino, Frederick of Lorraine, Stephen IX. And when Stephen died, very suddenly, seven months later, the new pope, Nicholas II, again was not the mere nominee of the court. This new pope was hardly installed before he settled, once and for all, the legitimate manner of choosing popes. This was the law enacted in a council at the Lateran in 1059, which restricted the election to the cardinals.[4a] To them alone it belongs, henceforth, to elect the pope, and a majority of their votes is essential and sufficient. The law makes no reference whatever to the emperor's approval or confirmation.

The first pope elected under the new system was Alexander II (1061), the second was Hildebrand, Gregory VII, in 1073. It was he who, two years later, issued the challenge to the whole system of lay investiture, the act that started the long war whose end the General Council of 1123 celebrates. This challenge was the pro-

---

[4a] Barry, no. 45, prints a translation of this decree.

hibition, in the Lateran Synod of 1075, to clergy of all ranks to accept an ecclesiastical appointment from the hands of a layman. If a bishop, for the future, has accepted a bishopric from the prince, the archbishop is not to give him consecration. Gregory VII makes no distinction between the bishopric considered as a cure of souls and as a feudal status. He has nothing to say of any claims the prince may make to share in the appointment because of the temporal possessions of the see. These are church property, given to the bishopric for the sake of God's poor, something sacred therefore. The bishopric is considered as a unity, and since it is a sacred unity the state must not touch it in any way. Free election of a good man by the lawful electors, confirmation of the election and sacramental consecration by the archbishop—this is required, and is all that is required.

The law does not provide penalties for offending princes. It is really no more than a restatement of the primitive ideal, the ideal for all future development. Nor did the pope send official notification of the law, as a kind of warning or threat, to the various kings. And in practice, his application of the law varied considerably, according as the abuses it was designed to check were more frequent or less, or nonexistent. What the pope was fighting was simony, and the only way (in some places) to put an end to this was to end all connection of the prince and ecclesiastical appointments. William of Normandy, a wholehearted supporter of the reform, with Lanfranc, the model archbishop of the century, at Canterbury, Gregory VII left wholly untroubled. Even for the German sees of the emperor, Henry IV,[5] a bad ruler, the pope did not take the aggressive line to which the root and branch declaration might have seemed the prelude. It was with the great sees of northern Italy, that looked to Henry as patron, and especially Milan, that the trouble began.

At Milan the bad men organised and fought back, supported by the emperor, and the good were extremely militant also. Whence a long history of rioting and, in 1075, half the city burned down, and the cathedral with it. The great events now follow rapidly: the emperor procuring the consecration of his nominee as archbishop (against the pope's express prohibition); the pope's severe reproof;

[5] Son of Henry III, emperor 1056–1106.

the emperor's bishops, in synod, depose the pope[5a]; and the pope replies with a sentence deposing the emperor, an act without any precedent in history. The extremes had at last collided. The emperor's bishops elected a new, carefully chosen, imperially minded "pope"—the lately deposed archbishop of Ravenna; the emperor came with an army to instal him in St. Peter's; and for years Gregory VII was besieged in Sant'Angelo. The Normans rescued him, in the end, and twelve months later he died, an exile (May 25, 1085), his soul and purpose unshaken. For three years the Holy See remained effectively vacant.

War, imprisonment, exile—we are seeing in operation, yet once again, the old tactics of the Catholic tyrant: Constantius against St. Athanasius, Constantine IV against St. Martin I, Justinian against Pope Vigilius, Leo III (had he been able) against Gregory II; no repudiation of the spiritual, but violence until the spiritual consent to be an instrument of the tyrant's government. And what the present tyrant, Henry IV, desires is a continuance of the bad system where he is absolute master of the Church, free to choose whom he will for bishops, and to fix their price, what time the revival of religion may take its chance.

At the election of Gregory VII's first effective successor, Urban II, in 1088, the end of the war is thirty years away and more—years in which popes could make serious mistakes in what they said and what they did: the costly, mischievous vacillation of the far from clearheaded Pascal II (1099–1118), for example, who moved from one extreme position to its very opposite. Meanwhile the trouble in France and in England had been ended by a logical, agreed solution where the true interests of both Church and State were protected, though the condemned investiture ceremony was given up. It was from the French intelligence that the ultimate solution came for the conflict with Germany, from the theologico-legal genius of Ivo, bishop of Chartres, and the realist sense of the newly elected French pope, Guy, archbishop of Vienne, Calixtus II (1119–24), a one-time extremist, and the bitterest of all the critics of his predecessor Pascal II, when that pope (under pressure) made his fatal wholesale surrender.

Ivo of Chartres (1035–1115) and his pupils drew attention to

[5a] Barry, no. 47, prints a translation of the letters of the emperor and his bishops to the pope.

the fact that simony is not heresy, and that no one had ever regarded the royal investiture as a sacrament. He stressed the reality of the distinction between the bishop's religious authority and powers and his temporal rights, duties, and properties; in all that belonged to the feudal side of the bishopric the king had rights, in what belonged to the spiritual side the king could have no right at all. It was this way of looking at the embittered problem which had produced the pact of 1106 that had ended the conflict in England between Henry I and his archbishop St. Anselm.

This new pope was a noble, from Burgundy, and kin to the emperor.[6] He had been archbishop of Vienne for thirty years and in all that time a leading reformer. He took up the great task where his short-lived predecessor, the strong-minded but conciliatory Gelasius II,[7] had left it, who had died at Cluny, on his way to a meeting with the French king. The first appearance of Calixtus II as pope was at a great council of the bishops of the south of France at Toulouse. A second council was summoned to meet at Reims in October, 1119. Meanwhile, the pope and the king of France met, and the emperor called a meeting of the German princes at Mainz, at their request, to consider how best to end the long civil war, and make a lasting peace with the Church. To this meeting came the messengers with the official news of the new pope's election, and the invitation to the German bishops to take part in the council at Reims. The emperor and the princes decided to await the council before making any decisions.

The pope, encouraged by these unusual signs of grace, sent two French prelates to the emperor, who could explain to him how, in France, the king enjoyed full feudal rights over the bishops and abbots as vassals without any need of an investiture ceremony. The emperor replied that he asked no more than this. Whereupon the pope sent a delegation with greater powers, two of his cardinals. An agreement was reached, formulae found, and a meeting arranged between pope and emperor at which both would sign. The emperor was now willing to say, explicitly, "For the love of God and St. Peter and of the lord pope Calixtus, I give up the whole system of investiture, so far as concerns the Church." And now came a hitch, owing to the pope's adding new conditions on the eve of the meet-

[6] Henry V, since 1106; the son of Gregory VII's adversary.
[7] Pope from January 24, 1118, to January 28, 1119.

ing, refusing to allow the emperor additional time to study these and, although the two men were actually on the ground, so to speak, refusing to meet him. More, the pope was so irritated that the emperor had failed to submit, that he renewed the excommunication.

What there was, in all this, besides personal temperament is not known. But the incident occurred while the great council was in session at Reims, with Calixtus presiding, seventy-six bishops from France, Germany, England, and Spain. It was between sessions of the council that he blundered into the new rupture, and it is recorded that when he returned from the adventure he was too worn out to proceed with the council business and took to his bed. Maybe the thought possessed the pope that the grim and treacherous emperor was about to repeat the treatment meted out to Pascal II, eight years before, whom this emperor had carried off a prisoner, and forced to sign away his cause.

It was only after another two years of war that the two parties came together again, when at a peace conference in Germany the princes asked the pope to free the emperor from the excommunication, and to summon a General Council, "where the Holy Spirit could solve those problems that were beyond the skill of men" (September 1121). The pope now sent to his imperial kinsman a kindly letter, the gist of which is the phrase, "Let each of us be content with his own office, and those who should show justice towards all mankind no longer strive ambitiously to pillage each other."

It was at Worms that the envoys of these high contracting parties met, and on September 23, 1122, they produced the two statements, papal and imperial, which, together, constitute the Concordat of Worms. The war about investitures was over, after forty-seven years.

At Worms the emperor, "out of the love of God and of the holy Roman church," said explicitly, "I give up . . . all investiture with ring and crozier and I promise that in all the sees of the realm and of the empire elections and consecrations shall be free. I restore to the holy Roman church the properties and temporal rights [*regalia*] of blessed Peter which have been taken away since the beginning of this quarrel, whether in my father's time or in my own. . . . I guarantee true peace to the pope Calixtus, to the holy Roman church and to all those who took that side. . . ."

The pope, for his part, "I Calixtus, the bishop, servant of the servants of God grant to you Henry, my dear son, by the grace of God emperor of the Romans, Augustus, that the election of bishops and abbots of the German kingdoms shall take place in your presence, without simony and without force . . . that the personage elected shall receive from you his *regalia* by the [touch of the] sceptre, and shall fulfil all those duties to which he is bound in your regard by the law. As to other parts of the empire, the bishop being consecrated, shall receive his *regalia* . . . by the sceptre, within six months and that he shall fulfil all those duties [etc., as above]. . . . I guarantee true peace to you and to those who belonged to your party in this quarrel."

The documents were duly signed, the cardinal bishop of Ostia —the pope's chief agent in all this—sang the mass, the emperor was given the kiss of peace and received Holy Communion. The usual ceremonies of humiliating public submission were, for once, dispensed with.

The great act had its imperfections—a certain vagueness in important matters, the king's share in the election for example. There was room for new troubles to grow out of it. But the great principle was safe that the king had not what he had claimed was his lawful right, the choice and appointment of his people's spiritual rulers and teachers. As to the settlement itself, as a whole, we may agree with the leading authority, "It was the common sense solution."[8]

This General Council of 1123 was, beyond a doubt, the grandest spectacle Rome, and the whole West, had seen for hundreds of years. Bishops and abbots together were reckoned at something like a thousand, there was a host of lesser ecclesiastics, and the vast train of knights, soldiers, and other attendants of these ecclesiastical lords, as well as of the lay notabilities who attended. So much we learn from the contemporary chroniclers. As to the proceedings of the council, what method was adopted for proposing new laws, for discussing them, for voting—of all this we know nothing at all, for the official proceedings disappeared long before the time when there was such a thing as posterity interested in the past. It is not even certain whether there were two or three public sessions. But

[8] Fliche, as before, 389. Barry, no. 48, prints a translation of the concordat.

the council opened on the third Sunday of Lent, March 18, 1123, in the Lateran Basilica, and the final session took place either on March 27 or April 6. The emperor had been invited to send representatives, and one of the acts of the council was the ratification of the concordat. The canons promulgated at the council, which cover all the social and religious problems of the day, are hardly of a nature to provoke discussion—remedies, sternly stated in the shape of prohibitions, for the various moral ills of public and private life. If Calixtus II adopted the simple method of announcing these canons, and asking the assembly to assent, it would be no more than what a series of popes and their legates had been doing, in one country after another, at all the councils of the last seventy-five years. There was nothing to surprise or provoke the bishops of that generation in thus following the practice that had been the means of so much improvement, in morals and in religious life. Calixtus II was no despot ordering submission to novelties now decreed, but the victorious leader of the episcopate, and the representative of other leaders now departed, thanks to whose intelligence and fortitude the episcopate everywhere had been liberated from the thrall of tyrants indeed, its dignity restored and its spiritual prestige renewed.

The twenty-two canons listed as the legislation of the council of 1123 are a curiously mixed collection. They indiscriminately treat of general matters and local matters; there are permanent regulations mixed up with temporary, set out in no kind of order; and almost all of them are repetitions of canons enacted in the various papally directed councils of the previous thirty years. With regard to the long fight against the lay lords' control, simony is again condemned, bishops not lawfully elected are not to be consecrated, laymen are not to hold or control church property, parish priests the bishop alone can appoint, they are not to take parishes as a layman's gift, the ordinations performed by the antipopes (and their transfers of church property) are declared null. A special canon renews the indulgence given to all who assist the crusade, and renews the Church's protection, with the sanction of excommunication, of the absent crusader's property. There is a law to excommunicate coiners of false money, and also (a reflection of the chronic social disorder) the brigands who molest pilgrims. A general rule is made about the new practice called "The Truce of God" —a practice designed to lessen, for the ordinary man, the horrors of the never ceasing wars between the local lords. By Urban II's law made at the council of Clermont in 1095, Monday, Tuesday, and Wednesday were the only days on which fighting was lawful, and this only between Trinity Sunday and Advent. The rule of 1123 only deals with the bishop's duty to excommunicate those who violate the truce. There are two canons about clerical marriage. The first (canon 3) renews the ancient law that those in Holy Orders must not marry. The second (canon 21) repeats this in so many words and adds that "marriages already contracted by such persons are to be broken, and the parties bound to penance."[9]

This law—which may not be a law of the ninth General Council at all, but a regulation of one of Urban II's provincial councils that appears in the list of 1123 by some confusion—is often regarded as the first beginning of the new rule in these matters that makes the contracting of marriage impossible for clerics in holy orders. At the next General Council this will be more explicitly stated.

[9] *Contracta quoque matrimonia ab huiusmodi personis disjungi ... iudicamus.*

10. *The Second General Council of the Lateran, 1139*

The tenth General Council, the Second General Council of the Lateran, took place only fifteen years after that just described. It was a council of much the same kind, in its procedure, in its legislation, and in the vast interest it aroused, and it should be seen as complementary to the council of 1123. As the reader may guess, it would never have been summoned but for a new crisis in church affairs. The crisis, this time, was a double papal election, at Rome, made by the cardinals, and an ensuing schism when for some years two rivals, each claiming to be the lawful pope, divided the Church.

When Calixtus II died, in 1124, there was elected in his place, the Cardinal Lambert who had negotiated the great concordat, a veteran of the papal service and one of the last survivors of the band who had stood around Urban II in the grim years that followed the death of Gregory VII. He took the name Honorius II, and lived out all his pontificate in Rome—the first pope to live continuously in Rome for nearly a hundred years. It was by no means a peaceful city. The old baronial feuds had revived during the years when it so rarely had a resident ruler. Here was the source of the double election after the death of Honorius in 1130. The Pierleoni brought about the election of one of that family—he took the name Anacletus II. The Frangipani faction elected Innocent II. That the better man of the two was Innocent seems certain. But which was the lawfully elected? Neither had been elected precisely as the somewhat vague law of 1059 prescribed.

Anacletus, however, the scion of a wealthy Roman clan, was master of Rome, and Innocent fled for support beyond the Alps. Thanks to Louis VI of France, and above all to the spiritual genius who towers above all the men of this age, St. Bernard, abbot of Clairvaux, he soon had the support of France and the empire, of

England, and of the Spanish kingdoms also. But, except intermittently, Innocent was never master in Rome—the Norman king of Sicily being the staunch supporter of his rival—until 1138, when Anacletus died and his successor, yielding to the influence of St. Bernard, made his submission to Innocent. Once again the spectacle of a wandering pope had been turned to the profit of the reform movement, and four great councils are associated with Innocent's presence, Clermont in 1130, Reims in 1131, Piacenza in 1132 and Pisa in 1135.

Rid of the burden of the schism, the pope now summoned the General Council of 1139, but in no such amiable spirit towards his late adversaries as Calixtus II had shown. St. Bernard pleaded for them, but in vain. Innocent showed himself a singularly un-Roman pope when he dealt harshly with the subjected foe.

There were more than five hundred bishops present at the council and, it is said, a thousand abbots—the mention of St. Bernard's rôle in the schism is a reminder that this is the century of the most remarkable sudden expansion of the monastic orders ever known, the Cistercian century. Again the *acta* of the council have perished. We know that it was opened on April 4, 1139, in the Lateran Church, and that there were three sessions. All that remains to us are the thirty canons enacted, and a chronicler's story of the pope's fiery reception of one of his recent opponents. This bishop made his way to the papal throne, and laid down his mitre at the pope's feet, in token of submission. But the pope arose, and kicked the mitre down the church, calling out, "Away, henceforth you are no bishop of mine."

The canons of this council, or the list as we possess it rather, is the same kind of *omnium gatherum* as the list of 1123. Of the thirty canons a half merely repeat the canons of that list, and a half of the remainder do little more than repeat verbatim the canons enacted by Innocent in the great provincial councils of 1130–35.

There are five new canons about clerical life. With regard to the old trouble of clergy who marry, there is the highly important declaration that these unions are not true marriages.[1] The faithful peo-

---

[1] *Huiusmodi namque copulationem, quam contra ecclesiasticam regulam constat esse contractam, matrimonium non esse censemus. Qui etiam ab invicem separati pro tantis excessibus condignam poenitentiam agant* (canon 7). This is a repetition of a canon enacted at Pisa, 1135.

ple are forbidden to attend mass said by such married clergy, whose sons are not to be ordained unless they become monks or canons regular. All are warned that in the Church there are no such things as hereditary benefices. Clerics who put forward claims of this sort will be severely punished for their impudence. Clerical dress must be seemly, no riotous colours or the indecent fashions of the day. And the cleric is protected by a law which strikes with an *ipso facto* excommunication whoever maliciously assaults him—an excommunication which the pope alone can remove.[2]

In what concerns the Catholic's relation with the world in which he lives—the virtue of social justice in the large sense—the council has six laws to propose. The ancient custom that the populace pillage the house of a deceased bishop is to cease. Usurers, i.e., those who—in this day when money is a nonproductive piece of metal, useful only in exchange for goods—charge a borrower interest for the convenience he has enjoyed, when he brings back the gold piece borrowed, are to be held (says the council) as they have always been held, as infamous and to be shunned by all. They are forbidden the sacraments, and if they die unrepentant are not to be given Christian burial. The "Truce of God" is now set out for the whole of Christendom in the detail of Urban II's law of 1095,[3] and the bishops are warned that slackness in excommunicating for breaches of the truce may cost them their place. There is a special prohibition against molesting merchants, country people engaged in agriculture and their stock, as well as the clergy. Another class of criminal (about whom there are three canons) is the incendiary. Those who repent of this crime are not to be absolved without heavy penance, i.e., a year's service with the Crusade, in Spain or in the Holy Land. Tournaments are most stringently forbidden. Knights killed in these "detestable jousts" are not to be given Christian burial. And the new military weapon of the catapult, that hurls immense masses of stone at the walls of besieged castles and cities, and over the walls, is condemned as a thing "detested by God." It is never to be used against Christian men under penalty of excommunication.

There are two canons that have to do with a Christian's belief. In one of these (canon 22) bishops are commanded to instruct their people that the outward acts of penance are of no avail with-

---

[2] The earliest example of a papal reservation of a censure by statute.
[3] See preceding page 196.

out true inward repentance. Practices of this sort are the straight road to hell. The second (canon 23) condemns a whole series of anti-Christian notions, the undercurrent that never ceased to affect medieval life. Those who hold these ideas present the appearance of great zeal for true religion, says the council, but they reject the sacrament of the Holy Eucharist, the baptism of infants, the priesthood, and marriage. Those who hold these heretical beliefs the state must coerce. Those who defend the heretics are excommunicated along with them.

11. *The Third General Council of the Lateran, 1179*

One of the disappointments as one studies the history of the Middle Ages is the scantiness of personal information about the great men whose acts, and effect upon subsequent ages, are yet really well known to us. Only too often is the personage himself a mere silhouette against the gold and scarlet of the event. Pope Alexander III, who summoned the eleventh General Council, is an instance in point, for in the history of the Church, by his effect, he stands out as one of the six or seven greatest popes of all, one whose laws and creative institutional work still influence the life of the Church. His reign, again, is one of the longest of all, close on twenty-two years. And yet, much as we know about his career, the man himself escapes us utterly.

As to what this pope accomplished, a French scholar of our own time, the author of the most complete study yet made of Alexander III, can say that he "is one of the chief founders of the Roman all-powerfulness over the clergy of the Church, with a very high idea of his office, ruling the clergy by the aid of trustworthy assistants, and thanks to means of government that are steadily being improved, intervening everywhere throughout the Church by his legates, setting in order and controlling the jurisdiction of the archbishops in their provinces and the bishops in their sees, and everywhere seeking to strengthen the links that bind the Holy See to the various local establishments"[1]; such is Alexander III, the first pope effective on the grand scale in the whole daily life of the universal church.

When, eighty years after his death, and after the more recent pontificates of Innocent III and Innocent IV, an ambassador writes

---

[1] Marcel Pacaut, *Alexandre III, Étude sur sa conception du pouvoir pontifical dans sa pensée et dans son oeuvre*, Paris, 1956, p. 301.

from Rome to his sovereign of the newly elected Urban IV, it is not to these famous men that he goes for a comparison. "Men here are saying," he reports, "that the new pope will be another Pope Alexander."

There was a special reason for this spectacular achievement of this great pope. He was one of those who, at a crucial moment of history, sometimes appear in the high places of government, with the very personality the time requires, and with the trained competence to make this effective. This rare combination is writ large, for the trained observer at least, in the laws of Alexander's General Council of 1179. These laws are the work of a legal genius; and they are but a fraction of what passed directly from him into the fundamental law of the Catholic Church.

Gregory VII, anxious to bring home to a world reluctant to be reformed, that what he demanded was not a perfection hitherto unheard of, but simply a return to what had always been, set in motion a great movement of research into the past legal history of the Church. And the age when, in a score of able legal-minded writers, these discoveries were attaining something like completeness, knew a still wider legal renascence, the rebirth of "the divinely reasonable" law of ancient Rome. Here was something that was a collection of laws, and a philosophy of law, and almost Law itself as a living creation, before which the reasonable man gladly bent in reverent acceptance, something than which nothing could be more welcome to rulers everywhere.

Also the age, the early years of the twelfth century, produced the man we know as Gratian, a monk who was a lawyer? a lawyer turned monk?—a legally trained mind, author of a book that was the first complete, scientifically planned epitome of the Church's law. On this scholar's work the whole magnificent fabric of the Canon Law was to be built—in his spirit and following his pattern. And the first part of the great work called the *Corpus Iuris Canonici*, which was the Catholic Church's law book down to 1918, is the *Decretum* of Gratian. Alexander III—Roland Bandinelli—was the pupil of Gratian, and the first of the hundreds of lawyers who were to publish commentaries on Gratian's book. And then, as pope, sitting in judgment on appeals of every kind that poured in from every part of Europe, he was so to decide the cases that, in judging them, he developed law, created law. It is simply not possible to exaggerate the influence of his twenty-one years of legal activity in the highest place of all. And yet, outside this work, and his other public activities as pope, we scarcely know the man.

The other public activities—a seventeen years' struggle against the determination of the emperor Frederick I (called Barbarossa) to make himself master of the Church, and reduce the papacy to an imperial dependency.[2]

This extremely serious affair was for Alexander III an inheritance from the days of his predecessor, the English pope Adrian IV. The emperor, young, ambitious, warlike, and crafty as a fox, allowed by two weak popes to do as he liked with the Church, now meant to make himself even more completely master of Italy than he was of Germany. Against the vast military power which he could assemble, the pope's main hope was the Norman king of Sicily. His own state, effectively, was little more than the city of Rome and its environs, and the city had for some time been enjoying the status of an antipapal republic. The only protection to the north was the fragile hope that the cities of Lombardy, Milan and the rest, would unite against their common foe. But upon Frederick's invasion in 1158 the cities everywhere had to yield, and submit to be ruled by governors he appointed. Lombardy was still seething with discontent, and Adrian IV meditating an alliance of the Lombards and Normans when September 1, 1159, he died, most unexpectedly.

And now the tragedy of thirty years before was repeated—a double election. The details of this affair are fairly well known, and what case can be made out for the lawfulness of the election of the cardinal who received only four votes, where Roland Bandinelli received twenty-two, depends in part upon a current idea that the election, to be valid, had to be unanimous, and in part upon the principle that the majority needs to be not merely the greater part, but the morally better part—a principle whose end is surely anarchy, but which then had its place in the general law about ecclesiastical elections, and had been successfully invoked by St. Bernard in the affair of 1130. But it was to matter much more that Roland Bandinelli had been Adrian IV's right-hand man in the contest with Barbarossa, and that his rival was the emperor's man.

Frederick did not now make the mistake of marching on Rome,

---

[2] These are the years, also (1163–70), of the dramatic contest of St. Thomas of Canterbury with King Henry II.

with what troops he still had in Italy. His policy was rather to suggest a kind of congress of princes before whom the rivals could state their case. The princes—Frederick, in his own mind—would then decide. To this Alexander III, from the first, opposed a blunt refusal, and from this position he never moved. His rival, who called himself Victor IV, accepted, and became henceforth all but a part of the imperial machine.

The schism lasted eighteen years nearly, "Victor IV" being followed by "Pascal III" (who, to make still more evident the sacredness of the emperor's cause, canonised Charlemagne for him in 1167) and he by "Calixtus III." For only two of these years was Alexander III able to live in Rome. The contrast between his masterly ruling of the Church, of which we have spoken, during these years, and his own personal insecurity is most striking. For years he lived in France, and then in the country to the south of Rome, close to the frontier of the friendly kings of Sicily, constantly in movement. At Rome the antipope was lord, and in St. Peter's he crowned Barbarossa and his empress.

This coronation was in 1167—the emperor's third or fourth invasion of Italy, and a highly spectacular success until, on the very morrow of the sacrilegious rite the plague struck his army, and troops and notables died like flies. The hated emperor had to disguise himself to get out of the country alive. Seven years later, after long preparation, Frederick returned, to meet at Legnano (in 1176) with a surprising and wholly disastrous defeat at the hands of the Lombard League. Of this league of city states Alexander III had been the real inspiration, and its steadfast counsellor in matters of alliance and diplomacy. The freedom of the Italian cities and the freedom of religion had become one thing in these tense years. For Frederick, Legnano was the end. He tried, of course, to make peace with the pope without the league, and with the league at the expense of the pope. But Alexander was loyalty itself. A peace congress came together at Venice, in 1177, terms were agreed, and the emperor made his submission to the pope—not, however, with the spectacular gestures of the frescoes that, at Siena and Venice, commemorate the event, for such was not Alexander's nature. The bad precedent of 1139 was not followed, and when the last of the antipopes came in to make his submission, in the following year, Alexander received him as a guest and provided for him. After all, in the distant days when Adrian IV was pope, had they not been cardinals together?

The General Council of 1179 was the outcome of these Venetian events, and it needs to be seen as such: as the council then promised to the emperor, in which, as will be understood, a whole world of reorganisation had to be faced—for example, Germany had, in a way, been out of the Church for nearly twenty years. And as well as reorganisation, there was the ever needed exhortation to reform, and the restraint of the abuses, ecclesiastical and lay, that are the perpetual scandal of church life.

Of the council itself we know all too little, for its acts have not survived. It opened March 5, 1179, and there were three public sessions, but whether the second and third were March 7 and 19 or March 12 and 23 is not certain. The number of bishops who attended was about three hundred. The greater part came from France and the various Italian states, but there were 19 from Germany and as many from Spain, 6 from Ireland and another 6 from the England of Henry II, with 12 from his French dominions. A Hungarian is mentioned and a Dane, and there were 7 bishops from the various Latin states of the Holy Land. Abbots and priors were still more numerous, and the bishop of Assisi in his sermon at the opening was able to say that the "universal assembly" could be seen to have been brought together from almost the whole of the world. There was even an observer from those Greek churches of the East with which, for generations now, there had been so little direct contact. "The senate of the whole Christian republic was come together," as the preacher said, "to consider and to give judgment to the universe. To Rome alone, of all the royal cities [Antioch, Alexandria, Byzantium, Jerusalem were the others] had it been given to rule with supreme power over all the other sees, with the power of the keys, the power to judge; Rome alone had the power to summon a General Council, to make new canons, to abrogate the old." As for the reigning pope, the benefits of his rule were felt as far away as the Indies.[3]

[3] Abyssinia rather, we should say, the mysterious land of Prester John, who had written to the pope about his desire to be better instructed in the Christian religion, and to whom Alexander had replied (1177). For all of which see Rousset de Pina, *Le troisième Concile Générale du Latran*, in F. and M., vol. 9, part 2, p. 160, n. 1.

In this rare sermon we are given, for a fraction of a second, a glimpse of the particular and personal. We could have exchanged it for some slight knowledge of how the council transacted its business. For of this we know just nothing at all. One of the chroniclers who treat of the council speaks of twelve canons proposed which the bishops rejected, and that is the only hint that has survived of all the discussions of those three weeks of March 1179. Were there no critics among the bishops? Was the pope's new system the very thing all of them desired? A passage in Alexander's letter convoking the council has been taken as a hint to the bishops that their presence was chiefly required in order to give the decrees a more rapidly effective publicity. Another critic was the English humanist John of Salisbury, present at the council as bishop of Chartres. He wondered whether there were not enough laws already. Was not the Church staggering under their weight? Would it not be better to keep to the simple Gospel, so long neglected these days by so many? Will our Lord not say to us also, "Ye let go the commandment of God and hold fast to the tradition of men"?[4] This curious anticipation of the simplist solutions of Erasmus is hardly likely to have influenced the world-weary and experienced old pope, who had twenty-seven canons[5] to propose to the bishops, practical regulations in all conscience, with appropriate punishments provided for those who ignored them. For the most part they concern the clergy, and especially bishops. Eleven are new laws, the rest repeat and renew canons already enacted.

The pope's first thought, naturally, is to amend the law of 1059 about papal elections. There must be no uncertainty about the meaning of such a law. As Alexander III now rewrote it the law has lasted until this present day.[6] Nor were there ever again disputed elections of the type of 1130 and 1159. What this first canon of 1179 decreed was as follows. Should the cardinals, through the malice of the devil, be unable to achieve a unanimous choice, and there be two thirds in agreement and the other third unwilling to join them, or presuming to choose another, then the one chosen by the two thirds is to be taken as the pope. Should it happen that, relying on his choice by one third only, a man usurps the

[4] Mark 7:8.
[5] They are translated in Schroeder, pp. 214–35.
[6] With a minor change introduced by Pius XII.

name of pope (for he cannot take the reality), both himself and all who take him as pope are excommunicated, and deprived of whatever ordination has given them, so that communion is denied them except as Viaticum at the hour of death. Should they die unrepentant their lot is that of Dathan and Abiron.[7] Moreover, if anyone receives a majority of the votes but less than two thirds, let him not dare to take on himself the office of pope, or he falls under all the penalties just mentioned. The law states that it does not affect the principle about "the morally better part" which rules in other ecclesiastical elections, for if disputes arise about these there is a superior who can decide the matter. "But in the case of the Roman see there is a special arrangement, since it is not possible here to have recourse to a superior."[8]

"Following the example of our predecessor Innocent [II]," all ordinations made by the antipopes, and by those whom these ordained, are quashed, and the benefices which these schismatics granted are to go back to their rightful owners. All who, of their own free will, took oaths to uphold the schism, are suspended from their orders and their dignity.[9]

As to bishops, no one is to be made a bishop who is under thirty years of age, of legitimate birth and demonstrably suited by his life and education. Elected, the election confirmed, the new bishop having taken over the administration of the see and received consecration, the superior whose duty it is will then fill the benefices vacated by his promotion. Archdeacons, rural deans, parish priests [i.e., pastors] are not to be appointed if under twenty-five, and the first named must at least receive deacon's orders and the rest the priesthood, within the time fixed by law. Clerics who elect contrary to this law lose all future right to elect, and are for three years suspended from their benefices.[10]

One never ceasing complaint is that bishops' official visitations tend to be ruinously expensive for the places they visit. Their train —officials, guards, servants—is now cut down: archbishops to a maximum of 40 to 50 horses, according to the country and its resources, cardinals 25, bishops 20 to 30, archdeacons 7; deans are

[7] For whom see Numbers 16:1.
[8] *In Romana vero ecclesia aliquid speciale constituitur, quia non potest recursus ad superiorem haberi.* Canon 1.
[9] Canon 2.
[10] Canon 3.

told to be contented with 2. No hunting dogs, no hawks and falcons. "And let them not demand sumptuous feasts, but gratefully take the seemly sufficiency set before them." Bishops are not to burden their subjects with taxes. Parents, as Scripture says, should enrich their children, not children their parents. What has been said about the prelate's train is, of course (*sane*), said as the maximum that is to be tolerated, something allowable in well-to-do places, parishes with ample revenues.[11] Should a bishop ordain anyone priest or deacon who has not any legal right to an ecclesiastical income, the bishop is to maintain him until he is placed.[12]

No cleric is to be appointed to a place which is not yet vacant, or to be promised appointment at the next vacancy—lest men begin to wish for the death of others. Promises of this kind were forbidden in the pagan laws of old. How shameful, and inviting the wrath of God, that there should be such expectations in God's Church. Bishops are to fill vacancies within six months. If they neglect to do so, the canons of the diocese are to appoint. If all concerned are negligent, the archbishop of the province is to act.[13]

There are "bitter complaints," says canon 9, from bishops about the way in which certain religious orders make a mockery of penitential discipline by so using the privileges granted them by the popes as to provide influential sinners with loopholes—they gladly accept from the lay lords grants of tithes and benefices, admitting these personages to the sacraments although excommunicated, giving them Christian burial, and where the order was allowed during times of interdict to have mass said once a year in that country, taking this to mean once in each of the monasteries of the order. The orders moreover had confraternities of laymen associated with them, and to these it was conveyed that such membership took them out of the bishop's jurisdiction. The new military orders, the Templars and the Knights Hospitalers, were especially complained of, regarding these gravely scandalous practices. The canon insists that in all these matters the bishop's authority holds good, over the priests who serve the parishes which the order "owns" and over the members of these various fraternities.

Two canons (16, 17) rule that in differences between the canons

[11] Canon 4.
[12] Canon 5.
[13] Canon 8.

of cathedral chapters and others the will of the *maior et sanior pars*[14] of the chapter is to prevail, and that where there are several patrons of a church the candidate who has the majority of the patrons for him is to be appointed: never are there to be as many pastors as there are disputing patrons.

Abuses in the matter of appeals from the lower ecclesiastical courts are corrected by canon 6. The legal trick of suddenly excommunicating the man thought to be about to appeal, is forbidden and, on the other hand, the man charged with an offence is not allowed to appeal before his case has been tried. Especially are monks and other religious not to adopt such a tactic as this against their superior correcting them according to the rule, "but let them humbly and devoutly receive what has been commanded for their spiritual good."

Canon 18 has a more general interest, and it touches on a problem of medieval history that has been all too little explored—the way in which the rank and file of the parochial clergy were trained. In order that all may have a chance of education, even the poor who cannot expect their parents to pay school fees, every bishop is to arrange that among the members of his cathedral chapter there shall be one who will teach gratis the clerics of that church and poor students too, and the same shall be done in other churches and in monastic churches. No one who is qualified to teach shall be denied permission. From the general terms of the canon, this is not the foundation of a system so much as an order for its restoration. There are as yet no universities in the formal sense of the word, but one has only to recall such a name as that of Abelard, dead now these thirty years, to be aware that in one cathedral city after another there were already remarkably flourishing schools of the liberal arts, and theology. This reforming pope sees no reason why there should not be at least the beginnings of such a school in every diocese.

Of the remaining canons which mostly renew the old laws, we may note how the clergy are now forbidden to accept offerings from the accursed gains of the usurer. Clergy who have accepted such offerings, or given a usurer Christian burial, are to be suspended until they have returned what they accepted.[15] Neither Jews nor

---

[14] "The greater and morally more respectable part."
[15] Canon 25.

Saracens are, on any pretext, to have Christian slaves. Christians who live with them are excommunicated. In all suits a Christian's word is to be preferred against the testimony of Jews, and whoever does the reverse of this is to be excommunicated, for Jews should be subject to Christians and be kindly treated by Christians from human kindness merely.[16]

There is a long and very detailed decree about the restraint of heretics,[17] declared to be numerous in Gascony, and around Albi and Toulouse, "Cathars as they are called," who make no secret of what they are and openly work to make converts. Both the heretics and those who protect them are excommunicated; no one is to give them shelter, or allow them in his territory, or to do business with them. If they die in their sin mass is not to be offered for them, nor are they to receive Christian burial. As to the wandering bands of marauders and plunderers, they are to be treated like heretics, and the pope calls on all good men to associate and, meeting violence with violence, destroy these pests of society; and to those who thus manfully organise all the indulgences are granted which the Crusaders in Spain and the Holy Land enjoy. The canon ends with an exhortation to the bishops to be brave themselves, in supporting this movement to protect the community from these powerfully organised hordes. Cowardly bishops and priests are to be deprived of their office.

The last of these laws that regard the social, as well as the spiritual, life of the Catholic, treats of the lepers—an increasingly large section of society since the crusades. Clergy are not to prevent lepers from having churches of their own, and cemeteries, and their own priest. And from the lepers no tithes are to be asked, whether of produce or of their beasts.[18]

[16] Canon 26.
[17] Canon 27.
[18] Canon 23.

12. *The Fourth General Council of the Lateran, 1215*

The long reign of Alexander III was followed by a period of seventeen years in which the Church saw a succession of no fewer than five popes—the faithful if aged coadjutors of the great legist. When the last of these died, January 8, 1198, the cardinals, that same day, elected the junior member of the college, Lothar, son of the Count of Segni, thirty-seven years of age. He took the name Innocent III. His reign of eighteen years is conventionally regarded—even by historians—as the summit of the papacy's achievement as a universal power, religious, social, political. The reality is a little more complex—or the true meaning of that remarkable hegemony. For our purposes, in this little book, Innocent III is the pope of the Fourth General Council of the Lateran, the greatest of all the councils (in its general effect) before Trent; in the pope's mind, no doubt, the most important event of his reign.

That reign had never for an instant been anything but eventful. There had been kings of France and Castile who had repudiated their wives and "remarried"—with public consequences of the first order; there had been the English king's rejection of the pope's appointment to Canterbury of the great cardinal, Stephen Langton —and the years of a papal interdict which followed; there had been in Germany the calamity of a double election to the empire, civil war—and the famous reasoned decision of the pope; there had been the crusade of 1204, which—partly because of the Venetians, partly because of the German prince against whose claims Innocent had declared—had never reached the Holy Land, but turned to the conquest of the empire of the Christian Greeks; there had been the foundation, upon the ruins of this, of the Latin empire of Constantinople, and a "reunion" of the churches in these lands under Latin bishops; there had been, in the south of France, the great drive to root out the deadly antireligious, antisocial revival of the organised, "mystical," pessimism of the Manichees, and growing out of this the long bloody war called the Albigensian Crusade; there had been the appearance of two great saints, Dominic and Francis of Assisi; there had been the "foundation" of the University of Paris. In every one of these great affairs Innocent III had played a leading rôle. Six thousand of his bulls survive to attest the universality of his interest, the effectiveness of his highly trained lawyer's mind, and the reality of his own spiritual life whose guiding star was his obligation as pope to forward everywhere the reign of Christ.

Innocent III had not been everywhere equally successful. Some of his plans had gone disastrously astray. Not always had his information been adequate. His coadjutors had more than once failed him badly. No historian has, so far, so completely studied the vast achievement in all its parts as to be able to strike the balance of success and failure with anything like finality.

In the opening months of his reign, and again at the great council held at its close, Innocent III declared that the two chief tasks before him were the recovery of the Holy Land and the reform of Catholic life. One clear evidence, in 1198, of the need for reform was the fact that great territories in the south of France seemed about to slip away from the Catholic faith. This menace of the growth of Manicheism, of the coming triumph of the Albigenses, was the occasion of the pope's main personal effort, and of a tragic failure also. For although, after several years of bloody warfare, all danger of a Manichee supremacy in the heart of Christendom was ended, the Catholic princes had behaved as all princes behave in wars of conquest, and so too had their armies. Nothing of Innocent's personal clemency was reflected in the crusade. And the remnants of the heresy went underground, to fester for centuries yet to come.

This grave peril conditioned two of the council's chief acts, its statement of Catholic belief and the law about the repression of heresy. What these heretics taught, whose organisation in France and Italy went back to the early twelfth century, was roughly as follows. Two supreme beings are at the origin of all things—and one of these is Evil. It is the evil principle that is the creator of the material world, of man's body for example. The Old Testament is a legacy from the evil principle, the New alone is from the good. Christ, the greatest creation of the good principle, was man in appearance only. He did not *really* suffer or die. The main duty of the believer is to avoid all possible contact with matter—food, for example, the possession of property, the exercise of sex. These heretics were organised in churches, where they formed two sharply divided classes. There were those called the Perfect, who lived with great asceticism, and acted as guides to the rest, and the ordinary believers who lived as they chose, but in what Christians called sin, as preferable to marriage—marriage, being a stable affair, was a greater enslavement to matter than promiscuous sex relations. The procreation of children was an evil and so, also, was life itself. For life is the imprisonment of the spiritual soul in the material body. To assist, or bring on, death is to perform the good work of liberating spirit from matter. And the sect had a kind of ritual suicide by starvation, called *Endura*, where during the long process the patient was surrounded by the Perfect, to prevent any fatal relapse once the decision was made. In order to be sure of a happy future life it was necessary to undergo the rite they called the Consolation. But this entailed the obligation to live as the Perfect—absolute continency, and an asceticism so strict in the matter of food that it amounted to semistarvation. And any falling away, after this rite, was irreparable: the rite then lost all its value, and it could not be repeated. With the vast majority the rite was put off until they were obviously dying, or else they were urged to the process of the *Endura*. As with almost all these medieval heresies the manual trades furnished disciples everywhere, the weavers, tailors, shoemakers. And they also recruited among the wealthy merchants.

By the time it fell to Innocent III to deal with them, these neo-Manichees had for many years conducted a successful propaganda, in which (apart from their attractively simple solution of the great question of evil) the ascetic lives of the Perfect and the organised charity of the brethren played a great part. The various counts and viscounts who governed these regions, themselves semi-Orientals in their way of life, given over often enough to the systematic dissolution of the harem system, made no effort to check the heretics. Along with the innumerable Jews and Saracens they were becoming a permanent feature of the exotic life of the country. The Catholic clergy were ignorant, and their prelates often corrupt. This, and

the great wealth of the prelates—rarely loved by their subjects—
offered the Manichee apostle one of his best openings. Innocent III
himself testifies to all this.

The bull convoking the fourth General Council of the Lateran
is dated April 19, 1213. It was to open on November 1, 1215. All
bishops were to attend, save two in each province, exempted in order to attend there to the general affairs of the Church. As many as
412 bishops went to the council, with some 800 abbots and priors
of the monastic orders. There were also present ambassadors from
the Latin emperor at Constantinople, from the kings of Germany,
France, England, Aragon, Portugal, Hungary, and Jerusalem, and
from the various Italian states.

Once again, it has to be said, we know all but nothing of the
way the council was organised, for the official proceedings have long
since disappeared. We have the pope's inaugural address, accounts
of one furious discussion at a public session, the text of the seventy
canons voted, and of the decree organising a new crusade. And this
is all. Of what discussions went on between the bishops in the intervals between the three public sessions, held on November 11, 20,
and 30, we know nothing, nor have we any knowledge how the
canons were drawn up or proposed to the council.

We do know that three matters of public policy were laid before
the council: Innocent III's choice of Frederick of Sicily as emperor;
his suspension of Cardinal Stephen Langton, archbishop of Canterbury, for refusing to publish Innocent's bull rebuking the barons of
England for forcing their king to assent to *Magna Carta*, and quash-
ing the charter; the claims of the victorious leader of the crusade
against the Albigenses, Simon de Montfort, to the territories of the
Count of Toulouse, their great protector. In the first two of these
matters the council readily ratified what the pope had done.

The commander in chief of the crusade, de Montfort, had been
as much interested in the spoil it brought as in the destruction of a
heresy. His powerful personality had dominated the legates whom
Innocent had sent to control the great affair. They were soon little
better than his accomplices. It was soon very evident that the pope
had let loose forces he was unable to control. Historians friendly to
Innocent describe what now happened as the pope's having no
choice but to submit to the *fait accompli*—the *fait* being de Mont-

fort's triumph over the Count of Toulouse, blessed as a religious act by the legates who had entirely disregarded the pope's mind.[1] All that Innocent was able to do, in the end, was to endeavour to save a part of Count Raymond's domains for his undoubtedly guiltless heir. At the council, when the pope's decision came up for confirmation, there were violent scenes between the partisans of de Montfort among the French bishops and those of the Count of Toulouse. But a part of the great inheritance was saved for the heir from de Montfort's fangs, as Innocent had hoped.[2]

Innocent III is usually held to be, with Alexander III, a "co-founder" of the Canon Law system as this has existed in the medieval and modern ages of the Church. The famous Lateran Council, regarded as a declaration of church law in all its universality—and of reforming laws—is in importance second only to Trent, among the twenty General Councils. For many generations to come it is "the General Council," referred to as the last decisive word on disputed points. What of its seventy canons?[3]

The first canon is a statement of belief, drawn up as a counter to the heresies of the time, of the Albigenses, Pantheists, and so forth. It stresses that there is only one true God, the one creator of all things, and that Christ our Lord is truly God and truly man. Also that in eternity there is a reward for the good, and for the unrepentant evildoer punishment. In this creed's exposition of the Holy Eucharist there occurs the first official use of the word henceforth famous, when the creed states that the bread and wine are *transubstantiated* into the Body and Blood of Christ.[4] Only priests duly ordained can bring this about. Baptism, by whomsoever administered, if it is rightly administered in the Church's form, is profitable to salvation, to little children as to adults. Sins committed after baptism can be made good by sincere repentance. Not only virgins and those who lead a life of continency can attain eternal

---

[1] Fliche speaks of the "political piece of double crossing" (*cette louche combinaison politique*) to which the legates lent themselves.

[2] The vast question that obviously palpitates behind these halting phrases is best summarised in the (somewhat apologetic) pages of A. Fliche, *La Chrétienté Romaine* 1198–1274 (i.e., F. and M., vol. 10), pp. 112–37, 201–2.

[3] Schroeder prints the whole of these and (pp. 237–96) translation. Barry, no. 76, translates a selection of them.

[4] *Transsubstantiatis pane in corpus et vino in sanguinem.*

happiness, by true faith and a good life, but married people also.

The council then turns to review the life of the Church, to denounce the weaknesses and the wickedness of its members, and to provide punishment for the obstinate. It begins with the clergy.

Clerics living in sin are to be suspended and, if they ignore the suspension, are to be deposed. Bishops who allow such scandals to continue—and especially if they allow this for the sake of money or some other advantage—are also to lose their office forever. The council makes laws against drunken clergy and those who never say mass—bishops amongst them. Hunting and fowling are forbidden, and to keep hunting dogs and hawks. There is a long catalogue of things which clerics must not do: civil employments, trade (especially if it is dishonest), miming, acting, frequenting taverns (absolutely forbidden save for the necessities of travelling), dicing and even looking on at games of chance. Clerics are to be soberly dressed, their garments neither too long nor too short, and fastened up to the neck, not of red or green cloth, no embroidery on gloves or shoes, no gilt spurs, bridles, saddles, or harness. Bishops are to wear linen unless they are monks, in which case they are to keep the habit of their order. Clerics are not to have any part in trials that involve the punishment of death. They are forbidden all military employment. They are not to act as surgeons. They are not to bless ordeals. This last prohibition, since it removed the one thing that gave the ordeal its value, was the beginning of the end of that superstition.

As to clerical appointments: Sees are not to be left vacant. If the chapter concerned does not elect within three months, the right (and duty) of providing the new bishop passes to the metropolitan. Whoever accepts election by favour of the lay power is not elected, and loses all right to be elected, to any post at all, in the future. Those who elect him are also to lose both office and income for three years, and to lose all electoral rights. If the metropolitan (whose duty it is to confirm the election) confirms an unsuitable choice, the confirmation is invalid, and the metropolitan is himself suspended until the pope absolves him.

The bishop's action in all such matters is supervised by the annual provincial council. There, bishops who have made unsuitable appointments are to be admonished, and if they do not act they are to lose all rights of patronage. If the negligent bishop is the metropolitan himself, he is to be denounced to the Holy See. The disability laid on such bishops, no one but the pope can remove.

The new papal centralisation gives the clergy protection against rapacious prelates. Bishops are warned that they must not rob the clergy who serve those churches which are in the gift of the bishop. The pope has heard of unfortunate priests who received only one sixteenth of the revenue due to them, the episcopal patron retaining the rest. Bishops are told that it is their duty to preach. If the diocese is too extensive, they are to choose suitable priests to assist in this work. It is the bishop who is responsible for the education of the future clergy, and the decree of 1179, about a school in each cathedral having, the present council states, been entirely ignored, is now re-enacted, and a lectureship in theology ordered to be founded in every cathedral. The bishop is specially warned to see that the clergy are trained in the administration of the sacraments.

Laws against clerical avarice follow. Bishops are forbidden to receive offerings of money from those they absolve from excommunications, or on the occasion of consecrations, blessings of abbots and ordinations. Convents of women are ordered for the future not to demand a premium, under the plea of the convent's poverty, from girls who wish to become nuns. The same is to apply to communities of men. Bishops are not to take advantage of a parish priest's death to tax the church beyond what the law allows, nor to enforce the payment of such taxes by laying an interdict on the church. For moneys thus obtained double restitution is to be made. With regard to the fees customary at funerals and marriages, while the clergy often ask too much, the laity as often offer nothing; but the sacraments are to be given absolutely without charge. On the other hand, the custom of the laity making a free offering is to be encouraged.

Complaints about clerical greed will be heard for centuries yet. And with them complaints about superstition. Here are three matters which will play a great part in the propaganda of the Protestant reformers—they are already a source of anxiety. A canon regulates the use of relics, and to check the trade in spurious relics orders that no new relics are to be exposed for veneration without the Holy See's authentication of them. Collectors of alms, again, are not always genuine or truthful. The canon gives a specimen of the letters of credence that for the future must guarantee them not to be frauds. The dress of such collectors is regulated, and they are to live religious lives. Bishops are warned not to grant extravagant indulgences.

A vast amount of Innocent III's time had been spent judging complaints of bishops against the religious orders. Several canons deal with this matter. It is now forbidden to establish any new orders. Those who wish to found a new house are to choose an existing approved rule. No abbot is to rule more than one monastery. Abbots are forbidden to judge marriage cases, to grant indulgences, or to allot public penances. Monks must respect the rights of parishes in the matter of funerals, and those privileged to give burial within the monastery to laymen who are oblates are told that an oblate is one who lives in the monastic habit, or has made over his property to the monastery; a mere annual subscription is not qualification enough. Monks to whom land charged with tithe has been given are not exempt from the payment of tithes. Still more important for the future of monasticism was the command to all monks to hold a triennial chapter, after the fashion of the Cistercians. All abbots and priors will attend this and thoroughly review the state of the province, and decide where reforms are needed.

The laity's sins are not overlooked. They are not to farm out benefices at a starvation rate, and are reminded that lay alienation of church property is null and void. They are warned against abusing their office of patron of a benefice to their own personal profit. Clergy are not to be taxed without a licence from the pope. Those rulers who levy such taxes without his permission are excommunicated, and all their acts are legally null. Should their successors not repeal such taxes within a month of assuming office, and give satisfaction for the wrong done, they fall under the same penalties. Another canon deals with evasion of tithe, and recalls that tithes have precedence over all other taxes and must be paid first.

The once famous law *Omnis utriusque sexus* now lays down that every Catholic, under pain of being debarred from church while alive and being denied Christian burial when dead, shall at least once a year confess his sins to his parish priest, and, if only at Easter, receive the Holy Eucharist. This canon concludes with a warning to confessors about the spirit in which they should receive confessions, and of the obligation not to reveal what is confessed to them. Offenders against this last prescription are to be thrust into a severe monastery, there to do penance for the rest of their life.

Three canons concern the sacrament of matrimony. Clandestine, i.e., secret, marriages are severely condemned and the clergy forbidden to assist at them, under pain of a three years' suspension. The impediments of consanguinity and affinity are notably restricted: henceforward they invalidate marriage only as far as the fourth degree, i.e., between those related through common great-great-grandparents. The tense business of the relations between Jews and Christians is also dealt with. Christians are to be protected by the State against the rapacity of Jewish moneylenders. Jews—and Saracens too—are to wear a special dress so that no Christian shall come to marry them in ignorance of what they are. During Passiontide Jews are to keep indoors; there have been riots caused by their mockery of the Christians' lamentations on Good Friday. No Jews or pagans are to be elected or appointed to a public office; it is contrary to the sense of things that those who blaspheme Christ shall hold authority over Christ's followers.

Seven canons deal with procedure in trials of one kind or another. Other canons regulate excommunication, rights of appeal, and the rules for the trial of clerics, the rights of chapters to correct their own members, and the rules for resignation of benefices. The clergy are forbidden to extend their jurisdiction by encroaching on that of the civil courts.

The most elaborate item of this part of the council's work is the third canon, on the pursuit of heretics. All who profess heresies contrary to the faith as this is set out in the first canon of the council, are condemned, and are to be left to the state to be suitably punished,[5] the officers of the state being present at the trial. If clerics they are to be first of all degraded from their orders; all their goods are to be given to the particular church they served. If laity, their goods go to the State. Those suspected of heresy are to prove themselves innocent. Should they neglect to do so they are excommunicated; if they continue in the excommunication for twelve months they are to be condemned as heretics. Princes are to be admonished, and if necessary compelled by threat of excommunication or interdict, to swear that they will banish all whom the Church points out as heretics. This oath, henceforward, all rulers

[5] *Animadversione debita puniendi.*

must swear on first assuming power. If within a year they have not sworn, they are to be reported to the pope, that he may free their vassals from their allegiance, and offer their territories to Catholics who will drive out the heretics. Catholics who take up arms against the heretics are given the privileges of the crusaders in the Holy Land.

All who, in any way, support heretics are excommunicated. If within twelve months they have not made their submission, they lose all power of testifying in lawsuits, and of holding public offices; they cannot make a valid will nor inherit; if they are judges their sentences are null and void; if notaries, the instruments they draw up are invalid; if clerics they lose both office and benefice.

As to the detection of heretics, bishops are now bound to visit, at least once a year, places where heresy is rumoured to exist. They are to take the sworn testimony of witnesses of good standing—if necessary the whole population is to be put upon oath. Those who know anything of heretics, or of any who differ in life or manners from the generality of the faithful, are to report at these visitations. The persons accused are to prove their innocence. If they refuse to take the oath they are to be presumed to be heretics.

There is nothing revolutionary in this law. It is, substantially, no more than what was decreed by Lucius III, in conjunction with the emperor Frederick Barbarossa, at the council of Verona in 1184, and what Innocent himself had been enforcing. As to the phrase about the "suitable" punishment (*animadversione debita puniendi*), this from 1184 is common form in all these laws, never defined but universally understood in the same sense. The first western legal text to prescribe burning at the stake is a law of Peter II of Aragon in 1197. It does no more, in effect, than revive a law about the Manichees that is as old as Diocletian, hardly a model for the Christian lay sovereign, but the beginning of the idea that fire is the fitting punishment for Manichees. Alexander III would never, it seems certain, have departed from the traditional papal policy not to proceed so far as the sentence of death for heresy, and Innocent III himself did nothing to encourage this particular development.[6]

[6] So Fliche, in F. and M., vol. 10, p. 201, "Innocent III who never envisaged the penalty of death for heretics would, no doubt, have disapproved of the [later] Inquisition." Readers interested in the story of the way in which public

The laws were made. How could the council secure that they would be observed, that the bishops, once retired into their distant sees, would put into practice all that they had voted? The sixth canon is an attempt to provide the means. It lays down that the bishops of each ecclesiastical province are to meet annually, for the correction of abuses—clerical abuses particularly—and for the express purpose of maintaining the discipline which this council establishes. Official investigators are to be appointed for each diocese, who shall report to the provincial council whatever they have found needing correction and uncorrected. Negligent bishops are to be suspended from office and from income, and the decisions of the provincial council are to be published in every see through the annual diocesan synod.

---

opinion gradually influenced ecclesiastical authority in the business of the repression of heresy, will find a documented summary in F. and M., vol. 7, p. 462; vol. 9 (part 1) pp. 95–96; vol. 9 (part 2) pp. 343–51; the work of A. Dumas and Raymonde Foreville.

13. *The First General Council of Lyons, 1245*

The vast achievement of the General Council of 1215—the fourth in ninety years—might have been expected to make further councils unnecessary for some generations. But General Councils have always been the product of historical accident. And who shall foretell when accidents will happen? The thirteenth General Council was to meet, in fact, just thirty years after the Fourth Lateran, and at Lyons in France. The purpose for which the pope called it together makes it a council apart—the trial of the emperor.

The emperor was Frederick II, that King of Sicily whom, as a child of three, his dying father, Henry VI, had made a ward of the pope; and whom, as a young man of twenty, Pope Innocent III had called to be emperor. Within four or five years of this, Frederick was launched on his great career as chief antagonist of all that the popes had been striving for since Hildebrand—the papal control (for protection's sake) of the papally reformed church, its total independence of the lay power, and the subjection of the lay sovereign, in regard to the morality of his rule, to the teaching of the Church, i.e., to the pope as teacher. Crises, all crises, develop character, and these long conflicts had developed a papal mentality vis-à-vis the empire, as surely as they had developed a *mens* in that corps of law-trained counsellors through whom princes were now governing their states. As well as personalities, rival doctrines of law were now in conflict, irreconcilable claims to supremacy, to independence of control, vested interests hostile by tradition. Frederick II, ward of Innocent III, was locked in conflict for a good thirty years with Innocent's three successors, Honorius III, Gregory IX, and Innocent IV. It was the last-named who called the first General Council of Lyons.

To understand the degree of the menace, we need to recall that Frederick was a unique figure, as a man and as a ruler, in all these years; "the world's wonder man," said the contemporary chronicler, Matthew Paris. And we need to say something of the kind of place Sicily was, where Frederick II was born and bred and where he lived for as much of his life as he could, of Sicily the kingdom and Sicily the island of that name. The kingdom then meant the island and all the Italian mainland from Sicily to about 80 miles southeast of Rome on the Mediterranean coast, and to about 130 miles northeast of Rome on the Adriatic. For the best part of two hundred miles the King of Sicily and the pope had a common frontier. Potentially, Sicily was the chief permanent menace to the pope's independence. All this territory, the island certainly and a good part of the southern mainland, had been for centuries, and until about the time of Hildebrand, a part of the Byzantine empire. In the eighth and ninth centuries it had been the object of continual Mohammedan raids, and the Saracens had settled there in great numbers. Then, halfway through the eleventh century, Norman adventurers had gradually wrested the whole from Saracens and Byzantines. Frederick II was, on his mother's side, the descendant of these Normans.

The social effect of this extraordinary history was to produce, in the island of Sicily especially, a culture richly diverse. Here, religiously, were Latin and Greek, Christian and Moslem and Jew; the Levant, the Mediterranean, the north of France; and eastern manners of life as deeply rooted as western, eastern vices and western vices, the culture of Syria and Egypt as of Italy and France. Frederick II grew up all but inevitably only half a western European, it might be thought; and even more orientalised by his own tastes than by the chance of the milieu where he was bred. He was extremely intelligent, interested in the arts, active, virile, ambitious, a strong ruler, utterly unscrupulous, and an accomplished man of pleasure. He was as much at home with Moslems as with Catholics, and lived in a half-Moslem court. Such was the prince on whom the popes chiefly relied, in the years that followed the council of 1215, to lead the great crusade that would reverse the long series of Saracen victories and once more restore Jerusalem to Christian hands.

Left to himself, and no pope interfering, what would Frederick II have done with the crusade? what would he have attempted? To make himself master of the eastern Mediterranean and of Italy, as his father before him had planned? The despotic ruler of a great state? And the Church in his dominions? with no rights, no property but what the state allowed it? the state controlling its whole life? With the papacy left at Rome in full independence?

What actually happened has often been told, and for the most part has best been told by writers whose sympathies are not with the pope.

It was in 1211 that the German princes elected the seventeen-year-old Frederick as "King of the Romans," that is to say, emperor-to-be. Innocent III acquiesced. But he demanded that Frederick, who as King of Sicily was his vassal (a feudal relation, pure and simple), should now make over that kingdom to his infant son: the all-powerful lord of Germany should not simultaneously be the lord of the realm which geography made the chief threat to the pope's independence. This arrangement was ratified by the act called the Pledge of Eger (1213), in which (among other matters) the suzerainty of the Holy See over Sicily was explicitly acknowledged. And Frederick, on the occasion of his receiving the crown of Germany, solemnly took the crusader's vow, before the tomb of Charlemagne at Aachen.

The crusade set on foot by Innocent at the Fourth Lateran Council was a fiasco. Frederick II took no part in it. He now began the most unusual part of his complicated policy, the dissolution of all the royal power that his father and grandfather[1] had built up in Germany, by surrendering to the multitude of ecclesiastical princes, archbishops, bishops, and abbots, all claim to control their temporalities, pledging himself to champion them against any usurpation by the lay princes. This was a preliminary to securing the election of his son, the nominal King of Sicily, as emperor-to-be. A massive violation, indeed, of the pact made with Innocent III. To the pope, Honorius III (1216–27), Frederick explained that the election had been made without his knowledge and that, moreover, the arrangement secured that Germany would co-operate more easily in the next crusade. He also asked that he might now be

[1] The emperors Frederick I (Barbarossa) 1152–90, and Henry VI 1190–97.

crowned emperor by the pope, and when this took place (1220), Frederick renewed his crusader's vow, fixing August 1221 as the date of his departure.

For six years Frederick continued to delay the sailing date, and each time the pope accepted the excuses he made. But in 1227 this pope died, to be succeeded by one of the toughest popes who have ever reigned, a relative of Innocent III who called himself Gregory IX. He immediately began to put pressure on Frederick, who responded by assembling a great army and a fleet of transports at Brindisi. On September 8, 1227, he sailed, but two days later put back into port—the plague had caught his troops, they were dying by the hundred. The pope simply ignored his explanation and excommunicated him for breaking his vow (September 29). Frederick replied by a violent attack on the pope. The Church, he said was a stepmother, not a mother. He would leave for the Holy Land in May next year. To which the pope retorted by renewing the excommunication, with the severe addition that wherever the emperor went an interdict would fall—for as long as Frederick stayed in any place the churches would close, there would be no mass and no sacraments, except baptism and the last rites for the dying. If he insisted on mass being said and was present (Gregory had already rebuked him for doing this), he would be treated as a heretic, and the Sicilians be freed from their allegiance to him.

Frederick organised his partisans in Rome, and soon Gregory IX was a fugitive. On June 28, 1228, the emperor sailed for the East.

There was nothing religious about this expedition, and it was (in one sense) completely successful, a diplomatic triumph. The emperor persuaded the sultan to cede Jerusalem, Bethlehem, and Nazareth and the route from the coast leading thither, with all the villages through which it passed. The Mohammedan inhabitants were to remain the sultan's subjects and have the free exercise of their religion. Also the great mosque of Omar, in the Holy City, was to be theirs and remain in use. Frederick, on the other hand, pledged himself to prevent any attack from the West during the next ten years. And in the church of the Holy Sepulchre the excommunicated emperor crowned himself King of Jerusalem, before an audience of his own soldiers and the Moslems. It was, indeed, wonderful. The Crusade principle, the Christian reconquest of the

Holy Land, had disappeared. The Christian no longer planned to drive out the infidel.

By June 10, 1229, Frederick was back in Sicily. He had been away all but twelve months.

It would be a pleasure now to tell the story of the sixteen years between the hero's return and his excommunication at Lyons, in some detail. But our business is merely to record the stages in his duel with the popes.

What Frederick II wanted to be, it seems agreed, was the Roman emperor of old, but a "Catholic" Roman emperor—claiming that the empire was created divinely, and that he was divinely commissioned to bring about the reign of justice and peace, and also to spread the gospel everywhere. The Church, as an institution wholly self-controlled (existing for the purposes of very much the same divine mission) and the pope as its single supreme ruler, could scarcely find any place in this fantasy. Which is why historians can say that Frederick could not have succeeded and the Church survive, except as a corps ministering and receiving sacraments within the four walls of the basilicas. So long as this man was in power there must be war—unless upon the Holy See there fell the misfortune of a succession of weakling popes, too simple to be able to read the signs of the times.

The emperor returned from the East to find the war already on in his kingdom of Sicily. He managed to drive out the papal army, punished his own rebels with shudderingly cruel executions—we are told of men he had skinned alive. Then he made a peace with the pope in which he conceded almost everything, and was re-instated in the Church—an essential need, if his gains in the Holy Land were to be maintained.

For six years after the treaty of San Germano (July 23, 1230) there was a kind of truce. Frederick in his kingdom of Sicily ruled pretty much as if he were already emperor and pope in one, building up his ideal of a strong central despotism, and in Germany bribing the princes with lavish surrenders of imperial rights; while the pope could barely maintain himself in his own ever turbulent capital, and was quieted (to some extent) by the emperor's exemplary, not to say bloody, repression of heretics, in Italy and in Germany too.

Presently Frederick was ready, and in 1236 he returned from Germany to make himself as truly master of Lombardy as he was of

Sicily. The pope's diplomacy was of no avail, nor the armies of the Lombard cities. At Cortenuova, near Bergamo, the emperor routed them utterly (November 27, 1237), reversing his grandfather's defeat at Legnano of sixty years earlier. To the Romans he announced his victory as a monarch writing to his own capital city. He reminded them, in fact, that Rome was just this, and spoke of celebrating a "triumph" there, in the antique fashion. Yet once again the emperor was to govern the empire from his capital, they were told; the ancient offices were to be revived and the Roman nobles be called to fill them. From Rome the proconsuls, once again, would go forth to govern the provinces, and to "infuse the blood of Romulus." The slender hold of the pope on the city and the surrounding lands was almost the only obstacle to the emperor's dream being realised.

But Gregory IX had already made clear his own conceptions of the relations between pope and emperor—conceptions just as extreme as those of Frederick, and presented with no less assurance that they were divinely willed. So long as he lived there would be no weakening. He listed Frederick's crimes against religion and once again excommunicated him with a personal interdict (March 24, 1239). Frederick had not waited to be attacked. He had already done his best to rouse the cardinals against Gregory, telling them that the pope was no more than a kind of chairman of their college, and appealing from his judgment to theirs. And his diplomats worked to bring into combination against the pope Henry III of England and St. Louis IX of France. All princes ought to unite to protest against a pope who had gone so far beyond the limits of his real powers. And the emperor also suggested to the cardinals that they call a General Council, and he would offer his case for the judgment of all the bishops of the world.

In reply to these manoeuvres the old pope replied in the tones of a very Lear:[2] "A great beast has come out of the sea . . . this scorpion spewing passion from the sting in his tail . . . full of the names of blasphemy . . . raging with the claws of the bear and the mouth of the lion, and the limbs and the likeness of the leopard, opens its mouth to blaspheme the Holy Name . . . behold the head and tail and body of the beast, of this Frederick, this so-called em-

[2] Gregory IX was something like 100 years old, if many historians are correct. It seems more likely that he was only 80.

peror. . . ."[3] Frederick was a heretic for his denial of the pope's authority, for his mockery of the virgin birth, and his declaring that nothing is to be believed that cannot be proved by the natural reason.

Frederick replied like a Father of the Church, pained at the pope's lack of charity—"the pharisee who sits on the plague-stricken seat, anointed with the oil of wickedness." He makes a most dutiful profession of faith and retorts that the pope is a liar. It is he who is the sole cause of the trouble, and the emperor too quoted the Apocalypse: "And a second horse came out fiery-red, whose rider was empowered to take away all peace from the world, bidding men slay one another."[4]

But if England and France held aloof from Frederick's invitation, they did nothing to protect the pope from what his power could do. Moreover all Germany—the ecclesiastical princes with the rest—stood by the emperor. By the summer of 1240 the pope was fairly isolated. But on August 9 he issued a summons to a General Council, to meet at Rome the following Easter. There was only one way for the bishops to come—by sea. Gregory negotiated with the Genoese for transports and protecting galleys. Frederick retorted by an alliance with Pisa, and at the sea fight of La Meloria (May 4, 1241) the Pisan fleet defeated the Genoese and took prisoner two cardinal legates and a hundred bishops en route for the council. It never met, and Frederick, moving ever closer to Rome, was all but prepared for the final assault when, August 21, Gregory IX died. For nearly two years the Holy See was vacant.

Gregory IX left twelve cardinals. Two of these were prisoners, a third, Colonna, had gone over to the emperor. The official who actually ruled Rome, the Senator Matteo Orsini, rounding up Colonna with the rest, locked them all up in the ancient Septizonium with the announcement that none should go forth until they had elected a pope. In this ruin they endured the horrors of a semi-imprisonment for a couple of months, then elected Celestine IV and —a number of them—immediately fled from Rome, as from the plague. Celestine was dead within the fortnight, from the effects of the weeks in the Septizonium. The cardinals refused to meet

[3] *Apocalypse* 13.
[4] Ibid., 6:4. Knox translation.

so long as Frederick held their two brethren captive. Then Louis IX intervened. Frederick thought it wise to release them, and on June 25, 1243, they elected pope the cardinal Sinibaldo Fieschi, a Genoese. He called himself Innocent IV.

This new pope was a man in the early fifties, vigorous, a practiced diplomatist and a born administrator, "the greatest lawyer that ever sat upon the chair of St. Peter."[5] His personal contribution to the strong drink of Gregory IX's ideas about the Pope-State relation, was to make the draught still stronger. God's mandate to the popes to govern men is absolute and universal. The pope is lord of all, in the temporal sphere no less than in the spiritual—the princes who rule the various states are, whether they know this or not, rulers by delegation from him to whom both swords were given.[6] Frederick's attempts to treat with this personage broke down at the outset, for the pope's first condition was the release of the hundred bishops. Nor would he make a peace without the Lombard cities.

In 1244 the negotiations were renewed, and in the midst of them the pope—did he fear a plot to kidnap him? it is not impossible—fled from Italy in disguise, to the city of Lyons on the very frontier of St. Louis' kingdom of France (December 2, 1244). A month later the summons went out for a General Council, to meet here on June 24, 1245, the feast of St. John the Baptist. In an address given in the cathedral of Lyons the pope called on the emperor to appear before the council, if not in person then by proxy, and clear himself.

The acts of this council have not survived. But from two contemporary accounts we know fairly well what happened at the three public sessions of June 28, July 5, and July 17.

The attendance of bishops (140–50) and prelates was notably smaller than at any of the earlier General Councils held in the West —less than half the number who came to the council of 1179, perhaps a third of those at Innocent III's council in 1215. Almost the only topic was the menace of Frederick II.

The emperor had not ignored the pope's summons, or challenge. To Lyons he sent one of his most capable legists, Thaddeus of Suessa. This personage, on the eve of the council (according to one

---

[5] F. W. Maitland, *Moral Personality and Legal Personality*, in *Selected Essays* (1936), p. 228.

[6] The reader will understand that these personal ideas of the medieval popes, whatever their worth, were never part of the universal teaching of the Church.

account of the affair), renewed in his master's name all the promises made so many times before, but refused the guarantees which the pope had demanded.

The council opened with an address by the pope on the five wounds of the Church. These were the sinful lives of the clergy (high and low), the recapture of Jerusalem by the Saracens, the Greek threat to that pitiful mockery the Latin empire set up at Constantinople these forty years now, the devastation of the Tartars in Hungary, and Frederick's persecution of religion.

As to Frederick, the pope recapitulated the whole long story of his cruelty and treachery, and put the case for his deposition. It was at the second session that Thaddeus made his defence, putting the best colour he could on the undoubted facts, and using all his skill on the points of law. Very notably he impressed the bishops by his argument that no man should be condemned as a heretic who had not been personally heard. Who else but the accused could really know his own innermost heart and mind? And so a delay was allowed for Frederick to put in an appearance—he was, at this time, at Verona, the key city which, from the Italian side, commanded the main route to Germany. Could the emperor have made the necessary arrangements and arrived at Lyons within the nine days allowed him? And if he had done so, would his known gifts of personality and oratorical skill have prevailed? Conjecture, reveries of wishful thinking, cannot fill the gaps in our knowledge.

It is said, by Matthew Paris, that the bishops were disturbed by the argument about condemning a man for heresy in his absence. And at the third and final session, on July 17, there was no general debate on the case. The pope had spent the interval between the sessions in personally interviewing the bishops, asking each whether he thought the case against Frederick had been proved. The emperor found none to defend him—not a single bishop had come from Germany,[7] by Frederick's own choice. At the third session his advocate had not a second opportunity to reply on the facts. All he could do was to raise the question whether this assembly was truly a General Council. Were there enough bishops present to make it such? The protest merely brought from Innocent the answer that Thaddeus must have expected—who but Frederick had hindered

[7] From the whole empire only Liège and Prague had come. Few Italians were present. The majority were from France and Spain.

the attendance of the bishops of Germany and Italy? And the pope proceeded to the inevitable sentence—excommunication and deposition.[7a]

Supposing the General Council had authority to pass such a sentence, was Frederick guilty of the crimes alleged? especially of the really fatal crime, that against the Faith? His own manifesto, a protest against the sentence and a defiance, can leave no doubt that the council had read his character and intentions truly. The emperor did not, by any means, straightway wither up and die. But the solemn act of the General Council was the beginning of the end, of himself and the whole great house of Hohenstaufen. Five years of bloody war followed, with the usual alternations of unexpected defeats and unexpected victories. But when Frederick II died, December 13, 1250, his cause was lost and the pope on the way to become (should he choose) King of Sicily as well as pope—a story that must be sought in the bitterly contested pages of Italian church history. Just four years after Frederick, Innocent IV too died.

There remain for consideration the twenty-two canons enacted by Innocent at Lyons, "the sacred universal council assenting." For once the laws are not concerned with the moral state of Christendom. What more could have been added to the seventy canons of the Fourth Lateran, barely thirty years old? Innocent IV is the jurist par excellence. To the new Canon Law—i.e., the great code promulgated by his predecessor Gregory IX in 1234, the Five Books of the Decretals [of the Popes]—he stands in the same relation as does Alexander III to the work of Gratian. Innocent was already a cardinal when this great act of Gregory's was accomplished,[8] but he somewhere found the time to write the first great commentary on it.[9] And when, forty years after his death, another papal legist, Boniface VIII, added a sixth book to the work, much of this was made up of Innocent IV's decisions. Among his legal works that then passed into the body of the Canon Law are these canons of 1245, almost wholly taken up with the details of judicial procedure, and no doubt a definite landmark in the history of church law.

For one who is not a lawyer to attempt to make clear to readers

[7a] Barry, no. 77, prints a translation of the bull.

[8] The actual author of the compilation was the Dominican canonist, St. Raymund of Peñaforte.

[9] *Apparatus in libros quinque decretalium.*

who are not lawyers the importance of a series of technical legal reforms, would be to waste their time and make himself ridiculous. But certain things may be said about these twenty-two canons, nevertheless. One explains the meaning of the technical term *quidam alii* ("certain others") in certain papal rescripts. There is the useful rule that suits are to be dealt with by professional lawyers —tried only in places where there is an adequate supply of legal talent. Only to dignitaries must the important office of Judge Delegate of the Apostolic See be committed. Judges against whom one of the parties to the suit raises an objection are given powers to act, in the case that the arbitrators chosen to judge the objection fail to act. Judges delivering an unjust sentence are, by the fact, suspended from office, and must make good the damage caused. They must not, while suspended, say mass, under pain of a censure from which only the pope can absolve them. Plaintiffs who fail to appear in court are to pay the costs of the suit. Excommunications are to be set down in writing, with the reason, and a copy given to the person affected. No judge is to excommunicate those who hold intercourse with an excommunicated person, except by process here provided. Otherwise the excommunication does not bind, and the judge is liable to a penalty. Bishops are not affected by suspensions or interdicts, unless the decree makes special mention of bishops. In appeals to the Holy See in suits about elections to benefices or provisions, the parties must set off for the Curia within one month from the date of the appeal. If within twenty days of the arrival of one party the other has not arrived, the case will be heard without him. "It is our ardent desire to lessen litigation," says the pope, in the manner of all good lawyers, and he proceeds to describe how appeals to his own supreme tribunal must be set in motion.

There is a canon about elections, which decides that conditional votes are invalid, and in the count are to be disregarded. And there is a canon about homicide—about the practice of hiring murderers to get rid of an enemy. "Prominent persons," says the canon, "have been reduced through fear of this danger, to pay money to the chief of the gang . . . not without detriment to their Christian dignity." So any prince or prelate, or indeed anyone at all, who makes such an arrangement with assassins, incurs by the fact excommunication, and deposition from his office—whether the murder takes place or not. Should it ever be established, in later years, that a man made such a pact, no new sentence of excommunication or deposition is needed in order to deprive him. The present suffices.

Finally the council enacted a lengthy decree about the need to deliver the Holy Land from the Saracens, calling for prayers, for volunteers, offering spiritual privileges, granting protection to the property of the crusader, and levying new taxes on all clerical incomes, 5 per cent per annum for three years. "We and our brethren the cardinals of the Holy Roman Church, will pay one tenth of our revenues." Deliberate tax-dodgers, those who make a fraudulent return of their income, are excommunicated. There are clauses releasing crusaders from paying the interest on money debts, and commands to creditors to release them from their oaths to pay the interest, and stringent excommunications of Christians who supply the Saracens with munitions of war, or give them advice and aid of any kind to the detriment of the crusade. If such are taken prisoner, all their possessions become the property of their captor, and they themselves become his slaves. For four years all trade with the Saracen lands is to cease, so that ships may be gathered for the expedition and the Saracens (it is hoped) be reduced to beggary meanwhile.

14. *The Second General Council of Lyons, 1274*

This council has the distinction that, in its inception, and in all that directed its activity, it was the work of a pope who was a saint—Tebaldo Visconti, known in the calendar of the Church as the Blessed Gregory X.[1] It might be said that, as with many another saint, his appearance in history is, to the experienced observer, a first indication of things seriously wrong and urgently needing correction, for the rôle of the saints in the Church has been very much that of the prophets in the older dispensation.

The quarter of a century since the disappearance of Frederick II had, indeed, seen a marked decline in the detachment of the popes from the things of this world. Not that Innocent IV, or any of his three next successors (1254–68), were what is called bad men—far from it. But they were increasingly caught up with the details of what we may term the international situation—with the political state of Italy, and above all with the affairs of the kingdom of Sicily which had now become their personal responsibility. The contest with Frederick and his sons, Conrad IV and King Manfred, involved the popes in unheard-of expenses. Nothing, then as now, so rapidly exhausts the treasury as a few good years of war, of just war no less than unjust. And from the church universal, which the popes, for the first time, now endeavoured to tax systematically and regularly, there arose a general clamour of discontent and anger; from England and from France especially, where the king, St. Louis IX (1226–70), while protecting the pope from the emperor's armies, most carefully gave the papal policy in these years not a shred of encouragement. Not even personal contact with the able Pope Innocent could move him to become an active ally; and to invita-

[1] Beatified by Benedict XIV (1740–58).

tions that his brother, Charles of Anjou, should accept from the pope the kingdom of Sicily, he remained resolutely deaf for nearly twenty years.

My kingdom is not of this world. Never had this truth been so evident, as when these popes had to face, as sovereignly responsible, the task—a layman's task and speciality—of ending the long anarchy in Sicily. "There is no supernatural way of washing a floor"—nor of finance, nor logistics. By the time Clement IV died, in 1268, the anarchy, after eighteen years and sundry campaigns, had not been reduced, and the strong man—Charles of Anjou—called in, somewhat fatuously, to be the tool of the popes was threatening to become their master.[2] At this crisis, following on the layman's destruction of the last Hohenstaufen,[3] the pope died,[4] and for three years the cardinals left the Holy See vacant. In these years the only man strong enough to control Charles also died—St. Louis (July 4, 1270). The prospect before the newly elected Gregory X[5] was grim indeed.

The new pope, a man of sixty—a great age in the thirteenth century—had never been a cardinal, nor a high official of the Curia Romana. At the moment when the cardinals chose him he was away in Syria, where for some years he had been aiding the crusade. His mind was henceforth wholly taken up with the menace from the East. The Italian question—as a matter of profit to the Holy See— did not interest him in the least. His own resolve, in such matters, was to take the papacy out of politics. That he feared Charles is unlikely, but he was aware of his strength and of the danger the king was, danger to the independent action of the Holy See, and to the pope's hopes for the East. For while Gregory X returned to Italy convinced that unless Latin and Greek were reunited there was no hope for the East, Charles now dreamt of little but a military conquest of the Greeks, a repetition of the crime of 1204, to end with himself ruling from Constantinople a new Mediterranean empire.

[2] In 1263 Charles was named King of Sicily by the suzerain, Pope Urban IV, St. Louis at last consenting, after two years of negotiations. It was only in 1266 that he was in a position to begin the war to drive out King Manfred. By 1270 Charles, a man in his early forties, was to all intents the master of Italy.
[3] Battle of Tagliacozzo, October 29, 1267.
[4] November 29, 1268.
[5] Elected September 1, 1271; consecrated and crowned March 27, 1272.

It was now just over two hundred years since the legates of Pope Leo IX had taken it upon themselves to excommunicate the patriarch of Constantinople, Michael Cerularius, in his cathedral of St. Sophia (1054)—an abrupt termination of a dispute that really concerned no one but that high personage and the pope. Without any further action from Rome, in a curiously indeterminate (and yet, perhaps, inevitable) way, the whole body of the eastern sees had then silently slipped away from their ancient allegiance. The real cause was that the chronic restiveness of the Greeks towards the Roman primacy—to the presence of which the history of the General Councils hitherto is witness—had now worked out to its inevitable end. The great flare-up preceding the council of 869-70 had provided future generations with an argued "case" against the popes, and with a hero, Photius. For the first time it had become settled belief, with the Greeks, that the Latins were heretics—their belief that the Holy Ghost proceeds from the Father and the Son was an untraditional innovation, and by adding the words "and from the Son" (*Filioque*) to the creed they had publicly announced their unorthodox doctrine about the Trinity. And every particular in which Latin customs and rites differed from the Greek were additional evidence that they had wandered from the primitive truth. Upon this situation, within fifty years, there had come the first of the crusades, and troubles of another kind altogether. The Latin world and the Greek were, from now on, in continuous close contact—the new Latin world, fruit of a social, political, and military renaissance. And the contact, the entry of the Latins into the internal political life of the factions at Constantinople, had intensified the division. So that, apart from the Latin charges, and the Greek countercharges, of treachery, of treaties not kept, of swindling in money matters, there was always the chance of a Latin party active in the succeeding *coups d'état* at Constantinople, and correspondingly intensified hatred from the mass of the Greek population. When, in 1204, the Fourth Crusade became the instrument by which the Latin state Venice which, above all others, had been for centuries in close contact with the Greeks, as their chronic danger, achieved the conquest of the city, the overthrow of the empire, and the installation of a Latin prince as emperor—once this had happened, it might have been judged that never again, unless by a miracle, would the Greeks even want to hear mention of the authority of the Bishop of Rome and his church.

That Innocent III, his dismay and anger at the crime once cooled down, could reconcile himself to the *fait accompli,* and crown it by the installation of a Latin bishop as patriarch, and by the creation of Latin sees, and by treating this as a reunion of the churches—that this did not help matters is certain. His more realistic namesake, the fourth Innocent, would have reversed this policy had his hands been free of other problems. He was willing to see the Greek emperor once more ruling in the capital and the Greek patriarch and, so long as the Greeks ceased to stigmatise as heresy the Latin way of setting out the mysterious doctrine of the Trinity, willing to put up with the Greek refusal to add *Filioque* to the creed. He even spoke of a General Council to regulate affairs, a council that should meet in the East, like the first eight councils whose history we have been reviewing. But Innocent died in the same year as the emperor John III with whom he had been negotiating.

And now there came on the scene in his place the capable Michael VIII, who in 1261 retook the great city. Henceforth the Latin was an emperor *in partibus,* as historians have noted. But Michael did all he could to keep on good terms with the pope, and to renew the negotiations. If the West felt it must hold Constantinople or give up its hope of regaining the Holy Land, the realist emperor was no less clear that without a permanent understanding with Rome his empire must disappear before the Mohammedan assaults. So, from the beginning, Michael VIII was ready for any concession that the popes demanded—especially once the sinister figure of Charles of Anjou began to dominate the Italian scene. And Michael—whose religious, or theological, interests were all but nil—was almost the only person of importance in his empire who did not heartily hate Rome and all that it stood for. The emperor persevered nevertheless, and his joy may be imagined when, after the long vacancy of the Holy See (whose other side was the opportunity of opportunities offered Charles of Anjou), the newly elected Gregory X, even before he had returned to Rome, sent ambassadors proposing the reunion of the Greek churches.

The first difficulty the pope had to face came from the group of Frenchmen among the cardinals.[6] The pope proposed to summon a General Council, and to send Michael VIII an invitation to at-

[6] Fruit of the pontificates of Gregory X's two French predecessors, Urban IV (1261–64) and Clement IV (1265–68).

tend. To this the French cardinals objected, no doubt in the interests of Charles. This delayed the pope's embassy for five months. It was the spring of 1273 before the emperor's enthusiastic acceptance reached Rome. Michael already wrote as though the reunion were accomplished; he was the pope's "most obedient son," and the pope was "sovereign bishop of the whole church, Peter's successor."

With Gregory's immediate predecessor, Clement IV, the emperor had already gone almost as far as this, in 1267. That pope, a saintly man if not a saint, who all his life had been a lawyer and a judge, had replied very tersely to the compliments, stating the terms of reunion as starkly as in an ultimatum, demanding "unconditional surrender" indeed. Only when he had received from the Greeks—the emperor, the bishops, and the faithful generally—an explicit acceptance of the primacy of the Roman see, and of the whole body of its teaching, would he summon a General Council. And what Clement IV asked he set forth in the form of a creed. Before, this plain-speaking Michael had to explain that the situation was a little complicated. But there had been no aggravation of the Roman attitude, when Clement suddenly died in 1268.

The new pope who had now, to the dismay of some of the cardinals, taken the initiative was then well aware of the delicate situation. In replying to the emperor he proposed, not to send legates to Constantinople in the spirit of Clement IV's letter, but that Michael should send envoys to the coming General Council, where the related matters of reunion and a military alliance against the Saracens could be discussed. It would simplify Michael's problem if he could present the Greeks with the double *fait accompli* of an alliance with the West (instead of the papal alliance with their dangerous enemy Charles) and their own acceptance by Rome as Catholics no less dear than the Angevin. Michael would meanwhile put his signature to the creed prepared by Pope Clement. And so it was done.

As the seat of the council the pope chose Lyons, as being a city beyond the influence—almost certainly malevolent—of Charles, and after some very delicate moves he secured from Charles a guarantee that he would not molest the Greek envoys as they passed through Italy.

The plight of the Christian East was not the sole anxiety of Gregory X. This pope is, in all things, first and foremost a priest and a shepherd of souls, and grieved (as his own words show) at the miserable degradation of Christian life throughout the West. The council, in his plan, is to inaugurate a real restoration of religious fervour. And here, in 1274, we have what is lacking for all the earlier General Councils held in the West, namely, documents to show the way the pope prepared for the council.[7] There was to be no merely mechanical repetition, word for word, of laws already enacted. But from various parts of Christendom reports were sought by the pope on abuses calling for correction, and the writers were asked to suggest how these should be remedied. Moreover, once the bishops had assembled, each of them was free to petition for new remedial laws. Many of these petitions still survive in the archives of the Vatican, and we also possess the reports from the bishop of Olmuč and from the master-general of the Dominicans, Humbert of Romans.

The Second General Council of Lyons, summoned in April 1273, opened on May 7, 1274, with five hundred or so bishops present[8]—the largest number since the Second Lateran Council of 1139—and some seventy lesser prelates, abbots, procurators of chapters, and so forth.[9] It opened with an address by the pope, dealing with the work to be done: the problem of the Holy Land, the reunion of the Greeks and, of no less importance, the general reformation of morals, especially in the lives of the clergy and of the bishops. In those bygone centuries the popes had all too little say in the actual selection of bishops. The kings and princes no longer (at least openly) named whom they would. But the popes, having secured the restoration of the rights to free election by the cathedral chapters, had been able to do little more than lay down conditions which the elect must fulfil on pain of his election being void, and to make laws with stiff penalties about episcopal sins, and to make an example of what wicked prelates came before them for

[7] For all this, and what follows, see the invaluable study by Stephan Kuttner, *Conciliar Law in the Making*, in *Miscellanea Pio Paschini*, Rome, 1949, pp. 39–81.

[8] So all the chroniclers. From the *acta*, and contemporary authors, we have details of no more than 126 "prelates and lords": 44 from Italy, 26 from Germany and the north, 21 from France, 19 Latins from Syria and the East, 8 from Spain, and as many from England.

[9] The pope, seemingly, had decided that not every monastery or chapter was to send a representative.

judgment.[10] Gregory X now said bluntly that it was bishops who were bringing the Church to ruin.[11] It was, he said, a matter of great surprise that they did not amend, and he gave them warning that he was about to take severe action in the matter of their reformation.

The Greek delegation was long delayed, and the council had been at work some six weeks by the time it arrived, June 24, 1274. In the name of the emperor, and with letters of procuration from fifty metropolitans and another five hundred bishops, there came the patriarch of Constantinople, Germanus, the Archbishop of Nicaea, Theophanos, and the chancellor, with two high officers of the court. And in the fourth session of the council, July 6, the reunion was accomplished.[12] Two memorials of this great day call for some quotations. First of all, the dogmatic constitution on the *Filioque* question, which ultimately was published as the first canon of the council, *Fideli ac devota*, and then the profession of faith made in the name of Michael VIII.

The definition of faith is as follows: "We firmly profess that the Holy Ghost proceeds eternally from the Father and the Son, not as from two principles but as from one principle, not as by two spirations but as by a single spiration. This is what the holy Roman Church, the mother and teacher of all the faithful has hitherto professed, preached and taught, this is what it holds, preaches, professes and teaches. This is truly what the unchanging judgment of the orthodox Fathers and Doctors, the Latins and the Greeks equally, holds. But since there are some men who through ignorance of the aforesaid unbreakable truth have fallen into various errors, We, desiring to close the road to errors of this sort, with the sacred Council assenting, condemn and reprobate all those who presume to deny that the Holy Ghost eternally proceeds from the Father and the Son, or who rashly dare to assert that the Holy Ghost

[10] Three bishops were deposed for evil lives in this very council.
[11] *Quod praelati faciebant ruere totum mundum.*
[12] Despite the demonstration of that prince of *érudits*, Dr. Heinrich Finke, made as far back as 1891, all who have written about the council of 1274—including the present writer—have repeated the centuries-old statement that the definition of faith was passed by the council before the Greeks arrived. My own enlightenment is due to Professor Kuttner's study, already referred to, who notes as a solitary exception in following Finke, the Dominican, Fr. H. J. Schroeder, so often referred to in these notes.

proceeds from the Father and the Son as from two principles and not from one [principle]."[13]

The emperor's profession of faith—it is that sent to him by Clement IV, as has been told—is too long to quote in full. The passages here translated are those with a direct bearing on the points in controversy between Latins and Greeks.

As to the doctrine of purgatory:

"But those who have died in a state of charity, truly repentant [for their sins] but before they have brought forth fruit worthy of repentance, their souls are purified after death by cleansing pains.[14] The petitions of the living, the sacrifices of Masses [for example], prayers, almsdeeds and other pious services, such as the faithful are accustomed to do for one another according to the established custom of the Church, [these] are profitable to them, [i.e., the dead persons mentioned] for the lifting of these pains."[15]

The sacrament of the Holy Eucharist:

"The same Roman church makes use of unleavened bread in the sacrament of the Eucharist, holding and teaching that, in the very sacrament there is truly transubstantiated the bread into the body of Jesus Christ our Lord, and the wine into His blood."[16]

Marriage:

"As to marriage it holds, that . . . when a lawful marriage has been dissolved by the death of one of the spouses, second, and third, and even further successive marriages are lawful, provided there is no canonical impediment from some other cause."[17]

The supreme authority of the see of Rome:

"This same holy Roman church itself, has over the whole Catholic Church the supreme and full primacy and sovereign authority;

[13] Denzinger, no. 460.
[14] *Poenis purgatoriis seu catharteriis.*
[15] Denzinger, no. 464.
[16] Ibid., no. 465.
[17] Ibid., no. 465.

which, it humbly and truthfully recalls to mind, [the Roman church] received from the Lord himself, with all fullness of power, through blessed Peter, the chief and the head of the Apostles, of whom the Bishop of Rome is the successor. And as before all else that church is bound to protect the true belief, so it is that whenever disputes arise about the faith they must be decided by the judgment of that church.[18] To which church any person troubled by any matter that belongs to the ecclesiastical courts, can make appeal, and have recourse in all cases that belong to the Church's supervision; and to this same [Roman] church, all the other churches are subject,[19] and their bishops owe to it obedience and reverence. The fullness of its authority is so constituted that it allows the other churches a part in these cares,[20] many of which churches, and especially the Patriarchal churches, the Roman church honours with divers privileges, its own special rights always respected, especially in what relates to General Councils and certain other matters."[21]

Among the thirty disciplinary canons of this council we may perhaps notice, first, a series of seven laws about elections of bishops and abbots. They are evidence of weaknesses inherent in the elective system—disputes as to the validity of the election once it is made are chronic and the lawsuits endless. So, appeals against elections (or provisions) to churches are to be made in writing, and to be countersigned by witnesses who swear they believe the objections are true and that they can prove this: penalties are provided for those who fail to make good their charges. The elect must await confirmation before taking up his office. Voters who knowingly vote for one who is unworthy sin mortally, and are liable to severe punishment. No voter is allowed to appeal against the one for whom he has voted—certain special cases apart. Where a double election has been made no objection will be allowed, for the future, against the majority on the score of lack of zeal, of worth, or of authority,

[18] The two first sentences of this quotation appear, as the testimony of this council, in the Vatican Council's constitution defining the infallibility of the pope's *ex cathedra* decisions (1870).
[19] In our more usual phraseology, seven hundred years later, "To this same Roman see, all the other sees are subject."
[20] *Ad sollicitudinis partem admittit.* The second word recalls St. Paul (II Corinthians 11:28): ". . . my daily pressing anxiety, the care of all the churches"; where the Latin Bible has *sollicitudo*, the English has "care."
[21] Ibid., no. 466.

where the majority numbers two thirds of the voters. Finally, to protect the successful against the malice of the disappointed, it is laid down that those who revenge themselves on electors for not supporting them by pillaging the electors' property or that of the electors' relatives, or who molest the electors or their families are by the very fact excommunicated.

Bishops who break the existing law about demanding money from the parishes where they make the canonical visitation, and who, within a month, have not given back twice the amount received, are forbidden to enter any church until this restitution is made, i.e., they cannot confer sacraments nor receive them, may not say mass nor hear mass; and this even though the money was the free gift of the parish.

Whoever, unauthorised, takes upon himself to administer the properties of a vacant see or abbey is *ipso facto* excommunicated—and so are the clergy or monks who abet him or connive at this usurpation. And prelates who, as the price of protection, hand over properties to some lay lord, retaining merely a right of use, are suspended from their office for three years, the pacts are null, even though confirmed with an oath, and the lay lord who does not restore the property is excommunicated.

The laws against usurers have not been sufficiently enforced. To make it easier to enforce them, no ruler is henceforth to allow usurers to come into his territory and settle there. All foreigners already practicing usury are to be expelled. As to the usurer, the penalties are increased. Not even though his will orders restitution to be made, is he to be given Christian burial until the restoration has actually been made. "All religious and others," who, ignoring this law, give usurers Christian burial now incur all the penalties enacted against the usurer. Wills of usurers that do not contain instructions about restitution have no legal value.

Lawyers who abuse their profession at the expense of their clients, are another subject of this council's legislation. "It seems to us," says the canon, "that it is most urgently necessary to correct the needless dragging out of lawsuits." All ecclesiastical advocates must therefore for the future take an oath every year that they will serve their client to the best of their powers, and that if they come to find out that his cause is not just they will immediately withdraw from the case. No advocate is to take more than the sum of

£20 (Tours reckoning) for his services. Anything accepted in excess of this he is bound to restore, and a breach of this law will be punished by three years' suspension from office.

The violence with which the faithful laity could react, in these ages of faith, against their spiritual fathers is a perpetual source of astonishment. To be, if not a bishop, then a bishop's official called for courage of every kind. We have here a canon enacting that absolutions from such penalties as excommunication and interdict which have been obtained by threats are null, and that those who brought the threats to bear on the official are excommunicated too. Also, those who, being excommunicated—"kings, princes, nobles, magistrates or their ministers," or indeed any excommunicated persons—instruct their servants to capture or kill either the judge who gave the sentence, or those who are observing the sentence and refusing to communicate with the man excommunicated—all such instigators of violence incur *ipso facto* a second excommunication.

There were three questions especially which provoked opposition and plain speaking in this council; the pope's proposal to finance the coming crusade by a 10 per cent tax for six years on all clerical incomes; the disputes between the bishops and the new religious orders called Friars; the new rules about how the pope should be elected. The first of these critical subjects the pope dealt with very diplomatically. He talked it over with the individual bishops, much as Innocent IV had discussed the deposition of the emperor thirty years earlier, and so avoided the risk of a storm in any public session.

With regard to the Friars, the pope showed himself the strong champion of the principle they represented, and of the privileges lavished on them by his predecessors. "What great services the Dominicans and the Franciscans have rendered the Church is too well known for them to need any defence," he is reported as saying. The complaints amounted to this, that the Friars were displacing the parochial clergy as the ministers of salvation to the ordinary man—Catholics were attracted away from their parish churches to the sermons in the churches of the new orders. The monks, for the most part, had settled in the deep countryside, as far away from towns as they could contrive. The presence of these new monasteries in the heart of a great city was a fascinating novelty. Also a novelty was the fact that in the Friars the ordinary Catholic had his first experience, as often as not, of a really trained preacher and director. The matter of alms and gifts now flowing towards the un-endowed Friars also played its part in the controversy. And the bishops complained that, by reason of the pope's exempting them from episcopal supervision, the Friars and their clients were beginning to be a church within the church. Also, it was becoming a kind of fashion for pious men to found new orders of Friars. The law of the General Council of 1215 forbidding the foundation of new religious orders had been generally ignored.

The canon now enacted justifies many of the bishops' complaints. The way in which new orders—not always authorised—had sprung up is described in pitiless language, principally orders who live on charity, on the alms they personally solicit. All orders founded since 1215 and not as yet approved by the Holy See are now forthwith abolished. Those founded since then, and approved by the Holy See, and which by their rule are dependent for their living on the alms of the public are provided for as follows: the professed members may continue to live together, but no new members are to be received and professed, nor may they accept any new foundations, nor sell what they already hold—these properties the Holy See reserves to itself to dispose of ultimately, either for the poor or some other pious uses. Members of these orders are forbidden absolutely to preach to the faithful, to hear their confessions, or to bury them. Then comes the explicit exception of the Dominicans[22] and Franciscans from this rule, with the encomium mentioned. As to the Carmelites and the Austin Friars, "we permit them to continue as they are till we ordain otherwise; for it is our intention to provide for these as well as for the others (including the non-mendicants) such measures as we deem expedient . . ." Gregory X was only at the beginning of his schemes of reform.[23]

The most striking of Gregory X's innovations was to institute, for papal elections, the régime familiar to all of us as the conclave—the rule by which the electors are locked up, separated from all contact with others, save for their servants, until they have chosen a pope. This is the purpose of the second, famous canon of this

---

[22] It is of interest that within two years of this the very pope was a Dominican, Innocent V.

[23] It was Boniface VIII who finally "stabilised" the Carmelites and the Austin Friars, in 1296.

council, *Ubi periculum*. Its opening words do not spare the cardinals—still alive—who lately had kept the Holy See vacant for nearly three years. In the severity of the discipline now imposed we may see reflected the natural indignation of a good man at this scandal. That the pope now proceeding to this reform had himself never been a cardinal was, no doubt, something of an aggravating circumstance to the cardinals, who steadily opposed his proposal. In this they had the support of many of the bishops.

Reason itself, says the pope, in the opening words of the canon, demands that we do something to provide a remedy for the greatest danger of all, now that we are busy with reforms. How teeming with dangers a prolonged vacancy is in the Roman see, the remembrance of what lately happened is witness. Therefore, in addition to what Pope Alexander III decreed, we now lay down as follows, with the assent of the holy council. The cardinals present in the town where the pope happens to die shall wait ten days (and no more) for the absent cardinals to come, and then, whether the rest have come or not, they shall assemble in the residence of the deceased pope, each with a single servant, clerical or lay. There in a single locked-up chamber (*in unum conclave*), they shall all dwell together. This place shall be so enclosed on all sides that no one can either enter it or leave it. No one is to have access to the cardinals, nor any means of secretly speaking to them, nor of sending in any written message. Whoever does anything in violation of these rules is, by the fact, excommunicated. If, which God forbid, the cardinals have not within three days chosen a pope, then for the next five days they are only to have a single course at luncheon and at supper. After these five days they are only to be served bread, wine and water. During the time the Holy See is vacant the cardinals are not entitled to any salary from the papal exchequer, nor any revenue from any other church source. And so the careful regulation goes on, with this command to the lord of the city where the conclave is set up, viz., to take full authority to see that these regulations are carried out. All pacts made between the cardinals are null and void, even though they have been confirmed with an oath. And in all cities, as soon as the news of the pope's death is known, and solemn masses have been sung for his soul, there are to be daily services for the blessing of God on the cardinals in the conclave, and solemn fasts.

The final session of the council took place on July 17. The pope said regretfully that there had not been the time to deal as fully with the reforms as he had hoped, but that he would see to this himself in some new constitutions. But no more than the crusade he planned were these ideas realised, for on his way back to Rome Gregory X died at Arezzo, January 10, 1276.

15. *The General Council of Vienne, 1311–12*

The legend dies hard of "the Middle Ages" as the golden age of the Christian faith, the time when popes gave the law to a lovingly acquiescent Christendom. This is to neglect such facts as that in one year out of two, of the two hundred years that followed the accession of Gregory VII—the High Middle Ages as the convention goes—the divine papal authority was fighting for its life with the Catholic princes. As many as four times in eighty years, during this period, the Holy See lay vacant for two and three years at a time, and the popes were nowhere less safe than in Rome, as the witness of their tombs in half a dozen Italian cities testifies to the tourist, in Viterbo, Orvieto, Arezzo, Perugia, and the rest. Never were there wanting, to threaten their freedom, not only warriors of the type of Barbarossa, but such stark and dangerous political princes as Barbarossa's son, the emperor Henry VI (1190–97), and the hard-faced brother of St. Louis IX, Charles of Anjou, King of Sicily (1265–85). In such contests with ruthlessness itself, it behoved the ecclesiastic to look constantly to what Monsieur Maritain has called "the purification of the means." Patriotism, so to speak, was not enough and the one hundred per cent righteousness of the cause. Woe to the pope who slipped! He inevitably contracted something of the enemy's coldheartedness. Such champions of the freedom of religion as Pope Innocent IV and Pope Boniface VIII were by no means *bon papa* all the twenty-four hours of every day. And the thirteenth, "greatest of centuries" in so many respects, ran out in the furious contest between the last-named pope and the most dangerous of all the medieval kings, the grim Philip IV of France (1285–1314), Philippe le Bel to his contemporaries, and the great mystery man of the Middle Ages still to the historians—a contest that culminated in a long blackmail of Boniface VIII's successor, the unfortunate, cancer-ridden French pope, Clement V. This is the setting of the fifteenth General Council, the Council of Vienne.

There is no council about whose history there is more obscurity than this Council of Vienne, summoned by Clement V under pressure from the King of France, in order to bring about the destruction of a great religious order. This is a pretty dreadful indictment —presuming that the order was not guilty of the crimes with which it was charged; and it seems generally agreed that it was innocent. And the story is the more horrible if it be true that, to wring from the pope a consent to the destruction of the Knights Templars, the King of France blackmailed him, holding over the pope the threat to start a campaign for the posthumous trial, for various alleged crimes, of his predecessor Boniface VIII. One of the crimes alleged was the manoeuvring by which Boniface became pope—or as the king would say, pseudo-pope. If Boniface had never been pope, what of the lawfulness of Clement's own election?

And why was the King of France so set on the condemnation of the dead Boniface? It was partly a question of the royal prestige— the king, as might be said nowadays, must not lose face—and partly a question of the binding force of various declarations of Boniface about certain public acts of the king. These were declarations of principle that condemned, in effect, the principles on which the king was reorganising the government of France. Were the condemnations valid? If so they still bound the king, i.e., in the eyes of those Catholics for whom the pope's sentences mattered, these acts of the king had no force.

Of the various causes of friction which, from before the election of Boniface VIII (1294–1303), had disturbed the relations of the king and the Holy See, two may be mentioned: disputes between royal officials and bishops over the frontier between their jurisdictions, and the claim of the king to tax the property of the Church as he chose. These troubles began around the years 1289–90. Boniface was elected in the last days of 1294. England and France being at war, both kings, desperate for money, plundered the Church revenues. There came a strong, general prohibition from Boniface to the clergy, in 1296, to pay these taxes,[1] and soon retaliation from

---

[1] This bull, *Clericis Laicos*, is printed in translation by Barry, no. 80A.

Philip IV, in the shape of protest at Rome, and intrigues with the discontented factions there—the Colonna cardinals, the little group of Franciscans known as the "Spirituals," and all the Apocalyptic-minded generally who were daily expecting the end of the world and their own triumphant reign over their fellow men, Catholic fanatics for whom Boniface was no pope, but rather Antichrist.

The French were successful in bringing the pope to his knees, for a time. Then, about the year 1300, weary of being "an obliging agent for the schemes of Philip the Fair,"[2] the pope in Boniface triumphed over the politician. The king's recent violation of all law in the arrest and trial of one of the French bishops, without any reference to the pope, moved him to renew his stand against the movement to make religion subservient to the state. In a series of private letters he seriously warned the king that what he was doing was mortally sinful, and that to continue was to risk the salvation of his soul. The pope asked that the bishop should be released, and sent to Rome, and he suspended all the privileges granted to the king allowing him to tax the Church. Moreover he summoned a council of all the bishops of France, to meet in Rome in November 1302. The king's reply was to organise the nation against the pope by a great propaganda campaign. This culminated in a national council—a parliament of an unprecedented kind—of clergy, nobles, and plebeians at Notre Dame, Paris, in April 1302. The king's case was put, and strong speeches made by his ministers about the pope's tyranny and usurpations, and how (thanks to the pope) true religion was in danger. Finally it was decided to send a national protest to the cardinals, setting down all the charges against the pope; "he who at this moment occupies the seat of government in the Church" is how they described him; and the word Antichrist was used.

Three months packed with drama followed. When the delegates from Paris presented to Boniface the letters from the clergy, in which they begged him to cancel the council, and spoke of the king's anger and the national feeling, the pope warned them that Philip was the most hated man in Europe, and that he was facing disaster. The king was, at this moment, at war with the communes of Flanders. Only thirteen days after that audience the French were

[2] *Un exécuteur complaisant des calculs de Philippe le Bel*—Digard's phrase, *Philippe le Bel et le Saint-Siège* (1936), I, 345.

unexpectedly routed, with great slaughter, at the Battle of the Golden Spurs,[3] and the three counsellors of the king whom the pope had denounced by name were among the slain. Whereupon a great change on Philip's part, permissions to the bishops to go to Rome for the council and an embassy to represent himself. There was not, at the council, any "trial" of Philip the Fair, nor sentence against him. All that happened, publicly, was the issue of a reasoned declaration about the pope's authority to correct what is morally wrong in a ruler's conduct as ruler. This is the famous bull called *Unam Sanctam* (1302).[4] Privately, the pope again warned the king, and sent him some kind of ultimatum to mend his ways.

In reply the king planned to arrest the pope and bring him before a council; and to prepare public opinion for this he organised a nation-wide propaganda, depicting Boniface as a heretic, an idolater, a man who worshipped the devil, and a man of evil life, whom the cardinals and bishops ought to bring to trial. There were, once again, great public meetings in Paris, where all estates were represented. The assembly adjured the king to bring about a council which should try this great criminal. And the king solemnly accepted this duty. Only one of the twenty-six bishops present refused to set his seal to the act. From Paris royal commissioners toured the country, organising like demonstrations everywhere.

As the news came in of what was afoot in France the pope began to prepare the bull excommunicating the king and threatening his deposition. But the king's chief executive advisor, William de Nogaret, with an armed troop broke into the papal palace at Anagni,[5] on the eve of the day appointed for publication of the bull. They found the old man seated on his throne robed, holding his crucifix. They demanded he should withdraw his sentence and submit himself to judgment. He replied that he would rather die. One of the Colonna offered to kill him, but was restrained. He then hit the pope in the face. And now the townsfolk broke into the palace and drove out the French. From this shock the pope never recovered. Three weeks later he was dead (October 11, 1303).

[3] Outside the city of Courtrai.

[4] Denzinger, nos. 468–69, prints the defining clauses of this bull, Barry, no. 80B the whole, in translation.

[5] Seventy miles or so southeast of Rome, the centre of the countryside whence Boniface (Benedict Gaetani) came.

There was only one way in which Philip the Fair could clear himself of a general reprobation that would last as long as life itself—have it proved in legal form that all the things charged against Boniface were true. And when he had succeeded in that, he would have brought low, not the dead man's memory only, but every shred of prestige that clung to his successors in the office. Such was the man and the mind whose political needs brought on the fifteenth General Council, which met just eight years after the death of Pope Boniface.

The truly saintly Dominican next elected pope, Benedict XI, reigned for eight months only. The conclave that followed lasted for all but a year, and it then elected, from outside the college of cardinals, a French subject of the English king, the Archbishop of Bordeaux. He called himself Clement V (June 5, 1305). This is the pope who summoned and presided at the Council of Vienne. Nothing would have more surprised him, as the news was brought to him from Italy, than to learn that he was destined never to see Italy as pope, and that his successors for the next seventy years and more would rule the universal church from France. For the so-called Avignon captivity of the papacy, it is now known, was not the outcome of any willed policy of this pope, but rather of a series of accidents. In the critical years of Boniface VIII, Clement had been one of the minority loyal to that pope, and he had taken part in the Roman council whence came the *Unam Sanctam*. He was an accomplished canonist and a man of long practical experience in church administration. But he was something of a ditherer by nature, vacillating to put it more formally, and in no way a match for the arts of Philip the Fair.

When the king and the pope met, at the pope's coronation at Lyons, it was suggested to Clement that he remain in France until a great scandal—now revealed to the pope for the first time—was investigated and dealt with. The scandal was the alleged condition of the military order of the Knights Templars.

These knights of the military orders, of which there were several, were religious in the full technical sense of the word, i.e., professed with the vows of poverty, chastity, and obedience, bound to a strict monastic round of prayer and penance, and to protect pilgrims and defend the Christian possessions in the Holy Land. Their monasteries were fortresses, and down to the time of the capture of St. Jean d'Acre, when the master-general of the Templars fell sword in hand (1291), they had been, along with the contemporary order of the Knights Hospitallers, the main defence, for 150 years, of what had been won from the Mohammedans.

Since the disaster of 1291 there had been no Christian forces at all in the East. The Templars, what remained of them, were lodged in their commanderies, in the various countries of western Europe. Their principal occupation had been finance. Their European castles had, for many years, been the places where princes, merchants, and the wealthy generally, could be certain their money was safe. And from being guardians of these deposits this international order had developed into something like an international bank, saving this nascent commercial world of the Middle Ages the dangerous necessity of transmitting boxes of coin from one country to another. The profits the Templars made were, it was alleged, enormous. It seems agreed that what really moved the King of France, at this moment, was the prospect of laying his hands on vast landed properties and a fortune in ready cash. The pope was told that it was being said everywhere that the Templars were utterly corrupt. They had long lost the faith, for they worshipped in their monasteries an idol, and this with obscene rites, formally denying Christ at their professions and spitting on the crucifix. In their masses the priest-members of the order—the knights' chaplains—always left out the words of consecration, and (the reader will be expecting this) unnatural vice was systematised as a kind of ritual. The pope was in no way impressed by this horrendous tale—no more than the King of Aragon had been impressed when it was told to him.

The French king set himself to "find" evidence which should bring the pope to order the suppression of the knights, and the confiscation of their property. This "evidence," from Templars already imprisoned for various offences, still left Clement V unmoved, but the menace of the campaign provoked the Grand Master of the order to beg the pope to order an enquiry (August, 1307). Seven weeks later the king regained the initiative when, on a single day, October 13, every Templar in France[6] was arrested by his orders and there began that systematic torturing to wring from them

[6] There were, it is thought, about 2,000, of all ranks, knights, sergeants, chaplains.

confessions of guilt that is still so sickening to read about, after six hundred years and more. The royal formula was simple—pardon and liberty for those who, self-confessed, were guilty of crime; death for all who maintained they were innocent. From the French Revolution until recently, evidence obtained by torture was what no man would consider seriously. But, just as universally, in the days of Clement V, torture was thought a reasonable and legitimate way of obtaining reliable evidence.[7] The pope was so impressed that he took the whole business into his own hands, and set up special courts throughout the church for the investigation: a court in each diocese where there was a house of the order, with the final authority to judge the knights left to the provincial council of the bishops; and a papal commission to consider what to do with the order itself; finally, the whole affair would be brought before a specially summoned General Council, which would meet at Vienne on October 1, 1310—two years and a half hence.

One feature was common to all these trials: whenever, in France, the knights, free of the king's jurisdiction, appeared before the bishops they immediately revoked their confessions. Describing the tortures they had endured they declared they would have sworn to anything, and that if the horrors were renewed they would again admit whatever their tormentors demanded. This revocation, of course, could be dangerous—among the charges was heresy, the worship of an idol. The punishment for heresy could be death, and for the heretics who, once self-convicted, retracted their confessions, death was certain. And so, in May 1310, fifty-four Templars were burnt in a single execution at Paris, on the sentence of the bishops of the Provincial Council. And, by a violent personal act of the king, the Grand Master himself was burnt, only a few hours after the ecclesiastical court had sentenced him to life imprisonment, because in his relief at the thought that his life was safe he solemnly retracted all his confessions, and vouched for the innocence of the order as such.

Outside France the Templars were everywhere acquitted, in Aragon, Castile, England, Scotland, the Empire. In Provence, Sicily, and the States of the Church, there were a number of con-

---

[7] An effect of the revival of Roman Law doctrines and procedures, *not* an invention of the Church.

demnations, but not many. As the date fixed for the meeting of the council drew near the order might, legitimately, have felt hopeful.

What, meanwhile, of the French king's other line of attack, his determination to blast the good name of his dead adversary Boniface VIII? He had first showed what he had in mind in one of his interviews with Clement V at Poitiers in the spring of 1307, eighteen months or so after the pope's coronation. Boniface VIII must be tried for his "crimes." All attempts to still the threats failed. The king demanded that the body of Boniface should be dug up and burned as that of a heretic, and that Celestine V—his alleged victim —should be canonised. In the end the pope pledged himself that the trial should take place, and fixed a provisional date two years hence, February 1309.

Clement V, like his namesake who had to deal with King Henry VIII two centuries later, had not the strength to say no to these requests to co-operate in a crime. He assented outwardly, and hoped the day would never come when he had to keep his promise. It was not until March 1310 that the misery began anew for him, when there appeared at Avignon to represent the king a team of lawyers headed by Nogaret, the hero of Anagni. All through that summer the lawyers fought, with the pope in person presiding and using every expedient possible to adjourn the court, finally deciding that both the "prosecutors" and the defence should state their case in writing and that the oral proceedings should cease. He also called politics to his aid, and the news that there was in contemplation the creation of a new kingdom on the eastern frontier of France—all the lands east of the Rhone, from the Mediterranean up to Besançon—now halted the French king. In February 1311, seven months before the General Council was due to meet, he agreed to call off his team. The order of Knights Templars, it was understood, would definitely be destroyed at the Council,[8] and Philip the Fair would

---

[8] Of this "understanding" there is no proof, nor is it (in the nature of things) provable. The Abbé Mollat, professor of History at the University of Strasbourg, says, "*Bien que la condition n'eût pas été explicitement exprimée dans les lettres royales, il fut convenu que le sort des Templiers serait reglé au Concile de Vienne,*" p. 260. But, surely, the pope had already arranged this in the bulls regulating the enquiries in 1308? The work quoted is Mollat's indispensable, *Les Papes d'Avignon,* 5me edition, 1924. Pages 229–56 of this book, *Le Procès des Templiers,* is the best of all short documented accounts, and it is the one generally followed in this chapter.

drop the case against Boniface VIII. On April 27, Clement V issued a series of bulls. Philip the Fair was cleared of any complicity in the Anagni incident, and praised for his good intentions. All the papal acts directed against him from November 1, 1300, to the end of the reign of Benedict XI were cancelled. Nogaret, too, was absolved, with the penance that he must go on pilgrimage to the Holy Land at the next crusade, and spend the rest of his days there, unless dispensed by the Holy See.

Even so, Clement V was to hear yet more of the case against his predecessor.

The General Council of Vienne was opened on October 16, 1311. The original convocation had been for 1310, but by a bull of April 4 of that year the pope postponed the opening. This second bull of convocation did something else. It made the singular innovation that not every bishop was summoned to the council, but only a chosen 231. And from these, 66 names were struck out by the French king. In the end there assembled 20 cardinals, 122 bishops, 38 abbots, with proxies, representatives of chapters and others that brought the number "assisting" at the council to around 300. The bishops had had ample time to prepare, as the pope following the precedent of 1274 had asked, reports on matters that called for reform. They found a new conciliar procedure awaiting them. For each of the main problems before the council a commission was named, representative of all ranks, and charged to find a solution. The solution then came before the pope and cardinals in consistory and, if they accepted it, it was presented to the council as a whole in the shape of a papal bull to be accepted and signed. There were to be no general debates in which the whole council took part.

The commission on the matter of the Templars reported in December. The knights should be heard before the council, it decided, and by a large majority. The pope, for the moment, set this embarrassing act aside. The bishops occupied themselves with schemes for the crusade and for various reforms, while the pope gave no sign of holding the next public session. Philip's representatives had only one comment to make, in all these discussions, "It must wait until our master arrives." The new year 1312 brought the king to Lyons—a mere twenty miles away, where the States-General of the realm were meeting (January to March). And from Lyons he played

upon the unhappy pope with threats to revive the campaign against
Boniface VIII. Towards the end of March he came in person to the
council, and brought it about that the Templars commission revoked their recommendation, and voted, by 4 to 1, that the order
should be suppressed (March 22, 1312). Two weeks went by, while
Clement struggled with the king about the order's vast properties.
Then, on April 3, the second public session of the council was held.
It began with yet another procedural novelty—the pope forbade
any member of the council to speak, under pain of excommunication. There was then read his bull, V*ox in excelso*, suppressing the
order. The pope gave no judgment about the crimes alleged—the
question, Guilty or innocent? was ignored. The bull explained that
Clement V was acting not as judge at a trial, but as an administrator
in the fullness of his apostolic authority. On May 3 the decision
about the Templars' property was announced. The pope had found
the courage to resist the king. The vast fortune was to go to the
order of the Knights Hospitallers, except in Spain where the beneficiaries were the three Spanish military orders.

Three days later, May 6, the council came to an end with its third
public session.

There is in the corpus of Canon Law a mass of legislation at-
tributed to this council, laws headed *Clement* V *at the Council of
Vienne*. It is by no means certain that all of this was there enacted,
nor do we know at what stage of the council what was certainly its
work was actually enacted. Of the official records of the council, we
have hardly a trace. And these laws of Clement V were not promulgated until the reign of his successor, John XXII, in 1317.

We can be certain of three decrees about the faith, definitions
of dogma. In one of these it is defined that the rational or intellectual soul is *per se* and essentially the form of the human body.[9] A
second condemns as heresy the statement that usury is not a sin.[10]
Thirdly, there is a decree listing various heresies of the people
known, if men, as Beghards, and, if women, as Beguines; theories
about what spiritual perfection is, and the obligations of those who
are perfect. Man can attain to such perfection in this life that it is
not possible for him to commit sin. Once he has achieved this a man

9 Denzinger, no. 481.
10 Ibid., no. 479.

is not bound to fast or to pray, his body being so spiritualised that he can freely grant it whatever he chooses. The perfect are not bound to obey any other human being, nor to keep the commandments of the Church, for—so they argue—where the spirit of the Lord is, there is freedom. Man can attain, in this life, to that perfection of happiness that he will enjoy in the life of the blessed. To kiss a woman, unless our nature prompts the act, is a mortal sin. But carnal acts are not sins, if done from the movements of our nature, and especially if done under temptation. No special act of reverence should be made at the elevation of the body of Jesus Christ [i.e., at mass], for it would be an imperfection in a man if he so descended from the pure heights of his contemplation to attend to the sacrament of the Eucharist or the passion of Christ's humanity.[11]

All these odd ideas are specimens of that false, self-taught mysticism that is ageless, and in every generation lurks in corners here and there. With these wandering, unauthorised, semi-religious[12] people the propagation of such notions could become a real social plague.[13] The severe prohibitions of General Councils to would-be founders of new religious orders are not unrelated to the fear that they would prove a breeding ground for cranks and fanatics.

The disciplinary decrees of the Council of Vienne take up, I suppose, a good thirty pages of the text of Fr. Schroeder's book. From the twenty-one certain decrees, and the eighteen less certain,[14] I select for notice the famous decree *Exivi de Paradiso*,[15] by which the council hoped to put an end to the disputes that were tearing the order of Franciscans apart, disputes as to the meaning of St. Francis' teaching about poverty. But the bulk of the decrees are what we have already met, rules about the duties of bishops, about the layman's usurpation of church jurisdiction and attempts to make church property his own, principles to settle disputes about rights of presentation to benefices and the like. The historical interest of these lengthy (and tedious) repetitions is that they are the outcome of the reports, brought in by the bishops and the re-

[11] Ibid., nos. 471–78.
[12] I.e., popularly regarded as a kind of monk or nun.
[13] See Cohn, Norman, *The Quest of the Millennium*, 1957.
[14] All the 39 passed into the Canon Law.
[15] For a translation of this (slightly abbreviated) see Schroeder, 407–13.

ligious orders from all over, on the state of the Church. As we read these decrees there is scarcely one of the disorders that troubled the generation upon which the Reformation came, two hundred years later, that is not to be seen already mischievously active. The remedies provided in the decrees are all admirable, if only they had been generally obeyed, and if, in those centuries of such miserable communications, there had been some way of enforcing obedience. What the decrees chiefly lack is any sense that the ills of the time call for new methods and new institutions. To read, in canon 15, the thirty complaints of the religious against episcopal oppression, or, in canon 16, the seven complaints of bishops and prelates against the religious, is to become aware of chronic weaknesses bound to drain away vitality like a running sore.

There is a story that as the Grand Master, Jacques de Molay, was fastened to the stake on that island in the Seine where he was done to death, he lifted up his voice and by name summoned his three oppressors to the judgment seat of God. Certainly they died within the year, the pope, the king, and William de Nogaret. Philip the Fair left three sons, young men, healthy, vigorous, well married. But not one of them had a son, and within fourteen years of his death the direct line of descent was extinct.

16. *The General Council of Constance, 1414-18*

There are three really remarkable councils in the fifteenth century
—councils of a new kind altogether—that took place all within
forty years: Pisa, where two rival popes were declared no popes at
all (on their refusal to resign) and a third was elected, a council
never reckoned as a General Council; Constance, which deposed
the pope who summoned it (the Pisan pope), accepted the resignation of one of those "deposed" at Pisa, deposed the third of the
rivals, and finally elected a pope whom the whole Church acknowledged as pope; Basel, a council lawfully called, dissolved, then revived, then dissolved again on its refusal to accept translation to
Ferrara, and finally—as a kind of rival to the Ferrara council—condemned anew, to be for all time henceforth (and especially for
the sixty years that followed) the very symbol of the theory that
popes are subject to General Councils, and to make the very word
"council" ominous in papal ears.

Once more we must look back, for our clue to the incredible, to
still earlier troubles, to the struggle between Pope Boniface VIII
and Philip the Fair of France (1285–1314). From this famous clash,
as a kind of by-product, there came, two years after the death of
Boniface, the election of a French pope, Clement V (1305–14).
He was the fifth French pope in less than fifty years, but he inaugurated a new tradition when he continued to reside in France, in
a tiny principality—the Comtat Venaissin—which was already papal
territory.[1] For seventy-three years all the popes were French, and
all but all of the cardinals. Then, in 1378, persuaded by St. Cather-

[1] The city of Avignon was an enclave in this territory, its sovereign the
Queen of Naples from whom, many years after the death of Clement V,
Clement VI bought it (1348).

ine of Siena, Pope Gregory XI returned to Rome, in the face of the almost unanimous opposition of his Curia.

Only two months after his return the pope died, and it was in a city dominated by mobs howling "Death to the French," and "This time pick an Italian" that the terrified cardinals (eleven French, three Italians, one Spaniard) chose for pope an Italian archbishop, Urban VI. It is necessary to bear all this in mind (and much more), for we are at the moment when the Great Schism of the West is about to happen, a régime when for nearly forty years, two sets of popes fought for the control of the Church, with half Europe backing each—a dreadful scandal, and a complicated practical problem of law and politics, for the thousands of anxious men in responsible positions who wished to restore unity. The three fifteenth-century councils, and all their turbulent revolutionary history, were the practical expression of this anxiety. It was the scandals, the spiritual tragedies wrought in every diocese of Christendom by the schism, for two generations, that fired the men who organised the councils, who had no precedent to guide them, who had no help from either of the papal rivals; and who by the time the schism was thirty years old, had no means of certifying themselves which line of popes was the true line, whether the Romans, descended through Urban VI, or the Avignon line descended from his rival Clement VII, elected five months after the election of Urban by the very cardinals who had elected Urban, by all of them.

At the outset of this story, the reader, so accustomed to national and international crises where public men give one another the lie, more or less, and where the newspapers supply an abundance of documentation, more or less complete—the modern reader must make the effort of realising this bygone world of 1400–50 with the restricted conveniences which were all that the men of the time possessed. He must realise that it was inevitable that, in the matter of good faith, there was soon nothing to choose between one side or the other. Here, to support this statement is the witness of a contemporary, who for his learning, his position in public life, and the integrity of his own life, is beyond all reproach, St. Antoninus, Archbishop of Florence, who was born in 1389. In his history of his own times he says, about the disputed point which of the two lines of popes was the true line: "There were many discussions about this matter; and many books were written in defence of both

sides. Through all the time that the divison lasted, both parts (or
obediences) could count among their supporters men exceedingly
learned, both in theology and Canon Law, and also men of most
holy life and (what is more striking still) outstanding by the miracles they wrought; yet it was never possible so to decide the question
that no doubts remained in the minds of the majority of men."[2]

From the very first months of the schism the one road to unity
seemed, to some of those best fitted to judge, to be through the
action of a General Council. Such was at any rate the suggestion
of the University of Paris to the French king in the year 1380. And
the cardinals of the Avignon pope, Clement VII, gave him the
same advice, some fourteen years later—somewhat to his dismay,
for he seems to have glimpsed behind their no doubt orthodox intentions, the dim line of the controversy that was about to shake
Christendom, viz., Are popes the ultimate master, or General Councils? Again, in the conclave of 1389 when the Roman pope Urban
VI died, and in that of 1404, the cardinals all swore that, whichever
of them was elected, he would summon a General Council, and
lay the great problem before it.

And in all these years there was a continuous discussion in the
world of theologians and lawyers and royal councillors, not only as
to ways and means, practical plans to end the schism, but as to
rights and duties: the rights of subjects to take control when rulers
show themselves incapable or unwilling, and the Church seems to
be drifting to its ruin; the rights of bishops vis-à-vis their chief, the
pope; the rights of the learned, expert in the theology of the Church
and its law; the rights of the clergy in general; the rights of the laity,
i.e., the vast majority of the members of the Church, if this needs
saying. All manner of theories, and interpretations of law, and of
past events, came in these desperate years into men's minds. The
new ideas, the suggested solutions, passed from one university to
another, and were passionately discussed at all levels of society. As,
no doubt, were the rival popes, of both of whom (long before the
crisis of 1408 which produced the first of these councils, Pisa) all
parties were heartily sick and tired—because of solemn promises to

[2] *Chronicorum* III, tit. 22; quoted by Edmund G. Gardiner, *St. Catherine
of Siena*, 252.

resign made only to be broken, promises to negotiate with one another followed repeatedly by endless justifying evasions.

What happened in 1408 was that the rival colleges of cardinals each deserted its pope, and coming together issued a joint summons to a General Council to meet in the Italian city of Pisa, November 1, 1409. And all Christendom responded, save the two kingdoms of Aragon and Scotland (which still stood by the Avignon pope) and southern Italy which still held with the Roman pope.

By the time the council opened at Pisa, almost the whole body of the followers of the rival popes had deserted to the neutral position of the cardinals and their council. It was numerically a splendid gathering, and very representative: 500 active members, that is to say voters, at the great sessions where the popes were condemned—of whom 84 were bishops and another 102 proxies of absent bishops. There were, besides, 100 representatives of cathedral chapters, representatives of 13 universities, and 300 doctors either of theology or of Canon Law—now, for the first time, here given a vote. The "General Council" had indeed a new look. It greatly resembled a parliament, a single-chamber parliament. Seventeen reigning princes sent ambassadors.

Another novel feature was the absolute unanimity of the council. There were no discussions, none were needed. All gladly assented to the forms in which the purpose that had brought them together was set out. The two rivals disposed of, i.e., excommunicated and deposed, it was the council that bade the cardinals set up a conclave and fill the presumed vacant throne. After ten days' seclusion they elected the archbishop of Milan, who took the style of Alexander V, and was duly crowned. He, too, was a very old man, and within the year he died. Whereupon the cardinals elected the strong man of the Council of Pisa, Baldassare Cossa, who called himself by a name that is lately familiar to all of us, John XXIII.

These elections, the first at least, were followed by a vast distribution of ecclesiastical spoil to all comers, and a generous renunciation of papal financial claims, and a lifting of excommunications levied for nonpayment of papal taxes. All through these thirty years of controversy—as in the history of the previous seventy years and more—two notes never ceased to sound against the popes: the way they used their right to appoint to all offices anywhere in the Church, and the increasing burden of the taxes they levied on the clergy and the harsh methods of their collectors. Nor will these complaints ever cease until, a hundred years or more later, the use of these powers really is abandoned.

It was Pope John XXIII who summoned the sixteenth General Council, the Council of Constance, December 9, 1413. It was to meet on the following November 1. The pope had not done this willingly and cheerfully, but compelled by the emperor Sigismund, at a crisis in John's own fortunes brought about very largely by his own evil life and by a curious loss of practical capacity that seemed to descend on him once he was elected. He was bound, by a decree passed at Pisa, to assemble a General Council in 1412. It met indeed, at Rome, but almost no one attended, and very soon John adjourned it. The faithful—those in a position to influence events —realised that this pope was no reformer. Gradually the whole body grew restive, princes began (for their own ends) to issue harsh threats, and when the King of Naples moved on Rome the desperate pope fled to Florence, whence he made an urgent appeal for help to the emperor Sigismund. His envoys and the emperor planned together the calling of a new council, and then Sigismund imposed this on the pope. As John XXIII made his solemn entry into the Swiss city, October 28, 1414, he was full of apprehension. He had helped two popes out of their place for far less shocking actions than what men were now alleging against himself.

The council that awaited him was made up after the new fashion inaugurated at Pisa. Not all its members by any means were assembled by the opening date. But ultimately there were present, it is held, over 600 ecclesiastics with a say in the council, 183 of them bishops, 300 doctors of theology and Canon Law; and an innumerable horde of less important clerics, and the suites of these magnificent ecclesiastical lords from Germany especially. Once again it was as the Estates of Christendom that the General Council presented itself.

The council's first task was to organise its procedure. As it turned out, all earlier precedents were abandoned. It was through entirely new machinery that the schism was to be ended and the Church reformed. With John XXIII there had come from Italy bishops enough to outvote the rest. They now overplayed their hand by proposing to limit the council's activity to organising the destruction of John's rivals. The English and the Germans arrived to find Italians and French already at odds about this, and they ranged themselves against the Italians. It was proposed that the council should be organised by nations, as the University of Paris was organised—Italians, French, Germans, English. In the decisive meetings—the sessions—each nation should have only one vote, and how that vote should be cast would be for the nationals to decide in separate preliminary meetings. In these national meetings not bishops only, and abbots, would have a vote, but the proctors of absentee prelates, the representatives of cathedral chapters and universities and all the doctors of theology and Canon Law—the parliamentary principle, once more. And John XXIII had no choice but to agree.

To work out this complex scheme, and secure its adoption had taken weeks of work. It was now March 1415, and a new crisis arose. The pope had been increasingly uneasy as his chances diminished. A pamphlet denouncing his sins in the plainest words unnerved him altogether, and on the night of March 20 he fled from Constance, with but a single attendant, to the dominions of Frederick of Hapsburg. The confusion he meant to produce was realised. While the mob pillaged the palace that had accommodated him, the bishops—many of them—thought only of returning to their homes. The council, as John had hoped, was going to break up. But the emperor's presence saved the day. He restored order in the town and persuaded the bishops to continue their work. The council met and in a violently antipapal mood it resolved that the pope's absence made no difference to the council's status and authority, that it would not break up until it had reformed the Church, and that it could not be transferred to another city without its own consent. Here was revolution—like that of the Tennis Court oath of the Third Estate in 1789.

The pope's reaction to the messages sent from the council only stiffened its determination. On April 5 resolutions were adopted that were a manifesto of antipapalism, and destined to be active in the Church for centuries. The first of them, the classic decree *Sacrosancta*, needs to be set out in detail. "This holy Council of Constance . . . declares, in the first place, that, lawfully come together in the Holy Spirit, being a General Council and representing the Catholic Church, it holds an authority directly [derived] from

Christ, which authority everyone, of whatever status or dignity, even the pope, is bound to obey in those matters concerning the faith, the extirpation of the said Schism, and the reformation of the Church in head and members. It declares, furthermore, that whoever contumeliously scorns to obey the commands and the laws of this holy council, or of any other General Council lawfully assembled [commands, etc. referring to the matters stated], he is to be duly punished, whatever his status or dignity, even though he is the pope."[3]

Another resolution stated that the pope's flight was a criminal act, rendering him suspect of heresy, and yet another that within the council there was full freedom of action.

This crisis that opened on March 20 lasted for ten weeks or so. The pope offered to resign—at a price: the red hat, control of Italy and Avignon, and 30,000 gold coins. He fled farther, was arrested, tried, and on May 29 deposed by the council, for the crime of his flight, for simony, and for his bad life. He accepted his sentence, and ratified it with an oath, and passed under guard to a German prison.

While this crisis kept Constance in an interested excitement, lovers of peace and unity in the tiny entourage of Gregory XII were busy negotiating with the council. The outcome of these delicate exchanges was the scene on July 4, when in a session not presided over by any ecclesiastic, but by a layman—the emperor—and so not (to all appearances) an assembled council of the Church, one of Gregory's cardinals, sent as legate, read a bull, dated three months earlier, not recognising the council but formally convoking it, and authorising it to work for the restoration of unity. This cardinal, the saintly Dominican, John Dominici, then pronounced the formula convoking the General Council, and the assembly consented to be convoked in the name (as it was expressed) "of the lord who, in his own obedience, is called Gregory XII." Next a second bull of Gregory's was read that authorised the second legate he had sent —the prince, Carlo Malatesta—to make in the pope's name a full, irrevocable resignation of the papacy. And Malatesta thereupon made the renunciation, and the council accepted it. The session

[3] Session 5, April 6, 1415. Mansi, XXVII, 590 f. Barry, no. 83A, prints a translation of the decree.

ended with a new summons to the third of the rivals, Benedict XIII, to yield to the council's authority.

But the Aragonese pope—who still had Spain and Scotland to support him—dwelt now in his family's ancient fortress of Peñiscola on the Mediterranean coast of Spain. His wits were as bright as ever, at eighty-six, and his determination to be recognised by all as lawful pope. All his great powers of manoeuvre came once more into play when the emperor, personally, now made the long journey to negotiate with him (July 14–October). But this time the famous ingenuity was too much even for Benedict's own royal supporters, and when he threatened to depose them if they dared to withdraw, the sovereigns accepted the challenge, and went over to the side of the council, December 13, 1415. It was now a year and a month since the council had opened, and the only man living who claimed to be pope actually ruled no more than his own personal servants and bodyguard. The council began the slow process of making a legal end of him. This called for—among other things—a second expedition to Spain to serve the citation. And before even this was despatched the council, in decency to the new fifth nation—Spain —could not act until the Spanish representatives had come to Constance. So that it was not until March 1417 that the trial really began. It ended, with a sentence of deposition, July 26—two years, almost to the very day, since the emperor took leave of the council, bound for Peñiscola and the attempt to win the pope's abdication. The council might now proceed to its second task, reform. But should it not wait until a pope was first elected? Or would it be easier—less embarrassing?—to push through the inevitably drastic reforms while the Holy See was vacant?

To set up a commission of thirty-five members to draft decrees reforming all that was amiss in the Church had been one of the council's first acts once it had disposed of John XXIII. And for seven months these grave matters were passionately debated. The core of the vast subject was the two-fold development of the papal authority in recent centuries, namely, the way in which the popes had come to intervene, in the matter of appointments to offices of every kind, in every diocese of the Christian world, and their highly developed, centralised system of the taxation of the whole revenues of the universal church. The question was raised whether the whole business of these papal appointments (more accurately *provisions*) should not be abolished, the system itself having become one vast abuse.

And here the reformers were divided. Against the bishops, who would have swept it away, the university interest—and there were three hundred doctors active members of the council—protested that the Holy See paid far more attention than the bishops to the claims of the educated clergy. And to those who would have swept away the whole taxation system, it had to be pointed out that the popes must have some fixed source of revenue to pay the immense cost of the general administration of the Church. Then, before the findings of the commission were ready for general criticism, the council found itself swamped by the practical matter of the general day-to-day administration of the Church.

From the date of Gregory XII's abdication there was, effectively, no pope reigning, and the Curia Romana had simply fallen apart. The parliamant, so to speak, now had no time for law-making so busy was it with problems of administration. There was also the matter of the two celebrated Czech heretics, John Huss and Jerome of Prague, tried by the council, condemned, and duly burned at the stake. There was the appeal to the council on the very lively controversy of the defence of the murder of the Duke of Burgundy by the orders of the Duke of Orléans—an incident in the history of the quarrel between the regents of France during the insanity of King Charles VI. From this murder a civil war had developed, and a new English invasion of France, which country, at this very moment, seemed from both these causes to have fallen into complete anarchy. One leading light of the French university world, John Petit, had written a book defending the murder; subjects (this was his theme) are morally justified who kill tyrants. The matter was referred to the council, and the discussion was not on purely academic lines. Ultimately it decided against the new theory that tyrannicide is lawful.[4] The negotiations that brought in the Spaniards as a fifth nation were another matter that distracted the council's attention from its second principal objective.

But at last, in the summer 1417, a new reform commission was

---

[4] For the text (Latin) of this decree, see Denzinger, no. 690.

set up. All the old controversies were immediately renewed, and by September the council seemed about to break up. There was an evident fundamental difference between the point of view of the cardinals and the council generally. And the bishops and doctors began to debate whether cardinals were of any value to religion, and whether the Sacred College should not be abolished. The council was not unanimous in its radical notions. The Italians, French, and Spaniards tended to support the cardinals. It was from Germany and England that the revolutionary ideas came. And leading the Germans was the powerful figure of the emperor, but for whom the council would never have held together so long.

One last cause of dissension in this same summer was the double question already mentioned, Should the pope be elected before the reform decrees were passed? and how should he be elected? The Council was loth to trust the cardinals with this, their essential function for centuries now. No question could be graver than this last. At all costs the coming election must be free from anything that might justify a future charge that it was not valid. There must not be a second schism. It was a highly placed English prelate who brought all parties to an agreement, Henry Beaufort, bishop of Winchester, and uncle to the reigning King of England, Henry V. He made three suggestions, which all accepted: the council to decree now that, once the pope was elected, reform would be its sole concern; to publish now the decrees it had ready; to set up a commission to decide how the new pope should be elected.

Five decrees were accordingly published on October 5, 1417. The first, and by far the most important in its consequences, is that called, from its first word, *Frequens*. It is a kind of practical corollary to the decree *Sacrosancta* already mentioned. Here is its text: "The frequent celebration of General Councils is the best of all methods for tilling the Lord's field, and for extirpating the weeds and thorns of heresy, schisms and errors. . . . This it is that brings the Lord's vineyard to the fullness of its fertility. The neglect to hold General Councils fosters and encourages all the disorders here spoken of; the history of former times and the events we ourselves are witness to make this very evident. Therefore, by this perpetual law, we command that, from this time on, General Councils shall be held as follows: the first within five years immediately following the close of this present council; the second within seven years of the close of the council immediately following this present council; and ever afterwards thenceforward every ten years; all these councils to be held in a place which the pope is bound to announce one month before the end of the council, and with the approbation and consent of the council. Should the pope fail to do this, then the council itself is to choose the place and time. So that, in this way, by a kind of continuity, there shall always be a council in session or the expectation of a council. The term appointed for the coming council the pope may, with the consent of the cardinals, shorten, but in no case may he make it any longer."[5] There is no need to explain what a revolution in the government of the Church was thus attempted.

A second decree of this same thirty-ninth session provides, with ingenious detail, a quasi-automatic way to prevent the spread of any future schism.[6]

At the fortieth session, October 30, a decree was passed binding the pope about to be elected to proceed, in collaboration with the council, to reform the Church "in its head and members" before the council is dissolved. Eighteen heads of reform are listed.[6a] Further than this list, the council had still not dared to go, so acute were the dissensions. But the Germans now suggested that the council confine itself to matters affecting the whole Church, while the new pope should, in conference with each of the nations, make a series of amendments to meet their particular needs. This was agreed to.

The scheme for the election of the new pope was also adopted at the fortieth session. For this time, and for this time only, said the council, there were to be added as voters to the cardinals, six deputies for each of the five nations. To secure election not only was a two-thirds majority of the cardinals required (the law of 1179) but the like majority in each of the five national deputations. The thirty deputies were elected, their names published, and with the twenty-three cardinals they went into conclave, on November 8, in the Merchants' Hall, around which the emperor set a strong guard of troops—no mobs were, this time, to play any part in the business. The conclave, despite the new complexities of its constitu-

[5] Sess. 39, Oct. 9, 1417. Mansi, XXVII, 1159. Barry, *op. cit.*, no. 83B, prints a translation of the decree.

[6] This decree, *Si vero*, far too lengthy to deal with here, will be found summarised in Hughes, *History of the Church*, vol. III, p. 298 note.

[6a] Barry, *op. cit.*, no. 83C, gives the list.

ents, did its work rapidly. On November 11 the new pope was announced, the cardinal Odo Colonna. He took the name Martin V —the day being the feast of that saint.

The advantage of an undoubted head to lead the council was now clearly seen. The Germans, French, and Spaniards each sent in a list of desired changes, and the pope, on January 20, 1418, sent in to the council a draft of eighteen decrees based on the eighteen points of October 30. From these the council worked out a set of seven decrees, and on March 20 they were published.

These seven decrees, *to which alone of the reforms of Constance the papal approval was given*, treat of the long-standing financial grievances of the bishops, and the question of appointments to benefices. All exemptions from the jurisdiction of the local bishop, granted since the death of Gregory XI in 1378 (i.e., granted by the popes of any of the various lines) are abolished, all unions of benefices or incorporations,[7] too, which they authorised, provided that the interested parties desire this. The pope promises there will be no more grants of exemption from jurisdiction without the local bishop's consent, and he also surrenders his rights to draw the revenues of sees, abbeys, and other benefices while they are vacant. All dispensations that allow a man to hold an ecclesiastical office without being ordained or consecrated as the office demands are revoked, and the pope promises that no more such will be granted. No more will the pope tithe the revenues of priests and bishops for the profit of lay princes, and Martin V pledged the Holy See never again to tithe the whole body of the clergy except with the written consent of the cardinals and of all the bishops he could consult in the emergency which moved him to act. As to special tithes—i.e., of a particular country—the pope promised never to levy such against the views of the majority of its bishops. And never would this ecclesiastical tax be handed over to laymen to collect. There is, too, a decree against simony of new and outspoken severity. This vice, the pope declares, no one has yet succeeded in extirpating. All simoniacal elections are henceforward, by the fact, null and

---

[7] An incorporation is the act by which for the individual benefice-holder there is substituted an ecclesiastical corporation, a university for example, a cathedral chapter, a religious community—to the profit of the corporation. It is to the abbey or college that the revenues now go, and out of these they pay a salary to the priest they hire to do the work.

void. Those who disregard this law, and possess themselves of the revenues of the office, are thieves, and must make restitution of the money taken before they can be absolved. All parties to the simoniacal pact are, also by the fact, excommunicated, even though (says the decree) it is the pope himself.

The Council of Constance was now practically over. It only remained to go through the formalities of closure.[8] It is matter for thought that what had chiefly occupied the minds of those who there gave so much time to the betterment of religious life, was the material organisation of religion—testimony to the extent to which, for generations, abuses of administration, the worship of administrators, had been choking the true life. The material reforms enacted at Constance were indeed essential, if religion was ever again to be healthy. But other things were needed also, were even more necessary, and of these there was no mention in the great debates: questions of the frequentation of the sacraments; of the way in which the truths of faith were explained, "in season and out of season," to the ordinary congregation; the education and training of the parochial clergy; the duties of bishops to reside in the diocese to which they were appointed, to visit regularly all its parishes and the religious houses under episcopal jurisdiction; their duty themselves to preach the gospel; renewed observance of the law about provincial synods, the great check on episcopal negligence; the state of theological teaching in the universities. There was an abundance of crying needs, and the bishops at Constance (to say nothing of the horde of learned clerics) were deaf; or if they heard they were too closely occupied with the great problem of securing that, in their respective spheres, each was more his own master than before.

The council is one of the great turning points of the history of the Church. After Constance things were never the same again in one very important matter. The ecclesiastical system, the system based on the hitherto unquestioned general assumption of the pope's right to rule the whole Church as its earthly master, this had there received a blow in the face as surely as Boniface VIII at Anagni. To change the simile, rough hands have been laid on the ark—hands of bishops, active in the cause of God (very ostenta-

8 The council ended April 22, 1418.

tiously so, sitting in a General Council); things have been done and things said—things impossible to harmonise with the tradition—with all the apparent prestige of a General Council. If scandal means a stumbling block, what were the three years of Constance to prove? The theologian will find it an easy matter to explain exactly how far this council, with its forty-six sessions, is truly a General Council lawfully summoned in the Holy Spirit, with a real claim to have been divinely guided in its acts. But at the time it dispersed, its prestige, immense and unquestioned, covered (for the ordinary man) all the council had enacted. No General Council had ever before sat continuously for so long a time; nor occupied itself with such a matter of public interest as the place of the pope in the Church's Constitution. And so delicate was the situation still, with decrees like *Sacrosancta* ringing loud in men's ears, that for years the very popes dared hardly do more than hint at the ambiguities which the prestige masked. The trouble engendered by the forty years of the schism was by no means at an end. It was indeed to endure for hundreds of years to come.

17.   *The General Council of Basel-Ferrara-Florence, 1431–45*

Martin V, before he closed the Council of Constance, duly announced that the General Council would meet five years thence, April 23, 1423, at Pavia. And at the appointed time he sent legates to preside at the council there in his name. They found awaiting them two abbots only. Gradually, as the months went by, a handful of bishops and lesser dignitaries straggled in—the number never exceeded twenty-five. Then the plague came to Pavia, and the council moved to Siena. Its members never got any further than a long-drawn-out discussion about the relation, in law, between the General Council and the papacy. Gradually the bishops began to leave, and just eleven months after its inauguration the council was dissolved. But, once again, the provisions of the decree *Frequens* were carried out. Before the last members of the council had departed it was announced to them that seven years hence, in 1431, the General Council of the Church would come together again, this time at Basel in Switzerland.

By the time that this council met, Martin V was no more. He had found it a very onerous task to set up anew the central administration of the Church in what was little better than a city in ruins. The animosities and personal rivalries of the curiously assorted cardinals who had elected him—relics of three rival papal régimes—naturally reasserted themselves. He added a fourth group to the Sacred College by his own nominations. Little wonder that this pope ruled his cardinals with a firm hand. Could the possibility ever be far from his mind that the schism would revive? Did he really lament, as he saw the council of Siena turn out a fiasco? There were elements in Rome whom it pleased to assert that Martin V dreaded the very thought of General Councils, and, as the date approached for that of Basel, insulting notices were placarded on St. Peter's, warning the pope of his duty in threatening terms. But death delivered Pope Martin from these anxieties, February 20, 1431.

His successor, elected almost immediately, was not one of the cardinals created since the restoration of unity, not alas the capable Giuliano Cesarini, but a nephew of Pope Gregory XII whose resignation had smoothed the path at Constance, sixteen years before—the cardinal whose creation, in 1408, had been the immediate occasion of Gregory's cardinals deserting him and uniting with the cardinals who had deserted Benedict XIII. The new pope took the name Eugene IV. He was to rule for sixteen years, and to die with the council now summoned, still active if excommunicated and, though long moribund, still rebellious. The history of the reign of Eugene IV is, in one respect, little more than the history of the Council of Basel.

Cesarini, appointed to preside over the council (by Martin V), had also been commissioned as legate to the Catholics of Germany, now engaged in a holy war against the Hussite heretics of Bohemia. The summer of 1431, which should have seen the hosts of bishops converging on Basel, was spent by the legate with the Catholic army. On August 14 it was wiped out, at the bloody battle of Taussig. Ironically, as it proved, the legate had had the new pope's permission to delay the opening of the council until the Hussites had been dealt with! Three weeks after the battle, a very much changed man, Cesarini reached Basel, to find what the other legates had found at Pavia. Almost nowhere, it seemed, were bishops interested in General Councils. The great wave of enthusiasm which had carried the decree *Frequens* had crashed more rapidly than it had risen. The Council of Basel opened on December 14, 1431, with a mere handful of bishops present.

One of the factors in the troubles that now began was the vacillation of the papal will, Pope Eugene reviving, in this, memories of his uncle, Pope Gregory. Another was the geographical distance that separated the pope's city from that of the council—a good seven hundred miles north to the frontier and then across all the mountains of Switzerland, fifteen to twenty days' journey, five centuries ago. In other words, the maximum of causality to bring about contradictory decisions in an anxiety-ridden superior. Four months after the first session, before the council had really begun its work, the legate received from him the surprising order to dissolve it and send the bishops home (January 10, 1432). The date of this bull was the previous December 18. But, despite the able and conciliatory Cesarini, the bishops refused to budge. They remembered the resolutions of Constance—had they not, at their first session, solemnly reaffirmed the decree *Frequens?*—and they reminded the pope of all this, by renewing the resolutions, and gave him sixty days to withdraw his bull. Otherwise . . . This was on February 10, 1432, at the second session of the council.

The pope's reason, given in the bull, was the invitation sent from Basel to the Hussites to attend and state their case. On this important issue there were now to be two policies, the papal and that of the council. With such a matter in debate, and the acutely critical state of Catholics in Germany and Bohemia, there was no saying how affairs would end—especially under so weak a character as this particular pope.

The King of France summoned his bishops, and they begged him to support the council. The emperor, Sigismund still, took the same line. The council "summoned" the pope to take his proper place at its deliberations, and the cardinals with him—the latter were given three months to appear. More, the council provided for the chance that the pope might die while it was in session, and it forbade him to create any new cardinals until the present crisis ended (June 20). This was the constitution of Constance in action, with a vengeance.

The pope was now all conciliation. In a bull of August 20 he gave the council leave to negotiate with the Hussites, and to make plans for the reformation of abuses in Germany. He had spoken of another council, to meet in Bologna in 1433, and he now left the choice of the place to the council. But the council (three cardinals at the moment, plus thirty-two bishops and abbots, plus a legion of doctors) was resolved that the pope should cry *Peccavi*, explicitly assenting to its doctrine that General Councils cannot be dissolved without their own consent. They told the pope explicitly that only General Councils are infallible.

The English king, Henry VI—or the regent who ruled in that child's name—now joined with the emperor and the French. It was quite a combination. The pope, out of his twenty-one cardinals, could only really rely on six, and in December the council gave him sixty days to withdraw his bull of dissolution explicitly, and to approve all it had done so far.

Long before this reached him Eugene had made another conciliatory move—the Bologna council would really be the Basel council continued, only in this sense had he ever dissolved the Basel council. When this decision reached Basel, during the fatal sixty days, it only stiffened the resolution of the little group to extort the fullness of what they insisted were their rights. The discussions with the pope's envoys were long and heated. Then on April 27—it is now 1433, of course—the council promulgated eight new shackling decrees about the papal authority. On July 13 it deprived the Holy See, forever, of all right to appoint bishops and abbots, and ordered that before being installed as pope the newly elect should, for the future, take an oath to observe this enactment—the enactment of a couple of dozen bishops plus a crowd of theologians and canonists. They reminded the pope how patiently they had so far dealt with him, and once more commanded him to withdraw his original bull.

And on August 1 the pope did precisely this.

Even so the council was not satisfied. The pope must admit that he was in the wrong when he issued the bull, and must accept the council as a true General Council and as having been such all through (September 11). And now, at the moment when Eugene IV was preparing a wholesale nullification of the council's antipapal decrees, he suddenly found himself a fugitive from his own state, a distinguished exile enjoying the hospitality of the Florentine republic. A Milanese army had invaded his state, giving out that it had come to punish the pope, and domestic treachery had helped it.

From Florence, December 15, the pope made what was to be his last surrender to the council. This bull acknowledged that the pope's dissolution bull of 1431 had been the cause of all the trouble. Eugene praised the council for the good work it had done, and bade it continue with the reform of the papacy as well as of the rest of the Church. All sentences passed against the council were annulled. This surely was the nadir of papal action.

When the bull was read to the council, February 5, 1434, it declared itself satisfied. Yet once again it renewed the decrees of Constance about the General Council's superiority to the pope, and on June 9, 1435, it abolished the main source of the Curia Romana's revenue, the taxes payable on a bishop's appointment (annates), declaring them to be simony—which was certainly not the case, however onerous they might prove.

The council, like its predecessor, now began to take to itself the general administration of the Church. It busied itself with the Jewish question, and legislated against clerical concubinage. It made useful changes in the procedure about excommunications, and about appeals from sentences given in the bishops' courts. In the face of all which, the pope gave not a sign that he knew what was afoot, except to notify the council that the pope is, nonetheless, its superior.

So the deadlock lasted through 1435 and 1436, by which time a new question had arisen—the Greek emperor, fearing the very days of his state were numbered, had for some years been making approaches to end the centuries-old schism. The council, as well as the pope, sent envoys to Constantinople to treat with him. The Greeks, not surprisingly, preferred to do business with the pope— the juridical position apart, what could the council do for the Greeks but pass resolutions? and how could the Greeks hope to achieve the aim of union with the pope by first making friends of the men who had all but dethroned him? Pope Eugene now had a new birth of courage. He denounced the council to the princes of Christendom for what it really was, arranged with the Greeks that Ferrara would be a suitable meeting place, and sent to Basel a bull transferring the council to that city (September 18, 1437). The legates left Basel, for Ferrara, in the December following—six years to a month since the council's first session—and many of the bishops left with them. The débris left at Basel was, by this, scarcely visible. Its arrogance and claims and language were, of course, more imperial than ever.

The attendance at the first eight General Councils had been all but wholly Greek—the legates of the pope the only Latins in the assembly. At the rest of the series, the attendance had been just as exclusively Latin. Only at the Ferrara-Florence sessions of this council of Eugene IV, did Constantinople and Naples, Milan and Ephesus ever sit down together. And the doctrinal business that brought them together was not the usual business of the condemnation of some new erroneous interpretation of the Christian faith, but Reunion, the demonstration—on the part of the Latins—that the Latin theology meant precisely the same as the Greek in matters where, for centuries now, the Greeks had been shunning the Latins as heretics.

Behind this interest in theological questions there lay, on both sides, the very urgent matter of the new Mohammedan threat to Constantinople, almost the sole remnant of the ancient empire still in Christian hands. These particular Mohammedans, the Ottoman Turks, had built up their vast power in the last eighty years or so, conquering various minor sultanates in Asia Minor, driving the Byzantines from the southern shores of the Black Sea, and from all that classic land of western Asia Minor where, of old, were such cities as Nicaea and Nicomedia and Chalcedon and Ephesus—occupying the countries that nowadays are Greece and Bulgaria and southern Yugoslavia. Constantinople was by this time a small island in a sea of Mohammedan territory. The population, 1,000,000 or so in the great days, had shrunk to a mere 50,000. The frontier was but a two days' ride from the walls.

It had at last been driven home to the great Christian state likely to be the next to be attacked, Venice, that it had been folly to allow the Turks to conquer so much almost unhindered, and, like any good state whose one real interest is commerce, to trust for its own security to good diplomatic and trade relations with them. And so the Latin power that had inflicted the death blow of 1204, was now coming forward, anxious to save the remnants. And in 1431, to quicken the chances of a new kind of understanding, a Venetian patrician had been elected pope—Eugene IV, cast for other rôles than the duel with the ridiculo-serious Council of Basel.

The Greeks themselves were divided, politically no less than theologically. The long-standing hatred of the Latins, burnt into their very nature by the crime of 1204, was as active as ever with many. The feeling of religious distrust—Latin help must mean Latinisation—was general. As to the imminence of the danger, no doubt, as with the imminent danger of secession a century ago, people were too used to the menace to realise it was a fact. When, finally, the papal envoys and the emperor John VIII and the patriarch of Constantinople came to an understanding, and the bishops were chosen, in a synod, to accompany them to the council, and all set off on the long ten weeks' sea voyage to Venice, they left behind them a city very largely hostile to their journey and its objectives. And the pro-Reunion emperor knew this only too well. And when, the great reconciliation effected, he returned to Constantinople he did not dare to publish the fact. Nor did his brother, the last of the successors of Justinian, Constantine XII, until 1452, the very eve of the final catastrophe.

The ceremonial splendour of the Venetian reception of the Greeks (February 8, 1438), the liturgical wonders at Ferrara, are in almost shocking contrast to the realities. They did not, for the emperor, mask the realities. He had come to do what lay in him for the religious reunion of the East and West, expecting then to discuss, for the common salvation of Christendom, a united military project. But not one of the kings of Europe, not a single leading prince, ever came to the council. To the hostile people awaiting his return, John VIII could not show a single treaty of alliance. The princes had remained fixed in that indifference to the fate of the East that had been theirs ever since the fall of Acre in 1291. The pope's appeal was but sounding brass to them, as in all the last hundred and fifty years. Is there ever a time when political situations are hopeless? If so, this was certainly one of them. Let a contemporary speak, a shrewd, professional diplomatist, later to be a pope and to organise the last of the crusades.

"The titles of pope and emperor are now no more than empty words, brilliant images. Each state has its own prince, and each prince his own special interests. Who can speak so eloquently as to persuade to unity under a single flag so many powers, discordant and even hostile? And even should they unite their forces, who will be so bold as to undertake to command them? What rules of discipline will he lay down? How will he ensure obedience? Where is the man who can understand so many languages that differ so widely, or who can reconcile characters and customs that so conflict? What mortal power could bring into harmony English and French, Genoese and Aragonese, Germans, Hungarians and Bohemians? If the holy war is undertaken with an army that is small, it will be wiped out by unbelievers; if the army is of any great size, it will court disaster just as infallibly through the insoluble problems of manoeuvre and the confusion that must follow. To whatever side one turns, one sees the same chaos."[1]

[1] Aeneas Sylvius Piccolomini (Pius II, 1458–64). Epist. CXXVII.

Such was the atmosphere in which, at Ferrara and at Florence, whither in January 1439 the pope transferred the council, the bishops discussed the theological matters that had divided East and West these many centuries.

The emperor John's disappointment at the council is understandable. That theological topics, once brought to the fore by the pressure of political necessity, would have so dominated the event that nothing but theology was spoken of in the council—who would have expected this? There was not a reference to the plight of the East, so far as we know, and not even the palest imitation of that papal speech at another council which had launched the First Crusade.[2] Most surprisingly, even to us, yet so it was.

In the first joint session, April 9, 1438, the council (117 Latins and 31 Greeks)[3] decreed, without any trouble, that this was a General Council. And then the theological tourney began. Despite the emperor—for so apprehensive was he that differences here would speedily end the council, that he had meant the plight of the East to be first discussed, and the means to remedy this. It was with the greatest difficulty that the Easterns were brought to the point of stating why they thought the Latins were heretics, and to a discussion of the Latin reply. The main dividing questions were the orthodoxy of the Latin theology about the relation of the Holy Spirit to the Father and the Son (the *Filioque* question), of the Latin theology about the purification of souls after death (Purgatory), of the Latin use of unleavened bread in the Holy Eucharist (the Greeks used ordinary bread), and of the Latin claim that the pope is, by God's ruling, the supreme earthly ruler of the whole Church of Christ.

As to procedure, the pope's plan was that a joint commission of ten Greeks and ten Latins should first study each topic and then their report be discussed. But the emperor's objection to all and any discussion of theology held up this plan. At last he agreed to the Purgatory question being debated. After two months of this (June–July 1438) the Greeks agreed that what the Latins taught was what they too believed. There was then a lull for a good three

[2] Urban II, at the Council of Clermont, 1095.
[3] The figures are from Gill, *The Council of Florence*, 110–11. There were 10 cardinals, 74 Latin archbishops and bishops, 20 Greek archbishops (i.e., metropolitans), and 2 Armenian archbishops.

months, and finally the emperor was brought round to consent to a discussion of the *Filioque*. This proved the most lengthy of the council's tasks—a thorough investigation and criticism of all the old writers, the champions of orthodoxy at Nicaea, and Ephesus and Chalcedon, Athanasius, Gregory of Nazianzen, Cyril, and the rest. By June 8, 1439, the Greeks had been satisfied that the Latins, despite their use of the words "and from the Son" (i.e., *Filioque*), did not hold a doctrine other than their own, and that the addition of the word *Filioque* to the original creed had been lawful since, at the time it was made, it was the sole means of warding off an heretical interpretation of the original text.

The question which, of all others, we might expect to have caused storms—the claim of the popes that their see is the mistress-see in fact, and not a mere primacy of honour—went through with comparatively little trouble, in little more than a week.

It took a week to draft the text of the decree setting forth the agreement—this took the form of a papal bull, *Laetentur Coeli*—and then on July 5 the 133 Latins and the 33 Greeks signed it, the pope also and the emperor. On July 6, 1439, it was promulgated in a solemn session of the council.

The definition about the kind of thing the pope's authority is, runs as follows: "In the name of the Holy Trinity . . . We, with the assent of the holy and General Council of Florence, define, in like manner, that the holy Apostolic See and the Bishop of Rome, have a primacy [*tenere primatum*] throughout the whole world, and that the Bishop of Rome himself is the successor of St. Peter and the prince of the Apostles, and that he is the true vicar of Christ, and the head of the whole Church, and the father and teacher of all Christians; and that to him in St. Peter there was committed by Our Lord Jesus Christ full power to pasture, to rule and to guide the whole Church; as is also contained in the acts of the General Councils and in the sacred canons."[4]

[4] Denzinger, no. 694, prints the Latin text. Especially in England was the reunion joyously celebrated. The papal envoy wrote from London of the processions of thanksgiving in all parts of the city and in other towns, and of sermons preached everywhere explaining what it was that was being celebrated (Gill, 299). Eighty years later, on the eve of Henry VIII's repudiation of the papal authority, Thomas More is quoting this passage of the decree of Florence in his reply to Luther's tract against Henry (1523) and referring Luther to John Fisher's book where it is all set out. May I refer to my own *Reformation in England*, I, 204.

And now the Greeks went home. The first of them left, for Venice, within the fortnight; the last—the emperor John—on August 26. They sailed from Venice October 19. Not until February 1 did they reach Constantinople. Most of them were still in Florence when there arrived another group of Orientals seeking reunion with the Roman see. These were Armenians from Constantinople and the Genoese colony of Caffa in the Crimea, but commissioned by their patriarch. They were Monophysites, their churches relics of the reaction that had followed the Council of Chalcedon, now a thousand years ago. "We have come to you our head," they said to the pope. "You are the foundation of the Church. Every member that has left you is sick, and wild beasts have devoured the flock that has separated itself from you. . . . You who have the power of the heavenly keys, open to us the gates of eternal life."[5] After weeks of daily conferences with the cardinals whom the pope appointed, an understanding was reached and the bull commonly called the *Decree for the Armenians* was promulgated, November 22, 1439.

It is of vast length, and begins with the verbatim repetition of the creeds of Nicaea and Constantinople (381). Next comes, also word for word, the definition of faith of the Council of Chalcedon, (the two natures of Christ our Lord) and of the General Council of 680–81 (the two wills and the two operations). There is also, for the acceptance of these Armenians, a specific declaration that Chalcedon is a true General Council and that St. Leo's teaching— the *Tome*—is authoritative. We know all too little of the later history of this group, but apparently they were still in communion with Rome when, thirty years later, the Turkish advance wiped out the colony of Caffa.[6]

Eugene IV had begun his negotiations with the Armenians somewhere around 1434. But it was only during the council that he made his first approach to the Monophysites of Egypt and Abyssinia (August 22, 1439), in the first weeks of the talks with the Armenians. The Franciscans who carried the pope's letters to "the Emperor of the Ethiopians," and also to "the Emperor of the Indians," were

---

[5] Gill, 306; i.e., my translation of texts quoted by Gill, as in subsequent quotations.
[6] Denzinger, nos. 695–702, prints only the summary about the seven sacraments.

many months on the road. In Cairo they delivered to the successor of St. Cyril his copy of the reunion bull *Laetentur Coeli*, who, acknowledging this, wrote to the pope that whoever did not accept what the holy synod at Florence had decreed should be held as a heretic. And in the same city these envoys met the Monophysite rival who also claimed to be the successor of St. Cyril—and of "St. Dioscoros" too. This personage, the patriarch of the Copts, was no less pleased at the message the Franciscans brought, and he appointed one of his monks, the abbot Andrew, to return with them to the pope. It was on August 31, 1441, that Andrew made his appearance in the council.

The Copt and the Latin bishops had no language in common. Andrew spoke in Arabic, which was translated first into Italian, and then into Latin. The gist of his address was a plea that the pope who had brought back the Greeks and the Armenians into communion with himself would do as much for the Copts. All the traditional complimentary language about the pope is brought into use—those compliments which are yet so much more, since they are made up of the popes' own descriptions of their unique rank; and since, also, they are never used by these Easterns to anyone but the popes. Eugene IV is here described as God's earthly vicar, St. Peter's successor, "head and teacher of the universal church."[7] At the same time another Coptic dignitary presented himself, sent by the Abyssinian abbot Nicodemus, from Jerusalem.

The linguistic difficulties, it may be imagined, caused much delay, and no doubt not all misunderstandings were cleared up. The bull of reunion (February 4, 1442) was, again, immensely long.[8] Once again the teaching of Chalcedon is verbally repeated—but, this time, with an explicit condemnation of Dioscoros. Of "the Emperor of the Indians" we know nothing at all; and of "the Emperor of the Ethiopians" only this that, eighty years later than the Council of Florence, Clement VII received a letter from his successor, saying that in the royal archives there was a letter from Pope Eugene IV to the emperor Jacob, and naming the Abyssinian monks who had brought it.[9]

[7] Gill, 323.
[8] Denzinger, nos. 703–15, gives a generous extract which is a synopsis of the condemnations of all the heresies from Cerinthus in the first century down to the Monothelites of 680.
[9] Ibid., 327.

Two years later than the reconciliation of the Copts, when the council had been translated (for the third time) to Rome,[10] the ghosts of yet another ancient council reappeared, when the Nestorian archbishop of Edessa, in the name of his patriarch, accepted the faith of the Council of Ephesus (431). Once again, what now bore fruit was the zeal of Franciscan missionaries, some of whom in the fourteenth century had made the long overland journey as far as the Nestorians of China.

Finally, in the same Lateran period of the council, two schismatic bodies from Cyprus were reunited—the Chaldeans (so-called) who were Nestorians, and the Maronites who were Monophysites (August 7, 1445).

This is our last date in connection with the council. At what date the pope formally brought it to an end, and why, we do not know. It is a most singular thing that no record has survived of a public act of this importance, in the history of the papacy, and in a century so well known to us.

But at Basel the little rump continued to sit, and for yet another four years.

The Basel reaction to the opening celebrations at Ferrara in 1438 had been to "suspend" the pope from the exercise of his functions. Eugene replied by an excommunication. The Baselites now proclaimed that the Constance decree, *Sacrosancta*,[11] about the autonomy of General Councils, was an article of the Catholic faith, and because of Eugene's ignoring this decree they deposed him (July 25, 1439).[11a] And then, once the complicated business of the reunion with the Greeks was settled, the pope, in the bull *Moyses vir Dei* (September 4, 1439), delivered judgment on these revolutionary acts of 1415. They were utterly null and void, he said, because they were the work of a "council" that represented not the Church but the "obedience" of "John XXIII, *as he was called in that obedience*,"[12] done at a time when, at Constance, the schism was still dominant.

Various European princes had seized the opportunity of the

---

[10] The bull translating the council is dated February 24, 1443.
[11] See p. 265 supra.
[11a] Barry, no. 85, prints a translation of this document.
[12] Italics mine. The sentence is a quotation from the bull, Gill, 312.

scandal to take sides with the Baselites (Aragon) or to declare themselves neutral (France and the Emperor)—always with the hope of "concessions" as the price of support, whether of church revenues or rights of jurisdiction. This was the beginning of a quiet blackmailing of the Holy See that went on for centuries, a permanent feature of international life indeed, whose greatest achievement was the supremely wicked suppression of the Society of Jesus, on the eve of the French Revolution.

At Basel the sacrilegious farce moved logically to the furthermost depths. The assembly elected a "successor" to Eugene, the widowed Duke of Savoy. He called himself Felix V (November 5, 1439). As there was but one cardinal at Basel, the legal problems of securing a clearly valid election will be obvious. They were solved by the expedient of creating, from the body of the council, an electoral college: the solitary cardinal, 11 bishops, 7 abbots, 13 theologians, and a licentiate of Canon Law; 33 in all.

Felix and his supporters were soon at loggerheads, about the simple, crude business of cash. And soon he had left them, to return to his princely solitude at Ripaille. The council found it had less and less work to do. When, after the death of Eugene IV (February 23, 1447) the emperor abandoned his pretence of neutrality, and came out on the side of his successor, Nicholas V, Basel asked the council to find another home. When Felix made his submission to the new pope, the council also gave in, going through a formal motion of accepting the "abdication" of Felix, and of "electing" Nicholas V, pope of course ever since the conclave two years before. Nicholas, once a poor scholar and now a princely-minded humanistic pope, was generous to these clerical pests in the hour of his triumph. He made Felix a cardinal and gave him a pension, and he restored the red hat to the late president of the council, who had crowned Felix and given him episcopal consecration, the archbishop of Arles, Louis d'Aleman.

18. *The Fifth General Council of the Lateran, 1512–17*

This Fifth General Council of the Lateran really originated in the tangled politics, national and international, of the last years of the reign of Pope Julius II (1503–13). It was called as the pope's reply to the summoning of an antipapal *conciliabulum* at Pisa, and this gathering owed its existence to an alliance of the French king, Louis XII, with a small group of cardinals hostile to the pope and his policies. This pope, a man of sixty years at his accession was, it is true, a politician born. Trained at the court of his uncle, Pope Sixtus IV, his Franciscan simplicity all too easily degenerated into the complicated outlook, political and cultural, of the typical Renaissance prince. In Italian history, in the popular saga, this pope, the patron of Michelangelo and Raphael, stands out as one of the *terribili* figures of the time, by which is meant a man possessed of awe-inspiring, demonic energy, in whom competence and high temper combine to force through the execution of great designs and the accomplishment of titanic ambitions. But the ambition of Julius II was not merely personal. He proposed to make the pope really master in his own States of the Church, ending once and for all the problem of the feudatories and the restive municipalities; and he hoped to free Italy from the yoke of "Barbarian" kings, thus making doubly secure the independence of the popes from all control by the lay power.

War was, more or less inevitably, the principal occupation of his ten years' pontificate and, given the age, this meant incessant diplomatic campaigns also, where, in a pattern of the greatest complexity, alliance succeeded alliance, enemies becoming friends and vice versa in rapid, bewildering succession, the elements in the pattern being, besides the pope, the emperor, the kings of Spain, France and England and the republic of Venice. One of these sudden

287

reversals by the pope, the peace with Venice of February 1510, brought Louis XII of France into the position of chief papal enemy. "These French want to make me a mere chaplain to their king," said Julius, "but I mean to be pope, as they will find out."[1] And now he threw into the dungeons of Sant' Angelo the French leader of a long-dissatisfied group of his own innermost council, the college of cardinals, threatening the rest with the like fate. Whence the ensuing alliance.

The fury of the French king drove him very far. If the pope could say to his ambassador, "I look upon your king as my personal enemy,"[2] Machiavelli could report from the French court to his own state, "You can imagine what is said here about the pope. Obedience is to be renounced and a [General] Council hung round his neck. The complete annihilation of his power, both temporal and spiritual, is the least of the penalties that await him."[3]

Louis XII was, indeed, about to summon a national council of his bishops. It met in September at Tours. In the presence of the king and the papal nuncio the bishops gave their verdict: the king was in the right, in this quarrel, and if necessary he could withdraw France from its obedience to the pope, and disregard any sentences of excommunication. They also advised that the king demand the calling of a General Council. Louis announced that he would march on Rome, and himself depose the pope. And five of the cardinals fled from Rome to join his army at Milan (October 1510).

By this time the pope had left Rome for the north and the seat of war. He fell ill and all but died (October to December), made a marvellous recovery and, in the snowy January of 1511, took part in the siege of Mirandola. But a change in the French high command now brought victories for Louis XII, and the papal negotiations to win over the emperor, Maximilian, failed. Bologna, the second greatest city of the pope's state, was captured and then, five days later (May 28), came the supreme insult and menace: Julius was served with the proclamation of the rebel cardinals, sent to all the leading princes of Europe, summoning a General Council to meet at Pisa, September 1, and citing him to appear.

---

[1] Quoted by Pastor, English translation of *History of the Popes*, VI, 326. The pope said this to the Venetian ambassador.
[2] Ibid., 327. The date is "beginning of July," 1510.
[3] Ibid., 329. The date assigned is July 21, 1510.

Louis XII was now master of northern Italy, the Venetian allies had been of no service. If the Pisa council was ultimately to end in something like farce, the move of the cardinals was, at the moment, heavy with menace. Canonists could be found everywhere who would assent to the principles on which the move was based: grave scandal given by the pope, a consequent "state of emergency" in the Church—these, according to the famous decree *Frequens* of the council of 1417, were the very matters that authorised cardinals to summon the General Council. The minor of the cardinals' argument was Julius II's disregard of the commands laid on him by *Frequens*, and his failure to keep the oath, sworn in the conclave, to call the General Council within two years. The cardinals had behind them the two principal rulers of Christendom.

An old, very familiar pattern was taking shape, and with a real uncertainty about the future in his mind, Julius made his way back to Rome—but only the more determined. What really saved him now was the wavering, vacillating character of the enemy. Louis, "whether from religious awe," or from fear of the reactions of other princes, made no use of his victory. But in that long march back, with such advisors in his company as the Dominican Master-General, Cajetan, the pope thought out carefully the details of his counterstroke. He reached Rome on June 26, and on July 18 he set his signature to the bull convoking the General Council. It was summoned for April 19, 1512, to meet in the pope's own cathedral church, the Lateran Basilica.

The rebel council was, by this time, in dire straits. It did indeed open its proceedings at Pisa, but on November 1. And with no more than sixteen French bishops; and not in the cathedral, for the canons had barred the doors against the assembly. Nor had the bishops been able to secure lodgings, until the Florentine government intervened forcibly. For ten days or so the motions of a General Council were gravely imitated while the citizens outside fought the French guards, and by night serenaded the cardinals with threats of death. On November 12 the bishops renewed the anti-papal decrees of Constance, pronounced that they would not separate until the whole Church had been reformed and peace established between all Christian princes—and also that the council, being in danger from the citizens of Pisa, would forthwith be transferred to Milan. And here, from December 1511 to June 1512, it continued its futilities, amid a population no less hostile, but protected from this by the arms of Louis XII. When, after the great French victory of Ravenna (April 11, 1512) the French cause, unexpectedly, fell into desperate straits, the council moved to Asti, and thence across the Alps to Lyons, where it finally petered out, without any particular final formalities. Its last definite act had been at Milan where, taking new courage from the victory of Ravenna, it had suspended Julius II and forbidden him to exercise any of his functions as pope.

This General Council which Julius had called was to last a good five years, until March 16, 1517, in fact—just seven months before Luther's dramatic defiance, the theses against Indulgences. The juxtaposition of these dates is, surely, significant. That, in the years when Luther was inwardly being turned from a Catholic friar into a Protestant apostle, a General Council should be in session whose *raison d'être* was reform—this is an historical coincidence that at first sight takes the breath away. It is no doubt true, as the modern historians seem to agree, that it was not the need of reform in church administration that started the engines of revolt in 1517, but a spiritual crisis in Luther wherein was mirrored the crisis in a myriad other souls. But why did the Fifth Council of the Lateran have all but no effect upon the life of the Church? Without professing to solve this question, we can examine how the council worked, what it actually decreed, and say something of the personages whose character influenced what was done.

There was an average attendance at the council of about 90 to 100 bishops, and almost all of them were from sees in one or other of the Italian states, subjects, that is, of the King of Spain, of Florence, Venice and the rest, as well as of the pope. There were no more than twelve public meetings of the council in all: four in 1512, four in 1513, and one in each of the years 1514, 1515, 1516, 1517. The legislation of the council appeared in the form of papal bulls, published in the several sessions. Of the organisation of the council, and the discussions that preceded the drafting of these documents, we know very little, save that it was the Curia that decided what was to be enacted in the sessions of the council, in detail; and that the bishops were allowed to elect a committee of twenty-four to discuss these drafts (or proposals) while in this formative state. The twenty-four were formed into three groups of eight, according to the matter to be studied: the question of the schism and of international peace; the reform of the Church; the faith, and the problem of the French law, called the Pragmatic Sanction,[3a] which for seventy years had, in effect, given indirect official recognition to the condemned Council of Basel. To each of these commissions of eight the pope added eight cardinals and two Generals of religious orders—a means of securing that the bishops should not overdo the business of radical reform in, say, the practice of the Curia or the life of the mendicant orders. Finally, the whole body of bishops debated the draft at a "general congregation."

These arrangements—which, from the bishops' point of view, were an improvement on those originally made—were the work of the new pope, Leo X, elected after the council had held six sessions. For Julius II died within a week of the sixth session, on February 22, 1513. The new pope, Giovanni de' Medici, thirty-seven years of age, and not yet ordained priest, was elected March 11, and first presided at the council in its seventh session, April 27.

The six sessions under Julius II were chiefly taken up with the leisurely business of the formal organisation of the council, with the condemnation of the schismatic manoeuvres of the rebel cardinals (sessions 3 and 4, May 17 and December 3, 1512), the appointment of a commission to study the question of the Pragmatic Sanction, which Julius was determined to bring to an end and, one of the spectacular events of the council, the emperor's formal repudiation of the Pisa Council and his solemn acceptance of the Lateran Council as a lawful General Council (December 3, 1512).

For the session of February 16, 1513, the pope had ordered the presentation of a bull against simony in papal elections. He was manifestly dying for some weeks before the day appointed came, but almost his last words were that this should be enacted. The bull provides briefly, among other things, that if anyone secures election as pope through simony, through bribes whether of money or of position or promise of favours, his election is null; and the

---

[3a] For a translation of this, see Barry, no. 87A.

elect, and those who have taken the bribes, are by the fact excommunicated, and they remain so until a pope lawfully elected absolves them. This bull, *Si summus rerum opifex*,[4] was the most useful piece of work accomplished in the council, and because of the way it was drawn, the one act wholly effective.

It is, however, with the successor of Julius that the Fifth Lateran Council is chiefly associated, through the twelve decrees promulgated in the four years 1513–17. Within two months of the first session of Leo's reign, the pope had the satisfaction of receiving the submission of the two surviving rebel cardinals, who (to their great chagrin) were commanded to make their public submission dressed simply as priests—their deposition by Julius II was no mere formality, and it was as priests they were received back, reading out a prepared formula of contrition and repudiation in which their great crime was explicitly set forth and the justice of their punishment acknowledged. And then the pope magnanimously restored them to their rank, but not to the benefices they had held, June 27. These, in the interval following their deposition, had been conferred on others. Thousands flocked to the Vatican to gloat over this spectacle of humiliation, so many indeed that officials feared that the stairs and the floors of the state apartments would give way.

It was next the turn of the King of France. The new pope came of a family traditionally friendly to France, and personally he was disposed to give up the cause of the Holy League that Julius II had formed. But on June 10, the pope's Swiss allies defeated the French so thoroughly at Novara (near Milan) that it was a mere remnant that got back to France. Louis XII was crippled, to the delight of all Italy and of Rome especially, where mobs paraded, crying "Victory" and "Julius II." The new pope did not dare to do more for Louis than to keep away from the victory celebrations. And soon the king, alarmed at the new anti-French coalition where the pope had no part, sent commissioners to Rome to treat of submission. A means was found by which the necessary act could be done with due "saving of face." On December 19, 1513, the French envoys appeared in the council, and announced their master's formal repudiation of the schism and his acceptance of the Lateran

---

[4] Not printed by Schroeder.

Council as truly a lawful General Council of the Church. This was but a more public repetition of what had taken place privately where, as the pope absolved the French king, he explained that this was only being done for the great safety of his soul, the sentence of Julius II against the Council of Pisa and its supporters not having been meant as against Louis XII. But the general opinion of the day laughed at the notion that there was any sincerity in the king's submission. And there still remained the question of the Pragmatic Sanction!

It is sometimes harshly said that almost more important than what was done at this council is the question why almost nothing came of its various activities. But in the first of the sessions under Leo X where decrees were voted, December 19, 1513, there is an important definition regarding the faith. The occasion of this was the reappearance of the atheistic philosophy of Averroës, particularly in the university of Padua in the teaching of a leading thinker of the day, Pietro Pomponazzi. The council now condemns (with no mention of any particular teacher) all who assert that the intellectual soul in man is mortal, or that there is but one single intellective soul [operating] for the whole human race. The intellectual soul is, *per se* and essentially, the form of the human body, as Clement V at the General Council of Vienne has taught already. This soul is immortal, and is single for each individual of the multitude of human beings. "Moreover, since one truth cannot contradict another truth, every assertion contrary to the truth of faith we define to be altogether false"—this against those who say that these errors about the immortality of the soul and its singularity (i.e., that for each human being there is a separate individual intellectual soul) are true, at least philosophically speaking. All who teach otherwise than the council are condemned as heretics and infidels, and must be punished accordingly.[5]

A second decree, published in the session of May 14, 1515, includes a declaration on a point of morals. This decree is meant to end a long controversy about practices in the loan offices set up by pious associations as a charity whereby poor people may borrow money and yet escape the usury of the professional moneylenders.

[5] For the text of the decree (from which the quotation is taken) see Denzinger, no. 738

The question has been raised whether these charitable agencies (called in Latin *montes pietatis*) are guilty of the sin of usury if they ask from their clients not only the full sum lent to them but also a small charge to help to cover the running expenses of the office (not however a profit in any way for the office). The bull gives the decision that this practice is perfectly lawful, and that such loans are by no manner of means to be considered an act of usury. All who, after this decree, continue so to stigmatise such loans, whether laymen, priests, or religious, incur the penalty of excommunication.[6]

Another decree of this same tenth session, after an eloquent compliment to the new invention of printing, establishes the principle of the censorship of what it is proposed to print—pornography has already begun its long, profit-making course, and books are appearing dangerous to a Christian's faith. We are, in 1515, only two years away from the great publicity campaign—Lutheranism—where, for the first time, the possibilities of the new invention will be shown in all their fullness. The censor, ex officio, of all books everywhere is the diocesan bishop, and his licence to publish the book is to be clearly printed in it. No charge is to be made for this censorship service.[7]

That preaching, at this time, had fallen on evil days we should know even though the council did not explicitly say so—it is a commonplace of all the contemporary literature. While too many priests are too ignorant to preach, says the council, very many others do no more than divert themselves, learnedly or foolishly, whenever they find themselves in a pulpit. So the council recalls the simple ideal and, passing to abuses that call for correction, it sharply forbids the common practice of preachers' prophesying, e.g., that the last day is at hand, that Antichrist is abroad, that the Divine wrath is about to consume us, etc. "Those who have made such predictions are liars." The preacher is forbidden to draw from Holy Scripture conclusions as to any future happenings, or to say he has been sent by God to say this, or that he knows it by a revelation. A second chronic source of mischief in the Middle Ages is also rebuked—preachers

---

[6] Ibid., no. 739 for the text.
[7] Bull *Inter sollicitudines*, May 4, 1515. Schroeder, op. cit., prints extracts from it, p. 504. This work never gives more than the essential passages in dealing with this council.

are strictly forbidden to preach about the sins of other clergy, "publicly defaming the character of bishops, prelates and others in authority." By "the preacher" is meant, given the age, a friar of one of the four mendicant orders, for almost the whole of what preaching was done was their work. Their superiors are now warned to see that they are fit and competent for the office, and the preachers are bidden to show the local bishop these testimonies to their piety and fitness. Preachers who offend against the decree are, of course, to be stringently punished.[8]

Leo X is a pope for whom the ecclesiastical historians have harsh words. This Lateran Council is never reckoned among his claims to a revised verdict. Nowhere is it a more tragic disappointment than in the reform decrees of its ninth and tenth sessions (May 6, 1514, and May 4, 1515). The parlous condition of ecclesiastical life at this time is a commonplace of all the historians. It was almost the single topic of the sermons preached to the council. And in no place was what was seriously wrong so indecently flaunted as in the city of Rome, and at the very court of Leo X. The gravest of all pro-papal historians, Ludwig von Pastor, presents the life of the court as the effect of a pope whose one interest in life was pleasure —intellectual pleasure, music, sculpture, painting, poetry, the drama; and the chase, for this seems to have been the first pope who hunted, it was his great passion. What are called the graver vices left him untouched—not so, only too often, the men whom he promoted to the highest ecclesiastical rank. As to public affairs, the pope's main problem was to maintain a balance in Italy between the foreign rivals who dominated, the kings of France and Spain. The papal policy was one of systematic deceit, the pope steering always by two compasses, as Muratori was to write, never trusted by either side. And behind all this diplomatic trickery— which failed more often than it succeeded—lay the timorous young pope's chief care, that his family's precarious hold on Florence should be transformed into a permanent, recognised, quasi-royal position. The thought of such a personage, "gilded butterfly" indeed, passing from the comedians and buffoons of his palace to the reform debates in the General Council leaves one aghast.[9]

---

[8] Bull *Supernae maiestatis praesidio*, Dec. 19, 1516, Schroeder, 505–6.

[9] For all this see the well-documented account in Pastor, op. cit., vol. VIII, 71–125.

Little wonder that, as the historians have read the decrees, they discount as platitude the conventional expressions of horror at abuses, and sneer at sternly worded reform laws which are peppered with exceptions, and legal loopholes to make disobedience lawful. The magnificent gesture, only too often, peters out in the feeble conclusion, "We therefore . . . repeating all our predecessors have said, renew all they have decreed. . . ." Certainly, to read the opening passage of the decree that is to provide better bishops for the future, and better abbots, is an experience to try one's patience; or to read the reforms imposed on the cardinals of the Roman Curia, solemnly saying their servants must not wear long hair or grow beards and the like, while at every step, in the gravest matters, the most extraordinary exceptions are legalised. All the main topics that had caused reformers and saints to groan for a good two hundred years and more are mentioned—benefices (sees among them, of course) given to bad men or to good men otherwise altogether unsuited; plurality of benefices (whose duties are incompatible) given to the favoured minority; abbeys given *in commendam,* that is to say to clerics not monks at all, whose sole purpose is to take from the monks their revenue, for the profit of the absentee secular priest or bishop. All these wonders by means of papal dispensations. So, no more abbeys are to be dealt with in this way, "unless" (almost the key word in this unhappy legislation) "in consideration of the present state of things . . . it should be considered expedient to do otherwise." Pluralities of incompatible offices—to be a bishop in Spain and at the same time an archbishop in France and an abbot in Italy, to hold canonries in half a dozen cathedrals at once—dispensations for these are to be limited, and so, "those who hold more than four such, are to resign all but four" within a given space of time, two years. Monasteries given *in commendam* for the future are to go only to cardinals and well-deserving persons, and the commendatory's financial hold on the abbey is somewhat restricted.[10]

There were two running fights through the greater part of this council, and it was one of Leo X's anxieties to keep them within due limits, the fight between the bishops and the cardinals of the Roman Curia, of which the reforms just mentioned are a faint echo, and the fight between the bishops and the orders of friars, which

[10] Bull *Supernae dispositionis arbitrio,* May 5, 1514, Schroeder, 488–98.

went on for a good three years and threatened, at one time, to wreck the council. Its monument is the decree of the eleventh session (December 19, 1516): *Dum intra mentis arcana.*[11]

The burden of the bishops' complaints was that the friars—thanks to the privileges lavished on them by pope after pope for centuries—had become a law unto themselves, and that their superiors were unable, or unwilling, to keep them in order. From time to time reform movements had sprung up in one order after another, and had received every encouragement from Rome, and the reformed had been given a kind of autonomy. But the original stocks, called the conventuals, were the cause of endless trouble. The bishops called for a wholesale cancelling of the privileges that put the friars outside their control, and even—some of the bishops—for the suppression of the conventual orders. It was the good fortune of the friars that, at this moment, two of the very ablest men in the Church were friars, and general-superiors of their respective orders: Cajetan, of the Dominicans and Egidio Canisio of the Augustinians—men for whom there were higher considerations than the mere prestige of their order.

It was an easy task for the friars to retaliate on these Renaissance bishops the charges of worldliness, materialism, and ill-living, and to ask how else (were the friars to disappear) the ordinary people would gain any knowledge of religion, or find confessors with knowledge enough to administer the sacrament properly. It was the pope's mediation that stilled the tumult, and Cajetan went so far as to say, publicly, that Leo alone at this crisis stood between the orders and destruction.

The new decree set out in great detail the rights of the bishops to intervene when religious superiors are negligent, and the limitations to the spiritual activities of the friars vis-à-vis the rights of the resident parochial clergy. Bishops are given power to examine those presented by their superiors to be confessors. Friars have no power to absolve from excommunications imposed by the bishop. It is to the diocesan bishop they must have recourse for ordination, consecration of churches, altars, cemeteries, and the like. They are not to marry people unless the pastor of the contracting parties consents. They are to remind those whose confessions they hear of their

11 Ibid., 506–9.

obligation to pay tithes to their pastor, and to instruct people about this in their sermons. And so the list goes on, twenty-two points in all. But whatever rights, whether of bishops or of friars, are not mentioned here remain unchanged. Also the new law applies to all the other religious orders.

The submission of Louis XII had left the question of the Pragmatic Sanction entirely untouched—for all that a commission of the council was studying it. Relations between king and pope were too tense, no doubt, for any mention of it to be safe. It was, however, to be solved very speedily and in a way none could have guessed. Louis survived his reconciliation just a year, dying on January 1, 1515. His successor was the somewhat distant cousin, the Count of Angoulême, who had married Louis' elder daughter— King Francis I, a young man just reaching his twentieth year. This new king took up his father-in-law's plans for a renewal of the Italian war, but with much greater energy, and without any of the older man's vacillation. In September 1515 he won a victory at Marignano that washed out all memory of the French disasters. All Italy was now at his mercy, Medici Florence of course, and even the Papal States. And it was the pope's misfortune that he had been leagued with the defeated Swiss. Leo X had no choice, as a temporal ruler, but to await the terms the conqueror would impose.

The two men met at Bologna, in December 1515. For a week they lived together in the same house, meeting daily for long conversations with not even a secretary in attendance. No detail of these momentous talks ever leaked out. But Francis left the Medici in Florence, and made no further advance into Italy. The coveted Duchy of Milan he, of course, took for France. And, in a bold gesture, he suddenly asked Leo to confirm the Pragmatic Sanction. It was an impossible request, and the king knew it. But it meant that the pope must make some settlement that would leave the king in possession. And so there came into existence one of the most famous treaties in all Church History, the French Concordat of 1516. By this the pope gave the kings of France the right to choose and present for appointment (which meant, in practice, to appoint) all the 93 bishops of France, all the 510 abbots and priors (with a few exceptions), and a host of other major beneficiaries—

offices whose revenues were almost equal to that of the nation itself. But in return the king abandoned the Pragmatic Sanction—
the Church in France would no longer be operating on a quasi-
schismatical basis, and its connection with the condemned schismatical Council of Basel would be at an end.

To the modern Catholic it is usually the pope's surrender that is
the striking feature of these arrangements. But to the French, in
1516, it seemed that the pope had got the better of the king. Their
fury rose to great heights, and the *Parlement de Paris* staunchly
refused to register the royal edict and thus give the arrangements
force of law. It took nearly two years of campaigning before Francis I overcame the opposition, and he only did so by an altogether
unusual act of the royal authority. Meanwhile, in December 1516,
the pope laid the two bulls before the council, explaining what
they effected, and asking the council to approve. There were critics
among the bishops and hostile speeches, but the council approved.

The bull *Pastor Aeternus* which records the surrender of the Pragmatic Sanction has a much wider interest than that of a mere change
in the local French situation. It was an opportunity for the pope
to reaffirm the doctrine that the Roman See is the mistress-see of
the whole Church of Christ, and so to describe the régime which
the Pragmatic Sanction had set up as an outrage on the divinely
founded authority of the papacy. None of the bishops named by
the various kings—in the years it endured—had been more than
"tolerated" by the popes. It was an opportunity, no less evidently,
to comment on the Council of Basel as it continued in defiance of
the translation to Ferrara, and to deny that it was then an assembly
with any authority at all. Like Pisa, in 1511, it was a mere conventicle (*conciliabulum*). The pope says plainly that the reigning pope
alone can call a General Council into being.[12] He can at will adjourn it or dissolve it. And the reminder that the Roman See is
sovereign in the Church was driven home by a renewal of the famous bull *Unam Sanctam* of Boniface VIII (1302). If such a
reign as Leo X's can be said to have a climax, this was surely the
day when the pope saw the General Council endorse this bull
Pastor Aeternus, and as it came to him to give his vote in the coun-

---

[12] Denzinger, no. 740, prints this section of the bull; Barry, no. 87B, a translation of the whole.

cil the pope could not contain himself. "*Non solum placet*," he called out, "*sed multum placet et perplacet*."[13]

Three months later the eighteenth General Council came to an end, March 16, 1517, with a decree forbidding the looting of the cardinals' palaces during vacancies of the Holy See, and a second that imposed a special tax on all benefices, for the expenses of the war against the Turks.

---

[13] The bishops voted "for," by rising and saying (each in his turn), *Placet*, i.e., "It pleases me." What the pope said was "It not only pleases me, it pleases me greatly, very greatly indeed."

19. The General Council of Trent, 1545–63

Martin Luther's revolt was, almost from the beginning, an essential matter, i.e., it was explicitly directed against the pope's essential claim that he is the ruler of the whole Church of Christ. He had already moved away from the Catholic belief, in certain matters regarding the divine forgiveness of sins, by the time he made the famous attack on Indulgences with which Protestantism began (1517). Within a further six months he was writing that the first thing needed in order to cure the manifold ills that afflicted religion was to overthrow the whole accepted system of theological teaching (1518). To the papal legate who now called on him, in the name of a fundamental papal law, to withdraw his teaching about Indulgences Luther replied by denying the validity of that law; and, within a few weeks, by appealing from the pope who had commissioned the legate, to the judgment of the next General Council whenever it should meet—an appeal made in due legal form, and in defiance of the papal law that forbade such appeals. The controversies continued without intermission, and a year later than the appeal (i.e., in 1519) Luther's mind had moved so far that he now denied that General Councils had any special divine protection that kept them from erroneous teaching when deciding questions about belief.

These rebellious principles were listed among the errors for which Luther was condemned by the papal bull *Exsurge Domine* (June 15, 1520). He was given sixty days to appear and publicly recant his sayings. Instead, he wrote two most violent—and exceedingly popular—pamphlets, the one to show how the popes had systematically corrupted the whole teaching of Christ for a thousand years and so led all the world astray, the other denouncing the papal institution as a vast financial racket which, for centuries, had been draining the life out of Germany. In impassioned phrases he called on the princes of Germany to destroy the papacy, and to wash their hands in the blood of the sacrilegious impostors at Rome. As to the bull *Exsurge*, Luther waited until the fatal sixtieth day, and then with a vast amount of public mockery, he threw it into the bonfire kindled on the town dunghill—and into the flames he threw, after the bull, the whole collection of the popes' laws binding the whole Church of Christ.

This was spectacular, and symbolical. Not for centuries had there been any defiance so far-reaching—and with the encouragement and protection of the state. To what means were the popes, drawing on a vast experience of crisis, now to turn and so avert the general destruction that threatened German Catholicism? There could only be one answer, since this was the opening of the sixteenth century. From all quarters came a demand for the classic panacea. The pope must call a General Council. And finally the General Council met, the Council of Trent—but not until twenty-five years after the great defiance of the appeal to the princes and the Wittenberg bonfire.

Since in all that long time the needed council never ceased to be talked of by Catholics and by rebels, by princes and by popes, and since it was amid the angry dissensions on the subject between Catholic princes and the popes that the men were largely formed who actually were the Council of Trent, to recall something of those twenty-five unhappy years is a first condition of understanding the history of the council, of its failures as of its splendid successes.

The sentences of bishops, and popes also, against heretics were mere noise until they were taken up by the State and put into execution. Luther was assured that his own sovereign, the elector Frederick the Wise, would not execute the bull *Exsurge*. It was however quite another thing to be assured that the sentence would remain a dead letter once the pope had appealed to the emperor and the princes of Germany, assembled at the first diet of the new emperor's reign. It met at Worms in January 1521, and in the way it both thwarted and supported the pope it was curiously prophetic of the history of the coming years. The princes accepted the papal sentence, and they made it their own by outlawing Luther. Whoever could, might kill him without fear of punishment, as though he were a dangerous bandit. But they ignored the papal sentence to this extent that they re-tried Luther; that is to say, they gave him a hearing, under a safe conduct, refusing to listen to the protestations of the ambassador whom the pope had sent to direct the action of the diet. The action of this solemn assembly was thus a great public flouting of the papal law, a serious repudiation, in a most serious matter, of the will of the man whom all these princes acknowledged to be the head of their church.

This is not the place in which to tell again the familar story of the events of the next ten years. But something must be said, however briefly, about the papal delay in applying the only remedy that could meet the German situation—the General Council.

The general attitude towards the plan of a General Council may thus be summed up: the man who was pope through the greater part of the period, Clement VII (1523–34), was at heart consistently hostile; the cardinals and other officers of his Curia were, for quite other reasons, still more hostile; the German Catholics were eager for a council, but a council in which they would really matter, a council fashioned rather after the pattern of a parliament than General Councils have usually been; the Catholic kings who enter the story are Charles I of Spain (just lately become the emperor Charles V), the life-long champion of the council idea, and Francis I of France, its bitterest opponent. And the history of Europe during the crucial twenty-five years, 1520–45, is little more than the history of the duel between these two princes. In their wars Clement VII, as often as he dared, sided with the King of France, for purely political reasons—it was, invariably, the side that lost.

The council problem comes to this, that a General Council was absolutely necessary, and that, for political reasons, it was just not possible to summon one. Whence, inevitably, on the part of Charles V, and of the German princes, a succession of schemes to bring back the Lutherans (for this, in the early years, is what it was hoped the council would achieve) by negotiations, conferences, local councils, informal councils, and the like. All of these failed and, in the long run, these ventures complicated the problem of reconciliation or submission; while the refusal of the Holy See really to take action gradually destroyed all confidence in its integrity among the Catholic princes of Germany. To such a depth, indeed, had the prestige of Rome sunk that when the successor of this timorous, vacillating, and all too worldly-wise pope announced, in the first hours of his reign, that he proposed to summon a General Council, the news stirred not a ripple among the Catholic reformers of Germany.

This second pope was Paul III (1534–49) and ultimately he lived to see the council he had dreamed of meet at Trent, but after bitter vicissitudes—for some of which history must hold his own personal failings responsible. The catalogue of these events needs to be set down.

By the time of the election of Paul III (October 13, 1534) the situation in Germany had radically altered since Leo X had first faced the problem in the Diet of Worms (1521). The Lutheran movement had long since passed from the stage where it was a matter of preachers and writers and the masses they influenced. The state was now in control of it, half a dozen princes in central Germany and a number of leading cities north and south. In all these places the adherents of the new religion and the preachers were organised into churches, installed in the buildings that had once been Catholic; monasticism had been abolished and the monks' properties taken over by the state; the clergy who wished had married, with the state's approval; the mass was everywhere forbidden and the new rites made obligatory; and these Lutheran states were banded together in a formidable military alliance, so powerful that it had been able (at a moment when a Turkish invasion threatened) to ignore the diet's summons to disband and submit, and furthermore it had won for their sect's new status in these regions a provisional acquiescence from the emperor.

One root of Clement VII's troubles had been his ambition to strengthen the hold of his family—the Medici—as rulers in what had been the republic of Florence. With Paul III there was the like family concern, to see his son, Pierluigi, established among the reigning families of Europe. In the end the pope succeeded, giving him in fief the duchies of Parma and Piacenza, carved out of the States of the Church, and marrying Pierluigi's son—Ottavio—to a natural daughter of Charles V. The intricate business of forcing his offspring into the charmed circle of royalty-by-birth, the negotiations with Charles for example over recognition of the new duchies, runs like a subtle poison through what was, despite the very evident Renaissance worldliness of this great pope, the leading policy of his reign, the calling of this council that would reform the life of the Church and heal the divisions in Germany.

Paul III's first obstacle was his cardinals, who voted unanimously against the plan to call a council, when he proposed it. After an exhaustive study of the situation in Germany—a matter where he had everything to learn—he despatched nuncios to all the courts of Europe, to the Lutherans as well, with invitations to attend. The French king was unfavourable, the German Protestants refused with insults. In these negotiations a whole year went by, and then, on June 2, 1536, the official announcement was made: the council would meet at Mantua, May 23, 1537. What followed next, however, was a whole series of postponements that finally brought the Catholics of Germany to feel that the new pope was as shifty as the old; postponements first to November 1537, then to May 1538, then to April 1539, and then a postponement indefinitely.

The reasons given were real enough, the steady refusal of the French king to co-operate (i.e., in practice, the impossibility of any French bishop or cardinal taking part in the council), the renewal of the war between France and the emperor, and so forth. But it came to be believed that the true cause was that the pope really preferred that the council should not ever take place.

Actually, as the years went by, Paul III came to understand that the task before the council was much more complex than he had conceived, or his official advisors. As was to be the case with the Vatican Council, three hundred years later, the official world began by oversimplifying the problem. The heresies, it was thought, could be simply dealt with by re-enacting the various decrees in which, at their first appearance, centuries before, they had been condemned. There would, of course, be no need to discuss such burning topics as the reform of the Curia Romana—that was not the business of any council, but a matter for the pope's personal action. The reform of Catholic life, again, called for no great research; the old laws were adequate, if only they were enforced. The council, once it met, would accomplish its task in a matter of weeks. Actually, the working time of the Council of Trent—to anticipate the story—was to amount to four and a half years; the constant hard work of the bishops and theologians who attended would produce a mass of decrees and canons exceeding in volume the whole of the legislation of all the previous eighteen General Councils.

What was also gradually borne in on Paul III was that the kind of council he had in mind—the traditional meeting of bishops—was not at all what Charles V was thinking of, nor the Catholics of Germany. Was the coming council to begin with a new religious crisis, with all these champions of the council demanding a say in how it should conduct its business, in what should appear upon its agenda? The Catholic critics of the intolerable abuses—for which the Roman Curia was generally held responsible—now expected to be heard, at the council. Luther's insistent cry, that there would never be any reform so long as Rome controlled the council, found echoes in the secret thoughts of many of Luther's Catholic adversaries.

And the achievement of the councils of Constance and of Basel, in those sessions ever since officially disregarded, came into the mind of more than one Catholic reformer as the obvious instrument to bring off the desired improvement. The acts of these councils, the wholeheartedly Catholic bishop of Vienna (for example) wrote to Rome, were indispensable as a guide to the council now under consideration. German bishops, supporting the pope's desire for a council, were taking for granted that just as they desired it should meet in Germany, so it would follow the pattern of these two classic German councils. How was the pope to accept this position, and not risk at the outset a new damaging controversy about the nature of his own authority? a controversy that might send thousands of Catholics in Germany, not, indeed, into the Lutheran body but into schism no less disastrous. Then there were the Catholics who, for years, had been thinking that unless the power of the Curia to grant dispensations were checked, reform legislation would be a dead letter from the day it was enacted.

"The pope was not merely having bad dreams when he saw these dangers."[1] And so he hesitated, time and again, and even when he did not hesitate he failed to be insistent. With all his gifts—and with the merit of the great reform he had achieved in his own personal life—Paul III was far from that perfect state where the supernatural controls every act and every thought. He was not a

[1] Jedin, *A History of the Council of Trent*, I, 351. These last two pages of my account are especially indebted to this great book. Cf. 346–54.

saint. And as his great servant Cardinal Girolamo Morone once expressed it, "He who conducts God's business must not be exclusively actuated by human considerations."[2]

The emperor now won over the pope to try what another, much lauded method might do to bring peace to Germany, the method of peaceful negotiation between the theologians of both parties, with reunion (perhaps) as the fruit of "a better understanding of what it is that divides us." For many years some leading Catholics had been urging that this way promised better results, some of them influenced in part—let it be bluntly stated—by the fatal delusion that the differences between the Church and the Lutheran bodies did not amount to a real separation. This seemingly incredible blindness had one source in the dangerous superficialities of Erasmus, who, for example, saw no reason why any differences mattered provided men agreed in accepting Christ, and who could not understand why either party would not accept as a sufficient statement of the Eucharistic mystery the unexamined ambiguity that Christ is here present somehow. The "appalling" intellectual confusion of which Jedin[3] speaks is indeed, by this time, a leading characteristic of the age among the Catholics.

Let it be remembered, also, that in the twenty years since the somewhat elementary directions of the bull *Exsurge*, Rome had not said a word about the divergencies. Lutheranism had, since then, developed all its doctrines, and a varied host of Catholic writers, each according to his lights and temperament, had, in criticising the heresiarch, offered his own solution for the new theological problems he had posed. For the Catholic princes and their political advisors the "conference" method offered this advantage that an official business like the General Council must result in clear-cut definitions of doctrine; in sentences, that is to say, and a summons to accept these or take the appropriate punishment; in strong resistance, and—who knows?—in civil war. And this with Francis I longing to renew the war against Charles; and the French ally, the Turk, already at the gates! Of the emperor's critical position, in the world of armies, of the grave risk of a Catholic defeat, the belligerents in the Sacred College and the Curia knew all too little.

[2] Ibid., 354.
[3] Op. cit., 369.

Paul III never lost sight of all this. His knowledge was one reason for his reluctance to act with decision.

The high-water mark of the reunion-through-negotiation movement was the conference held at Ratisbon in the summer of 1541, about which historians are still arguing. This history is of interest because it does much to explain what, at first sight, is utterly incomprehensible, viz., that nearly thirty years went by before the vitally necessary council met, and also because it reveals the nature of one serious weakness that hampered the Catholic champions in these critical years.

To Ratisbon, where most of the princes of Germany attended and the emperor himself, there came two of the principal reformers, Philip Melanchthon and Martin Bucer, the last-named bringing with him a reformer of the second generation who was soon to eclipse in influence all the rest, the young John Calvin. The pope sent, as legate, the Venetian Gaspar Contarini, theologian and statesman, the greatest figure the Curia had known for generations, and a man of saintly life. If Contarini, a steady opponent of extreme solutions, went to Ratisbon still really believing that disagreement about the essentials was not so serious as many believed, he was soon enlightened. Though he contrived an apparent, momentary harmony on the question of Justification, there was no resolving the flat contradictions he encountered on the doctrines of the Eucharist and of the sacrament of Penance. The conference failed utterly, and when Paul III announced that the preparation for the General Council would be resumed the emperor did not dissent. The conference had had this useful result: it demonstrated to the "practical" minds the truth which the controversial theology of twenty years had ever insisted on, that Catholicism and the new theologies were contradictory, and impossible to reconcile.

The bull convoking the council is dated May 22, 1542. It was to meet on November 1 following, at the episcopal city of Trent, the first town outside Italy on the great road along which for a thousand years and more the traffic had travelled between Rome and Germany. Trent was a city of the empire, a German city where the bishop was also the reigning prince. Eighty miles to the north, along the same road, is Innsbruck, the capital of Charles V as Count of Tyrol.

The three legates appointed to preside arrived at Trent on November 22. They found scarcely a single bishop awaiting them. In January 1543 the representatives of the emperor arrived, and very slowly bishops came in—very slowly, for by May there were no more than a dozen. The fact was that four months before the summons of Paul III's bull, the long-expected war had broken out between France and the empire. Francis I had explicitly refused to countenance the council, and had forbidden the hundred bishops of France to leave the country. The emperor, driven to fury by the pope's determined neutrality in the war, had taken a similar course, barring out thereby any participation of the bishops, not only from Spain, but from his kingdom of the Two Sicilies (110 bishops), from the Netherlands, from Austria and Hungary; and affording an excuse for all the bishops of the empire. A General Council, at a time when three fourths of the bishops of the world were violently prevented from attending? By July 1543 there was only one thing to be done, suspend the council yet once again.

How, upon the peace between the rival sovereigns (September 1544), Francis I withdrew his prohibition, while Charles was reconciled to the pope, and how next there supervened the new trouble over the investment of the pope's son with the duchies of Parma and Piacenza—all these highly relevant matters must be studied elsewhere.[4] But in November 1544 Paul III revoked the suspension of the council, and on March 13, 1545, the legates once more made their entry into Trent.

The council was solemnly opened there on December 13, with thirty-one bishops in attendance and forty-eight theologians and canonists, technical experts, summoned to assist them.

It will perhaps help the reader if, before the attempt is made to convey what is contained in the legislation of Trent—itself equal in volume to this present work—it is stated, once and for all, that the various political difficulties that had delayed the council's meeting for so many years never ceased to harass it during its entire progress. Here, of course, lay the cause of the two long suspensions which the council suffered—one of four years and one of ten. The council's history has, in fact, three chapters: sessions 1–10, Decem-

[4] Pastor, *History of the Popes*, XII, chaps. 4, 5; a masterly summary in Jedin, *A History of the Council of Trent*, I, 490–544.

ber 13, 1545, to June 2, 1547; sessions 11–16, May 1, 1551, to April 28, 1552; sessions 17–25, January 17, 1562, to December 4, 1563.

What I now propose to do is to explain how the council organised itself, how the bishops and the technicians did their work, and then to show, by some examples, the tone of the council's treatment of the twofold task before it, viz., the restatement of belief in opposition to the new theologies, and the reformation of Catholic life.

The direction of the council was in the hands of the three cardinal-legates. Of these the senior, Gian Maria del Monte, a man of fifty-eight, had been in the service of the papal curia for well over thirty years. He was esteemed one of its leading canonists and had a vast experience of administration, civil and ecclesiastical. He was the practical man of the trio, level-headed, firm, and a good manager of men. The second in rank, Marcello Cervini, was another type altogether, a theologian primarily and a man of rigidly austere life, dedicated passionately to the extirpation of the abuses that had almost become an ecclesiastical institution. He was not really a curialist at all, and had come to the notice of Paul III as a tutor to the pope's two grandsons whom the old man had made cardinals, at the age of fifteen, in the opening weeks of his reign. The third legate was the solitary English cardinal, Reginald Pole, the near kinsman of King Henry VIII, and an exile for his faith this many a year. His mother, and other relations, had some years before been executed by the king, and the cardinal was continuously in danger from the Italian bravos whom Henry hired to assassinate him. Pole, at forty-five, was roughly Cervini's contemporary, a scholar primarily, the Christian humanist indeed, and learned in the Fathers, in the new Renaissance manner. With his great friend Contarini, whom a premature death had carried off in 1542, he was regarded by all as the very embodiment of the Catholic Reformation. It fell to him to write the opening address of the legates to the council—a frank admission that it was clerical sin mainly that had brought religion to this pass, and a passionate plea for sincerity in the deliberations. One who was present has recorded that as the secretary of the council read the speech, the bishops instinctively turned to look at Pole, recognising from its tone and content who was its actual author. Paul III could have given no clearer sign of his own sincerity than in this association of Cervini and Pole in the direction of the longed-for council.[5]

As to procedure, the bishops decided that only bishops and generals of religious orders should have the right to a vote. The question whether to treat doctrinal matters first (as the pope required, to the anger of Charles V) or the reforms, they settled by treating both simultaneously—along with each decree about a doctrine called in question by the reformers there would be enacted a definite law about reforms. After some experiments the following system of work was adopted. The technicians would debate the proposed decree with the bishops assisting as an audience. This was the meeting called the "particular congregation" of the council. Next the bishops, meeting alone, discussed the matter under the presidency of the legates—the "general congregation"—and came to a final conclusion about the text. Then, in a public meeting called a "session," an open vote was taken and the decree read out as the council's definition. In the first chapter of the council's history the public sessions took place in the cathedral of Trent, later in the church of S. Maria Maggiore. The particular congregations were held in various mansions of the little city. Of the twenty-five public sessions between 1545 and 1563, seventeen were devoted to definition of doctrine and the promulgation of reform laws. The rest were ceremonial occasions for the transacting of the inevitable legal formalities—the opening of the council, the various suspensions, and reopenings, and so forth.

The technical work done by the bishops, the theologians, and the canonists was of a very high order, and the work was done thoroughly. It took, for example, seven months to hammer out the decree on the key doctrine of Justification, forty-four particular congregations and sixty-one general congregations. The decrees about belief especially are evidence of the theological revival that had begun with the emergence of the great figure of Cajetan, and is marked by the teaching of Francis de Vittoria and Soto—the last named of whom actually took part in the council. The language of the decrees, again, is that of men influenced by the new classical

[5] Del Monte is the future pope Julius III (1549–55), Cervini the all too short lived Marcellus II (1555) commemorated in the title of Palestrina's fine mass, and Pole only failed to become pope in 1549 through his refusal to take the least step—he would not even say he was willing—on his own behalf in the conclave.

learning of the Renaissance—as is that other literary monument of the council, the so-called *Catechism of the Council of Trent*. And, all in all, the theological achievement of Trent is a memorial to the small band of competent writers who, from Luther's first adventure, had never ceased to examine critically and to expose the weaknesses and the mischievousness of his theology.

It was a small band also who, at Trent, whether of the theologians or of bishops, brought about this great result. The modern French historian who, to a statement similar to this, appends the word *heureusement* was not merely cynical. The comparatively small number of bishops made for manageable discussions. When, three hundred years later, there appeared at the Vatican Council some seven hundred or so bishops and, in the early days, the drafts of decrees prepared proved inadequate, and debates dragged on endlessly, a prelate who knew his history said, feelingly, "If the Fathers of Trent could rise from their graves, they would disown us." The number of bishops present at the Tridentine sessions varied greatly. At the opening of the council there were, besides the legates, 32. During the remainder of this first (1545–47) period the numbers gradually increased to 68. In the two sessions of the second (1551–52) period there were 44 and 51, respectively. The third (1562–63) period began with 105, and rose to 228 at the session of November 11, 1563. At the closing session there were 176. As well as the bishops, there were also present the generals of five religious orders, who were full members of the council, with the right to speak and to vote. Two of these played a principal rôle in the council, the Augustinian Girolamo Seripando[6] in the Paul III period of the council, and the Jesuit, Diego Lainez in the two closing years.

Throughout the council, the great majority of the bishops were from Italian sees—which does not imply that they were all equally at the disposal of the Curia Romana. The Italy of the sixteenth century was not, of course, a single unified national state. In central Italy—one sixth of the whole Italian territory—the pope was the sovereign. To the south and in Sicily and Sardinia, it was Charles V (as King of Naples) who ruled, and he also ruled the Duchy of Milan in the north. Whether the 110 bishops of the kingdom of

---

[6] Seripando, created cardinal by Pius IV (1559–65), later served as one of the presidents of the council, 1562–63.

Naples were likely to favour papal policies against those of their king needs no telling. To the east of Milan lay the Venetian Republic, one of the most powerful states in Europe which, notoriously and for generations, had taken its own line in ecclesiastical affairs. In a list of 270 bishops present, at one time or another, during the third period of the council, 187 are set down as "Italians," 31 are Spaniards, 26 French, with no more than 2 from Germany.

The various orders of friars played a great part in the council, furnishing the bulk of the theological experts, and—many others of them—sitting as bishops. There were no fewer than 23 Dominican bishops at the council, for instance, and a total of 28 Dominican theologians besides. It was at Trent that St. Thomas Aquinas first really came into his own as the *doctor communis* among the theologians.

The prestige of the Council of Trent was to approach the fabulous in the ensuing centuries. And not surprisingly. In answer to the challenge of the reformers it had surveyed anew the greater part of the Christian belief and had reaffirmed it, always with an especial explicitness about the points where Luther and the rest had gone astray. It had looked directly in the face the dreadful disorders that had for centuries disfigured the practice of religion, and had laid the axe to the root of the tree. It had no less boldly innovated in the remedies it provided. The decrees of Trent "remain to this very day, the most noble part of all the Church's legislation," a modern authority can say.[7] All this is what every man knows about the Council of Trent. It remains for us to examine, a little more in detail, what those scores of pages of reform decrees contain. Perhaps the summary will be less deadly if it follows the simple historical fact that the council abolished altogether many practices hitherto lawful, and introduced much that was new, and that it hoped to secure the future observance of what it now decreed by the related legal devices of a new kind of power for the diocesan bishop and of penalties for wrongdoing that would work automatically. The summary list of the achievements that follows is not, of course, complete, and it does not follow the chronological order of the sessions.

[7] Maroto, *Institutiones Iuris Canonici* (1919), I, 87.

Of all the chronic scandals of the fourteen to the sixteenth centuries none had given rise to more continuous resentment than the papal licences to ecclesiastics to hold more than one see, or abbey, or parish simultaneously—scandals connected with what is called, compendiously, the benefice system. Trent utterly forbade this practice—even where the beneficiaries were cardinals—and the council ordered all existing pluralists to surrender all but one of the benefices they held. It abolished, also, all expectatives, that is to say, all grants of posts when they next fell vacant; and, with these, "coadjutorships with the right of succession," the practice whereby the benefice-holder secured, in his own lifetime, the nomination of his successor (a relative usually) to whom, when something better for himself turned up, he could surrender the parish, or canonry, or see. The choice of coadjutors to sees was strictly reserved henceforth to the pope. Meanwhile the third chronic benefice scandal was checked—the absentee priest or abbot or bishop, who never even saw his flock but merely drew the profits while a hireling tended them at a salary. Dealing with which the council roundly says, "The law about residence has become in practice a dead letter." The new method of dealing with this old trouble was to forbid all licences allowing clerics with a cure of souls to reside away from their posts, to set out in detail the limits of the temporary leave annually allowed them, and to provide an automatic penalty of loss of right to the income—so that the delinquent who managed to get the income was, in effect, stealing it and bound to restitution. No more were there to be sees where, like Milan, no archbishop had resided for a hundred years.

Other dispensations, to the profit of the benefice-hunting cleric, which were now abolished were the permissions which enabled newly appointed bishops to delay their consecration all but indefinitely, so that boys could be appointed to sees, draw their revenues (or their parents draw them in their stead), and, when arrived at an age to be ordained and consecrated, could remain in their semilay state until, succeeding to some lay dignity, they chose to resign an abbey or see, marry and found a family. No one, henceforward, is to be appointed to a see who has not been in Holy Orders for at least six months, and he must be consecrated within six months, or the appointment lapses. For lesser clerics, the dispensation, so often given, to delay receiving the orders which were the very condition of holding the post was likewise abolished; and also licences to be ordained by whatever bishop the cleric chose. Bishops were now told that it was their duty to ordain personally all the clerics destined to work in their own particular sees. The benefice-holder not yet ordained must go for ordination to the bishop of the diocese where his benefice lay.

Money—the cleric's need and desire for more and more of it— was certainly one main cause of the religious malaise whence Luther's chance came. Trent cut away two perennial sources of trouble by abolishing, under most stringent automatic penalties, the custom by which bishops, making the visitation of their dioceses, either levied a tax on the parishes visited, or were given tributes of affection, free gifts, etc., in the shape of money, and otherwise. And it abolished similar age-long customs for the benefit of the bishop at ordinations. Finally the council remembered Luther, and how his revolution had started, in 1517, with a declaration against Indulgences which stressed the scandals deriving from the connection between these and the Christian duty to give alms to pious causes. The council speaks of these abuses as the occasion of heretical blasphemies, and of the wickedness of the alms collectors' practices being the source of great mischief to the ordinary Catholic. The very office—name and thing—of clerical "alms-collector" (*questor* in Latin) is therefore abolished, the council bluntly stating that after two centuries of lawmaking there seemed to be no hope of their amendment. The duty of announcing Indulgences was reserved henceforward to the bishop of the diocese, and, for the future, the giving of an alms was never to be the necessary condition for the gaining of an Indulgence.

Finally, in the matter of marriage, the council restricted the force of the law which forbade marriage between in-laws (so to call them) related through sinful sex relations,[8] between those related through a brother or sister's solemn espousals (*sponsalia*), or by the spiritual relationship set up through the sacrament of baptism —the council frankly admitted that the number of these prohibitions had become an occasion of sin to very many, of invalid marriages, for example, contracted in ignorance, which the partners refused to abandon, and which could not be broken off without dan-

---

[8] As King Henry VIII was "kin" to Anne Boleyn through his sinful association with her older sister, Mary.

ger of further sin. The council also abolished secret marriages—marriages where none need be present but the man and woman who contracted the marriage. Such marriages—provided the parties were really free to marry—were true marriages. But since the fact of the marrying could not be proved by independent testimony, and since the mutual contradiction of the two partners (should one of them choose to abandon the other) was not capable of resolution, these secret marriages were a chronic source of trouble. The Church, says the council's decree (*Tametsi*, November 11, 1563), "has ever held the practice in detestation, and strictly forbidden it." To contract a marriage in this way was, generally speaking, a grave sin. Those married in this clandestine fashion were, once the fact was discovered or admitted, condemned to a public penance in reparation of the scandal, and compelled to renew their matrimonial pledges in due form in the parish church. The council's proposal, to decree that clandestine marriages were, by the fact, not marriages at all, met with strong opposition. All, of course, acknowledged the terrible evil they had caused from time immemorial, but many bishops doubted whether the Church had the power to make the declaration which, for the future, nullified all marriages but those contracted before three witnesses, one of whom must be the parish priest (*parochus*, i.e., "pastor" in the modern American parlance) or a priest licensed by him or by the bishop.[9] The reader will perceive, behind the objection, the shade of a doctrinal controversy about the power of the Church of Christ with reference to the matter and form of the sacraments. To avoid the chance of a debate about this, the council dealt with the practical problem only, and it is among the disciplinary reforms, and not among the decrees on doctrine, that the great change was placed. At the same time the council refused to declare null for the future marriages of young people made without the consent of their parents. "Had there been no other reason for calling this council," said a bishop who took part in it,[10] "this task alone, the condemnation of furtive marriages, would have justified its being summoned, for there was

[9] The new law was passed by 155 votes to 55, G. H. Joyce, S.J., *Christian Marriage* (1933), 127.
[10] Jerome Ragazzoni, coadjutor to the see of Famagusta, preaching the sermon with which the council closed, December 4.

not a corner of the world that this plague had not infected, the occasion, for generations, of an infinity of wicked deeds."[11]

The bishop's arm as a reformer is strengthened, time and again, in the Tridentine reforms, by the clause that he acts "as delegated for this by the Holy See." This in such matters as these: the visitation of all chapters within his diocese, of all monasteries which are held *in commendam*,[12] and of all "pious places," i.e., places of pilgrimage, shrines, and so forth; for the examination of all dispensations sent through him, from Rome, to his subjects (and henceforth it is always to the petitioner's bishop that dispensations will be sent), of all Roman permissions to change the terms of wills; the examination and correction of all notaries, a race whose costly incompetence is frequently complained of; the correction of all secular clerics who live in his diocese, and of all regulars there who are not living within a monastery; for the summary, out-of-hand correction of notorious and defiant concubinary clerics, and for the suppression of all abuses and superstitions centering round the mass.

In all these cases the bishop's sentence takes effect immediately. He is given the like power to unite neighbouring parishes, and to divide parishes that are, geographically, too large, and this whether the priests are willing or not, and he may finance the new from the revenues of the old as he judges best. Where the priest is too ignorant to preach, the bishop may provide him with a better instructed curate, fix his salary and compel the parish priest to pay it. Dilapidated churches are a frequent subject of comment in all medieval church records. The bishop's powers "as delegated," etc., make it possible to compel the repair of churches, i.e., to compel those to whom the parish revenues are paid to finance the repairs, even the repairs of monastic churches where the superior of the local abbot is negligent in this duty. Finally, he may use the same power to

[11] These summaries, as has been said, are only of the principal matters. But among these surely is, also, the change by which the council abolished the age-long right of metropolitans (archbishops) to make the visitation of all the sees of the bishops of their province, the local bishop's jurisdiction suspended the meanwhile, and the archbishop correcting what he found amiss and ordering the penalties this called for.

[12] A monastery was said to be *in commendam* which was granted as his benefice to a cleric who was not a member of the community or of the order or even of any religious order. These commendatory abbots, who were not bound to reside at the monastery, were sometimes not even in major orders.

finance, out of the revenues of the cathedral chapter, the new public lectureship of Sacred Scripture which he is ordered to institute in his see-city, the Scripture teaching in the diocesan "high school," and the diocesan seminary which he is now ordered to found. One sometimes hears the nonsense that never have bishops really been bishops since the Council of Trent. Actually, with Trent there came to an end, once and for all, that reign of the exemptions from episcopal authority which had plunged the Church into an anarchy that had well nigh destroyed her religious life, so that Pole, as legate at the council, could speak of "the almost ruined Church."

There are three phrases that continually recur in this new legislation, *tamquam delegatus*, *deinceps* (i.e., henceforward), and *ipso iure*, a phrase of the same force as our own common expression, English now as well as Latin, *ipso facto*—the fact here, being the law in which the phrase appears. This is the magical automatic penalty. The law issues an order, and states a penalty, and the delinquent incurs the penalty immediately he breaks the law, sometimes a spiritual penalty such as excommunication, sometimes the loss of a title to income. Some of these penalties we have met already, incidentally, on our voyage through the forest. Here are more specimens. It is the bishop who is the subject chiefly affected. The bishops at Trent are legislating about their own order; they are reforming bishops, securing to the best of their powers that "Never again," etc., etc. It is with laws providing against the catastrophe of bad bishops that the council's reforms, indeed, begin; to which the blunt honest words of Pole's keynote speech, at the opening of the council, all but compelled them. "Let us come to what are called abuses. . . . It will be found that it is our ambition, our avarice, our cupidity that have wrought all these evils on the people of God." Trent may indeed have been the glorious triumph of orthodoxy over the new heresies, but we shall fail wholly to understand the real changes it brought about, unless we see also in the council the repentant episcopate, sitting in sackcloth and ashes. "Before the tribunal of God's mercy we, the shepherds, should make ourselves responsible for all the evils now burdening the flock of Christ . . . not in generosity but in justice. . . ." So Pole, once more.

These reforming bishops, then, use the device of the "automatic" penalty so that the absentee bishop loses the right to his income, and the pluralist is deprived of sees he will not resign; that the

concubinary prelate who defies the warnings of the provincial council loses his see; that the bishop becomes (in law) a thief who
accepts gifts from those he ordains or from the parishes and other
churches where he is making the visitation; and that the metropolitan is deprived of his right to officiate who fails to report to Rome
the fact of a defiantly absentee suffragan. It is in the same way,
too, that the pluralist of lesser degree is reached, and the non-
preaching parish priest is fined.

The simplest remedy for whatever has been amiss in these matters is to appoint to the office none but good men, competently
endowed with the needed natural gifts and technical training. And
on this subject the council has much to say, about preliminary enquiries before the appointments are made. Ultimately the responsibility lies with that supreme authority whose bulls are the essential
element in all these appointments. The council ventures to hint at
negligence here as the chief source of the evils. "In the last place,
this holy synod, troubled by the number of these most serious evils,
cannot refrain from putting on record, that nothing is more necessary for the Church of God than that the most blessed pope of
Rome, who by his office is bound to the care of the whole Church,
should give this particular matter his closest attention, [namely]
to associate with himself, as cardinals, only men of exceptional
character and gifts, and to appoint as diocesan bishops the very
best and most suitable; and this all the more because our Lord,
Jesus Christ, will require at his hands the blood of those sheep of
Christ who have perished through the wicked misgovernment of
neglectful bishops unmindful of their duty."[13]

Both cardinals and bishops are explicitly warned that the natural
affection of a man for his kinsfolk breeds nepotism, that this affection can be "a seeding-plot of many evils in the Church." So the
council forbids these personages to provide for their relations out of
church revenues. If they are poor folk, they may, of course, be suc-

[13] Postremo eadem sancta synodus, tot gravissimis ecclesiae incommodis com-
mota, non potest non commemorare, nihil magis ecclesiae Dei esse necessarium,
quam ut beatissimus Romanus Pontifex, quam sollicitudinem universae ecclesiae
ex muneris sui officio debet, eam hic potissimum impendat, ut lectissimos
tantum sibi cardinales adsciscat, et bonos maxime atque idoneos pastores
singulis ecclesiis praeficiat, idque eo magis, quod ovium Christi sanguinem, quae
ex malo negligentium et sui officii immemorum pastorum regimine peribunt,
Dominus noster Iesus Christus de manibus eius sit requisiturus. Session 24
(Nov. 11, 1563) *De Reformatione*, chap. 1, the final paragraph.

coured like other poor folk. And one of the most obnoxious troubles of the past centuries is faced when the council begs bishops to be moderate in the use of excommunication, "for experience teaches that if this penalty is inflicted rashly, and for slight offences, it provokes contempt, not fear, and works harm to the offender rather than good"—excommunication being, in the mind of the Church, not a vindictive act but medicinal, something done to bring a man to his senses. Bishops are warned especially not to allow themselves, in this matter, to be made the tools of the state, excommunicating according to the wish of the prince.

Two more items in this lengthy selection and we have done; one of them about the layman—a rare subject for direct notice in these Canon Law sections. The subject is duels, the use of which, as an acknowledged social convention among the nobles—and what a curse it was to be down to the mid-nineteenth century!—is now first establishing itself. The council's principle is that the man who kills another in a duel is a murderer. The man killed dies with the stigma that his last intention, too, was murder. The seconds are accessories to murder, and the friends of the parties who assemble to see the duel are approvers. All, then, are henceforward punished by *ipso facto* penalties: the principals and the seconds are excommunicated, and incur the legal penalty of "perpetual infamy"—never again will a court of law consider their testimony in any case before it; they rank as professional criminals, and are all to be held as murderers. If one of the party is killed in the duel he is not to be given Christian burial. All who encourage the duel, and the spectators, are also, by the fact, excommunicated. Rulers, whatever their rank (and the emperor is explicitly mentioned), who make provision for the fighting of duels—providing a kind of official duelling ground (for example) are *ipso facto* excommunicated, and lose all their jurisdiction over the place where this is situated, if it is a fief of the Church; if it is held by a lay prince, the place reverts to the suzerain.

"With regard to the ordination of priests, Holy Father, no care whatever is taken," the cardinalitial committee on reform had reported to Paul III, eight years before the council met. "The most ignorant of men," they said, "and sprung from the dregs of society, and even themselves depraved, mere youths, are everywhere admitted to holy orders." We touch on one of the great mysteries of medieval Catholicism, not that there were bad priests, but that the Church never faced the problem of training and educating the rank and file of the parochial clergy—and this in the centuries which saw the rise of such remarkable formative institutions as the monastic orders and the orders of friars. Here, more than in any other point, with Trent a new age begins. "Youth, unless rightly trained, sinks to the pursuit of the lustful pleasures of the world," say the venerable Fathers of the council. "Unless a boy has been formed in habits of prayer and religion from his tenderest years, before the habits of adult vice can take root, he will never perfectly persevere in ecclesiastical discipline, unless by some very great and more than ordinary grace from God." So the council now decrees that every bishop shall set up a special college where picked boys shall live and be given a religious training, be taught to live the clerical life. These are to be boys who give promise of perseverance in the Church's service, poor boys preferably. They must be twelve years old at least, and able to read and write well, and of legitimate birth. This college "will become a permanently fruitful seed-bed (*seminarium*) of ministers of God."

The council, in this aside, has given the new institution the name it will henceforward always bear—the seminary. The programme of studies is next set out, and the way of life: daily mass, monthly confession, Holy Communion as often as the boy's confessor judges. On Sundays, and at the great feasts, the seminarians will assist at the services in the cathedral, hard by which the college is to be placed, or in other churches in the town. Unsuitable boys, the incorrigible above all and the troublemakers, are to be sent away. As the years pass, they receive minor orders and go on to their professional studies, Holy Scripture, ecclesiastical treatises, the administration of the sacraments (especially the hearing of confessions), the Church's ritual. They will receive Holy Communion more frequently once they are in minor orders, and will begin to be associated with the practical work of the parish clergy. Once they receive the subdiaconate they are to communicate every week. For this first of the major orders they must be twenty-one years of age completed, for the diaconate twenty-two, for the priesthood twenty-four. The foundation of these new colleges the bishops are to take in hand *quam primum*—at the earliest opportunity.

The remainder of this very long decree is taken up with rules about the choice of teachers, and their needed academic qualifications. As to finance, the bishop is given exceptionally wide powers to call upon all the ecclesiastical revenues of his diocese, of the regulars (even the exempt) as well as the diocesan clergy, the mendicant orders alone excepted. Special provision is made for the diocese that is too poor or too small to provide its own seminary.

These clergy, thus carefully trained, and now duly ordered, how are they to live? The sixteenth-century parish rarely needed more than one priest to attend to it—so numerous were the parish churches, even in the cities.[14] In most churches there were chapels built by pious men of means, where mass was daily offered for the repose of the souls of themselves and their family—the chantries. The funds left were sufficient to keep the priest appointed to the duty—this was his benefice. Very often also he served as schoolmaster. Now one of the trials of the pious man down to the end of the Middle Ages had been the sight of the horde of beggar-priests—priests without any benefice at all, driven to live by their wits out of the general benevolence of the laity. As well as founding the seminary system, Trent forbade bishops to ordain candidates who could never be of service, and also all who were not able, at their ordination, to bring legal proof that they were in peaceful possession of a benefice the income of which was enough to support them. Even good, suitable candidates are not to be ordained, says the new law, if they are lacking here. This benefice, if it is the only one the priest possesses, he is never allowed to resign without expressly stating that it is the benefice by title of which he was ordained.

The sixteen dogmatic decrees of the council, for all their terse style, would run to some sixty pages of this size even in a terse translation. Little more can be done than to list them, and for the student of history especially, to point out the excellent starting point they are for the study of the Catholic religion as it was in the early sixteenth century, and of the theological case between the Church and the reformers. It is a statement of that case as simple and as clear as it is authoritative. These decrees are, in form, miniature theological treatises, and they are carefully *not* written in the

[14] In London, for example, a city of about 100,000 people at the beginning of the 16th century, there were 93 parish churches alone.

technical language theologians use. To each decree there is a list of canons annexed, statements, that is to say, of some point of the reformed teaching which is contrary to the teaching set forth in the decree and therefore condemned.

Here, in chronological order, is the list of the dogmatic decrees, with the dates of the sessions when they were passed, and a note of the number of the canons attached to them and of the length (in printed pages) of the decrees:

Doctrine.	Session.		Date.	Canons.	Decrees.
The Holy Scriptures	4	1546	April 8		1
Original Sin	5		June 7	5	4
Justification	6	1547	January 13	33	16
The Sacraments in General	7		March 3	13	1
Baptism	7		"	14	None
Confirmation	7		"	3	"
The Holy Eucharist I[15]	13	1551	October 11	11	8
Penance	14		November 15	15	15
Extreme Unction	14		" 4	4	3
The Holy Eucharist II[16]	21	1562	June 16	4	3
" " " III[17]	22		September 9	9	4
Holy Orders	23	1563	July 15	8	3
Marriage	24		November 11	12	1
Purgatory	25		December 4	None	1
The Cult of the Saints, of Relics and Images	25		"	"	3
Indulgences	25		"	"	1

It will be observed that more than half of the text of the decrees is given to the doctrine of the sacraments. This, indeed, ever since Luther's famous tract, *The Babylonian Captivity of the Church* (1520) had been the main point of the Protestant assault, in this sense, that what was challenged here was what every man could appreciate immediately, namely, the actual practice of the religion instituted by Christ our Lord. All could see here the difference between the old and the new, where only a select few were in a position to judge the implications of the new key-doctrine that

[15] The doctrine of the Real Presence; the worship of God present in the sacrament; the use of the sacrament.

[16] On Communion under both kinds, and the Communion of little children.

[17] On the Sacrifice of the Mass.

Justification is through faith alone. With this heresy the council dealt very faithfully, in a single decree of sixteen chapters that takes up one-quarter of the whole text.

Trent, it is sometimes said, put an end once and for all to the indefiniteness and confusion of thought among Catholics—to their comparative freedom to believe pretty much what they liked, in one version of the criticism. But this matter of terminating differences, when true at all, is true only with a great reservation. The confusion, or division of opinion, was not about traditional doctrine but about the problems raised by the new theories, differences in part related to the practical problem how best to deal with the points raised by Luther, and how to reconcile the Lutherans by so stating the tradition that it would satisfy them also. The idea that the Catholic unity in the fundamentals of belief about grace, original sin, justification, and the sacraments is the fruit of the Tridentine restatement of Catholic doctrine, is too grotesque for patience to bear. Nowhere does the council say—in effect—so far some Catholics have believed it is X, others that it is Y, but from henceforth, all shall believe it is Y. It is, on the contrary, forever using such phrases as, "following the teaching of the Fathers we define . . ." Where is the doctrinal definition of this council, for comment on which the theological lecturer will not turn for guidance to St. Thomas, to say nothing of one or other of the Fathers?

Trent is a witness to the age-long tradition, to the Apostolic tradition, as truly as Nicaea twelve hundred years before or the Vatican Council three hundred years later. It never does more than state, with the peculiar authority and explicitness of a General Council, what the body of the teaching theologians had been agreed on for centuries and the Church as a whole had implicitly accepted and practiced. As to questions which do not touch the substance of a particular doctrine, but regard methods of explaining and defending it, questions of its history, its relation to other doctrines, questions arising from the various ways in which different ages have set it out, the council decides nothing. From the learned warfare of the Catholic theologians about such matters, it carefully distinguishes its own rôle, which is not theological scholarship but the preservation of the traditional belief, and the exposure, and condemnation therefore, of whatever contradicts this. As to the theological views put forward in the council, and rejected, in, e.g., the

long discussions that preceded the decree on Justification, when
what was called the theory of the double Justification was proposed
as an orthodox solution that might reconcile Lutheranism and
Catholicism—how new such ideas were among Catholic theologians is illustrated, it may be suggested, from the fact that when the
leading theologian of the age, Cajetan, was dealing, in 1507,[18]
with St. Thomas' refutation (two centuries in advance) of Luther's
basic theory, he has no comment to make about this that would
suggest that anywhere among theologians was there any division
of opinion on the essence of the question.

The decrees restate the whole doctrine; they are not merely a
contradiction of the reformers' innovations. The canons attached
to the decrees are short summary condemnations of heresies that
contradict the doctrine set out in the decree, and not of the new,
contemporary heresies only. Thus, along with the Lutheran theories about Original Sin, there are also condemned (yet once again)
the heresies of Pelagius. To show something of the council's teaching, the canons on the key doctrines of Justification, the Sacraments in General, and the Holy Eucharist will now be summarised.

In the matter of Justification, a doctrine which now makes its
first appearance—in its own right—at a General Council, *these new
errors are condemned:*[19] the theory that man is passive, like a stone,
under the influence of grace; that since Adam's fall there is no real
freedom in the human will, this last idea being an invention
brought into the Church by the devil; that the good works done by
man before he is justified are sins meriting damnation; that nothing
but faith is requisite to achieve Justification; that man can be justified otherwise than through the justice of Christ;[20] that man is

[18] Just ten years before Luther's 95 Theses appeared.
[19] Session 6, January 13, 1547. The Latin text of the canons here summarised is in Denzinger, pp. 277–81. With respect to the phrase "all are condemned," which continually recurs in these canons, it is to be observed that
the council has in mind Catholics and the ex-Catholics who, abandoning the
traditional doctrines, founded the various reformed bodies. The bishops at
Trent were not addressing that multitude of later, non-Catholic Christians
who, born and bred in these forms of belief, worship God and keep His law
after a non-Catholic fashion in all good faith. To these, the personal condemnation was not addressed, although the condemnation of the theories inevitably stands.
[20] A heretical caricature of traditional doctrine, found useful in the Reformation propaganda.

justified by the imputation only, of the justice of Christ—Justification being no more than God showing favour to a man; that the faith without which man cannot be justified is the trustful confidence that the divine mercy has forgiven his sins for Christ's sake; that it is a condition for a man's sins being forgiven that he believes, without any hesitation, that his sins have been forgiven; that no one is justified unless he believes he is justified, this belief being what brings about absolution and justification; the justified man is bound to believe, as of faith, that he is numbered among those predestined [to eternal life]; that all men except these are, by the Divine Power, predestined to evil; to believe is the only thing commanded in the Gospel, all the rest being neither commanded nor forbidden, the Ten Commandments having nothing to do with being a Christian; Christ our Lord was sent as a Redeemer to save, not as lawgiver to be obeyed; man, once justified, cannot sin or fall from grace; there is only one sin that is mortal, the sin of not believing, and through no other sin can grace once attained be lost.

This is not a complete account of what the thirty-three canons about Justification contain. It omits some more subtle statements that would call for a lengthy explanation, and it omits canons which state, not a theory the reformers put out, but Catholic doctrine which they deny.

As to the new theories about the kind of thing sacraments are, the canons[21] *condemn* those who say: that there are more or less than seven sacraments instituted by Christ our Lord—baptism, confirmation, the Eucharist, penance, extreme unction, order, marriage —or that any one of these is not truly a sacrament in the full sense of the word; that these sacraments only differ from the sacraments of the Jewish dispensation as one ritual from another; that the sacraments are not a necessity of salvation, but that through faith alone, and without the sacraments at all, man can obtain from God the grace of Justification; that the sacraments were instituted for the purpose of nourishing only faith; that the sacraments do not contain and confer the grace which they signify—as though they were but outward signs of the grace or justice received through faith, badges of Christian profession that mark off the believer from

21 Session 7, March 3, 1547. Latin text ibid., 281–82.

the infidel; that the sacraments do not themselves confer grace by the very activity of the sacrament (*ex opere operato*), but that only faith in the divine promises is sufficient to obtain grace; that all Christians have the power to administer all the sacraments; that any pastor of the Church can change the received and approved rites used by the Church in the solemn administration of the sacraments.

As to the doctrine called the Real Presence,[22] the council *condemns:* those who, denying that Jesus Christ, God and Man, is truly, really, substantially present in the sacrament of the Holy Eucharist, hold instead that He is only present as in a sign or image or manifestation of power (*in virtute*); those who say that the substance of the bread and the wine remains along with the body and blood of Christ, denying that marvellous and unique changing of the whole substance of the bread into the Body [of Christ] and the whole substance of the wine into [His] Blood, while the appearance of bread and wine still remain—the change which the Catholic Church most suitably calls *Transubstantiation;* those who say that the Body and Blood of Christ is not there following upon the consecration (*peracta consecratione*), but only while the sacrament is in use, while it is being received, that is to say, but not before this or after this, and that in what is left over of the consecrated hosts or particles after communion has been administered, the true Body of the Lord does not remain; who say that the main fruit, or the sole fruit, of this sacrament is the forgiveness of sins; or that Christ the only begotten son of God is not to be adored in this sacrament with the externals of the reverence called *latria*,[23] and that those who do so adore Him in this sacrament are idolaters; that Christ is shown forth in this sacrament to be received [by the communicant] in a spiritual manner, and not also sacramentally and really; that only faith is sufficient preparation for receiving this most holy sacrament.

The Council *denies*[24] that there is a divine command that all shall receive Holy Communion under both the forms, i.e., of wine as well as of bread, and that it is a necessary sacrament for little

[22] Session 13, October 11, 1551. Latin text ibid., 290–91.
[23] That homage due to God alone, as the Creator of all.
[24] Session 21, June 16, 1562. Latin text ibid., 310.

children. It *condemns* those who deny that the whole Christ is received when Holy Communion is received under the form of bread alone.

There remain the canons attached to the decree about the sacrifice called the Mass,[25] clear statements in everyday language. The Council *condemns* those who say: there is not offered in the Mass, a true and proper sacrifice to God; nothing more is meant by this word "offered" than that Christ is given to us to be eaten; Christ, by the words *Do this in commemoration of Me*,[26] did not constitute the apostles priests, or ordain them, so that they and other priests should offer His body and blood; the sacrifice of the Mass is a sacrifice of praise and thanksgiving only, or a mere commemoration of the sacrifice offered on the Cross, but not a sacrifice whereby God is appeased; [the sacrifice] profits only those who receive [Holy Communion]; Mass should not be offered for the living and the dead, or for sins, penalties, satisfactions, and other necessities; a blasphemy is inflicted, through the sacrifice of the Mass, on the most holy sacrifice wrought by Christ on the Cross; the Mass takes away from the sacrifice on the Cross; the Canon[27] of the Mass is full of errors and should be done away with; the masses where none but the celebrating priest receive Holy Communion are unlawful and should be abrogated.

It has been a simpler task to tell the story of what the council accomplished, without any reference to the contemporary events of those eighteen years, 1545–63. But, without requiring anything like the history of those years, the reader is entitled to ask, Why was the council twice interrupted, and for so long a period? In 1547 the cause was the outbreak of the plague at Trent. The council hastily voted an adjournment to Bologna (March 10) to the fury of Charles V (who took for granted that the plague was mere excuse) and to the embarrassment of Paul III, who realised he would be held responsible for what was, in fact, in no way his doing. Several sessions were held at Bologna in 1547, a mere marking of time. Meanwhile the emperor carried his attack on the pope to the utter-

[25] Session 22, September 9, 1562. Latin text ibid., 314–15.
[26] Luke 22:19.
[27] The long prayer which is the core of the rite, during which the consecration takes place.

most limits—ordering his own bishops not to leave Trent, proclaiming that this handful was the real council and the majority at Bologna a mere conventicle.

This crisis had come, in fact, at a moment when the political relations of emperor and pope were at their worst. The opening of the council in 1545 had found them allies in Charles' often-delayed, but now about to be executed, war against the German Protestant league. But by the time of Alva's crushing defeat of the princes at Mühlberg (April 24, 1547) relations between the chiefs were strained. The pope's unsatisfactory son, Pierluigi, whom he had invested with the duchies of Parma and Piacenza, against the emperor's will (and possibly against his rights) in 1545, was a thorn in the emperor's side. The imperial viceroy in Milan arranged the duke's assassination (September 10). Was Charles V privy to this? It is hardly likely, but he had assented to the plan to expel Pierluigi by force (May 31). This crime was committed in the early weeks of the Bologna period of the council. Charles, by virtue of Mühlberg, was master of Germany as no emperor had been for hundreds of years. A brittle glory it was to prove, but the threat of this prince, already ruler of half of Italy, to the independence of the pope was real indeed. And the emperor used his mastery to impose on Catholic and Protestant, in Germany, a religious settlement of his own, the so-called *Interim*. Was Charles now going to prove himself a Spanish Henry VIII? The old pope found somewhere a reserve of patience, and the explosion never happened. The bishops went home from Bologna, and from Trent, and then in November 1549 the pope died.

There followed the long dramatic ten weeks' conclave of 1549–50, in which Pole almost became pope, and from which the senior president at Trent, Del Monte, emerged as Pope Julius III. And now began the old weary business of persuading Charles to cooperate in the reassembly of the council, and the French king too. Charles had a new point to urge—the reassembled council should be a new council altogether; the Protestants would be pleased if all the matters defined at Trent were treated anew as open questions. The French king, Henry II, whose reign[28] had barely begun utterly refused to have anything to do with the council. He was, in

[28] Francis I died March 31, 1547.

fact, on the verge of war with the pope, the *casus belli* being the revolt of Paul III's grandsons against the new pope. The French king had taken up their cause. Julius III, as more than one incident at Trent, especially with Charles V's bullying commissioners, had shown, had one of the great tempers of the day. But somehow he managed to stifle it, and despite some bad blunders and vacillation he managed to get the council on its feet again in 1551. It was in this period that the Protestants accepted the invitation to come to the council—an incident which merely showed beyond all doubt that the new doctrines were not reconcilable with the old.

And now in Germany the war with the Protestant League took up once more. This time it was the emperor who was defeated, and his army destroyed, in southern Germany. The pursuit was so hot that Charles himself narrowly escaped capture, and as he made his way over the mountains to a precarious safety at Innsbruck, the bishops of the council decided it was high time they, too, moved south. So ended the Julian period of the Council of Trent.

Julius III died in 1555, to be succeeded by his one-time colleague at Trent, Cervini, whose reign lasted but a short three weeks. Then came Gian Pietro Caraffa—Paul IV—a hale old man of seventy-nine, the grimmest reformer who ever sat in St. Peter's chair. As a young bishop, forty years earlier, he had sat in the all but futile Fifth Council of the Lateran. Perhaps it was here that he developed his strong belief that little good came of councils. He had other methods, and for heretics they were simple enough—the stake. Paul IV's four years of government in Rome was a reign of terror for evildoers and lawbreakers of every sort, clerical as well as lay.

His death was followed by a conclave that lasted four months. From it came forth a pope as great a contrast to this passionate, unbalanced Neapolitan as could be imagined, Gian Angelo de' Medici, a Milanese, who took the name Pius IV. He was by training a lawyer, and by his career a professional administrator, who had governed one city after another for Clement VII and Paul III; and for his moderation he had found it prudent to leave Rome, in the days of Paul IV. His election had produced the ideal character for the delicate business of reconciling to Rome the various Catholic princes recently alienated—particularly the Hapsburgs for whom Paul IV had had an unconcealed personal hatred.

Charles V had died a few months only before Paul IV. In the

empire his brother, Ferdinand I, had replaced him; in the rest of his dominions his son, Philip II. In France too there was a new ruler since June 1559, when Henry II was killed in a tournament—his fifteen-year-old son, Francis II. This boy, whose wife was Mary, Queen of Scots, lasted barely a year and a half, and the sovereign with whom Pius IV had to treat was this boy's mother, Catherine de' Medici, the queen-regent for his still younger successor. Add that in England the short-lived Catholic restoration of Mary Tudor had just ended, and that Pius IV faced the *fait accompli* of a restoration of the entire Protestant régime, with Catholicism proscribed utterly in legislation that culminated in the death penalty, and with all the bishops the new queen's prisoners. The queen was, of course, Elizabeth I.

Given this unusual array of talent among the leading princes, and the fact that all the old prepossessions of those who were Catholics still survived—the instinct to take control of the religious crisis into their own hands, to settle the problems of their own realms, for example, by a national council not under papal influence—given all this, the fact that Pius IV succeeded in reassembling the council, at Trent, within little more than two years would suggest that he is a more important figure than has usually been recognised.

With patience and prudence and a constantly firm purpose, he guided the council through what proved to be the major part of its work, and through a continuity of passionate discussions where Spanish and French bishops, as well as Italian, had to be considered and managed. The most dangerous moments were when the Spaniards strove for a decision that the personal obligation of the bishop to live in his diocese was an obligation of divine law, and not merely of synodal legislation. The danger was that this excellent idea masked a point of theology, and was meant to lead to a discussion of the loaded question, Is the pope the superior of the General Council or its servant? the question that had racked the Church of the previous century, and for a renewal of which the Church of the sixteenth century was by no means yet sufficiently healthy. That the premature discussion of this particular application of the defined doctrine of the papal supremacy was averted was due, in especial manner, to the great cardinal whom Pius IV sent to preside at the last months of the council, Girolamo Morone.

The great council[29] ended with what jubilation about the work done may be imagined. The pope by a special bull confirmed all it had decreed, and by a second bull forthwith abolished all privileges and exemptions previously accorded by his predecessors which went contrary to the decrees; and to settle authoritatively all questions arising out of the interpretation of the decrees he created a permanent commission of cardinals, the Congregation of the Council of Trent, a body which developed into a kind of permanent Ministry of the Interior of the Catholic Church, and which functions to this day as one of the most important instruments of the government of the Church. The matter of providing the revised edition of the official Latin translation of the Bible, a revised Breviary and Missal, a Catechism and an Index of books dangerous to Faith and Morals, the council had left to the pope.

It was the immediate successor of Pius IV who saw to all these, except the new Bible. This successor was the Dominican, Michele Ghislieri, known to history as Pius V (1566–72), in whom the aspirations of good men for centuries were realised, a living saint ruling the Church. Of all the services rendered by St. Pius V (he was canonised by Clement XI in 1712) none was greater than this, that in his ruling of the Church he was as scrupulously obedient to the laws of Trent as he had been obedient to the Dominican constitutions during his long life as a friar. He set an example which none of his successors could ever ignore; and perhaps nowhere more powerfully than in what he did with the task from which the council, in its last moments, shrank—the reformation of the Catholic Princes, i.e., the defence of the rights of religion against the encroachment of the Catholic state. But to say more about this would be to write the tragic history of the seventeenth and eighteenth centuries, of a fight where there were defeats, but no surrenders. The ideal of the example set by St. Pius V was at times obscured. It was never forgotten. And never, since his time, has there been any such moral falling away—nor anything remotely recalling it—as what, in almost all his life before his election, he himself had been witness of in the highest place of all.

[29] December 4, 1563.

20. *The First General Council of the Vatican, 1869-70*

It is not to the nineteenth General Council that, in this summary, we dare propose to link the history of the twentieth, which followed it almost exactly three hundred years later. If we are to see the Vatican Council of 1869–70 in relation to any great formative world movement, it is with the French Revolution that our business lies.

How the great crisis that opened in the year 1789 found the Catholic religion everywhere in chains, in the various European states, its vitality low indeed after generations of captivity to the Catholic kings, is one of the commonplaces of history. And the death of the aged Pius VI, in 1799, the actual prisoner of the French Republic, was hailed pretty generally by the observant as the end of the spiritual empire he had ruled so long. But this funeral of Christianity, as Chesterton once wrote, was interrupted by the least expected incident of all—the corpse came to life.

The world, as the Revolution and Napoleon left it, would indeed be a new world. But in the new world the Catholic Church, and its popes, would be readily discernible. In that new world there would begin, on the very morrow of the settlement of 1814–15, a grim struggle between the dispossessed of 1789, now once more in the saddle, and those who had for a quarter of a century kept them out. The struggle would be political, social, cultural; and religion would sensitively react to every shift and turn of the contenders. One political feature, common to the new world everywhere, was the presence, now permanent, of the new idea that "subjects" had a right to a say in the way they were governed—and over a great part of western Europe the right was recognised. The "subjects" had votes, they were citizens; there were parliaments, elections, parties, public controversies, a political press; and everywhere politicians, able and less able, endlessly planning, infinitely ambitious, and passionately idealistic—the first, and romantic, generation to operate an organ of national life still with us, and as important as ever, if long dulled and mechanical, for us, after the daily use of a century and a half.

At the time of the Vatican Council the men were still alive, and active, who in France and Belgium and Prussia and Austria and Italy and Spain had seen this new thing come into existence, and in a hundred passionate fights had brought it through its adolescence to a somewhat blasé maturity. The pope's call in 1869 to the bishops of the world to meet in a General Council interested all these men enormously, for no subject had more passionately possessed, and divided, the statesmen of the new Europe in the first half century of its existence than the astonishing return to life of the Catholic Church: the real revival of religious life, of practice and belief, to which no country in Europe was a stranger; and with this, the reappearance of those age-old claims—that the religion of Christ is a thing *sui iuris*, independent of all earthly power, not to be controlled by the state whether royal and absolutist or democratic and republican. Nowhere had the struggle in the post-Waterloo world been tougher than where the political reorganisation (of one school or another) had clashed with this renascent Catholicism, in Prussia, in France, in Italy, to say nothing of Latin America where the conflict seemed part of the national life.

We are in a better position to know what exactly happened at the council of 1869–70, and to understand why things then happened in a particular way, than is the case for any of the General Councils that preceded it. It is an event that belongs to the age in which we ourselves have grown up—ninety years old though the event be. For if it belongs to the age of parliamentary democracy, it belongs also to the new age of speedy, safe, and reasonably cheap travelling: the bishops who made their way to Trent made the journey with all the discomfort and hazards that were the lot of the bishops who attended Nicaea, twelve hundred years before—and they travelled at about the same speed, fifty or sixty miles a day if they were lucky, and not too old to stand such a strain. By 1869, however, the great revolutionary invention we call the railroad, barely forty years old, had already linked all the principal cities and seaports of western Europe; and the Atlantic passage had shrunk to a matter of days. And not only could bishops, and statesmen, diplomatists and revolutionaries, travel now at many times the speed of their own fathers, but the news of their doings went even more swiftly. The electric telegraph, as it was called, had been in operation for twenty years; and to spread the latest tidings (and the rumours) and the desired commentary on all this, there was the highly organised business of the modern newspaper—the daily press. Already the power of this over public opinion had been demonstrated when, for example, in 1855, the greatest of all the journals of the day, *The Times* (of London) had, in the midst of a war, brought about a change of government by the stories it published of tragic incompetence in the army medical services. And in this country, on the very eve of the council, the extensive, detailed, daily reporting of the battles of the Civil War had revealed to the discerning that here was a new force which rulers—and indeed the great men in all walks of life—must henceforth reckon with. Scarcely had the official announcement been made that a General Council was to meet, than from every country a host of special correspondents descended on Rome—to create, by their inevitably incomplete stories, an unexpected problem for the council's "publicity" chiefs, if this wholly anachronistic term be allowed.

The reigning pope, Pius IX,[1] had, for nearly twenty-five years, been a leading personage in the eyes of the newspapermen. Whether admired or hated he had always been "news"; for in all that time he had never ceased to denounce the wrongs done the Church by the revolution, or the Catholic state's habit of ruling as though there were no God. Like all his predecessors for a thousand years, Pius IX was also a temporal prince, with a territory of some 18,000 square miles that, very strategically, covered central Italy from the Mediterranean to the Adriatic. To the north of this important state, there were the provinces of Lombardy and Venezia, annexed in 1815 to Austria, where, naturally, patriots never ceased in their schemes to drive out the foreign ruler. To the south there was that comic-opera kingdom of Naples whose government had, to the best of its power, deliberately restored in 1815 all the crazy incompetence of the years before 1789—and all the petty restrictions that brought home to nineteenth-century man that, in the eyes of his rulers, he was a mere child. Here, too, for fifty years the national life never ceased to heave with discontent. From both north and

[1] John Mastai-Ferretti, born May 13, 1792, elected pope June 16, 1846.

south defeated conspirators were forever crossing the borders of the Papal State, in flight from their oppressors. And in the northern part of that state—with Bologna its chief city—the papal rule was as well hated as that of the Hapsburgs at Milan, or of the Bourbons at Naples. For all the long reign of Pius IX, Italy had continued to be the stage upon which the greatest opera of all time was played, with all Europe for audience. Little wonder, then, that the Vatican Council was "news" everywhere.

To the mind of the general reader, mention of the Vatican Council will usually recall two facts: that it was the occasion of the definition of the doctrine popularly called Papal Infallibility, and that many of the bishops present were opposed to the definition. The more erudite will add that their opposition was not to the doctrine itself, but to the policy of choosing this present moment to proclaim it—the definition, they would say, was held not "opportune." These are, indeed, important considerations for the historian of the council, but they are far from the full tale of what the council accomplished, and still further from what the Pope had in mind when he called it; nor did the matter of Papal Infallibility figure in the original programme. How this particular question came to take such a prominent place in the actual proceedings is a matter that is bound up very closely with the history of the general Catholic revival in the years immediately preceding the council. As the reader may have already discovered, a good part of the story of any council must necessarily be the story of what caused it to be summoned, and of the forces that shaped the men who played the leading rôles in it. How best to describe this, briefly, in the case of the Vatican Council, is something of a problem. The leading critics of the "definition policy" were French, German, and Hungarian—how much can here be told of the Catholic history of these countries in the twenty years between, let us say, the great revolutionary year 1848 and the calling of the council?

We might begin with a truism: religious revivals are times of enthusiasm, and enthusiasm is not a critical thing. This particular Catholic revival was very consciously, in France, a militant reaction against the classical rationalism of the eighteenth century, the deism, the naturalism, the atheism; and it found congenial allies among the new romantic writers—Chateaubriand is one obvious example of this. Romantics also were the two writers who, for the generation after 1815, most influenced the Catholic mind, Joseph de Maistre and de Lamennais. That mind, when it turned from the practice of religion to its defence, was all too easily satisfied that with these magnificent rhetoricians the last word had been said. Seminaries and schools of theology had been swept out of existence after 1789. Nor was the long break in the traditional scholastic formation repaired by the time the council met. Almost the only thinkers now were the apologists—amateurs as always, whatever their intentions; the victory over the old adversary seemed an easy business; and (what concerns us very closely) the Catholic was regarded suspiciously who asked whether these literary superficialities could really suffice, or who shifted uneasily as he heard these comforting extravagances that no official voice ever rebuked.

"Inopportunism," when it arrived, would be, in great part, a reaction against these extravagances. The prelates who were inopportunists at Rome had long been fighting at home superficial untrained zealots, who not only attacked the anti-Christian intellectuals of the nineteenth century with the weapons of the eighteenth, but attacked no less violently their fellow Catholics who refused to follow where they led; and in the press they controlled they made no secret of their distrust of the very bishops. The bitterness of the spirit that animated this faction-fighting in France, at the time of the Second Empire, is hard to exaggerate. Here is one principal cause, it might be argued, of the least pleasing incidents of the great council of 1869-70.

In the country we today know as Germany, and in Austria, the reaction was spared some of the weaknesses of the romantic literary apologetic. And the theological formation of the clergy—including the bishops—was here more solid. The divisions, which appeared here too, were divisions rather between the various schools of theology, in the universities of Mainz, Tübingen, and Munich, for example. But the German Catholics, from 1848 onward, began to organise nationally and in their annual congresses to work out in open debate their attitude to all the questions of the day—very notably to its social problems. One feature this revival had in common with that in France—a dislike and suspicion of the Roman Curia's known desire to centralise still more the general administration of the Church. Particularly in the Austrian Empire was this feeling strong, where the bishops still reigned over their sees very much as in feudal times, great lords who were, socially, quasi-omnipotent. But although there was public discussion and controversy between the various groups, these German and Hungarian churches were spared—until Döllinger emerged as the anti-Roman champion—the bitterness that aggravated the situation in France. Nowhere was there in the German press such a scandal as the constant reviling of bishops as untrustworthy religious guides.

What Pope Pius IX had in mind in summoning the council is set forth in his bull convoking it (*Aeterni Patris,* June 29, 1868): to restate the faith in certain matters where it had been attacked or misunderstood; to review the whole matter of clerical life and its needs; to provide new safeguards for Christian marriage and the Christian education of youth; and to take up in this new age the ancient problems of the relations of Church and State and provide appropriate guidance, so as to promote peace and prosperity in the national life everywhere. That the state, everywhere, is labouring under an infinity of ills, the pope says, is known to all, and the Church is at the mercy of terrible storms. In fact, the malice of God's enemies continually assails the Church's teaching, and the authority of the Holy See; it has robbed the church of vast properties, brought about the dissolution of religious orders, exiled and imprisoned bishops, set up systems of education where the name of God is never even mentioned, allowed the publication and sale of wicked books, and the organisation of societies whose purpose is to spread these evils still further. This succinctly describes what, in the reign of Pope Pius IX, had taken place at one time or another in France, and Spain, and in every country of Latin America, and in Italy too—even in what, until 1860, were the pope's own territories. It is the pope's bounden duty to take counsel about these matters in consultation with the whole body of his brethren, the bishops of the Catholic Church. Whence this summons to the General Council, which will meet at Rome in the Vatican Basilica (St. Peter's Church) on December 8, 1869.

In the twenty-three years he has reigned Pius IX, as he truthfully recalls, has never failed to protest each time the rights of religion have been violated. And if a reader would see, formally set forth, the anti-Christian ideas whence these crimes derived he has only to read the great series of the pope's encyclical letters and his public addresses; or he may find it all succinctly stated in a kind of *aide-mémoire* which Pius IX had sent to the bishops in 1864, the document known to history as the *Syllabus*.

Pius IX had had the idea of a General Council in his mind for many years. He was from the beginning of his reign consciously dedicated to the general restoration of Catholic life, and the coming council should do for the post-revolutionary world what Trent had done for the sixteenth century. It was in 1864 that he laid the matter before the cardinals resident in Rome. The majority favoured the idea (13-8) and a few months later the pope set up a commission to study ways and means. He also consulted between thirty and forty diocesan bishops in various countries as to the questions the council should consider. Almost all of these, too, favoured the project.

What all wanted from such a council was the formal condemnation of the various anti-Christian philosophies of the time, and of the new rationalistic interpretations of Christianity and its sacred books. They asked for a restatement of the Catholic faith, particularly about the kind of thing the Church of Christ is, and about the rights and prerogatives of the pope; only ten, out of the fifty or so consulted, referred to the definition of infallibility. Another general demand was for the revision of the Canon Law—a dense forest that had been growing unsystematically, and unpruned, for hundreds of years. They wanted a reorganisation of clerical life and of the religious orders; the regulation of all the host of such new "inventions" as missions, sodalities, "devotions"; and a single official catechism for the use of the whole Church. And they wanted, finally, a statement about the relations of the Church to the new modern democratic state, something that would show that the Church was not hostile to all but absolutist régimes.

A body of a hundred experts, theologians and canonists for the most part, was formed to prepare the first drafts of the laws which the council would discuss; sixty of them were Italian "professionals," the rest called in from elsewhere. The industry of this host of experts produced 51 drafts of decrees, 23 relating to Catholic belief and 28 to what may be briefly described as reorganisation of Catholic life. All that the council brought to the stage of sanctioning, out of this vast mass, were two definitions of belief: that called *Dei Filius* (a restatement of the fundamental truths of the Christian religion against the new rationalism) and that called *Pastor Aeternus* (that the pope is supreme head of the whole Church of Christ and cannot err when as shepherd and teacher of all Christians he defines a doctrine concerning faith or morals to be held by the whole Church). The council, it will be seen, had indeed barely begun its work when, after seven months of laborious discussions, political events brought it to a halt.

The preparations for the council were interrupted for a time by the political crisis of 1866–67,[2] but on June 29 of this last year the pope made the first public announcement that the council would be held. One of the men who did most to overcome his hesitation was the bishop of Orléans, Félix Dupanloup. He was to be a leading figure in the next four years. The first effect, in France and Germany, of the pope's announcement was to bring to a head all the agitation of the previous twenty years. For the two years and more that elapsed before the council met, the controversy was, in both countries, continuous and acrimonious. The leading prelates on both sides of the coming debate, "Is it opportune?", arrived at the council, then, already well known to each other, and to the rest, as opponents through their remarkable pamphleteering activities; the French bishop Dupanloup very notably, the Englishman Manning, and—the most competent of all these contestants, the most level-headed—the Cardinal Archbishop of Mechlin, Victor Dechamps.

Something like a thousand personages had the right to take part in the council, once the pope decided that titular bishops should be convoked as well as bishops actually ruling a territory. Of these thousand, some 75 per cent actually attended the council, 744[3] of them, at one time or another, during the seven months it sat (December 8, 1869–July 18, 1870). Of these 744, 643 were bishops actually ruling a territory, and a bare 43 were bishops either retired

[2] The leading events of which were the withdrawal from Rome of the French troops that protected the city from attack by the new Italian state, and the Seven Weeks War between Prussia and Austria.

[3] Aubert, R. *Le Pontificat de Pie IX* (vol. 21 of F. and M., *Histoire de l'Église*), 1952, 324.

from active work or consecrated as auxiliaries to some diocesan bishop, or because their high position in the Curia Romana carried with it the episcopal dignity. The balance of the 744 was made up of cardinals resident in Rome and the general superiors of the religious orders.

As many as 200, and even more, of these diocesan bishops were from Italy itself where, alone, the custom of the primitive church had continued, that each city should have its bishop. Over 120 were English-speaking (from England 12, Ireland 19, the United States 46). From France came 70, Germany and the Austrian Empire 58, Spain 36, Latin America 30. There were 50 bishops from the various churches of the Oriental rites, and 100 missionary bishops from Asia, Africa, and Oceania.

Exactly how many of these bishops took the view that it was not opportune to define the infallibility of the pope, it is not easy to say. The highest number ever claimed for the inopportunists was 200.[4] In the last of the meetings called General Congregations (July 13, 1870) they mustered 88 votes, while another 76 stayed away rather than vote.

The procedure—devised for the council by the Curia[5]—was simple enough. A draft of the proposed definition of belief, or of the reform (in the case of ecclesiastical discipline), was sent to each of the bishops, and a day fixed for the opening of the discussion. These discussion-sessions were officially styled General Congregations. Bishops who wished to speak at them sent in their names beforehand to the presidents of the council, five cardinals appointed by the pope. There was no time limit fixed for their speeches. When the discussion petered out, any changes they wished to see made in the draft were studied by one of the four committees of the bishops, elected by the general body for this purpose. Of these four committees (for matters of the Faith, for disciplinary questions, Religious Orders, the churches of the Eastern Rites) the only one which actually played any great part in the council was the first named. These

[4] David Moriarty, bishop of Kerry, to Newman, Feb. 3, 1870, quoted Butler, *Vatican Council* (1930), II, 29.

[5] Its actual author was Carl Joseph Hefele, the historian of the councils, whom the pope had early called in as an advisor. He became bishop of Rothenburg in time to take part in the council, and on the issue of infallibility was a leading force in opposition. He was, apparently, one of the very few bishops who had not already accepted the doctrine.

committees, which had power to call in the experts who had prepared the draft, made a technical report on the amendments to the council and prepared the amended draft. This, together with the amendments and the report on them, were circulated to the bishops in advance of the final discussion at which a vote was taken. When the council had passed the definition, a day was appointed for what was called a Public Session of the council. Here it was the pope who presided. The draft as the bishops had finally adopted it was read, and each bishop, rising in his place, gave his vote, saying *placet* or *non placet*. Then the pope read the formula of definition, to which all the bishops said "Amen." The only time the pope appeared at the council was at these Public Sessions, of which there were four in all: December 8, 1869, the formal opening of the council; January 6, 1870, when the bishops one by one made their formal public profession of faith; April 24, for the definition of the decree against rationalism; and July 18, for the definition of the papal primacy and the infallibility. Of General Congregations, amendments and speeches there was, as will be seen, almost no end.

The first business of the bishops after the opening solemnities was to elect the four revising committees mentioned (they were officially known as *deputations*). There was a fifth committee, named by the pope, whose business it was to decide whether new matter proposed by a particular bishop or a group—subjects additional, that is to say, to what the drafts prepared by the theologians contained—should come before the council. This fifth committee was known as the deputation *Pro Postulatis* (For Requests), and it was a great series of petitions by bishops to this deputation that brought the infallibility question before the council. It has often been said that too little initiative was left to the bishops in 1869–70, but there was sufficient for them to make the council what had never been intended originally, viz., the council of the Infallibility of the Pope.

To the great annoyance of many of the bishops, these preliminary elections took up the best part of a month. It was only on December 28 that the council really got to work, when the debates opened on the draft of the statement of Catholic belief which ultimately emerged as the Dogmatic Constitution, *Dei Filius*. Each bishop had had three weeks to study his copy of this draft. The general feeling was that the theologians had made a bad job of it. It was, the bishops thought, "too long and elaborate,[6] too abstract and obscure, and it did not meet the needs of the time."[7] The bishops spoke their minds about this very bluntly, the Archbishop of Vienna[8] leading, in the first speech the council heard. There was nothing to be done with the draft, said Archbishop Connolly, of Halifax, but "to bury it with honour." For six days—four hours a day—the bishops, thirty-five of them in all, had their say and on January 10, "mangled and pulled to pieces . . . bleeding in every limb,"[9] the unfortunate draft was sent back to the deputation *For the Faith* to be redesigned.

The deputation, despite the objections of the Jesuit theologian Franzelin who was principally responsible for the draft, decided it must be drastically remodelled. It gave the task to one of its own members, Conrad Martin, bishop of Paderborn, a very distinguished theologian and a man with an organising mind. With the help of another Jesuit, the great Kleutgen, and a Frenchman Charles Gay,[10] he accomplished the task in something like seven weeks. The deputation then spent eight sessions debating the text, amending it in various ways, chiefly in matters of language, and on March 14 sent it to the bishops.

The general debate opened four days later. It did not end until April 19—seventeen General Congregations, in which 107 bishops made speeches, many proposing still further amendments, 281 in all. On April 12 a "trial voting"[11] on the text as a whole showed 510 *pro*, and none *contra*; but another 85 voted *pro* with reservations, i.e., these bishops still had 148 amendments to urge. These they had to put in writing, with their reasons. The deputation took a week to consider them, recommended the adoption of two (to

[6] Fifteen folio columns as printed in Mansi, vol. 50, 59–74.

[7] So Butler, I, 198.

[8] Cardinal Rauscher (1797–1875), archbishop since 1853, once the tutor of the emperor Franz Joseph; austere, a first-rate mind, and a prodigy of learning. Said to be worth all his colleagues put together, Rauscher *was* the Catholic restoration in Austria.

[9] The words (Butler, I, 198) are from William Bernard Ullathorne, O.S.B., bishop of Birmingham (1850–88) whose letters and diaries are a leading source of Butler's work. According to Butler, the fate of the schema was a great surprise to the Roman authorities. "It was not anticipated that the bishops were going to take things so seriously." Ibid.

[10] Later a bishop, and noted for his spiritual writings.

[11] Butler's term, I, 281.

which the bishops unanimously agreed) and reported the rest as merely stylistic or as reopening points already discussed. On April 24, Low Sunday, at the third Public Session, the final voting took place, the pope presiding, and the 667 present unanimously approved.[12]

The ten pages of text of this constitution are so closely knit as to defy summary. To give the reader a general idea of the subject matter it seems better to print the canons attached—these are statements condemning, point by point, all Catholics who say otherwise than the council, about the doctrines it has just defined. In place of the conventional formula, "If anyone says," or "If anyone denies," it makes easier reading to write "It is an error to say," or "It is an error to deny," and this has been changed accordingly. Given the importance of the matter, and the occasion, the word "error" is, of course, charged with the maximum of seriousness, and each canon ends with a malediction on the offender. There are eighteen canons in all. The grouping and the headings follow those of the constitution, and are the work of the council.[13]

I. GOD THE CREATOR OF ALL THINGS

It is an error *to deny* that there is one true God, Creator and Lord of all things visible and invisible.

It is an error *to say* that nothing exists that is not matter; or that the substance and essence of God is one and the same with the substance and essence of all things; or that finite things, both corporal and spiritual, have emanated from the divine substance; or that the divine essence, by the manifestation and evolution of itself, becomes all things; or that, lastly, God is universal or indefinite being, which by determining itself constitutes the universe of things, distinct according to genera, species, and individuals.

It is an error *to deny* that the world and all things contained in it, both spiritual and material, have been, in their whole substance, produced by God out of nothing; or *to say* that God created, not

[12] The text of this "Constitution" is printed (with an English translation) in Butler, II, 247–75. Denzinger, nos. 1781–1820, prints the Latin text.
[13] The translation is that of Manning's *Pastoral Letter* (1870) printed in Butler, II, 269–75.

by His will free from all necessity, but by a necessity like to that by which He loves Himself. It is an error *to deny* that the world was made for the glory of God.

II. REVELATION

It is an error *to say* that the one true God, our Creator and Lord, cannot be certainly known by the natural light of human reason through created things; or *to say* that it is not possible that man can be taught by divine revelation, nor suitable, about God and the worship to be paid to Him.

It is an error *to say* that man cannot be raised by divine power to a knowledge and perfection higher than the natural, but that he can, and ought, by a continuous progress, to arrive at length, of himself, at the possession of all that is true and good.

It is an error *to deny* that the books of Holy Scripture, entire, with all their parts, as the holy Council of Trent has listed them, are sacred and canonical; or that they were inspired by God.

III. FAITH

It is an error *to say* that the human reason is so independent that faith cannot be enjoined it by God; or that divine faith is indistinguishable from the natural knowledge of God and of moral truths, and that, therefore, it is not a requisite of divine faith that the truth revealed is believed on account of the authority of God who is revealing it.

It is an error *to say* that divine revelation cannot be made credible by outward signs, and that men therefore must be moved to faith solely by the internal experience of each, or by a private inspiration.

It is an error *to say* that miracles are not possible and that, therefore, all accounts concerning them, even those contained in Holy Scripture, are to be dismissed as fables or myths. It is an error *to say* that miracles can never be known with certainty, or that the divine origin of the Christian religion cannot be truly proved by miracles.

It is an error *to say* that the assent of Christian faith is not a free act, but is produced inevitably by the arguments of human reason; or *to say* that the grace of God is only needed for living faith, the faith which works by charity.

It is an error *to say* that the condition of the believers is on a par with the condition of those who have not yet attained to the one only true faith, so that Catholics can have a just cause for doubting, with suspended assent, the faith which they have already received under the magisterium of the Church, until they shall have obtained a scientific demonstration of the credibility and truth of the faith.

IV. FAITH AND REASON

It is an error *to say* that in divine revelation there are no mysteries, truly and properly so called, but that all the doctrines of faith can be understood and demonstrated from natural principles, by properly cultivated reason.

It is an error *to say* that human sciences are to be so freely treated, that their assertions, even if opposed to revealed doctrine, may be held as true, and cannot be condemned by the Church.

It is an error *to say* that it is possible that sometimes, according to the progress of science, a sense is to be given to dogmas propounded by the Church different from that which the Church has understood and understands.

The story of this first definition has been told at disproportionate length in order to show how the Vatican Council actually functioned, as well as how thoroughly the bishops did their work. Nor had they been idle while the deputation *De Fide* was busy remodelling the draft of *Dei Filius* at their behest. Only four days after they had sent back that draft, the bishops received the first drafts of the proposed reforms in ecclesiastical discipline, January 14. These were to occupy them for the next six weeks, and to provoke criticisms still more outspoken, and some of the best constructive speaking the council heard.

The subject matter of these two first drafts was bishops, synods, and vicars-general; also the vacancies in episcopal sees. The first speaker was the Cardinal Archbishop of Prague,[14] who complained that the reforms should have begun with the Roman Curia which, it was common knowledge, many bishops thought should be reorganised. A French cardinal[15] and the primate of Hungary[16] supported this. The great speech was that of the Archbishop of Paris[17] who took the opportunity to criticise the whole scheme of procedure drawn up for the council. Why was not a complete agenda sent to the bishops of what it was proposed to enact, not in the form of rhetorical exercises, but set out with businesslike brevity? The drafts now before the bishops were filled with trivialities, fit only for professional canonists to discuss. The council's business was with more fundamental things. Those who had drafted these schemata were utterly out of touch with realities. Melchers, of Cologne, complained of the tendency to overcentralisation, and bishops being given faculties, not for life, but for five years only at a time. In something of the same spirit one of the Orientals—the patriarch of Babylon of the Chaldeans—also spoke, begging that the Easterns should not be subject to a régime suitable only for the West, and that the composition of a code of law for the East be left to the eastern bishops. This was a protest against changes recently made by the Congregation of Propaganda. And the patriarch spoke of the oath he had sworn at his consecration to preserve and transmit intact the privileges of his see. Ketteler, of Mainz, spoke in this debate and also Dupanloup, at whose appearance hundreds of bishops left their seats and crowded round the pulpit, anxious not to lose a word, Manning (his chief adversary) in the first ranks of them.

Other bishops raised the question of changes in the Breviary, the official prayer book for clergy and religious. Finally there appeared a fourth draft which renewed all the liveliness of the discussion at a moment when, after "five weeks of interminable oratory,"[18] the mass of the bishops were beginning to tire. The subject of this was the Catechism, a proposal to have a single catechism—Bellarmine's —for the whole Church. In the six meetings when this was debated,

[14] Frederick Schwarzenberg (1809–85), archbishop since 1850.
[15] Mathieu, Archbishop of Besançon.
[16] Simor, created cardinal in 1873 by Pius IX.
[17] Georges Darboy (1813–71).
[18] Aubert, 334.

forty-one bishops spoke. The Germans especially were hostile. It was impossible to put anything in the place of the catechism of Canisius, used all over Germany since the time of its author. And a Hungarian archbishop, Haynald, spoke of the right of every bishop to settle the question for his own diocese. "If a catechism is dictated to us, our sermons will next be dictated," he boldly said.[19] To the end, this opposition to surrendering the work of Canisius was maintained, reinforced by objections to the proposed new catechism being drawn up by Roman theologians and imposed without a vote of the council. Whence, in the "trial voting" (May 4), while there were 491 votes *pro*, another hundred bishops voted either *contra*, or *pro* with a reservation. But none of these four disciplinary drafts, discussed, amended and then discussed anew, ever became law. The infallibility question had now been placed before the bishops, and for the rest of the council this absorbed all their time.

Before entering on the exciting events of the next nine weeks,[20] something needs to be said about the "Minority" bishops. Not altogether accurately they are often spoken of much as we speak of the opposition in a modern democratic parliament. This image was continually in Butler's mind as he described the proceedings of 1869–70, and we sometimes find Ullathorne, also, thinking of the council in terms of the English House of Commons.[21] The Minority, made up of bishops from many countries,[22] was never of course anything like the closely organised, disciplined political parties of the democratic state. In the first place, no one of these bishops was in any way bound to another, or subject to any discipline beyond his own sense of what was right, as was true of all the seven hundred or more bishops who attended. For as a bishop, each

[19] Butler, I, 229.

[20] The council had now been in session 22 weeks. It had only another nine weeks to run; though, of course, none of its members, nor the pope, knew this.

[21] It is also interesting that this shrewd, level-headed man, "the only man who kept his head in the Second Spring," thought that the most effective speakers at the council (whatever their views) were those who came from the democratic countries, bishops familiar with the way men go to work with their fellows in representative assemblies.

[22] ". . . Hungary, Germany, half of France, England [with two or three exceptions], all North America." Moriarty's estimate to Newman, Feb. 3, 1870, Butler, II, 29.

bishop in the Church is equal to any other bishop. The only superior any diocesan bishop has is the pope.

Again, the bishops who opposed the definition were not all moved by the same kind of reasons. Bishops from Great Britain and from the United States, for example, argued that the definition would not be understood by the vast Protestant population amidst which the Church was painfully making its way; it would create yet another stumbling block in the way of the Protestant attracted towards the Church and still influenced by the mental habits of his upbringing. In France the difficulty alleged had to do with Catholics. So loudly and so generally had the party that favoured infallibility cried out their extravagant, untheological, untrained ideas of the nature of the pope's prerogative, that—so the Minority feared —it was just not possible that, for generations, the true meaning of the definition would be understood. The definition, for years and years to come, would be read in the light of the prevailing popular Catholic misconceptions[23]—such misconceptions, all of recent growth, as that infallibility was tantamount to a divine inspiration, that the pope had but to express a wish or the hint of a wish and it was the Catholic's bounden duty to think as he thought, to act as the pope would (presumably) want the Catholic to act, in every walk of life. If the rationalists rejoiced, as the greater part of the Catholic press poured out this flood of affectionate adulation—protestations of loyalty to the pope seen as besieged for twenty years by all the powers of hell—rejoiced at the chance it offered to proclaim that the Catholic thought his pope a God on earth, who shall be surprised? No matter in what terms the definition be couched, said an English bishop, William Clifford, it will be said that we have made the pope a despot.[24] Another aberration of leading Catholic publicists—clerical no less than lay—disturbed many of the bishops: namely, the idea that the council would be wasting its time examining and debating the pros and cons of the infallibility. Did the Holy Ghost need time to think? they said explicitly. The doctrine should be defined by acclamation. There was something lacking in the faith of bishops who wanted the question studied and discussed.

This last extraordinary idea had been given the greatest possible

[23] Newman recalled the disastrous years that followed Chalcedon.
[24] Speech in the council, May 25, 1870. Butler, II, 49.

prestige when, just ten months before the council met, a Roman review, the *Civiltá Cattolica*, popularly identified with what was current thought in the highest circles, stated in an article headed "Correspondence from France" (February 1, 1869), that the bulk of the Catholics of France were hoping that "a unanimous outburst of the Holy Spirit would define [the pope's infallibility] by acclamation by the mouth of the Fathers [i.e., the bishops attending the council]."[25] This, to men already alarmed by what lesser lights had been allowed to publish unreproved, sounded like the beginning of official encouragement for this dangerous nonsense.

In German-speaking countries there had been nothing like these excesses. Here the reluctance of the bishops was bound up partly with the idea that the doctrine, although true, was not "definable." It was also thought that the definition would make for papal interference with the freedom of theological teaching, along the lines of Rome's recent reproof of the congress of Catholic savants at Munich.[26] And there was a kind of fear that the new prestige which would come to the papacy from the definition would inevitably strengthen its hand in the unmistakable move towards a closer Roman control of the general life of the Church. Also there were, in Germany, a very small number of really great scholars who definitely held that the pope was not infallible, and who grew more and more antipapal with each year that passed. Of all parts of the Church, it was Germany that was distinguished by an ecclesiastical scholarship equal to the best scholarship of the day. The article in the *Civiltá Cattolica* provoked from Döllinger (or gave him the excuse to write) the famous letters of Janus,[27] "the gravest and severest attack . . . on the policy of Rome for a thousand years," said Ullathorne.[28] Immediately Germany was all ablaze. A Catholic gathering at Coblenz asked their bishop, in effect, for reassurance that no new spiritual despotism was in preparation. The Catholics of Berlin followed suit, and fourteen German bishops sent a joint, private letter to the pope saying that, in view of the rising excite-

[25] Butler, II, 109.

[26] September, 1863. Döllinger presided. The letter of Pius IX, *Tuas Libenter*, is dated Dec. 21, 1863. The text (Latin) is in Denzinger, nos. 1679–84.

[27] *The Pope and the Council*, by Janus.

[28] Butler, I, 111.

ment in Germany, they thought any definition of infallibility would be inopportune.

The Minority bishops felt, often enough, that to the bishops of lands like Italy and Spain their anxieties were simply not intelligible, for these were "men who had never come into conflict with the unbelieving mind, or into contact with the intellectual mind of the time."[29] "When I read the school of theology in which they were trained," said this Irish bishop, "I am not surprised that they treat every doubter as a heretic."

A last word, before we return to the council's proceedings—the bishops debated amid a storm of excitement that held all western Europe. The chief forces in the public life of Europe were hostile, not merely to the idea of infallibility, in so far as they understood this, but to the whole vast effort of Pius IX to rebuild the Church around a stronger central headquarters. More than one government was "willing to wound, but yet afraid to strike." Tentative gestures were in fact made by Austria and Bavaria and France. In London even, Gladstone brought the question before his cabinet. And some of these governments were encouraged, nay urged, so to act, by Catholic subjects so hostile to the prospective definition that they would gladly have seen it prevented by governmental threats to the pope. So Döllinger worked at Munich, and Acton upon London, and one or two of the French bishops at Paris.

These manoeuvres, known in great part at the time—for Rome, inevitably, was the great whispering gallery of Europe in the winter of 1869–70—reflected unfavourably, in the eyes of many Catholics, upon the whole company of the Minority bishops, and most unfairly. When Wilfrid Ward, forty years after the council, came to write his great life of Newman, he felt it still necessary to spend time explaining that, until the council had defined the doctrine, it was not a defined doctrine, and that a Minority sympathiser was not, *ipso facto*, a less good Catholic than a man of the Majority. And twenty years later still, Abbot Cuthbert Butler considered it not time wasted to deal at length with the same point. So long lasting, both these writers felt, were the effects of the slanderous campaign waged against their Minority opponents by those extremists whom Ullathorne, at the time, made no difficulty of calling plainly,

29 Moriarty to Newman, Feb. 3, 1870, Butler, II, 29.

"fanatics." "I think myself," he wrote,[30] "that the opposition is in the order of Providence, both to ensure searching investigation, and a proper balance of expression in the decrees." This was very far from the view taken by the quasi-official *Tablet,* of London, and its special weekly supplement, *The Vatican,* the writers of which laid about them unsparingly, all too little concerned with the origin of the stories they published or the theological accuracy of their criticisms. The American Bishop of Rochester, McQuaid, writing of the like extravagances of the *Freeman's Journal,* of New York, could say, "He draws all his facts or supposed facts from the London *Tablet* and *Vatican.* Many of these *facts* amuse us at the power of invention, if not of malice, they display."[31]

It must not, however, be thought that these ultras were the only ones to write rashly. Moriarty wrote to Newman: "On the other hand, if the Pope's cause has been damaged by the intemperate advocacy of the *Civiltá, Univers* [Paris], and *Tablet* [London], we have been damaged also by some of the pamphlets on our side. . . . They furnish our adversaries with arguments for the necessity of an immediate definition."[32] Also, it needs to be pointed out that, too often, Minority bishops wrote as though the views of the extremists were shared by the Majority of the council.[33]

What the council's problem really was is put very simply by Ullathorne: ". . . at a distance nothing could seem easier to a theologian than to word it [i.e., the statement defining the pope's infallibility]; but with the rapidly accumulating knowledge that springs up in the conflict of minds and the very varied local bearings of the question with respect to different regions, the same theologian, were he here, would find his cleverness considerably tamed."[34]

As to the doctrine itself—that the pope is divinely preserved from error when he makes a declaration, addressed to the whole Church, as to what is the belief of the Church—no less authoritative a theologian than Canon Aubert can speak of it as "in the back-

---

[30] May 19, 1870; Butler, II, 64.

[31] April 25, 1870. *Letters of Bishop McQuaid from the Vatican Council,* ed. Henry J. Browne, in *Catholic Historical Review,* Jan. 1956, p. 425.

[32] May 14, 1870, Butler, II, 62.

[33] Cf. Aubert, 353.

[34] May 19, 1870, Butler, II, 64.

ground for centuries"[35] at the time when Pius IX began his reign. What the position was a century earlier, no less an authority than the then reigning pope can inform us, Benedict XIV, who is rightly considered as one of the glories of Catholic theological scholarship. Writing on July 13, 1748, to the Grand Inquisitor of Spain, he says that the doctrine is held by the whole Church with the exception of France.[36] And as to the France of those days, a Benedictine writing in 1724[37] of the French attachment to the view that "infallibility in dogmatic judgments has been given only to the body of the bishops,"[38] gives the warning that at least one half of the bishops, university dignitaries, and clergy of France of all ranks held the doctrine of papal infallibility. By the time the Vatican Council was summoned, it seems safe to say that quasi the whole body of the French bishops accepted the doctrine, and their people with them. The so-called Gallican theology on the matter—as in the phrase just quoted—had by now all but withered away.

[35] ". . . Obscurcie depuis des siècles," p. 294, by which (I take it) is meant that it was not in the forefront of people's minds. It had its place in the textbooks of Theology, set out in the Euclidean terseness of the genre, with the classic texts quoted in support as for centuries already.

[36] Quoted Billuart, *Cursus Theologiae* (Paris edition, 1878) V, 176.

[37] Abbot Matthieu Petit-Didier, O.S.B., *Traité de'Infaillibilité du Pape*, quoted Butler, I, 34.

[38] This phrase is quoted by Butler, I, 30, from a standard manual of Catholic doctrine which ran to seven editions between 1768 and 1792. Its author was a Benedictine of St. Maur, Jamin. The most important statement of this view is that contained in article 4 of the *Declaration of the Clergy of France about Ecclesiastical Authority*, made in their General Assembly, March 19, 1682. It runs as follows: "Also, in questions of belief the principal rôle is that of the pope, whose decrees are binding on all sees, but his judgments are not irreformable unless [to them] there is added the general agreement of the Church"; Mirbt, no. 535, prints the full text of the Declaration. In 1690 Pope Alexander VIII reproved this Declaration stating that oaths sworn to accept and observe it were null and void (Denzinger, 322–26). All those who signed it retracted their signatures in 1693, at the demand of Innocent XII, with an explicit, personal acknowledgement that the Assembly had no power to decide such questions. And Louis XIV revoked the edict which made the teaching of the Four Articles obligatory. See Pastor, *Lives of the Popes*, vol. 32, pp. 595–603. But the doctrines implied were never condemned as heretical. These Gallican theories had their effective origin in the troubled times of the so-called Schism of the West (1378–1417), when theologians and canonists, driven desperate by the long crisis, were willing to consider any theory that would give the Church a means of ridding itself of the contending popes. The classic work on this subject is V. Martin, *Les Origines du Gallicanisme*.

It was in the second month of the council, January 1870, that the "infallibilist" bishops began to move, various groups sending in petitions to the pope that the question be added to the agenda. In all, nearly five hundred bishops signed one or another of these petitions. There were five petitions in the contrary sense, signed by 136 more. The pope sent the petitions to the deputation *For Requests*, and after some debate the deputation, by a vote of 25 to 1, advised the pope on February 9 to add a statement about the infallibility to the draft *On the Church* already given out to the bishops on January 21.[39] On March 1 Pius IX accepted their advice, and five days later the new addition was in the hands of the bishops. It was not a satisfactory text at all. Drawn up months before the council met, in case some such draft would be needed, it was inevitably not suited, from its extreme tone and indefinite terminology, to the hour in which it now appeared. And almost simultaneously rumours began to spread among the bishops that the extremists were working for a decision "by acclamation," and without any debate. Four bishops,[40] thereupon, sent in a protest to the presidents, saying that if this were to be allowed they would immediately leave the council "and make public the reason of our departure." To whom the presidents replied that the "acclamation" scheme none but madmen (*insensati*) would even think of, while the text now sent out was but a draft for the bishops to shape as they chose. But it is a fact that some of the madmen had actually sent in petitions to this effect.

There was, it may be imagined, less and less of "the coolness of the unconcerned spectator" among the Minority bishops at this unhappy coincidence, and from this moment many of them hardened considerably. They also began to organise in earnest—a few of them outside the council as well as within.

The leaders of the extreme right, heartened by their success in bringing the great question before the council, now made a second move. They asked that the question be taken out of its proper place in the draft—according to which it would scarcely be discussed for another twelve months and more—and laid before the council im-

[39] The deputation included several Minority leaders. The solitary voter was the Archbishop of Vienna, Cardinal Rauscher.

[40] The four were the archbishops of Cincinnati (Purcell) and St. Louis (Kenrick), the bishops of Little Rock (Fitzgerald) and Kerry (Moriarty); Butler, II, 33.

mediately, i.e., as soon as the constitution *Dei Filius* (at present in the hands of the revisers) had been dealt with finally. Some two hundred bishops signed the petition prepared to this effect. But there were many counter-petitions, and not from the Minority only. There were "infallibilist" bishops who thought that common prudence forbade such an appearance of forcing the pace, and others who were shocked at the patent violation of the logical order of the important draft *On the Church*. Among the Italians who protested was the cardinal who was to be the next pope, Leo XIII. Another to object was the greatest of all the French champions of the definition policy, Louis Edouard Pie, bishop of Poitiers. The five cardinal presidents also objected to this change.

But the small inner group who were the heart of the extreme party—led by Manning and the bishop of Regensburg (Senestréy) —did not give up. They took their petition to the very presence of the pope (April 19) and, mistakenly, thought they had won him over. But the opposition of so many of the officials was impressive, and it was not until April 29 that Pius IX consented. A greatly amended text was prepared, the draft of a separate, short Dogmatic Constitution that would deal only with the pope's primacy of jurisdiction over the whole Church and with the prerogative of infallibility. This new text suffered from none of the blemishes of the old. There was much greater care in the terms used, the drafting of what was proposed to be defined was more precise—ruling out, inevitably, the chances that extremists would be able easily to claim it as sanctioning their own loose statements. Let one example illustrate this, where the words in italics show the changes now introduced. The pope is declared to be infallible when he declares to the Church: "Whatever in matters of faith and morals is by the whole Church to be held *as part of the faith* (*tamquam de fide*) or rejected *as contrary to the faith* (*tamquam fidei contrarium*)."

The Minority—seventy-one of them—sent in a petition against this plan to discuss a doctrine about papal prerogatives before determining the doctrine about the Church generally. But the next day, May 9, the new text was delivered to the bishops, and on May 13 the great debate began—the debate in which the greatest speeches of the council were made.

The debate was in three "acts," so to speak: (I) the discussion of the draft as a whole, May 13–June 3, 15 meetings of four hours each in these three weeks, with 65 speakers in all, 39 *pro* and 26 of the Minority; (II) the detailed discussion of the text dealing with the primacy of the pope, June 6–13, 5 meetings, 32 speakers; (III) the detailed discussion of the text of the infallibility proposal, June 15–July 4, 11 meetings, 57 speakers, 35 *pro*, 22 of the Minority. The bishops were fortified for the work before them by a folio of 104 pages that contained the amendments proposed by various of them to the original draft of the primacy section of the Constitution, and a second folio of 242 pages with the like amendments to the section on the infallibility. With the amendments were printed the comments of the theological experts.

The proceedings began with a masterly recommendation of the text as amended, delivered by Pie, bishop of Poitiers, on behalf of the deputation *On the Faith*. Very speedily the debate developed into a battle over the previous question, Was it opportune to define the prerogative of infallibility? Feeling ran high from the outset, and after ten days of it the bishop of Nancy, Foulon, could write, in a private letter, "Some speakers give one the impression they speak with their fists clenched, or with their finger on the trigger of a revolver."[41]

It would be unprofitable as well as tedious to name the sixty-five speakers, and quite impossible to give anything like a résumé of their arguments.[42] Not all were masters of the art of oratory, nor all gifted with original ideas. With the bores, as the days went by, the bishops began to grow impatient; and the presidents with the irrelevancies. Of the great speakers, Cardinal Cullen of Dublin, Manning of Westminster, and Dechamps of Mechlin, seem to have most impressed the bishops, among the "infallibilist" orators; and Hefele from the ranks of the Minority, made "probably the most impressive adverse speech."[43] But the great historian, who cited Chalcedon[!] in proof[!] that the pope was never held to be in-

[41] Aubert, 351.

[42] Butler, II, 43–55, mentions, with an occasional comment, 46 of the 65. Of these 46, 7 are French; the Austrian Empire, Ireland, and the U.S.A. each produced 5; Italy and Spain 4 each; Germany 3, England 2, with one from each of the following: Canada, Chili, Belgium, Holland, and Switzerland. Of the 8 from Germany-Austria all are of the Minority, as are 6 of the 13 from English-speaking countries. Two prelates of Eastern Rites also spoke, the Armenian patriarch *pro*, and the Melchite Patriarch of Antioch with the Minority.

[43] Butler, II, 47.

356

fallible, found himself corrected in detail by the next speaker, the Archbishop of Saragossa. And Manning's extraordinary slip—that the infallibility was already an article of the Catholic faith—was immediately picked up by the learned bishop of Galway, Mc-Evilly.[44] A third Irishman to distinguish himself was the Archbishop of Cashel, Leahy, Newman's erstwhile colleague in the Catholic University,[45] while Clifford, of Clifton in England, roused strong grunts of disapproval by his blunt description of the likely effect of the definition on the non-Catholic world. One American bishop also drew blood when, pleading against the definition, he spoke of the battles of the churches placed among aggressively hostile and prejudiced Protestants, and the present good hope of making converts, which the definition, he feared, would destroy. In another forty years, said this bishop of Pittsburgh, there will be more Catholics in North America than in Italy, "and they will be not mere nominal, but real practicing Catholics."[46] For this he was called to order, and bidden speak more carefully about the faithful of Italy. With Vérot, the French bishop of Savannah, it was his sense of humour that got out of control. He alternately annoyed and amused his audience, and was told, "If you have nothing more to say except jokes, there is no use your occupying the pulpit any longer"; at which, "Many Fathers: 'Come Down.' "[47]

Such human incidents must, however, have been something of a relief as, with the rapid onset of the torrid Roman summer, these hundreds of elderly and aged men endured day after day speeches that rarely did more than repeat the centuries-old arguments, or correct the ancient errors still repeated. "Many bishops are getting leave to go home, unable to stand the heat, or pressed by affairs," Ullathorne wrote on May 17. Others, in the end, took advantage of a new regulation and, to the number of 150, besought the cardinal-presidents to use their powers and bring the debate to an end. There were still another forty bishops who had put down their names as intending to speak, besides the sixty-five who had spoken, when on June 3 the presidents put it to the council whether they

[44] A one-time professional from Maynooth.

[45] "The Archbishop of Cashel threw Cardinal Cullen into the shade." McQuaid, May 24, 1870, *Letters, etc.*, p. 432.

[46] This bishop, Michael Domenec, was a Spaniard by birth. The quotation is Butler, II, 54.

[47] Ibid., 53.

wished to hear any more, and by a huge majority the council voted that it had had enough, and the presidents formally ended this preliminary discussion. "These words were received with general applause," says the official record, "but there were not wanting those who showed their displeasure. . . ." And the Minority sent in a formal protest, signed by eighty prelates, among them three cardinals.[48]

Act II of the debate was the detailed consideration of a proposed definition on the subject of the Papal Primacy over the whole Church of Christ, i.e., that the pope is, by divine arrangement, the supreme ruler of the Church, with full authority over every part of it. This doctrine, no less vital than that about the prerogative called infallibility, had never entered into the controversies which in recent years had occupied the energies of so many Catholics; and while, as the debates in the council had revealed, there were actually some bishops, Hefele for one, who doubted that the pope was infallible, not a single bishop questioned the doctrine of the primacy, whether in principle or in its practical implications. There was here no question of the Minority, any more than there had been a Minority movement re the definition *Dei Filius*. And with good reason—the primacy had been defined doctrine for over four hundred years, ever since the General Council of Florence, 1439[49]; and it had been the general belief of the Church and the constantly asserted teaching *in act* of the popes, as far back as history goes.

The discussion, in the next five General Congregations, turned on the words now to be used to express the matter defined; and the critics of the draft were moved by the fear that the phrases used might lend themselves to misconstruction. They also regarded it as a serious blemish that this section on the pope's over-all authority had not a word to say about the complementary Catholic belief that the diocesan bishop's authority is also divine in its origin, that the bishop is not a mere vicar or delegate of the pope. Some of the 140 bishops who had sent in reasoned amendments to the deputation *On the Faith* also feared, it must be said, that this seemingly one-sided statement was part and parcel of the Curia's desire to de-

[48] Mathieu, Archbishop of Besançon, the leader of the French Minority group; Rauscher and Schwarzenburg.
[49] See above p. 282.

velop still further the administrative centralisation of the universal church.[50] A much more likely cause of their fears, it would seem, was the suddenness of the resolve to change the order of the topics, and the consequent proposal of this question outside its natural setting in the general order of the theology regarding the Church. The council had been in session now for six months, and no member of the Curia could have had any doubt as to what the bishops would do with drafts that did not please them.

The most important speech made in these five congregations of June 6–13 was perhaps that of Cardinal Rauscher, who improved the text of the definition by introducing phrases already used by Innocent III in the General Council of 1215. Cardinal Dechamps, injudiciously, surely, and uncharacteristically, proposed a censure, in the very decree, of a new work by a bishop present at the council, Maret, dean of the faculty of Theology at the Sorbonne, the leading theologian of the Minority on the infallibility question. This move fell flat, before the silence of the startled bishops, and the hostility of the presidents. The bishop of Nice also attracted the personal attention of these officers by explicitly denying that the pope's power in sees other than Rome was "episcopal, ordinary or immediate." The spokesman of the presidents interrupted to say this doctrine was inadmissible. A Hungarian archbishop, Louis Haynald, also proposed that these same words be left out—seemingly as not a suitable description of the supreme authority. The Melchite Patriarch of Antioch pleaded that, in order not to create new obstacles to the reconciliation of the Orthodox Churches, the decree of Florence should be repeated but nothing more, with no new anathemas, and that something should be added explicitly safeguarding the rights of the patriarchates.

The last—thirty-third—speaker was the newly consecrated bishop of Angers, Freppel, fresh from his chair of Theology at the Sorbonne, and about to begin his great career in the hierarchy of France. He did the debate the service of showing that there could be no clearer term to safeguard the rights of the bishops than these traditional words, "ordinary," which goes back to the Council of 1215, and "immediate," which has the authority of St. Thomas behind it; terms with a history, then, in the technical commentaries of

50 Aubert, 352.

six hundred years. He derided, in a learned way, "the fantastic despotism or absolutism, that we have been hearing about." Absolutism was the classic law of the ancient Roman Empire, yes. "But who has ever said that the Roman Pontiff may govern the Church according to his own sweet will, by arbitrary power, by fancy—that is, without the laws and the canons? . . . Is power arbitrary because it is supreme? . . . Let us make an end of this confusion of ideas."[51]

So the debate ended, in its own time,[52] and to the bishops of the deputation *On the Faith* the seventy-two amendments proposed went for consideration. They reported to the council on July 5— the report being made by the bishop[53] in whose diocese the future St. Pius X was a newly appointed parish priest. The deputation proposed to reject all but four of the amendments, and the bishops, sometimes by unanimous vote, and always by huge majorities, supported their judgment.

Meanwhile, July 4, in the debate on the infallibility—i.e., on the proposed text—the fifty-seventh speaker had just come down from the pulpit, and the other sixty-three who had proposed to speak had, to the general relief, nobly foregone their rights to immortal fame in Mansi.

Act III—the debate on the text of the infallibility decree—is what most people have in mind when they speak of the Vatican Council. It began on June 15 and occupied eleven meetings of the council, 120 of whose members proposed themselves as speakers. Actually no more than 57 were heard, and as, by the time the debate began, all the generalities of the subject had been exhausted, the bishops were treated to a vast deal of rambling exhortation and its repetition. The presidents, in this last section of the council, were daily calling speakers back to the matter in hand, the suitability of the proposed text. But nonetheless the text was thoroughly discussed, and it was amended out of recognition.

The general sense of the directing mind of the council was to produce a text of the strictest theological accuracy, that no particu-

[51] Butler, II, 78–85 for details of the debate.
[52] On July 3 an attempt was made to invoke the closure procedure. The presidents ignored it.
[53] Zinelli, bishop of Treviso.

lar party would be able to cite as a warranty for the condemnation of other parties, the subject of the definition being, as Cardinal Dechamps had already said, not the controversial ideas of the moment but the traditional belief of the Church, the belief set out by such classic teachers as Bellarmine and St. Thomas. A powerful influence in all this was the Archbishop of Bologna, Cardinal Guidi, a Dominican who spoke on June 18. He proposed to make the title of the decree more exact—not to use in such a document the loose phrase "the pope's infallibility," which might be taken to mean a permanent quality in the pope. The divine assistance which preserves the pope as universal teacher from error is a transient divine act, he pointed out, making the pope's act infallible but not his person. It is the definition that is infallible and not the person. Therefore, let the title be "The infallibility of the pope's dogmatic pronouncements." To those more at home with pulpit oratory than such cool theological analysis, this was far from pleasing, and the cardinal was violently interrupted. Despite this opposition—and the resentment of Pius IX, that a cardinal from the Papal State should have opposed him[54]—the title of the decree was changed in Guidi's sense, and so voted, and so promulgated, by the pope.

There were two other remarkable speeches, each time from a member of the deputation *De Fide* that was responsible for proposing the definition, each speaker desiring to amend it still more seriously. The first of these was Cullen of Dublin, who proposed an entirely new form of words for the definition itself. It is the form as it actually stands.[55] The other speaker was a German, Martin, bishop of Paderborn, who proposed that the whole section on infallibility (and not merely the definition itself) be rewritten, and a long historical passage be written into it to make clearer still what the definition did *not* do, e.g., confer new powers on the pope,

---

[54] Pius IX, now in his 79th year, was of the temperament that is always liable to be swept away by emotional storms, cf. Aubert, 227: "l'homme essentiellement émotif," and also, "n'écoutant comme toujours, que sa première impression," 208. He sent for the cardinal and, it is said, replied to the explanation that Guidi had been explaining how the bishops were witnesses to the tradition of faith, "I am tradition." The authority quoted by Butler, II, 98 is Dupanloup's private diary. For other sources cf. Aubert's account, 353–54.

[55] Cardinal Cullen seems to have been, rather, the spokesman of a group in the *De Fide* deputation, the most prominent of whom was the president of that body, the gifted Cardinal Bilio.

extend papal power in a way never before heard of, do away with the traditional safeguards.

By this first week of July the heat was such that the official records speak of it. The practical men on both sides began to meet behind the scenes—Manning and Haynold are especially named—and a joint effort was made to induce the remaining sixty-three speakers to desist. It was successful, and on July 4, after the speech of the bishop of Oran, the presidents announced that as no one else wanted to speak, the debate was closed—this, says the record, "amid general shouts of joy, and applause."

Before the deputation *De Fide*, however, there still remained many laborious hours, studying the ninety-six amendments proposed by the speakers, and another forty-eight sent in in writing. With the aid of their theologians they had sorted it out, and were ready with their recommendations to the council, by July 11. They then proposed, following Guidi, to change the title and, following Martin, to put in the historical section. They accepted the new—Cullen—wording of the definition, and so were able to refuse the hundred proposed amendments of the old formula. The explanation and justification of all this was left to the bishop of Brixen, Vincent Gasser, "the most prominent theologian in the council,"[56] to whose great speech Butler gives a whole chapter of his book. The council, without more ado, voted as the deputation proposed.

The way was now open for the "trial voting" on this second Dogmatic Constitution, *Pastor Aeternus*, the classic definition of the papal primacy and the infallibility of the popes' *ex cathedra* pronouncements. This took place on July 13. The votes were: *Pro*—451, *Contra*—88, *Pro* with some reservations—62. There were another 76 bishops who, though still in Rome, did not attend and vote.

Those who voted *pro*, but with a reservation (*placet iuxta modum*), had to send in a note of the reservation, i.e., the change they wished to see made. The schedule of these, prepared now for the use of the council, ran to as many as 160 items, 200 alterations in all. By no means all of these were from the Minority. The changes made in the text of the proposed constitution had greatly displeased some of "the extreme papal school"[57] among the bish-

[56] Butler, II, 134.
[57] Butler's words, II, 153.

ops, and they called for the suppression of the new historical passage, and asked that the infallibility be explicitly declared to extend beyond the field of faith and morals. The deputation recommended that all but two of these suggested changes be rejected. The two were, first, the suppression of two quotations, from St. Augustine and St. Irenaeus which were not really relevant to the matter they were introduced to support, and secondly, a clause to make clear that the infallibility of *ex cathedra* pronouncements did not depend on the assent of the Church to them. These decisions of the deputation *On the Faith* the whole body of bishops accepted, in the eighty-sixth General Congregation, July 16. The solemn Public Session of voting and definition was announced for Monday, July 18.

Meanwhile, what of the 88, who on July 13 had voted *non placet*? For them this had been a week of anxiety and distress. They made every effort to secure modifications that would save them from the need to vote *non placet* at the coming solemn session. On July 15 they sent a deputation to the pope. Ketteler, it is said, fell on his knees and with tears besought the pope to make himself the changes which the council had rejected, chiefly the addition of a phrase explicitly mentioning the rôle of the bishops and the Church in the "evolution" of an infallible pronouncement. So little, it may now seem, ninety years after the event, separated the Minority, at the crucial hour, from their brethren—the question which is the better form of words.[58] On the day after their audience some of the Minority were surely among the 552 bishops who took part in the last General Congregation. Then, on the very eve of the definitive voting, they met to decide finally on their action. They were by no means unanimously resolved. Haynald won them over to his idea of solemnly closing their long campaign of protest by a public vote *contra*. And then came Dupanloup, very late, and, told of the decision, he reopened the discussion, and carried the day, reversing the Haynald plan. The bishops should keep away from the morrow's event. "We could not vote *placet*," he urged, "for nobody would believe us. We could not vote *non placet*, for the sake of the Catholic world, which would not understand us, and which might be scandalised." By 36 votes to 28 the bishops accepted this idea, and in a letter to the pope they explained their action. "Filial piety

[58] Butler, II, 157.

and respect," they say, "do not allow us, in a cause so closely affecting Your Holiness, to say *non placet* openly, face to face with our Father."[59] Fifty-five signed, and eight others wrote individually to the pope.

The great day came in with heavy showers of rain. It has often been described how the long hour and a half of the voting—each of the 535 bishops present, vested in cope and mitre, called on by name, rising and pronouncing his vote—took place to the accompaniment of a wonderful July thunderstorm. "Nothing approaching to the solemn splendour of that storm could have been prepared," wrote the correspondent of *The Times*, the Rev. Thomas Mozley, Newman's brother-in-law and erstwhile pupil. At the close, it was so dark in the basilica that lights were needed for the pope to read the authoritative phrases, "We define and confirm by our apostolic authority, the sacred council approving," the Dogmatic Constitution[60] as it has been read. And then, from their places among the bishops, two figures made their way to the foot of the papal throne, the two bishops who had voted *non placet*. "Holy Father, now I believe," each of them said. One was the bishop of Cajazzo in southern Italy, the other Edward Fitzgerald, Bishop of Little Rock, Arkansas.[61]

Meanwhile, the fortnight between the close of the debate and the promulgation of the constitution *Pastor Aeternus* had seen, in the world outside the council, the swift emerging of a first-class international crisis. When Dupanloup and Darboy met Melchers and Ketteler in that last conference, the evening before the final session, their two countries were already on the verge of war. Two days later the fateful Franco-German war had begun. Napoleon III must now perforce recall his troops that were the pope's protection against United Italy. On August 4 they began to embark. From the Italians came a request that the pope would bless the now inevitable invasion, and surrender Rome like a good Catholic and a good Italian. On September 11 the invasion began, and on September 20 Rome capitulated to the army of Cadorna—something like three

[59] The full text of the letter is in Butler, II, 158–59.

[60] The text of this, known as *Pastor Aeternus*, is printed (with an English translation) in Butler, II, 276–95.

[61] One of the youngest bishops in the council, born 1833 at Limerick in Ireland, consecrated May 26, 1867.

weeks after a revolution in Paris had overthrown the empire of Napoleon III. In all these weeks of crisis the work of the General Congregations had continued, the 120 bishops who had not availed themselves of the "vacation" granted by the pope toiling steadily through August at the unfinished project on ecclesiastical discipline. But just a month to the day after the Italian capture of Rome Pius IX suspended the council, indefinitely. It has never been reassembled since.

The Minority bishops, once returned to their flocks, published their belief and acceptance of the decree against which they had voted—some half dozen of them after severe interior struggles. The Holy See bore no ill will for their opposition. Of the Austro-Hungarians, Simor, Haynald and von Fürstenberg were made cardinals within the next few years; and had their respective governments not hindered it, Leo XIII, it is said, would have given the hat to Dupanloup and to Strossmayer.

It had ever been a very general consideration with the Minority prelates that a definition of infallibility would be followed by schisms and individual defections everywhere. An American bishop may be quoted as an example: ". . . The damage to the Church will be immense. In some countries there will be large schisms, and great losses to the Church in all countries except Italy, Spain, and Ireland and among our poor people at home."[62] But none of these fears were realised. Only in Germany and Switzerland did a group of clergy—professors of Theology and Canon Law in various state universities—win over a number of Catholics who organised themselves as the Old Catholic Church. Since no bishop patronised the little movement the chiefs were driven, for ordinations and the rite of episcopal consecration, to the schismatic Jansenist bishop of Utrecht. And although various governments gave the movement recognition it languished from its birth. Nowhere in the Church, from the beginning of the Catholic revival, had the renewed activity of the papacy been anything but welcome to the generality of Catholics. Their whole-hearted acceptance of the decrees of 1870 was natural, inevitable. It was an acceptance that was in the nature of things, and that meant no more change than that they now believed explicitly what, like their fathers for centuries, they always implicitly had taken for granted.

[62] McQuaid to Rev. James M. Earley, [May] 1870, in *Letters, etc.,* p. 430.

Appendix I

SOME NOTES ABOUT FURTHER READING

There are two indispensable tools for the serious student of the history of the General Councils, one of them a source book and the other a history. The first, referred to always as Mansi, is a collection of all the known documentation of councils of every kind, made by John Dominic Mansi, archbishop of Lucca, and published in 31 folio volumes in the eighteenth century, 1759–98, *Sacrorum Concilium Nova et Amplissima Collectio*. A new, revised edition was prepared and published 1899–1927. This includes the nineteenth-century councils and runs to 60 volumes. The second indispensable work is the *History of the Councils* by Carl Joseph Hefele, who later, as has been related, played a part in the Vatican Council. This work goes as far as the Lateran Council of 1517. It was, many years later, translated into French and brought up to date, in the matter of research, by the Farnborough Benedictine, Henri Leclercq, in eight[1] volumes (1907–21). This is the work cited as *Hefele-Leclercq*.

The reader will see that to make use of these "indispensables" our serious student needs at least a reading knowledge of Latin and French. And there is the same need of foreign languages for all of us whose curiosity about this history takes us any appreciable distance beyond such a book as mine. The exiguity of Catholic scholarly work, in the English language, in the field of Church History is notorious and, considering the fact that English-speaking Catholics must number a good 60 or 70 million, is very little to our credit. For far too long now we have left it all to the "heretics." Indeed, I can think of only one figure who can be ranked with the great French and German scholars, from Döllinger to Duchesne and Batiffol, and that is Newman. This, in explanation of the character of the books I am now going to suggest "for further reading."

[1] Since several of these volumes are in more than one "part" the bulk is really considerable.

As to the general history of the Church there are now available in translation, published by Herder (St. Louis) several volumes of Mourret's *Histoire de l'Église*—very thoroughly done, and scholarly indeed, but a little out of date after nearly sixty years. A more succinct account, not yet (I trust) to be labelled, "somewhat out of date," is my own *History of the Church*, in three volumes, which goes down to the end of the Fifth Lateran Council, 1517. Volume I tells the story of the councils as far as the sixth (680). In Volume II are the last two eastern councils (787 and 869) and the medieval councils from First Lateran to First Lyons inclusively. In Volume III, Lyons II to Lateran V are dealt with. I mention these two, somewhat detailed, general works[2] because it is not possible to understand the councils without some knowledge of the general history, and because unless history is read in considerable detail it not only raises more questions than it answers, and risks all the time being a distortion or a caricature of the truth, but is horribly dull and dreary work. Who is there who ever got any satisfaction, for example, out of these terrible survey courses of the history of our civilisation, one massive (splendidly produced) volume that begins with the Egyptians (and earlier) and tells us all about it, down to the conventions of 1960? What a dreadful prostitution of a great branch of learning! What a fraud on the young people! There are no short cuts in history; from the nature of the matter there cannot be.

As to the special works on particular councils, they are not so numerous as might be expected. I should like to begin with Newman's *Arians of the Fourth Century*, for the first two councils—a book greatly admired by the nineteenth century for its classic purity of style, and which (after 130 years) has not ceased to be very useful indeed. The fifteenth centenary of Chalcedon (1951) produced *Das Konzil von Chalkedon, Geschichte und Gegenwart*, edited by A. Grillmaier, S.J., and H. Bacht, S.J., in three volumes. The next council for which I can suggest a special *ad hoc* work is the "Photius" council of 869–70, for which see Fr. Francis Dvorník's book in the list that follows. No one has written a specialist general work on any of the next six councils. But for the Council of Vienne (1311–12) we possess *Das Konzil von Vienne* by E. Müller, O.F.M. (1934). About the so-called Conciliar Theory which underlay the activities whence came the troubles of the next two General Councils, we have two very remarkable books, *Foundations of Conciliar Theory* by Brian Tierney (1955) and *Studies in the Conciliar Epoch*, by E. F. Jacob (1943). Although no one has yet

---

[2] Needless to say, for those who read French the great Fliche and Martin series offers a means of study far beyond anything so far attempted. See the list in Appendix II.

attempted to sum up, for their own sake, the history of the councils of Constance and Basel, mention must be made of two great pieces of scholarship, re—the proceedings on both these occasions, viz., *Acta Concilii Constantiensis*, 4 vols. (1896–1928), due primarily to Fr. H. Finke, and *Concilium Basiliense*, 8 vols. (1896–1936), the work of J. Haller and others. From the Papal Oriental Institute in Rome there has now come a similar work on the Council of Florence, *Concilium Florentinum*, 6 vols. (1940–55); one of the scholars engaged on it, Fr. Joseph Gill, S.J., is the author of the work noted in the list that follows.

As to Trent, the greatest council of all, the history of its history has indeed been one of conflict. The first account, the basis of the anti-papal view that has coloured almost every account since given, published (in Italian) in London in 1619 was the work of a Servite friar, Fra Paolo Sarpi, who certainly had access to many of the closely guarded documents and the diplomatic correspondence. He was a Venetian, and a kind of literary bravo in the service of the Serenissima during its conflict with Pope Paul V (1605–21) who had laid Venice under an interdict. This partisan and highly damaging work went unanswered for forty years, when Cardinal Pallavicini, S.J., specially commissioned by the pope, and with access to all the papers, produced his *Istoria del Concilio di Trento*, in three volumes. Ranke's critical comparison of these two works is one of the classic feats of his well-known *History of the Popes*. But in our own time the real history of the council has at last appeared, Monsignor Hubert Jedin, modestly announcing himself with a finished history of the History of the Council of Trent, *Das Konzil von Trient. Ein Überblick über die Erforschung seiner Geschichte* (1948). There have now been published also the first two volumes of his *History of the Council of Trent*, the first of which has also appeared in an excellent English translation by Dom Ernest Graf (1957). Msgr. Jedin comes to his task after a hard apprenticeship in the service of the great German enterprise which, for sixty years and more, has been classifying and critically editing the documents of the council. Of this work, *Concilium Tridentinum*, twelve volumes have so far been published. Meanwhile, for the reader who needs today to know this history, there remains the much neglected account of the Council of Trent to be found in Pastor's *History of the Popes*, the details of which I transcribe: vol. 10, 106–69, 221–29; vol. 12, 124–408; vol. 13, 76–128; vol. 15, 216–65.

The Vatican Council was scarcely more fortunate than Trent in the way the forces hostile to it in the intellectual world were allowed a good fifty years start in their commentaries. Given the notorious fact of the bitter feeling, it is somewhat surprising that twenty years went by before, in vol. VII of the Jesuit work on councils, *Collectio Lacensis*, the essential documentation began to appear (1892). This was, again, a German enterprise, and it was a German Jesuit also, Granderath, who in 1903–6 published the first history, *Geschichte des Vatikanischen Konzils*, 3 volumes. For this work the author was given all the papers he desired to see. In 1923–27 the whole of the papers were published as volumes 49–53 of the new edition of Mansi. Then, in 1930, appeared Butler's book, noted below, which Canon Aubert generously calls "the best account," to be himself rewarded (so to say) for his own account, noted below, by a like word from Msgr. Jedin. As an introduction to the socio-religious history of the years 1789–1870, I cannot too highly recommend two books by E. E. Y. Hales, *The Catholic Church in the Modern World; A survey from the French Revolution to the present* (1958) and *Pio Nono; Creator of the Modern Papacy* (1954); *Revolution and Papacy; The Papacy and the Revolutionary Movement in Europe, 1769–1846* (1960).

Appendix II

WORKS CITED IN THE FOOTNOTES.

AMANN, E., *see under* F. and M., vols. 6, 7.

AUBERT, R., *see under* F. and M., vol. 21.

BARDY, G., *Les Luttes Christologiques après le Concile de Chalcédoine, see under* F. and M., vol. 4.

BARRY, COLMAN, O.S.B., *Readings in Church History*, 1960.

BATIFFOL, PIERRE, *L'Église Naissante*, 1908.

———, *La Paix Constantinienne et le Catholicisme*, 312–59, 3rd edition, 1914.

———, *Le Siège Apostolique*, 359–451.

BREHIER, L., *La Quérelle des Images*, *see under* F. and M., vol. 5.

BUTLER, CUTHBERT, O.S.B., *The Vatican Council*, 2 vols., 1930.

CHAPMAN, JOHN, O.S.B., *The Condemnation of Pope Honorius*, London, 1907.

COHN, NORMAN, *The Quest of the Millennium*, 1957.

DENZINGER, *Enchiridion* [A Handbook of Creeds, Definitions and Declarations of the Popes about Faith and Morals—Latin and Greek texts].

DUCHESNE, LOUIS, *L'Église au VIme Siècle*, 1925.

DVORNÍK, FRANCIS, *The Photian Schism: History and Legend*, 1948.

F. AND M., *Histoire de l'Église* edited by A. Fliche and Msgr. V. Martin.

———, Vol. 4   395–590 by various authors.

———, Vol. 5   590–757 by various authors.

———, Vol. 6   757–888 *L'Époque Carolingienne* by E. Amann.

———, Vol. 7   888–1057 *L'Église au pouvoir des Laiques* by E. Amann.

———, Vol. 8   1057–1123 *La Réforme Grégorienne et la Reconquête Chrétien* by A. Fliche.

———, Vol. 9, pt. 1   1123–53 by various authors.

———, Vol. 9, pt. 2   1153–98 by various authors.

———, Vol. 10   1198–1274 *La Chrétienté Romaine* by A. Fliche.

———, Vol. 21   1846–78 *Le Pontificat de Pie IX* by R. Aubert.

FLICHE, A., *see* last entry, vols. 8 and 10.

FINLAY, G., *The Byzantine Empire, 717–1057*, Everyman's Library edition.

GILL, JOSEPH, S.J., *The Council of Florence*, 1959.

JAFFÉ-WATTENBACH, *Regesta pontificum Romanorum*, 1888. [A catalogue of all the existing papal letters down to 1198.]

JALLAND, T. G., *The Church and the Papacy*, 1944.

JEDIN, HUBERT, *A History of the Council of Trent*, vol. I, London, 1957. This is the best survey yet made of the general history of the Church in the 150 years before the council actually met.

KIRCH, C., S.J., *Enchiridion Fontium Historiae Ecclesiasticae Antiquae.* [Handbook of sources for the history of the early Church: 600 pages of texts, Latin and Greek, from various writers, and councils, from A.D. 80 to 750.]

NEWMAN, JOHN HENRY, CARDINAL, "Apostolical Tradition," in *Essays, Critical and Historical*, vol. I.

——, "Causes of the Rise and Successes of Arianism," in *Tracts, Theological and Ecclesiastical.*

——, "The Heresy of Apollinaris," in *Tracts*, etc.

——, "St. Cyril's Formula," ibid.

——, "The Trials of Theodoret," in *Historical Sketches*, vol. II.

PASTOR, L. VON, *History of the Popes*, vols. 6, 8.

ROUET DE JOURNEL, M. J., S.J., *Enchiridion Patristicum.* [Handbook of extracts from the Fathers of the Church and other ecclesiastical writers, A.D. 90 to 600, Latin and Greek texts, 760 pages.]

SCHROEDER, H. J., O.P., *Disciplinary Decrees of the General Councils, Text, Translation and Commentary*, 1937. [Ends with the Lateran Council of 1517.]

TIXERONT, J., *Histoire des Dogmes*, 6me edition, 1922, 3 vols. English translation, *History of Dogmas*, 2nd edition, 1926, 3 vols.

WATERWORTH, J., *The Canons and Decrees of the Council of Trent.* [The whole of the Tridentine laws translated into English.]

Index